Indian Models of Economy, Business and Management

Indian Models of Economy, Business and Management

Third Edition

P. KANAGASABAPATHI

Director
Tamil Nadu Institute of Urban Studies
Coimbatore

New Delhi-110001
2012

₹ 275.00

INDIAN MODELS OF ECONOMY, BUSINESS AND MANAGEMENT
Third Edition
P. Kanagasabapathi

ISBN-978-81-203-4563-8

Fifth Printing (Third Edition) ... ... **February, 2012**

Published by Asoke K. Ghosh, PHI Learning Private Limited, M-97, Connaught Circus, New Delhi-110001 and Printed by Mudrak, 30-A, Patparganj, Delhi-110091.

CONTENTS

List of Figures

List of Tables

List of Boxes

PREFACE

After completing my doctorate in finance, I came to be associated with the stock markets. Soon I realized that the theories I had studied were insufficient in explaining the ground realities prevalent in the field of investments in India. After a few years, when I became the president of an agricultural cooperative bank, I started studying the saving pattern of the people of western Tamil Nadu. Among other things, it came to my knowledge that the average household saves higher amounts of money in avenues that are not discussed seriously by the finance professors and investment experts. These initial experiences taught me that there are gaps between the theories presented in textbooks and the practices adopted by the people, at least in the field of finance.

When I started analyzing these aspects and began to interact with the practitioners at the field levels, I came to understand that some of the differences between the theories and practices were really true. Then, accompanying my students and associates, I began to take up studies in different economic centres, including the major industrial and business clusters. We tried to know more about the functioning Indian models, covering different aspects of the economy, business and management. These studies showed us that the functioning models of India were in many ways different from the popular textbook models that were taught in universities and they possessed unique features that we do not normally observe. We also began to feel that these models had roots in the native soils, shaped primarily by the social and cultural factors.

After fifteen years of empirical and research studies in diverse situations, it is becoming clear that the Indian economic, business and management models are indeed unique and they operate on a different set of paradigms. A comparative study with the models of other countries, especially the popular ones of the western world, shows that most of the Indian models are quite different, much simpler, more sustainable and designed for better results. The Indian society appears to be self-dependent, effectively working its way in the midst of limitations and disturbances. It seems to be capable of achieving success, using the resources available at local levels through social capital and native practices.

India was a poor and underdeveloped country at the time of independence. In a span of just sixty years, India has emerged as the fourth largest economy with a lot of potential to grow further in the coming years. What could be the reason for such a turnaround in six decades? The field studies indicate that the major reason for such a performance is the functioning Indian models. India has generally been associated with poverty and underdevelopment. But when we go back and study the functioning of the economic and business systems of the earlier centuries, we come to know that India remained as the most prosperous country for many centuries. A true history of the Indian economic, business and management models seems to be missing in our country.

It is time that we studied the functioning Indian models especially at a time when India is emerging as an economic and business power. The need of the hour is to understand the ground realities to plan and make better use of the resources and methods available for creating a prosperous and peaceful society. It is important that we undertake this exercise now, as the popular western models are not able to provide solutions to many of the contemporary problems. This book is an attempt to present the functioning Indian economic, business and management models in the right perspectives.

After introduction, the book begins with the Indian economic models. Here the economic systems of ancient India, British India and post-independent India are presented. The details and data quoted in the book, many of which are not widely used, emphasize the special nature of the Indian economic systems. The third chapter briefly discusses the Western economic models beginning from feudalism. The next chapter presents the basic features of the Indian and the Western models for the purposes of comparison and proper understanding. The subsequent three chapters deal with the Western and the Indian business models. The fifth chapter gives an introduction to the types of different business models and their 'universality'. The next chapter discusses the Indian business models since the ancient days. It would be interesting to note here that the corporate form of organization was in existence more than two thousand years ago. The salient features of the Indian and Western business models and the uniqueness of the Indian models are discussed in the seventh chapter.

The eighth chapter explores the management models of India and the Western countries, the origin and the present position of management thought and education in India and the West. It also includes the basic factors underlying the Indian management thoughts and practices, and the need for an India-oriented approach in management education for a better and smooth functioning of our economic and business systems. The ninth chapter presents basic details that characterize the emerging India, underscores the need to understand the performing models and explains the opportunities available for the Indian models to emerge as the alternatives at the global level. Conclusions are given in the ninth chapter.

Though the book is primarily designed for the postgraduate students of Management, it is hoped that this would reach a wider audience including students of Economics and Commerce, business professionals, policy makers and research bodies.

I thank the academic and professional communities for their encouraging response to the first two editions of the book. The present edition has been updated with recent developments, latest data and new information.

P. Kanagasabapathi

Acknowledgements

A study of this type which involves frequent field visits and interactions with different groups of people across the country cannot be possibly done by a single individual and this work is not an exception. Therefore, I would be failing in my duty if I do not express my sincere gratitude to the people who have helped me in shaping my ideas, visiting different industrial and business centres, arranging meetings and collecting materials. Many industrialists, businessmen, entrepreneurs, office-bearers of industry and business associations, community leaders and academic institutions in different places across the country have helped in providing information and collecting details. Many of my students at the P.S.G. Institute of Management, Coimbatore who have been with me for the past ten years have helped me in my field studies. It is difficult for me to enlist all those who were associated with this endeavour as the list would be very long. I thank all of them for their whole-hearted cooperation.

During the course of these studies and earlier, I was fortunate enough to interact with a few experts who were involved in studying many of these aspects more deeply at a macro level for a long time. The noted corporate advisor S. Gurumurthy gave me critical inputs sparing his valuable time and helped me in undertaking studies in different centres. Dr. R. Vaidyanathan, Professor, Indian Institute of Management, Bangalore provided me insights into the functioning of our economic systems and allowed me to freely use his writings relating to the non-corporate sector. I had the opportunity to meet and interact with many industrial, business and social leaders, many of whom are either pioneers in their chosen areas or representatives of different industries and business associations in different centres across the country.

My special thanks are due to the following persons without whose help this book would not have been possible.

M.N. Arun Kumar, Michel Danino, B. Siva Kumar, Dr. R. Shanmugam, N. Subramanian, P. Thangavelu, B. Krishna Kumar, S. Muralidharan, C.G. Mohan, R. Sundaram, R. Srinivasan, R. Rajalakshmi, M.D. Shankar, Yugandar, Ranjan Kumar Sinha, Sharad Patel, S. Chandra Sekaran, A. Geetha, P. Rathishree, K. Manickam, K. Vinayagam, Sivaranjani, Aarthi, Vijay, Vish Trivedi, G. Karthikeyan, M. Gopinath, C. Balasubramaniam, Shanthi, S. Shantha Kumari, R. Prakash, N. Vivek, R. Sujatha and P. Tamilselvan. In addition, I would also like to gratefully acknowledge the support of the management and my friends at the P.S.G. College of Technology. And last but not least, I am thankful to the editorial and production staff of PHI Learning who have helped me in bringing out this edition in time.

P. Kanagasabapathi

1

INTRODUCTION

India is fast emerging as a powerful nation. The Indian economy has been growing at a steady pace for more than a quarter century and its performance during the recent years has been very impressive. The average rate of growth of GDP during 2003–04 to 2007–08 was 8.9 per cent [1]. The growth rate declined to 6.8 per cent in 2008–09 due to the impact of the global economic crisis. Subsequently, the economy started recovering in 2009–10 and achieved a rate of 8 per cent during the year. The performance improved much better during the next year with a rate of growth of 8.5 per cent. The Reserve Bank of India notes: "The Indian economy rebounded strongly in 2010–11 from the moderation induced by the global economic crisis.[2]" Earlier, the *Economic Survey 2010–11* mentioned: "This has been a classic year of economic recovery for India. The economy remained on the path of rapid resurgence which began in 2009–10 and has virtually returned to the growth path that it had achieved during 2005–08, before the global financial crisis and economic meltdown. India's growth story this year has been remarkable by any standards.[3]"

The higher performance of the economy during the past decade has placed India among the fast-growing and most potential economies in the world. The International Monetary Fund (IMF), in its *World Economic Outlook 2005*, had noted: "India's recent growth performance places it among the world's fastest growing economies. ....[4]" It is important to note that India has emerged as the second fastest growing economy in the world during the last few years.

With regard to the performance of the Indian economy during 2011–12, the Reserve Bank of India notes: "After the above trend growth during 2010–11, growth is expected to decelerate but remain close to the trend of about 8 per cent in 2011–12. Growth prospects for the year 2011–12 seem to be relatively subdued compared to the previous year due to a number of unfavourable developments. Global uncertainties have increased.[5]" In spite of the uncertainties and problems, India is widely expected to perform better in the coming years. India remains one of the very few countries least affected by the global economic crisis. Almost all the international organizations, economists and research bodies unanimously agree that India would soon be one of the top economic powers in the world. An increasing number of assessments point out that India would emerge as the leading performer of the world in future. Hence, the Indian economic systems are closely observed throughout the world.

Indian businesses are gaining worldwide recognition during the recent decades. Many companies are emerging as world-class performers. Out of the 100 local companies identified by the Boston Consulting Group as the new global challengers from 12 rapidly developing economies, there were 21 Indian companies[6]. Some of the Indian companies have been setting new benchmarks in the international markets. An increasing number of our companies are going out in different directions to establish, expand and diversify their businesses during the recent years. Overseas investments from India have increased from $14.3 billions during 2006 to $18.4 billions in 2008[7]. Meanwhile, more foreign companies have been scouting India to establish ties and increase their businesses. Reflecting this trend, *The Economist* stated: "Long neglected in Western boardrooms in favour of China, its yet more gigantic neighbor, India now appears on every corporate to-do list. Even in the furnace of pre-monsoonal heat, linen-suited Westerners (and Easterners) are appearing in Mumbai, Bangalore and Chennai, anxious not to miss out[8]." Many of the industrial and business centres of India, run by the family-based non-corporate sector, are emerging crucial to the global businesses. As a result, more and more up-country centres are becoming significant to the international markets.

While the Indian economic and business systems are being increasingly recognized and respected, the western systems are facing serious problems. The globalization model, as advocated by the West, is facing serious challenges in the recent periods. While the rich countries have been affected by the crisis, the poor have become poorer. The standard sets of policies prescribed by the multilateral agencies have worsened the situation in many developing and poor countries. Even in the richer countries, the divisions within the societies have widened. Modern economic theories are not in a position to provide solutions to many of their problems. The business models of the West are in difficulties. Recent years have witnessed the biggest failures in the western corporate system. Their management system is losing the confidence of the society as the top managements seem to be more interested in self-aggrandizement and personal benefits at the cost of the larger interests of the stakeholders.

In this scenario, it has become important to study and understand the functioning of Indian economic, business and management systems. Study of the 'business models'* requires an understanding of the 'economic models'.† Business models are influenced by, and depend on, the economic models. Hence, an understanding of the background of the economic models is necessary before studying the business models. In the contemporary world, no country is an island. Every country is influenced by the developments in other countries. So when we want to study India and her models, we need to have an idea of the major economic and business models of the other countries, especially the influential ones. Hence the study of the Indian economic models, in comparison to the western models, would help us to get a comparative view of the different systems, as the western approaches have been dominating the economic thinking of the rest of the world since the emergence of Europe in the eighteenth century. In the life of nations, the present era is a continuum of the past. Moreover, like all living beings, countries also mature and evolve over the years. Hence, the study of the present state alone may not be sufficient; rather an understanding of the historical developmental process would be necessary to get a clear picture. So the background of the economic systems of the past is required to get a clear view of developments.

Study of businesses cannot be undertaken in isolation; it requires a background of the economy, society and other relevant factors that influence business systems. Comparison of businesses between two or more countries without taking into account the other relevant factors would not be a complete exercise. Business models are complex and dynamic. Even within a country one could notice differences in business models. Cultural values, social behaviour, community norms and other factors seem to influence business models, apart from the economic ideologies of the countries. India is a country that nurtures diversities and accepts differences since the ancient days. So in a country such as India, one might see the existence of different kinds of systems. Moreover, India is a nation with a long history. The experiences of many centuries and historical developments over these periods would also have an impact on the economic and business systems.

* Business models are taken as the broad frameworks within which the businesses operate.

† Economic models are taken as the broad frameworks within which the economic systems operate.

All the available evidences portray India as a prosperous economy for hundreds of years. India was known as an important trading nation in different parts of the world for a long period. During this period, the economic and business models of the country were unique and largely driven by higher principles. The advent of the British, however, dramatically changed its position resulting in the decline of her economy and businesses. The native models were also destroyed to such an extent that at the time of independence it was a poor country.

For more than three decades after its independence, the policy-makers of India largely believed in socialistic-oriented approaches. Resultantly, the economic model of those years emphasized a greater role for the state and the public sector. Since the 1980s, policies were framed to ease restrictions and liberalize the environment. The beginning of the 1990s witnessed a drastic change in the attitude of the state, with policy initiatives being planned more in tune with the popular western economic thinking. All these developments have influenced the functioning of Indian models in different ways.

The western economic thinking has undergone many changes in the last five centuries. The colonial policies of the European powers helped them prosper and move ahead of India and China in terms of the global economic position. The later part of the eighteenth century witnessed the capitalistic ideology as propounded by Adam Smith. During this period, the United Kingdom began to emerge as an important economy. In less than a century after Adam Smith's advancement of the capitalist model, Karl Marx and Frederick Engels advocated the communist philosophy. Subsequently, in the later decades, the economic power shifted to the United States of America. The first communist government came to power in the Soviet Union in 1917.

After the Second World War, the International Monetary Fund and the World Bank were promoted and they began seriously advising different governments, especially since the 1980s. Meanwhile, the neo-classical economic theories, placing the market at the centre, became prominent. Unfortunately, the market fundamentalist theories, as they are called, could not prove to be a better alternative. Of late, the World Trade Organization has been facing serious difficulties as the agreements between the countries remain elusive. Consequently, their economic and business models have been facing serious challenges.

The management models* of different countries are influenced

* Management models are taken as the broad frameworks within which the management systems function.

by their economic and business models. Apart from these basic variables, the social and cultural backgrounds, historical experiences and other factors that are peculiar to different countries and regions might also influence the management systems. In the United States of America, for example, one could notice more of an individualistic style of management, while Japan nurtured more of a paternalistic system. In some cases, one could also observe a synthesis of the native and foreign management styles.

An objective analysis of different models with a historical background is needed to understand India's position in the emerging global scenario. A comparative study of different approaches would help us to learn about the strengths and weaknesses of different models. The ultimate purpose of this exercise is to examine and evaluate different models properly so that one could get the right perspective. This is a historic moment for India. A country that was poor and underdeveloped with a big population sixty years back, is now expected to play a dominant role in the global economy. This is not a small achievement. Not many countries in the world would be able to reach such a level within such a short period.

So it is the time now to understand and analyze the working of the Indian models from realistic perspectives, instead of looking at them through the theoretical points of view based on western assumptions and experiments. We need to understand the ground realities and functioning models of India and realize how they are managing to perform in the fast changing circumstances. Earlier, Peter Drucker had asserted that "the dominance of the US is already over... There is no one centre in the world economy... India is becoming a powerhouse very fast[9]." The contemporary global developments indicate that the world is expecting more from India than any other nation. Hence, there is an urgent need to understand the functioning Indian models in a better way and evolve suitable methodologies so that India could go forward and prove her mettle at the world level.

REFERENCES

[1] *Annual Report 2010–11,* Reserve Bank of India, Mumbai, p. 168.

[2] *Annual Report 2010–11*, Reserve Bank of India, p. 1.

[3] *Economic Survey 2010–11*, Ministry of Finance, Government of India, New Delhi, p. 23.

[4] 'Is India Becoming an Engine for Global Growth?', *World Economic Outlook,* September 2005, International Monetary Fund, Washington, p. 36.

[5] *Annual Report 2010–11,* Reserve Bank of India, p. 6.

[6] The Boston Consulting Group, 'The New Global Challengers-How 100 Top Companies from Rapidly Developing Economies are Changing the World', *BCG Report,* The Boston Consulting Group Inc., May 2006.

[7] *Report on Currency and Finance 2008–09*, Reserve Bank of India, p. 101.

[8] 'Can India Fly?', *The Economist*, June 3, 2006, p. 11.

[9] 'Peter Drucker Sets Us Straight', Interview by Brent Schlender, *Fortune 2004,* January 12, 149(1), pp.114–118.

2

INDIAN ECONOMIC MODELS

Indian economy had witnessed dramatic changes during the past centuries. As a result, the economic systems of India had also undergone notable changes. This chapter discusses the position of the Indian economy over the years.

2.1 ANCIENT INDIAN ECONOMY

India is an ancient nation. Evidences in India indicate human occupations ten thousand years ago[1]. We get to know about the economic activities of the earliest periods through archaeological evidences. For the later periods, the status of the Indian economy is gathered from different sources such as records, inscriptions and writings. The impressions of the foreign travellers, scholars and for the latest centuries, the English officials, who had seen and studied India for various purposes, also help us to find out the position of the economy. We do not have the quantitative and financial details for all those years, in the way we now have different sets of data to measure economies, as the present system of calculations is a product of the development of the last few decades.

Fortunately, we now have the Gross Domestic Product (GDP) figures for India since the beginning of the Common Era (CE). Hence it is possible to know the economic performance of India with the help of the contemporary quantitative figures at least for the past 2000 years. Noted economic historian Angus Maddison[2] has provided these details and his works have assumed significance because for the first time that certain vital economic data for different countries and the world are provided.

2.1.1 World GDP during 0 CE

The GDP figures of the world and different countries/regions during

0 CE reveal clearly the predominance of Indian economy*. Table 2.1 presents the details.

Table 2.1 World GDP (0 CE)

(million 1990 international $)

Year	0 CE
Total western Europe	11,115
Eastern Europe	1900
Former USSR	1560
Total western offshoots	468
Total Latin America	2240
Japan	1200
China	26,820
India	33,750
Other Asia	16,470
Total Asia (excluding Japan)	77,040
Africa	7013
World	**1,02,536**

Source: Maddison, Angus, *The World Economy—A Millennial Perspective*, 1st Indian Ed., Overseas Press (India) Private Limited, New Delhi, 2003, p. 261.

Table 2.1 shows the total GDP of the world at $102.5 billions. India was the largest contributor to the global GDP at that time with $33.75 billions. China was following India with $26.82 billions. Africa's contribution was $7.01 billions, while that of Japan was $1.2 billions. The GDP figures are not available for other countries individually, as they came into existence in their contemporary forms only in the later centuries.

Let us look at Table 2.2 to understand the shares of different countries/regions in the GDP of the world during those times.

Table 2.2 clearly illustrates the predominant position of India in the international economy during 0 CE. It shows that India's share of world GDP was 32.9 per cent 2007 years earlier. It means that India alone was contributing almost one-third of the global GDP, while all the countries in the rest of the world were jointly contributing the remaining two-thirds. China's contribution during

* Indian economy denotes the economy of undivided India as existed during 0 CE. The GDP figures for many other countries that exist today are not available individually since 0 CE, as they came into existence or were born as separate nations only in the later centuries. While Maddison (2003) has given details since 0 CE, Maddison (2007) uses 1 AD to denote the period 0 CE, and uses AD instead of CE for the subsequent years. However, this book uses CE for AD.

Table 2.2 Share of Countries/Regions in World GDP (0 CE)

Year	0 CE
Total western Europe	10.8
Eastern Europe	1.9
Former USSR	1.5
Total western offshoots	0.5
Total Latin America	2.2
Japan	1.2
China	26.2
India	32.9
Other Asia	16.1
Total Asia (excluding Japan)	75.1
Africa	6.8
World	**100**

Source: Maddison, Angus, *The World Economy—A Millennial Perspective*, 1st Indian Ed., Overseas Press (India) Private Limited, New Delhi, 2003, p. 263.

that period was 26.2 per cent. India and China together were contributing 59.1 per cent to the global economy. While the other countries in Asia were contributing 16.1 per cent, Japan's share was 1.2 per cent. The total contribution of Asia including Japan to the world GDP was an astonishing 76.3 per cent. While the total western Europe was contributing a share of 10.8 per cent, Africa's contribution was 6.8 per cent. It is significant to note that India's GDP was slightly more than three times of the GDP of the total western Europe. No country or even geographical region was anywhere nearer to India, except China. Even when compared with China, India's GDP was more than 125 per cent. Today when countries with much lesser share of contributions are called superpowers, how should one call India of 0 CE?

Now let us look at Figure 2.1 to understand the economic performance of India and China with the rest of the world.

Figure 2.1 clearly shows that while the rest of the countries in the world were contributing about 41 per cent to the global GDP, India's share as a single nation was about 33 per cent, with China following India with a share of 26 per cent. This demonstrates the superior economic performance of India more than two millennia earlier. We see India as an outstanding performer in economic affairs when the contemporary GDP methodology is applied to measure the position of different countries. It is important to remember here that India could not have garnered a one-third share of the global economy suddenly in 0 CE. India must have had strong fundamentals and a well-developed economic status many centuries ago.

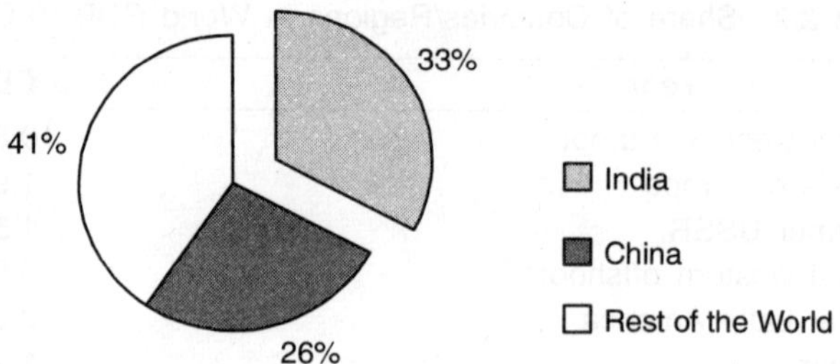

Figure 2.1 Share of India, China and the rest of the world in world GDP (0 CE).
Note: Percentages in the figure are in round figures.

2.1.2 Indian Economy Since the Ancient Periods

What could be the reason for such an excellent performance during 0 CE? A country could not have remained in such a high position without high levels of performance of different sectors. Such performance would not have been possible without strong fundamentals including high levels of skills and talented citizens. Moreover, a strong foundation must have been necessarily laid many centuries earlier, to be at such a high level at 0 CE. Since we do not have the GDP data for periods earlier to 0 CE, we have only to rely on the performance details of the different sectors that make up the economy. The living conditions of citizens and the functioning of the society would also enable us to know the status of the economy. From such details, we can certainly understand the economic position of India in the earlier millennia. So let us see the position and performance of the vital sectors that contribute to the growth of an economy. First, let us take the three major sectors of the economy, namely agriculture, industry and trade.

2.1.3 Agriculture and Food Production

Jean-Francois Jarrige[3], the French excavator, had noted that by 6000 BCE, Mehrgarh, one of India's most ancient settlements, had "a veritable agricultural economy solidly established." Agricultural scientists show that Indians cultivated wheat, barley, peas, date palms and cotton, among other items, more than 4500 years ago[4]. The earliest sample of cotton cloth discovered in India was in the ruins of Harappa around 5000 years ago[5]. Evidence of rice cultivation in India goes back to 4300 years[6]. Hence, India seems to have been engaged in cultivating different varieties of cereals, cotton and other items at least a few thousand years ago. Much later, the Greek historian Megasthenese, who visited India about 2300 years ago from now, had noted: "The greater part of the soil is under irrigation, and, consequently, bears two crops in a year[7]." In fact, it is clear that the foreign travellers who had visited India were surprised to see the agricultural prosperity of the country. Diodorus Siculus, who visited India later around the first century BCE, had particularly mentioned the fertility of lands and production of different varieties of cereals and fruits. Siculus had noted: "India has many mountains which abound in fruit trees of every kind, and many vast plains of great fertility, which are remarkable for their beauty and are supplied with water by a multitude of rivers. The greater part of the soils, moreover, is well watered and bears two crops in the course of a year... . In addition to the cereals, there grows throughout India much millet, which is kept well-watered by the profusion of river streams, and much pulse of superior quality, and rice also... as well as many other plants useful for food, of which most are native to the country. The soils yield, moreover, a few other edible fruits fit for the subsistence of animals...[8]."

The knowledge in agriculture, acquired over many years of experience, must have helped Indians to develop superior techniques and tools necessary for higher and sustainable production. Writing on Indian agriculture around 1820, Major General Alexander Walker who had served in the East India Company, had noted: "The Hindoos have been long in possession of one of the most beautiful and useful inventions in agriculture. This is the Drill Plough. This instrument has been in use from the remotest times in India[9]." But it is said to have been first used in Europe much later in 1662. "Its first introduction in England dates to 1730. But it took perhaps another 50 years before it was used on any scale[10]." The western agricultural scientists of the twentieth century mention as to how the Indian farmers used compost and organic manure which ensured that they could continue farming on the same land for more than 2000 years without a drop in yields[11]. The noted agricultural scientist, Albert Howard regarded the Indian farmers as 'professors' and "decided that he could not do better than watch their operations[12]. He openly admitted that "from them, he learnt how to grow healthy crops, particularly free from diseases, without the slightest help from artificial manures or insecticides[13]." This stands testimony to the practical wisdom of Indians in the field of agriculture.

Food is the basic necessity for all living beings. The ancient texts from different regions of India insist that abundant production of food crops is the foremost duty of the society. *Thirukkural,* written by the Tamil sage Thiruvalluvar more than two thousand years ago, emphasized farming as the foremost vocation and underlined the need for bountiful yields for a country[14]. Evidences indicate that there was neither famine nor scarcity of food in ancient India.

Siculus had mentioned: "It is accordingly confirmed that famine has never visited India and that there has never been a general scarcity in the supply of nourishing food[15]." By different accounts, the agricultural prosperity seems to have continued throughout the centuries. Ibn Battutah, the Arab scholar who travelled during the fourteenth century CE had noted that rice was sown three times a year[16]. *Food for All* notes the higher levels of agricultural production and productivity till the early nineteenth century. "Historically, India had been known to be a country of agricultural abundance. Epigraphic information available from about 11th century onwards from different parts of the country indicates a very high level of agricultural production and productivity. And, European observers of the early nineteenth century repeatedly report levels of productivity that are high not only in comparison with the Europe of that time, but also with the best of today[17]."

It is proud to know that Indians of the ancient days were able to achieve a world class performance in agriculture. How could they have achieved such high levels of production? Apart from utilizing all the natural facilities, they seemed to have developed and used all possible techniques to get maximum possible production. In this connection, it is pertinent to quote a few lines on tanks from the '*Cambridge Encyclopedia of India, Pakistan, Bangladesh and Srilanka*', *1989*. It says: "The whole of South India is dotted with tanks. A British expert writing in the 1850's estimated that the total number of such tanks in the Madras Presidency to be over 50,000. Another estimate indicated that in the eighteenth century, there were more than 38,000 tanks in the region that later constituted the Mysore State. The state had an area of around 29,000 square miles. It is, therefore, a fair estimate that there were over a lakh tanks in the whole of South India. These tanks were constructed and maintained by local effort. Together they formed a closely-knit whole so that the outflow from the one at a higher level supplied the one at a lower level, and so on[18]." We have to note here the perfect planning that existed to conserve water in those days. The *Encyclopedia* further continues to say: "This chain of tanks was so complete and inter-related within itself that British engineers of the nineteenth century felt that it would have been impossible to add another tank to the chain or to take out one from it[19]."

It was not just more production, but maximum productivity that seemed to be the hallmark of those days. We are surprized to see the higher productivity levels even in the not so high fertile regions as late as the eighteenth century. It was noted: "We have detailed information about the state of agriculture in 1760's for about 2000 localities of the Chengalpattu region around the city of Chennai in

South India. In this relatively difficult region, and in that period of extended war and great disturbance, average productivity of land was near 2.5 tons per hectare. Even more strikingly, the localities of relatively intensive agriculture, that covered about a sixth of the cultivated land, produced as much as 5 tons per hectare on the average. Per capita production of food grains in this region, covering about 45,000 households, was nearly a ton per year. This is five times the production per capita in India of today[20]."

2.1.4 Industry

India was an industrial and a manufacturing country from the ancient times. Different types of industries, including the highly specialized ones, have functioned since the earlier days. The eminent archaeologist Chhabra[21] had noted: "It may be a surprise even to an Indian today to be told that in the ancient world, India was in the forefront in the field of shipbuilding. Her ships flying Indian flags, sailed up and down the Arabian sea, the Indian Ocean and far beyond. Her master-mariners led the way in navigation. Riverine traffic within the country, shipping along the entire length of India's coastline and on high seas, were brisk until as recently as the days of the East India Company." Writing about the Mauryan state that existed about 2300 years ago, Basham[22] mentions that there were different sizes of industries. "Though the basis of ancient Indian industry was at all times the individual craftsman, aided chiefly by members of his own family, larger manufactories, worked chiefly by hired labour, were by no means unknown. Not only did the Mauryan state own spinning and weaving workshops, but also shops for the manufacture of weapons and other military supplies, employing salaried craftsmen. The larger mines were also owned and worked by the state. But though the economic order approximated to a sort of state socialism in the time of the Mauryas, it always left scope for the individual producer and distributor. We read here and there of private producers who had far transcended the status of the small home craftsman, and who manufactured on a larger scale for a wide market. Thus an early Jaina text tells of a wealthy potter named Saddalaputta who owned 500 potters' workshops, and a fleet of boats which distributed his wares throughout the Ganges valley; there a few other references, which confirm that large scale production for a wide market was not unknown in ancient India, though such industrialists as Saddalaputta were no doubt comparatively rare." *The Arthashastra,* written about 2300 years ago, had clearly divided and documented the responsibilities of the heads of various departments of industries during those periods. The list of heads of departments of industries included Chief Controller of Mining and Metallurgy, Chief Salt Commissioner, Chief Textile Commissioner and Chief Controller of Shipping[23]. It only shows that there were various types of specalized industrial activities and a well-defined demarcation of duties and responsibilities with regard to each department. All these would not have happened without a developed industrial sector. In those days weaving was a national industry that employed qualified labourers to manufacture yarns, shirtings, clothing and ropes[24].

Different sources note that India was well known for her manufacturing expertise throughout the world. Montgomery Martin, who had compiled the first complete history of British colonies in 1840, had noted: "India is as much a manufacturing country as agricultural, her manufactures of various descriptions have existed for ages, and have never faced competition from any nation, whenever fair chance has been given to them." Business historian Agarwala[25] notes that a large proportion of the population was engaged in various industries till the beginning of the nineteenth century. In his book on the business history of India during the last 5000 years, Agarwala[26] states: "A large proportion of the Indian population was engaged in various industries up to the first decade of the 19th century. Weaving was still national industry of the people; millions of women eked out their family income and their earnings from spinning. Dyeing, tanning and working in metals also gave employment to millions."

Kennedy[27] has presented the shares of manufacturing output of different countries/regions in the world during 1750. Even at that time, India's share in world manufacturing was almost one-fourth of the global output. Table 2.3 presents the relevant figures.

Table 2.3 Relative Shares of World Manufacturing Output (1750)

Europe as a whole	23.2
United Kingdom	1.9
Hasburg Empire	2.9
France	4.0
German states	2.9
Italian states	2.4
Russia	5.0
United States	0.1
Japan	3.8
Third World	73.0
China	32.8
India	24.5

Source: Kennedy, Paul S., *The Rise and Fall of the Great Powers—Economic Change and Military Conflict from 1500–2000*, Fontana Press, London, 1988, p. 190.

We have to note here that India's share of global manufacturing was more than that of Europe as a whole, and was next only to China. India and China together contributed 57.3 per cent of the global manufacturing output. Among the western nations, the share of the United Kingdom was only 1.9 per cent, while France contributed 4 per cent. The share of Japan, that emerged as an industrial power later, was 3.8 per cent. It is important to note that the Third World countries were contributing 73 per cent of the global output during the middle of the eighteenth century.

Figure 2.2 illustrates the position of India, China, UK and the rest of the world in the world manufacturing output in 1750.

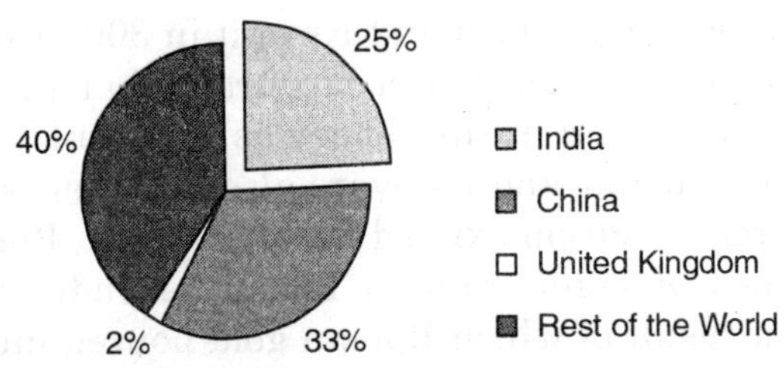

Figure 2.2 Share of India, China, UK and the rest of the world in world manufacturing output (1750). *Note:* Percentages in the figure are in round figures.

2.1.5 Trade

Trade was considered the most important activity after agriculture and industry in ancient India. Writing in the context of South India, Mukund[28] notes: "In South Indian ethos, trade is recognized as one of the most important economic activities after agriculture and crafts, which also signifies the sequence in which the economy diversifies into more specialized activities beyond subsistence." Agarwala[29] mentions that there was a vast network of trade 5300 years ago and quotes: "Even some 53 centuries ago, the people were linked in a vast trade network, much of Harappa's trade undoubtedly travelled along the Ravi river, eventually reaching the Indus. And some surely went by that main stream river to Mohenjodaro, Harappa's sister city some 400 miles to the south. Traders from the north waited to present turquoise and lapis lazuli to a Harappan merchant weighing beads." Trade was not confined to the borders. It extended to many countries around the globe. Even sea trade was very much in vogue. In this connection, it is useful to take note of the following lines. "The history of India's trade and commerce goes back to the Phoenician times when spices, ivory, silks, fine cottons and precious stones were carried by intrepid

Indian merchants to Egypt, Mesopotamia, the countries of Asia Minor and the near East and later to Greece and Rome. Indian silks and fine muslins were highly prized and there is contemporary evidence of a flourishing trade between India and the distant European countries since pre-Christian times. Indian merchants also used to navigate many sea routes and the start of the caravan was an important event for the merchant community. Excavations in Ur, Chaldian, Babylon, Assyria, Sumer, Petra, Persia and Lebanon testify to trade exchanges with India. Archaeological excavations testify to the existence of the ports at Lothal (Gujarat) and Rann of Kutch (Dholavira) which had extensive trade exchanges in the time of the Indus Valley civilization with the Dilmun civilization of Bahrain and Kuwait in 3000 BC and later[30]."

India seems to have enjoyed a favourable balance of trade from the beginning and as a result she was accumulating gold. "The Yemenites, Nabataeans, and Himyars also had their share in Indian trade. Commercial relation existed between India, Rome and Greece and the balance of trade was in favour of India from the very beginning, as a result of which Roman gold poured into India[31]." In this context, it is interesting to note the statement of Pliny on the drainage of Roman wealth into India. Trade historian Chakravarty[32] mentions this point while writing as to how the historians were made to take note of India's position in international trade. To quote: "The famous statement of Pliny that the love of gain brought the Roman Empire nearer India, his lamentation for the drainage of huge wealth to India to meet the affluent Romans' demand for luxuries, the descriptive geography of the voyages and the Indian coasts in the *Periplus of the Erythraean Sea* and the mention of a Temple of Augustus at Muziris (Cranganore, Kerala) in the *Tabula Peutangariana* spoke for themselves." The ancient texts emphasized that the basis of foreign trade was earning profits. *Arthasastra* said: "A crucial injunction regarding trade with foreign countries given to the Chief Controller of State Trading was: 'generate profits; avoid losses[33].'"

Agarwala mentions that in the ancient times, both the internal and external trades were at their peak. To quote: "In ancient times both the internal and external trades were at their peak. The trade in textiles was very brisk. Silks were imported from China, and from Central Asia came pearls and very fine wool. India mainly exported cotton cloth. The articles of export and import consisted of seashells, areca nut, sandalwood, gold, silver, pearls, precious stones and coral. India also had a large trade with Iran[34]." Hence trade, including international trade, was not new to India. In fact, India was a successful exporter from the earliest times. Economic historian Frank[35] notes that during the period from the fifteenth to the beginning of the nineteenth century, "...India had a massive balance of trade surplus with Europe and some with West Asia, based mostly on its more efficient low-cost cotton textile production and also of course on pepper for export. These went westward to Africa, West Asia, Europe, and from there on across the Atlantic to the Caribbean and the Americas... . In return, India received massive amounts of silver and some gold from the West, directly around the Cape or via West Asia, as well as from West Asia itself." India was the economic centre of the Indian Ocean region during this period. "The geographical and economic centre of this Indian Ocean world was the Indian subcontinent itself. Much of it was highly developed and already dominant in the world textile industry before the Mughal conquest[36]." An important point that we learn here is that India seemed to be a successful player in international trade with a favourable balance of trade from the very beginning.

India seems to have excelled in all the three crucial economic sectors, namely agriculture, industry and trade. India was a pioneer in developing new tools and technologies since the ancient days, when no country had any idea of them. Agricultural production and productivity were world-class. The observations of many foreign travellers and scientists in the later periods vouchsafe the superior performance of the agricultural sector. All the available evidences place the performance of the industrial sector at higher levels. India was a significant player in international markets, even five thousand years ago. Khanna[37] notes that "ancient India not only had business forms that easily met the notion of a contracting entity, but also had business forms that went considerably further with many features that are common to more recent organizational forms such as corporations." The trade relationships with many countries show India as a major trading power. Details regarding the three major economic sectors indicate high levels of performance for many centuries before the beginning of the Common Era.

2.1.6 Other Critical Sectors

Education and science and technology

A nation could emerge powerful only when there is widespread education and arrangements for imparting high quality skills and knowledge. A superior economic status demands new developments in science and technology leading to social and economic benefits. So education and science and technology could be considered the vital sectors for development. It is accepted that India was contributing one-third of global economic output more than 2000 years ago. But what was the level of education in olden days? Was there any possibility for a higher level education? What was the position of science and technology? Was there any development worth mentioning in different fields of science? Let us see the position of education and science and technology in the earlier days.

Education: The traditional Indian system divided a person's life into four stages. The first stage, namely, *Brahmacharya* was devoted to education. Hence, education was the first and most significant part of one's life. Records show that the first university in the world was established in India, in Takshila, about 2700 years ago. It means that India was a pioneer in higher education in the world. At that time, there were more than 10,500 students in the Takshila University pursuing studies in more than 60 different subjects. Such a high number of students indicate widespread education at the lower levels and a thirst for higher level of knowledge among a large number of people. Offering more than 60 different courses in various fields such as science, mathematics, medicine, politics, warfare, astrology, astronomy, music, religion and philosophy shows the expertise of ancient Indians in diverse subjects and the requirements for such specialized courses in the society. We come to know that the Takshila campus had students from Babylonia, Greece, Syria, Arabia and China[38]. It only proves that the university was internationally renowned, as candidates from all the other ancient civilizations had studied here. The presence of students from all the important countries of those times demonstrates that India was the centre of higher education in the world. Nalanda University, established during the fifth century CE, remained the centre of education for scholars from different countries in Asia for many years. There were a number of students from Persia, China, Japan and Korea. There were continuous contacts between Nalanda and China over many years. On the demand for Nalanda education in foreign countries it was noted: "The success of Nalanda as a seat of learning is singularly demonstrated by the demand of foreign countries for the services of its trained scholars...[39]." Nalanda is said to have contained the largest collection of books numbering over ninety lakhs[40]. Universities were functioning successfully in different centres including Vikramashila, Nadia, Mithila and Jagadda during the earlier periods.

An important point to be remembered here is that without a high level of economic and social development, higher education of international quality would not have happened in those times. High quality education in different fields must have led to further developments during the subsequent periods in the society. It is significant to note that specialized industrial and technical education was offered in the ancient periods. One could notice, for example, the school of sculpture. What is significant is the contribution of education to the development of the economic prosperity of the country. Mookerji[41] notes: "Ancient Indian literature ... does not furnish much evidence on the subject of industrial and technical education, though it is upon the basis of such education that ancient India was able to build up her own economic life and prosperity, and figured in the ancient world as the chief exporting country..." The artisans and the guilds of various kinds functioned as schools for imparting necessary skills to the entrants. "While the house of artisans functioned as the school for imparting education in the particular craft..., the collective interests of craft as a whole in a particular area or region were administered by an organization like a guild... The guilds were of various kinds like the crafts and were like so many industrial schools[42]."

Even after invasions from foreign lands and continued disturbances in the society during the later centuries, literacy levels were reported to be highest in the world during the eighteenth century. Makkhan Lal[43] notes: "Literacy was widespread; it was probably as high as 75 per cent at the beginning of the 18th century. In the contemporary world, no other country had such a high percentage of literate population." In the nineteenth century, the British conducted studies on the prevailing indigenous educational system. Surveys were made in the Bombay Presidency during 1820–1830 and the Madras Presidency during 1823–1826. A limited semi-official survey was also conducted in the Presidency of Bengal ten years later by a former missionary W. Adam, and his findings were published in 1835. His first report was followed by two more reports, published in 1836 and 1838[44]. These studies were revealing.

In 1931, while he was in London, Mahatma Gandhi noted that the education system in India before the arrival of the British was like a "beautiful tree". Later, the noted Gandhian, Dharampal took upon himself the responsibility of studying the Indian education system from the archival materials. He published his works under the title '*The Beautiful Tree.*' In his work, Dharampal[45] writes on the Adam's report: "In his first report which is a general statement of the situation and a presentation of the data which he could derive from post-1800 official and other sources, W. Adam came to the conclusion, firstly, that every village had at least one school and in all probability in Bengal and Bihar with 1,50,748 villages "there will still be 1,00,000 villages that have these schools. Secondly, on the basis of personal observation and what he had learnt from other evidence, he inferred that on an average there were around 100 institutions of higher learning in each district of Bengal, and consequently, he concluded that the 18 districts of Bengal had about 1,800 such institutions. Computing the number studying in these latter at the lowest figure of six scholars in each, he also came to the conclusion that some 10,800 scholars should be studying in them." Dharampal[46] noted that almost similar conclusions were given by the British officials. "Similar statements had been made, much before W. Adam, for areas of the Madras Presidency by men like Thomas Munro, that "every village had a school" and for areas of the newly extended Presidency of Bombay around 1820 by senior officials like G.L. Prendergast, "that there is hardly a village, great or small, throughout our territories, in which there is not at least one school, and in larger villages more." Observations made by Dr. G.W. Leitner in 1882 show that the spread of education in the Punjab around 1850 was of a similar extent. The Survey Reports prepared by British district officers between 1813 and 1830 show that almost every village had a school, financially supported by the villagers themselves[47].

Based on details, Dharampal[48] mentions that the education system in India in 1800 was much better than that of the British. He also notes that the Indian method of school teaching that prevailed here for centuries had helped the introduction of popular education in England. To quote: "According to this hard data, in terms of content and proportion of those attending institutional school education, the situation in India in 1800 (and it should be remembered that it is a greatly damaged and disorganized India that one is referring to) does not in any sense look inferior to what obtained in England then; and in many respects Indian schooling seems to have been much more extensive. The method of school teaching was the method which is said to have greatly helped the introduction of popular education in England but which had prevailed in India for centuries". This is because 'school education, especially education at the people's level was rather an uncommon commodity till around 1800' in Britain[49]. During that time, there were a number of institutions of higher learning, enumerated under the term 'colleges'. Dharampal gives details of the number to 'what was then known as the Presidency of Madras.' "The largest number of 'colleges', 279, were in the district of Rajahmundry with a total of 1,454 scholars, Coimbatore coming next with 173 such places (724 scholars). Guntoor had 171 (with 939 scholars), Tanjore 109 (with 769 scholars), Nellore 107, North Arcot 69 (with 418 scholars),

Salem 53 (with 324 scholars), Chengalpattu 51 (with 398 scholars), Masulipatnam 49 (with 199 scholars), Bellary 23, Trichnopoly 9 (with 131 scholars), and Malabar with one old institution maintained by the Samudrin Raja (Zamorin), with 75 scholars[50]."

The above details show India as the pioneer in education since the ancient periods. Education was widespread; literacy rate was very high. India was the centre of higher education for all the countries about 2700 years ago. Education was offered in different technical and specialized areas through localized institutions. All these must have helped in the development of the economy and society. Probably, it was with this background that Voltaire was 'convinced of the pre-eminence of Indian achievement in the areas of secular learning and world culture[51].'

Science and technology: India's performance in different areas of science and technology, including mathematics, medicine, chemistry, physics, astronomy, architecture and metallurgy, is amazing. In fact, India had been making original and pioneering contributions in different fields of science and technology since the ancient periods. Apart from the fact that these contributions were made during the earlier periods, they have also laid the foundations for modern science. Speaking on just one aspect, one of the greatest scientists of the modern times, Albert Einstein had noted: "We owe a lot to the Indians, who taught us how to count, without which no worthwhile scientific discovery could have been made." India's contribution to the field of mathematics over many centuries is astonishing. India had produced many renowned mathematicians since the ancient days. Baudhayana (800 BCE), Manava (750 BCE), Apastamba (600 BCE), Panini (520 BCE) and Katyayana (200 BCE) were the well-known mathematicians who contributed before the beginning of the Common Era. In the subsequent periods, there were many great mathematicians such as Aryabhata I (476 CE), Bhaskara I (600 CE) and Bhaskara II (1114 CE). Many of their achievements are path-breaking. Experts point out that the inherent taste of the Indian mind towards science is responsible for these achievements. Georges Ifrah[52] notes: "The Indian mind has always had for calculations and the handling of numbers an extraordinary inclination, ease and power, such as no other civilization in history ever possessed to the same degree. So much as that Indian culture regarded the science of numbers as the noblest of its arts... . A thousand years ahead of Europeans, Indian *savants* knew that the zero and infinity were mutually inverse notions..."

Amercian writer Dick Teresi's book titled *"Lost Discoveries"* deals with the ancient non-western foundations of modern science.

Quoting Teresi's references to India, Shashi Tharoor[53] notes: "India invented modern numerals (known to the world as 'Arabic' numerals because the West got them from the Arabs, who learned them from us!). It was an Indian who first conceived of the zero, shunya; the concept of nothingness, shunyata, integral to Hindu and Buddhist thinking, simply did not exist in the West. "In the history of culture, wrote Tobias Dantzig in 1930, the invention of zero will always stand out as one of the greatest single achievements of the human race." The concept of infinite sets of rational numbers was understood by Jain thinkers in the sixth century BC. Our forefathers can take credit for geometry, trigonometry, and calculus; the 'Bakhshali manuscript', 70 leaves of bark dating back to the early centuries of the Christian era, reveals fractions, simultaneous equations, quadratic equations, geometric progressions and even calculations of profit and loss, with interest.

The Sulba Sutras, composed between 800 and 500 BC, demonstrate that India had Pythagoras' theorem before the great Greek was born, and a way of getting the square root of 2 correct to five decimal places. (Vedic Indians solved square roots in order to build sacrificial altars of the proper size.) The Kerala mathematician Nilakantha wrote sophisticated explanations of the irrationality of 'pi' before the West had heard of the concept. The Vedanga Jyotisha, written around 500 BC, declares: 'Like the crest of a peacock, like the gem on the head of a snake, so is mathematics at the head of all knowledge.' Our mathematicians were poets too! But one could go back even earlier, to the Harappan civilization, for evidence of a highly sophisticated system of weights and measures in use around 3000 BC.

Archaeologists also found a 'ruler' made with lines drawn precisely 6.7 millimeters apart, with an astonishing level of accuracy. The 'Indus inch' was a measure in consistent use throughout the area. The Harappans also invented kiln-fired bricks, less permeable to rain and floodwater than the mud bricks used by other civilizations of the time. The bricks contained no straw or other binding material and so turned out to be usable 5,000 years later when a British contractor dug them up to construct a railway line between Multan and Lahore. And while they were made in 15 different sizes, the Harappan bricks were amazingly consistent: their length, width and thickness were invariably in the ratio of 4:2:1."

"Indian mathematical innovations, writes Teresi, had a profound effect on neighbouring cultures. The greatest impact was on Islamic culture, which borrowed heavily from Indian numerals, trigonometry and analemma. Indian numbers probably arrived in the Arab world in 773 AD with the diplomatic mission sent by the Hindu ruler of Sind to the court of the Caliph Al-Mansur. This gave rise to the famous arithmetical text of Al-Khwarizmi, written around 820 AD, which contains a detailed exposition of Indian mathematics, in particular the usefulness of the zero. With Islamic civilization's rise and spread, knowledge of Indian mathematics reached as far afield as Central Asia, North Africa and Spain. In serving as a conduit for incoming ideas and a catalyst for influencing others, Teresi adds, India played a pivotal role[54]."

There are many path-breaking achievements in different areas of science and it is difficult to point out all the contributions of ancient India in these pages. But it is necessary for us to understand that the contributions are in diverse fields of science ranging from mathematics to medicine and astronomy. For example, Sushruta defined the function of the heart 2600 years ago. In the West, Harvey could do it only during the seventeenth century. It is said that Sushruta conducted surgeries even in those days[55]. A *chaturyuga* or cycle of four ages in the ancient Indian system, is supposed to last 43,20,000 years, almost exactly the age of the earth. Aryabhata I made many contributions such as giving the accurate value of Pi and suggesting that the earth is a sphere. In the technological fields, we again find superior levels of performance. For example, when we take metallurgy, smelting of metals and derivation of alloys were already in vogue in India since 3000 BCE. Texts suggest that steel was exported to Europe, China and Middle East from South India. British records show that even in the eighteenth century, there were 20,000 furnaces operating in India[56]. It only shows the development of industries related to metallurgy.

India's achievements in science and technology are outstanding. For a long time, India had pioneered innovations in various fields of science. All the accomplishments in the fields of education, science and technology must have helped in the economic and social developments of the country.

2.1.7 Predominance of the Indian Economy

Hence, ancient India was not just the most prosperous nation. It was also the nation of the intellectual and scientific achievements of highest calibre. Moreover, these achievements demonstrate that India must have had a developed economic status for at least many centuries before 0 CE. Performance details regarding different sectors of the economy, including international trade five thousand years ago, indicate that a sound economy should have functioned even in those days. Detailed studies would be able to provide a clear picture. In the ancient periods, agriculture was the main occupation with crafts, manufacturing and trade following it. The economy was mostly village-based and the villages were largely self-sustaining. There were also well-developed cities with perfect planning about five thousand years ago. Agriculture supplied the raw materials for textiles and crafts, apart from meeting the requirements regarding food. There seemed to be a fine balance among different sectors of the economy as we see the developments of all the sectors in the country. Moreover, India seemed to have developed a scientific system for running the government and managing economy. This is evident from the *Arthashastra,* considered to be the world's first comprehensive book on economics and politics. The ancient society encouraged economic activity for current prosperity and future growth. *Arthashastra* advised: "The root of wealth is economic activity and lack of it brings material distress. In the absence of fruitful economic activity, both current prosperity and future growth are in danger of destruction[57]." *Thirukkural,* written in deep south, exhorted people to make wealth in plenty[58]." It is significant to note that the ancient Indian society considered making wealth as the most important activity.

2.1.8 Ethics in Economics

There seems to be a higher ideal in all the economic activities of ancient India. The objective of Indian agriculture was not just high levels of production and higher levels of productivity. The ultimate aim was to make food available to all. Hence, sharing of food was part of the life of the society. The following lines explain this noble practice of sharing in Tamil Nadu. "Another striking feature of the Chengalpattu information is the extensive sharing of the produce that was practised then. The sharing arrangements of the Chengalpattu society covered almost every institution and every household of the region[59]." While sharing food, the concern of the ancient Indians was not only the human beings, but all the living beings. See further: "On looking at India of classical times, we find an extraordinary emphasis on production and sharing of food. The classical texts unanimously insist that abundance of production and sharing is the essential condition of *dharma.* For classical India, a state or a society tolerating the hunger of even a single individual commits an unthinkable sin. This discipline of taking care of the hunger of all encompasses not only human beings, but also animals, birds, insects and, in fact, all aspects of nature[60]." It is important to take note of two points here. One is that the abundant production and sharing of food was insisted as the essential condition of *dharma,* the noblest ideal in life. The next point is that the discipline of taking care encompassed not only human beings, but also animals, birds, insects and all aspects of nature. The rulers in those days saw to it that those who traversed through their lands were provided with food. In this connection, it is worth reading the extracts of the letter written by the Sarfojee Maharaja of Thanjavur (in Tamil Nadu) in 1801 on the arrangements made regarding food in *Chatrams.** "All travellers..., pilgrims of every description ... are fed with boiled rice; those who do not choose to eat the boiled rice receive it unboiled with spices etc. These distributions continue till midnight when a bell is rung and proclamation made requiring all those who have not been fed to appear and take the rice prepared for them[61]."

While discussing the structure of business in ancient India, Basham[62] notes that the ancient Indian business functioned on higher ideals, even when making money was the objective. To quote: "Thus the ideals of ancient India, while not perhaps the same as those of the acquisitive West, by no means excluded money-making. India had not only a class of luxury-loving and pleasure-seeking dilettanti, but also one of wealth-seeking merchants and prosperous craftsmen, who, though less respected than the brahmans and warriors, were honoured in society." Even while encouraging wealth creation, the ancient society emphasized higher principles. The ancient texts and literature exhorted people to follow higher principles in business and creating wealth. *Thirukkural* cautioned people to avoid making wealth through wrongful methods. It underlined that earning wealth without human principles is a disgrace. Ancient India emphasized the significance of earning wealth through proper methods in all possible ways, through texts, sages and common sayings in the local languages. Thiruvalluvar[63] had allotted a separate chapter in his classic with the title 'means of wealth'. In one of the couplets he said: "For those who earn wealth in abundance through right means, virtue and happiness follow."

The Jainese texts advised their community men 'to follow truthful and peaceful means of earning wealth.' Jain[64] notes: "A large number of traders in western India during the eleventh–thirteenth centuries were *Jainas*. They were exhorted by their teachers and preachers to follow truthful and peaceful means of earning wealth. Jinesvara Suri (eleventh century), in his *Satsthanakaprakarana,* dilates upon the code of conduct which a merchant was expected to follow. He advises that a merchant should

* *Chatrams* are rest houses for travellers.

neither weigh less nor charge more. He should deliver the goods of the same quality as seen and approved by the customer, and should never indulge in adulteration. Jinesvara Suri, suggests that a merchant should not hoard grain as it could be destroyed by worms, but may store such goods as cotton, yarn, cloths, coral, pearls, madder, areca nuts, etc. which could be kept in godowns for a long period without the fear of physical loss. Since a king could be of great service or disservice to merchants, he advises that a merchant should call on the king frequently and flatter him by reciting his good qualities; a merchant should never refute him or keep the company of his opponents. To the money-lenders he advises that a loan should never be advanced for the sake of greed, and that the creditor must not use the pledged items such as carriages, bullocks, etc. for his personal benefit without making a payment. He adds that if a wicked debtor refuses to return the loan or turns violent, the creditor should be prepared to forego his money rather than fight with him. Hemacandra also advises merchants to remain calm and peaceful in provocative circumstances, and points out that heroism must not be shown by a merchant, even though he is heroic. Since peace is essential for the promotion of commercial activity, merchants at large were advised to avoid all strife, strain and provocation in the interest of their profession."

2.1.9 Government and Business

There were different forms of businesses in ancient India. "Along with the family-run business and individually owned business enterprises ancient India possessed a number of other forms of engaging in business or collective activity, including the *gana, pani, puga, vrata, samgha, nigama,* and *sreni*[65]." The most common economic entity in those days was *sreni,* containing features similar to the modern corporate form of organization.* There seems to have been codes of conduct and general rules regulating businesses, though they were not written down in the form of documents most of the times. For the *sreni* forms of organization, there were clear rules that were upheld by kings. "...the customs, traditions and usages of the *sreni* (very frequently put down in writing) generally had the force of law and were upheld by the monarch even if they had punitive elements, absent them being against royal interest of

* Khanna, Vikramaditya S., op.cit., p. 8. Khanna writes that generally a *sreni* is a legal entity composed of a collection of people who were normally engaged in a similar trade. It is similar to the modern corporate form of organization, though there are certain differences.

the scriptures. These rules, called *sreni dharma*, could cover a number of topics including production practices, prices, quality controls and so forth[66]."

Evidences show that there were arrangements in the society to take care of all the travellers, including those with merchandise. Well-defined systems were in place to see that those who travelled were not allowed to suffer any expenses, including towards carriage of their merchandise. While explaining the condition of India under the native rulers, Naoroji[67] makes the following observations collected from different sources. These observations explain the responsibilities of the Government and the society with regard to all travellers, including those with merchandise, in Bengal. To quote: "The traveller, either with or without merchandise, becomes the immediate care of the Government, which allots him guards, without any expense, to conduct him from stage to stage; and these are accountable for the safety and accommodation of his person and effects. At the end of the first stage he is delivered over, with certain benevolent formalities, to the guards of the next, who, after interrogating the traveller as to the usage he had received in his journey, dismissed the first guard with a written certificate of their behaviour and a receipt for the traveller and his effects, which certificate and receipt are returnable to the commanding officer of the first stage, who registers the same and regularly reports it to the Rajah. In this form the traveller is passed through the country; and if he only passes he is not suffered to be at any expense for food, accommodation, or carriage for his merchandise or baggage; but it is otherwise if he is permitted to make any residence in one place above three days, unless occasioned by sickness, or any unavoidable accident. If anything is lost in this district, for instance a bag of money or other valuables, the person who finds it hangs it on the next tree, and gives notice to the nearest chowkey, or place of guard; the officer of which orders immediate publication of the same by beat of tomtom, or drum."

At the same time, the Indian system permitted interference of the government in business in the interests of the society. It required the traders and businessmen to follow the basic norms in the interests of the society at large. Any misuse or exploitation by the merchants and traders was considered a serious and punishable offence. "The testimony of Megasthenes, corroborated by the *Arthashastra*, shows that in Mauryan times, prices were regulated by market officials. The latter text suggests that, as a further effort at maintaining a just price, government officers should buy on the open market when any staple commodity was cheap and plentiful, and release stocks from government stores when it was in short supply, thus bringing down the price and making a profit for the kind into the bargain[68].” It seems that moral, social and state mechanisms were used to see that the economics worked in the overall interests of the society.

2.1.10 Character and Principles in Business and Trade

Available information shows that the conduct of Indians in economic activities was appreciable and fair. Quoting sources, Jain shows us as to how the foreign merchants preferred to do business with Indians for their character and helpful tendencies. Writing in the context of western India, Jain[69] writes: “The character and conduct of traders in western India generally receive high acclaim from foreign travellers. Al Idrisi tells us that a large number of Muslim merchants visited Nahrwara (Anahilavada) because the people of the town were ‘noteworthy for their excellence of justice, for keeping up their contracts, and for the beauty of their character’, and adds that the people of the region practiced truth and abhorred falsehood. Marco Polo bestows yet more generous praise on the merchants of Lata, whom by a curious mistake he calls Abraiaman or brahmanas. He says, ‘you must know that these Abraiaman are the best merchants in the world, and the most truthful, for they would not tell a lie for anything on earth,’ and ‘if a foreign merchant who does not know the ways of the country applies to them and entrusts his goods to him, they will take charge of these, and sell them in the most loyal manner, seeking zealously the profit of the foreigner and asking no commission except what he pleases to bestow. These observations of the foreign travellers may reflect the general ethos of the mercantile community in western India.”

2.1.11 Superior Society Backed by Economic Prosperity

Ancient India does not seem to be just the wealthiest country; but also a nation whose people seem to have possessed high character and pleasing manners. The people of those days seemed to have lived their lives full of generosity and kind feelings. We could see different scholars and visitors repeatedly emphasizing the higher human qualities that prevailed among people. Basham[70] had recorded his feelings of appreciation for these qualities through the following words: “India was a cheerful land, who’s people, each finding a niche in a complex and slowly evolving social system, reached a higher level of kindliness and gentleness in their mutual relationships than any other nation of antiquity. For this, as well as for her great achievements in religion, literature, art and mathematics, one European student at least would record his admiration of her ancient culture.” The higher human qualities seem to have extended beyond personal relationships and a fair and humanitarian approach guided the lives of people in all their activities, including warfare. Basham had underlined this aspect when he wrote, "...our overall impression is that in no other part of the ancient world were the relations of man and man, and of man and the state, so fair and humane. In no other early civilization were slaves so few in number, and in no other ancient law book are their rights so well protected as in the '*Arthasastra*'... In all her history of warfare, Hindu India has few tales to tell of cities put to the sword or of the massacre of non-combatants... To us the most striking feature of ancient Indian civilization is its humanity[71]."

By all accounts, the society seems to have functioned with a higher orientation, driven by noble ideals, even in economic affairs. A spiritual orientation seems to have guided all the activities of the society. While we could see different and varied economic activities with high levels of perfection, we notice that there were arrangements to take care of the overall interests of all sections of people. This is not to say that everything must have been perfect in the ancient days, as only detailed studies would provide us with more inputs. There may be different views on some of the issues related to the ancient periods. But the broad details provided by different sources over a long period of time presents India as the most prosperous economy with people of high calibre and superior qualities. The economic philosophy of ancient India seems to be a unique one that took the welfare of all living beings as supreme, even while providing opportunities to the citizens to produce maximum wealth through fair methods. It is neither the present day capitalism which tries to exploit others at the slightest opportunity, nor communism where the state dominates and interferes in every activity.

The western society gives its own name to anything with which it gets acquainted. The earlier American countries that were in existence for a long time, many of them with prosperous civilizations, were called "new lands" when the Europeans first came to know of them. Indians are however slow in giving names. Most of them even name their children only after three to six months of birth. Even after sister Nivedita compelled scientist J.C. Bose, he refused to get a patent for his discovery. With the result, Marconi was identified with wireless communication, till it was proved otherwise after so many years. This is basically because Indians have never tried to own their knowledge and practices, as they believe everything is the sum total of the accumulated experiences of the society. So they have never really thought of giving any name to their economic system. We can only say that the ancient economic model was neither the modern day capitalism nor communism, but a different and unique one. The ancient Indian system cannot be compared with the modern economic theories of the West, as the foundations and approaches are basically different.

2.1.12 GDP of India and Other Countries/Regions from 0 CE to 1700

Now let us see in Table 2.4, the GDP of different countries/regions for the periods, from 0 CE to 1700, to get an understanding of the movement of GDP for India and the World.

Table 2.4 GDP of India and Other Countries/Regions (0 CE to 1700)

(million 1990 international $)

Year	0	1000	1500	1600	1700
Austria			1414	2093	2483
Belgium			1225	1561	2288
Denmark			443	569	727
Finland			136	215	255
France			10,912	15,559	21,180
Germany			8112	12,432	13,410
Italy			11,550	14,410	14,630
Netherlands			716	2052	4009
Norway			192	304	450
Sweden			382	626	1231
Switzerland			482	880	1253
United Kingdom			2815	6007	10,709
12 Countries Total			**38,379**	**56,708**	**72,625**
Portugal			632	850	1708
Spain			4744	7416	7893
Others			590	981	1169
Total Western Europe	11,115	10,165	**44,345**	**65,955**	**83,395**
Eastern Europe	1900	2600	6237	8743	10,647
Former USSR	1560	2840	8475	11,447	16,222
United States			800	600	527
Other western offshoots			320	320	300
Total western offshoots	468	784	**1120**	**920**	**827**
Mexico			3188	1134	2558
Other Latin America			4100	2623	3813
Total Latin America	2240	4560	**7288**	**3757**	**6371**
Japan	1200	3188	7700	9620	15,390
China	26,820	26,550	61,800	96,000	82,800
India	33,750	33,750	60,500	74,250	90,750
Other Asian countries	16,470	18,630	31,301	36,725	40,567
Total Asia (excluding Japan)	**77,040**	**78,930**	**1,53,601**	**2,06,975**	**2,14,117**
Africa	7013	13,723	18,400	22,000	24,400
World	**1,02,536**	**1,16,790**	**2,47,116**	**3,29,417**	**3,71,369**

Source: Maddison, Angus, *The World Economy—A Millennial Perspective*, 1st Indian Ed., Overseas Press (India) Private Limited, New Delhi, 2003, p. 261.

Table 2.4 shows that while the GDP of India had remained the same in terms of dollar values for thousand years since 0 CE, there was a small decline in the case of China as well as the total western Europe. Only the share of Africa had increased notably during this period. During 1500, while the GDP of India had increased to $60.50 billions, the GDP of China touched $61.80 billions. There are two notable developments in this period. One is for the first time in the previous two thousand years, India's position as the number one economy was overtaken by another country, namely China. The other one is that for the first time in history, the UK and the US enter the GDP map of the world along with many other western countries.* At that time, while the GDP of the United Kingdom was $2.81 billions, that of the US was $800 millions. The data for the next two hundred years reveal that in 1700, India again becomes the number one country in terms of economic performance in the world. So the contemporary economic figures clearly reveal that India had remained as the premier economic power almost till 1700, with declines during 1500 and 1600.

To understand the comparative performance of different economies during the above periods, let us see in Table 2.5 the shares of GDP of India and other countries/regions.

Table 2.5 GDP Share of India and Other Countries/Regions (0 CE to 1700)

Year	0	1000	1500	1600	1700
Austria			0.6	0.6	0.7
Belgium			0.5	0.5	0.6
Denmark			0.2	0.2	0.2
Finland			0.1	0.1	0.1
France			4.4	4.7	5.7
Germany			3.3	3.8	3.6
Italy			4.7	4.4	3.9
Netherlands			0.3	0.6	1.1
Norway			0.1	0.1	0.1
Sweden			0.2	0.2	0.3
Switzerland			0.2	0.3	0.3
United Kingdom			1.1	1.8	2.9
12 Countries Total			**15.5**	**17.2**	**19.5**
Portugal			0.3	0.3	0.5
Spain			1.9	2.1	2.2
Others			0.2	0.3	0.3
Total western Europe	**10.8**	**8.7**	**17.9**	**19.9**	**22.5**

(Contd.)

* Columbus 'discovered' the present United States of America in 1492. Later it became a British colony and got Independence in 1776. In 1500, it was predominantly a country of the natives.

Table 2.5 GDP Share of India and Other Countries/Regions (0 CE to 1700) (*Contd.*)

Year	0	1000	1500	1600	1700
Eastern Europe	1.9	2.2	2.5	2.7	2.9
Former USSR	1.5	2.4	3.4	3.5	4.4
United States			0.3	0.2	0.1
Other western offshoots			0.1	0.1	0.1
Total western offshoots	0.5	0.7	0.5	0.3	0.2
Mexico			1.3	0.3	0.7
Other Latin America			1.7	0.8	1.0
Total Latin America	**2.2**	**3.9**	**2.9**	**1.1**	**1.7**
Japan	1.2	2.7	3.1	2.9	4.1
China	26.2	22.7	25.0	29.2	22.3
India	32.9	28.9	24.5	22.6	24.4
Other Asia countries	16.1	16.0	12.7	11.2	10.9
Total Asia (excluding Japan)	**75.1**	**67.6**	**62.1**	**62.9**	**57.6**
Africa	6.8	11.8	7.4	6.7	6.6
World	**100**	**100**	**100**	**100**	**100**

Source: Maddison, Angus, *The World Economy—A Millennial Perspective*, 1st Indian Ed., Overseas Press (India) Private Limited, New Delhi, 2003, p. 263.

Table 2.5 shows the share of global GDP for different countries for the first 1700 years in the previous 2000 years of world history. The position of India as the topmost economic power had continued uninterrupted, for the longest period during the last two millennia, till 1500 CE. Even during 1500, China's GDP was only more than 0.5 per cent of India's GDP. Such a high performance testifies that India was the sole economic power of the world for fifteen centuries of the previous twenty centuries, without any competition from any other nation in the world. But, there is a real decline in 1600 CE and thereafter India regained her position as the top economic power in 1700 CE, leading China by a margin of 2.1 per cent. So it could be said that for about 80 per cent of the time in history of previous two millennia, India was the premier economy. This is an excellent and unparalleled performance in the history of world.

During 0 CE to 1700, while the share of India in global GDP had declined from 32.9 per cent to 24.4 per cent, the share of China had declined from 26.2 per cent to 22.3 per cent. As a result, in the same period, the share of Asia had declined from 75.1 per cent to 57.6 per cent. But at the same time the share of the total western Europe had increased during the above period from 10.8 per cent to 22.5 per cent. While the share of Africa had slightly decreased during the above period from 6.8 per cent to 6.6 per cent, Japan had increased its share from 1.2 per cent to 4.1 per cent. The share of increase for the total western Europe is more from 1000 CE onwards. In fact, it was only this region that had gained the most during 1000 CE to 1700 CE. The share of UK had shown an increase of 264 per cent in just two centuries, between 1500 CE and 1700 CE, with its actual share moving from 1.1 per cent to 2.9 per cent. This is a high increase for a country that first appeared in the global GDP map only in 1500 CE. It is interesting to note that the share of the US had declined from 0.3 per cent to 0.1 per cent during 1500 CE to 1700 CE. The share of India was the highest in the world in 1700 CE, followed by China. There was an important development in the economic history during this period. For the first time in history, the share of the total western Europe was more than the share of China.

The GDP shares of India, China and UK in the World GDP during 0 CE to 1700 are presented in Figure 2.3 to help us understand their movements better.

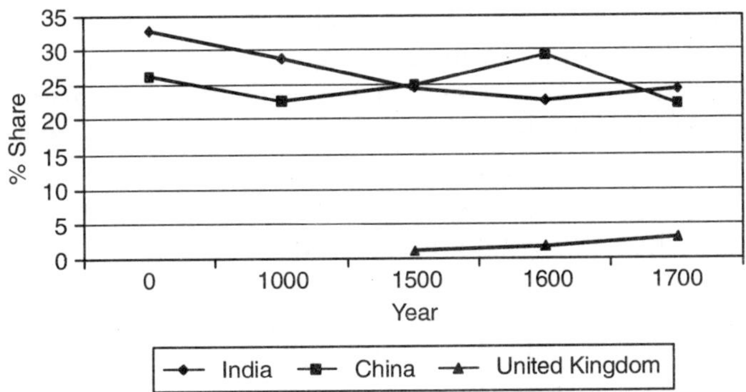

Figure 2.3 GDP shares of India, China and UK in World GDP (0 CE to 1700).
Note: The years in the figure are not as per scale.

We could observe here that India's share had been declining continuously since 1000 CE. In fact, Naoroji[72] noted that "India had gradually declined in civilization from the date of the invasion of Alexander up to the time of first Mussulman conquest; but we have abundant testimony to prove that, at that date, and for centuries before it, here people enjoyed a high degree of prosperity, which continued till the breaking up of Moghul empire in the eighteenth century." The disturbances caused by invasions and the governance of the country by rulers from foreign lands seemed to have affected the economic superiority of India. But even then India had maintained her supremacy for centuries. Writing on the position of economies during 1400–1800, Frank[73] notes: "The two major regions that were most "central" to the world economy were India and China. The centrality rested primarily on their outstanding, absolute and relative productivity in manufactures. In India, these were primarily its cotton textiles that dominated the world market, and to lesser extent its silk textiles, especially in Bengal, India's most productive region. Of course, this competitiveness from manufacturing also rested on productivity of the land and in transport and commerce. They supplied the inputs necessary to supply raw materials to industry, food to workers, and transport and trade for both, as well as export and import."

The details from other sources and observations also indicate India's high levels of prosperity till the eighteenth century. The noted American author Sunderland[74] had underlined the prosperity of India at the time of the arrival of the British in the following words. "This wealth was created by the Hindus' vast and varied industries. Nearly every kind of manufacture or product known to the civilized world—nearly every kind of creation of Man's brain and hand, existing anywhere, and prized either for its utility or beauty—had long, long been produced in India. India was a far greater industrial and manufacturing nation than any in Europe or than any other in Asia. Her textile goods—the fine products of her loom, in cotton, wool, linen, and silk—were famous over the civilized world; so were her exquisite jewellery and her precious stones, cut in every lovely form; so were her pottery, porcelains, ceramics of every kind, quality, colour and beautiful shape; so were her fine works in metal—iron, steel, silver and gold. She had great architecture—equal in beauty to any in the world. She had great engineering works. She had great merchants, great businessmen, great bankers and financiers. Not only was she the greatest ship-building nation, but she had great commerce and trade by land and sea which extended to all known civilized countries. Such was the India which the British found when they came." As a result, as the data provided in Table 2.4 shows India's GDP was the highest in the world with $90.75 billions even in 1700. It only shows the capacity of the Indians to function and produce, irrespective of the disturbances and difficulties.

2.2 INDIAN ECONOMY UNDER THE BRITISH

Britain is a small and new country compared to India. Experts opine that even its national identity was quite unclear until the middle of the fifteenth century. Maddison[75] notes: "From the eleventh to the mid-fifteenth century, British national identity was ambiguous. The monarchy and the ruling elite were Anglo-French warlords whose property rights and income derived initially from territorial conquests in England and France. The resources which the state could mobilize came from tribute received from feudal vassals and their servile peasantry." It could be observed that there was the feudal system in existence during those times and the resources for the state came from vassals and servile peasants.

The British Empire began during the period of mercantilism. The theory of mercantilism emphasized competition between nations for a fixed amount of wealth. Maddison mentions that "from the sixteenth to the nineteenth century, commercial policy was dominated by mercantilist assumptions. In England and in continental Europe, it was taken for granted that international competition was beggar-your-neighbour proposition[76]." The modern Empire of the British took the initial shape in the early seventeenth century, with the settlement of the eastern colonies of North America, parts of Canada and the colonization of the islands of the Caribbean. In the beginning, the sugar-plantation islands were Britain's most important colonies. In 1750, the percentage of slaves in nineteen Caribbean sugar islands was as much as 85.3[77]. The colonies producing tobacco, cotton, rice and other items in Americas had large areas of good agricultural lands and a number of Britishers went and occupied them. In 'the seventeenth and eighteenth centuries, Britain became the main slave shipper[78].'

Having learned about the prosperity of India, many European merchants began trying hard to reach the country. Agarwala[79] notes that "it was the search for an alternative route to India for spices that led to the discovery of America by Columbus in the closing year of the fifteenth century and also brought Vasco de Gama to the shores of Malabar in 1498." Once the sea route was known, the Europeans from different countries started coming. Even during the earlier times, India was attacked by the alien forces and lots of wealth was taken out of the country. India was known for its abundant wealth that 'to shake the pagoda tree' became a phrase in the foreign lands. But in spite of the invasions, difficulties associated with the governance by the outsiders and disturbances caused to the national fabric, India remained an economic power. The entry of the European countries however changed all that and even more. Agarwala[80] notes: "The first Portuguese vessel appeared in the Indian water at the end of the fifteenth century and, within a short time, the concept of a new type of a colonial empire, the like of which Asia had not experienced in her recorded history before, was manifested."

The East India Company was formed in England for trading in this part of the world in 1600. The Englishmen came to India in the beginning of the seventeenth century as traders. The Company acquired its first settlement in Surat in 1613. It fought wars with the local kings and began conquering territories to increase its business. For the first time in India, the country witnessed foreign merchants using physical force to expand their businesses. They were fully supported by their distant government in all their efforts. This was something totally new to the Indian culture, where businesses were always conducted through fair means, even with outsiders. The Company strengthened its stronghold after it won the Plassey War in 1757, as Bengal came under its domination. In the subsequent periods, there were a lot of complaints against the Company and its officials. As a result the queen of England took over the power from the Company and the Government of England established its rule in India in 1858. By the 1860s, they had taken control of most of the regions of India, and had established their supremacy. India henceforth remained under the gripping power of the British Crown until 1947.

John Sullivan, who had worked in India in various capacities including that as a member of the Madras Council, was examined on the occasion of the renewal of the Company's charter in 1813. The noted economist Dutt[81] quotes one of the questions directed to him during the official examination and his answer to the question. Sullivan's answer gives us an indication of the state of prosperity of India for a long time before the arrival of the British. It is as follows:

Question: "Do you suppose that they [the people of India] have the traditions among them which tell them that the economic conditions of the population was better in former times under their native rulers than it is now?

Answer: "I think, generally speaking, history tells us that it was; they have been in a state of the greatest prosperity from the earliest time, as far as history tells us."

2.2.1 GDP of India and Other Countries (1700–1950)

Against this background, let us now see in Table 2.6 the GDP of India along with that of the other countries for the years, 1700 to 1950.

Table 2.6 GDP of Different Countries (1700–1950)

(million 1990 international $)

Year	1700	1820	1870	1913	1950
Austria	2483	4104	8419	23,451	25,702
Belgium	2288	4529	13,746	32,347	47,190
Denmark	727	1470	3782	11,670	29,654
Finland	255	913	1999	6389	17,051
France	21,180	38,434	72,100	1,44,489	2,20,492

(Contd.)

Table 2.6 GDP of Different Countries (1700–1950) (*Contd.*)

(million 1990 international $)

Year	1700	1820	1870	1913	1950
Germany	13,410	26,349	71,429	2,37,332	2,65,354
Italy	14,630	22,535	41,814	95,487	1,64,957
Netherlands	4009	4288	9952	24,955	60,642
Norway	450	1071	2485	6119	17,838
Sweden	1231	3098	6927	17,403	47,269
Switzerland	1253	2342	5867	16,483	42,545
United Kingdom	10,709	36,232	1,00,179	2,24,618	3,47,850
12 Countries Total	**72,625**	**1,45,366**	**3,38,699**	**8,40,743**	**12,86,544**
Portugal	1708	3175	4338	7467	17,615
Spain	7893	12,975	22,295	45,686	66,792
Others	1169	2206	4891	12,478	30,600
Total western Europe	83,395	1,63,722	3,70,223	9,06,374	14,01,551
Eastern Europe	10,647	23,146	45,448	1,21,559	1,85,023
Former USSR	16,222	37,716	83,646	2,32,351	5,10,243
United States	527	12,548	98,374	5,17,383	14,55,916
Other western offshoots	300	941	13,781	68,249	1,79,574
Total western offshoots	827	13,489	1,12,155	5,85,632	16,35,490
Mexico	2558	5000	6214	25,921	67,368
Other Latin America	3813	9120	21,683	95,760	3,56,188
Total Latin America	6371	14,120	27,897	1,21,681	4,23,556
Japan	15,390	20,739	25,393	71,653	1,60,966
China	82,800	2,28,600	1,89,740	2,41,344	2,39,903
India	90,750	1,11,417	1,34,882	2,04,241	2,22,222
Other Asian countries	40,567	50,486	72,173	1,46,999	3,62,578
Total Asia (excluding Japan)	2,14,117	3,90,503	3,96,795	5,92,584	8,24,703
Africa	24,400	31,010	40,172	72,948	1,94,569
World	3,71,369	6,94,442	11,01,369	27,04,782	53,36,101

Source: Maddison, Angus, *The World Economy—A Millennial Perspective*, 1st Indian Ed., Overseas Press (India) Private Limited, New Delhi, 2003, p. 261.

During this period of 250 years, many significant changes had taken place in the world economy. The western countries became economically powerful. By 1820, China replaced India as the largest contributor to the global economy. Asia had to lose its long held supremacy as the economic powerhouse of the world. By 1913, the US became the largest contributor to the global economy.

Let us now see in Table 2.7 the GDP share of different countries in percentage figures to get a comparative view.

Table 2.7 Share of Different Countries in World GDP (1700–1950)

(Per cent of the world total)

Year	1700	1820	1870	1913	1950
Austria	0.7	0.6	0.8	0.9	0.5
Belgium	0.6	0.7	1.2	1.2	0.9
Denmark	0.2	0.2	0.3	0.4	0.6
Finland	0.1	0.1	0.2	0.2	0.3
France	5.7	5.5	6.5	5.3	4.1
Germany	3.6	3.8	6.5	8.8	5
Italy	3.9	3.2	3.8	3.5	3.1
Netherlands	1.1	0.6	0.9	0.9	1.1
Norway	0.1	0.2	0.2	0.2	0.3
Sweden	0.3	0.4	0.6	0.6	0.9
Switzerland	0.3	0.3	0.5	0.6	0.8
United Kingdom	2.9	5.2	9.1	8.3	6.5
12 Countries Total	**19.5**	**20.9**	**30.7**	**31.1**	**24.1**
Portugal	0.5	0.5	0.4	0.3	0.3
Spain	2.2	1.9	2	1.7	1.3
Others	0.3	0.3	0.4	0.5	0.6
Total western Europe	22.5	23.6	33.6	33.5	26.3
Eastern Europe	2.9	3.3	4.1	4.5	3.5
Former USSR	4.4	5.4	7.6	8.6	9.6
United States	0.1	1.8	8.9	19.1	27.3
Other western offshoots	0.1	0.1	1.3	2.5	3.4
Total western offshoots	0.2	1.9	10.2	21.7	30.6
Mexico	0.7	0.7	0.6	1	1.3
Other Latin America	1	1.3	2	3.5	6.7
Total Latin America	1.7	2	2.5	4.5	7.9
Japan	4.1	3	2.3	2.6	3
China	22.3	32.9	17.2	8.9	4.5
India	24.4	16	12.2	7.6	4.2
Other Asian countries	10.9	7.3	6.6	5.4	6.8
Total Asia (excluding Japan)	57.6	56.2	36	21.9	15.5
Africa	6.6	4.5	3.6	2.7	3.6
World	100	100	100	100	100

Source: Maddison, Angus, *The World Economy—A Millennial Perspective*, 1st Indian Ed., Overseas Press (India) Private Limited, New Delhi, 2003, p. 263.

Table 2.7 shows that since 1700, the contribution of India to the global GDP had been continuously falling. As a result, within a period of just 120 years between 1700 and 1820, more than one-third of India's economy was wiped out. By 1820, India's GDP had declined to around 66 per cent of what it was in 1700. India that remained the leader, far ahead of the others as an economic superpower since the ancient times, had to lose her long held premier status in 1820. Thereafter, the decline was steady, and in the next 130 years, nearly 75 per cent of her economic worth of 1820 was again wiped out. In just 250 years about 83 per cent of India's economy was completely ruined. By 1950, India's share of GDP became nearly one sixth of what it was in 1700. Even though China took over the position of India as the largest contributor in 1820, its share had also declined very fast. As a result China's contribution to the global GDP was 4.5 per cent in 1950, just 0.3 per cent more than that of India. The share of Asia declined to 15.5 per cent from 57.6 per cent in 250 years. By 1913, Asia had lost her status as the largest contributor of the world economy to the total western Europe.

The contribution of the UK to the world economy in 1870 was 319 per cent of what it was in 1700. Thereafter, the share of UK declined to 6.5 per cent in 1950. The share of total western Europe had increased from 22.5 per cent to 26.3 per cent during this period of 250 years. The US had emerged as the largest contributor in 1913 with a share of 19.1 per cent and its contribution reached 27.3 per cent in 1950. The biggest gainer during this period of 250 years was the US. The share of Africa had declined from 6.6 per cent to 3.6 per cent during the period. It is important to note that while the shares of traditional powers led by India and China had drastically declined, the shares of the western nations led by Europe and later US had increased manifold.

Figure 2.4 illustrates the shares of India, China, UK and US in the world GDP from 1700 to 1950.

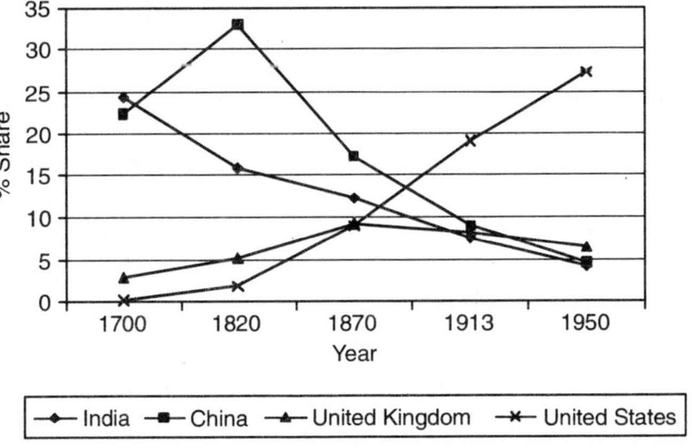

Figure 2.4 Share of India, China, UK and USA in world GDP (1700 to 1950).
Note: The years in the figure are not as per scale.

What could be the reason for such a drastic decline of the Indian economy in just 250 years? India was not just another economy; it was the world's most superior economic power with strong fundamentals. India is the most ancient economy in the world and had been maintaining her supremacy for many centuries in spite of numerous difficulties over the years. Then what brought about her sudden decline in such a short span of time? Let us see a few important developments during the British period to get a clearer insight.

To begin with, we shall see the critical sectors of the economy, namely Industry, Agriculture and Trade.

2.2.2 Industry

Maddison[82] notes that "Moghul India had a bigger industry than any other country which became a European colony, and was unique in being an industrial exporter in pre-colonial times. A large part of this industry was destroyed as a consequence of British rule". The noted freedom fighter Surendranath Banerjea had underlined the motives of the Britishers through the following words: "It had been the settled policy of England in India ever since rise in political power, to convert India into a land of raw produce for the benefit of the manufacturers and operatives of England[83]." Pherozeshah Mehta had articulated the policy of the Britishers more clearly. "That principle and that policy are that the infant industries of India should be strangled in their birth if there is the remotest suspicion of their competing with English manufactures[84]."

Kennedy presents the decline of Indian and Chinese manufacturing (in percentages) since 1750 in Table 2.8.

Table 2.8 Relative Shares of World Manufacturing Output (1750–1900)

	1750	1800	1830	1860	1880	1900
(Europe as a whole)	23.2	28.1	34.2	53.2	61.3	62.0
United Kingdom	1.9	4.3	9.5	19.9	22.9	18.5
Hasburg Empire	2.9	3.2	3.2	4.2	4.4	4.7
France	4.0	4.2	5.2	7.9	7.8	6.8
German states/Germany	2.9	3.5	3.5	4.9	8.5	13.2
Italian states/Italy	2.4	2.5	2.3	2.5	2.5	2.5
Russia	5.0	5.6	5.6	7.0	7.6	8.8
United States	0.1	0.8	2.4	7.2	14.7	23.6
Japan	3.8	3.5	2.8	2.6	2.4	2.4
Third World	73.0	67.7	60.5	36.6	20.9	11.0
China	32.8	33.3	29.8	19.7	12.5	6.2
India	24.5	19.7	17.6	8.6	2.8	1.7

Source: Kennedy, Paul S., *The Rise and Fall of the Great Powers—Economic Change and Military Conflict from 1500–2000*, Fontana Press, London, 1988, p. 190.

Table 2.8 shows that in 1750, India's share was 24.5 per cent of the world's manufacturing output. But, thereafter, there had been a continuous decline. Between 1750 and 1880, in just 130 years, the share of India had decreased by nearly eight times. The steepest decline had occurred in just 50 years, between 1830 and 1880, with a decline of more than five times. Overall in just 150 years, the share of India had come down from 24.5 per cent to 1.7 per cent, a decline of more than 13 times. In the case of China too, there was a decline; but the proportion was many times less. Resultantly, the premier status of the Third World as the dominant player in manufacturing came to an end. During the same time the share of UK went up from 1.9 to 18.5 per cent, nearly nine times an increase in 150 years. The steepest increase was from 1830 to 1860, with a rise of more than 100 per cent. There were increases in the shares of other European nations too, but UK accounted for the highest increase. As a result, Europe had come to reach a dominant position in the global manufacturing scene by 1900. US had emerged from nowhere to the first position during this period. The share of US in 1900 was 23.6 per cent, the highest for any nation.

Figure 2.5 shows the movements of relative shares of world manufacturing output for India, China, UK and US during 1750–1900.

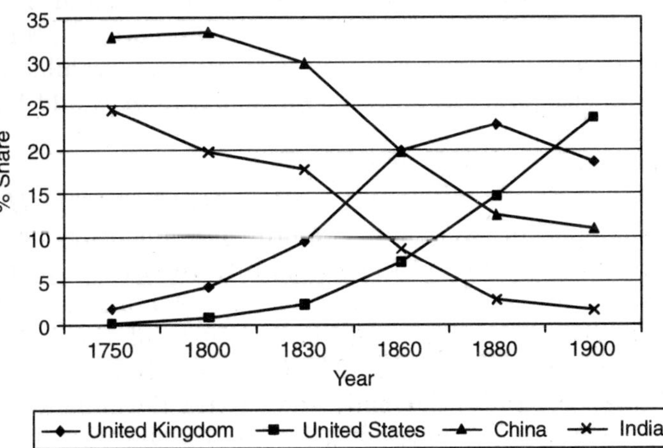

Figure 2.5 Share of India, China, UK and USA in world manufacturing output (1750 to 1900). *Note:* The years in the figure are not as per scale.

Figure 2.5 shows the steep fall in the relative share of manufacturing output for India. The figures for per capita levels of industrialization during 1750–1900 show that while the level of industrialization for India had declined by 86 per cent, for UK the level had increased by 870 per cent[85].

Many of the observers, including a number of British officials, expressed their views against the colonial policies with regard to Indian industries. GG de H Larpent, the then Chairman of the East India and China Association, had openly stated that "we have destroyed the manufactures of India[86]." Sir John Malcolm, the Governor of Bombay in 1830, noted with consternation the ruin of Indian industries[87]. Sir Charles Trevelyan had noted that "We have swept away their manufactures; they have nothing left to depend upon but the produce of their land[88]." He recommended that at least the raw produce of India should be freed from all unequal duties in the English market.

The British used the duty system to destroy the Indian industries. As a result, the position of India as an exporter changed. "Up to 1800, India was the largest producer and exporter of textiles. Within the first three decades of the nineteenth century, Indian textiles were completely wiped out from the international markets[89]." In a significant work on political economy, written in 1844, the German economist Fredrick List pointed out the grave injustice done to Indian textiles: "Had they sanctioned the free importation into England of Indian cotton and silk goods, the English cotton and silk manufactories must, of necessity, soon come to a standstill, India had not only the advantage of cheaper labour and raw material, but also the experience, the skill, and the practice of centuries. England strove for commercial supremacy[90]." H.H. Wilson, a historian, noted that without such prohibitive duties and decrees, "the mills of Paisley and Manchester would have been stopped in their outset and could scarcely have been again set in motion even by the power of steam[91]."

Romesh Dutt's monumental work, "*The Economic History of India*", published in two volumes more than a century ago, vividly describes the destruction of Indian manufacturing. To quote: "India in the eighteenth century was a great manufacturing as well as a great agricultural country, and the products of the Indian loom supplied the markets of Asia and of Europe. It is, unfortunately, true that the East India Company and British Parliament, following the selfish commercial policy of a hundred years ago, discouraged Indian manufacturers in the early years of British rule in order to encourage the rising manufacturers of England. Their fixed policy, pursued during the last decades of the eighteenth century and the first decades of the nineteenth, was to make India subservient to the industries of Great Britain, and to make the Indian people grow raw produce only, in order to supply material for the looms and manufactories of Great Britain. This policy was pursued with unwavering resolution and with fatal success; orders were sent out, to force Indian artisans to work in the Company's factories; commercial residents were legally vested with extensive powers over villages and communities of Indian weavers; prohibited tariffs excluded Indian silk and cotton goods from England; English goods were admitted into India free of duty or on payment of nominal duty[92]."

Wilson made it clear when he wrote that the British manufacturer "employed the arm of political injustice to keep down and ultimately strangle a competitor with whom he could not have contended on equal terms[93]." The authorities took all steps to kill competition. They even took the extreme step of cutting off the thumbs of weavers, the very thumbs that were respected throughout the world for centuries for the highest quality of work. Dutt had written on this: "Weavers, also, upon their inability to perform such agreements as have been forced upon them by the Company's agents, universally known in Bengal by the name of *Mutchulcahs*, have had their goods seized and sold on the spot to make good the deficiency; and the winders of raw silk, called *Nagoads*, have been treated also with such injustice, that instances have been known of their cutting off thumbs to prevent their being forced to wind silk[94]." This was surely an inhuman method of preventing manufacture to kill competition from an enslaved nation.

Resultantly, "By the end of the 19th century, however, most of the indigenous industries of India had either decayed beyond recovery or were on the road to ultimate ruin, while the modern industry was yet to reach considerable proportions[95]." The destruction of the industries compelled people to go to rural areas in search of jobs and depend on agriculture for livelihood. This resulted in the breaking up of the 'harmony and balance that existed between agriculture and industry' for many years in the past, and had created a new situation in which there were more hands than what was necessary for agriculture. Historian Bipan Chandra[96] writes: "The Indian leaders maintained that this disruption of the balance between the agriculture and industrial sectors of the economy and the consequent industrial depression not only destroyed a very important source of national income but also deprived millions of workers of their traditional occupations and forced them to fall back, in the absence of other avenues of employment, more and more upon agriculture, the one remaining source of subsistence in sight. Thus the decadence of handicraft industries produced an increasing pressure of population on land. The result was the increasing ruralization of the country and dependence of the people of India upon 'the single and precarious' resources of agriculture."

The consequences of the British policies were severe. Dutt[97] noted that millions of Indian artisans lost their earnings; the population of India lost one great source of their wealth. He went on saying that "it is a painful episode in the history of British rule in India; but it is a story which has to be told to explain the economic condition of the Indian people, and their present helpless dependence on agriculture[98]."

2.2.3 Agriculture

After the collapse of the Indian industry, to use the words of Dutt[99], "Agriculture is now virtually the only remaining source of national wealth in India, and four-fifths of the Indian people depend on agriculture." But there were interferences in the agricultural sector also. Maddison[100] notes that "The colonial government modified traditional institutional arrangements in agriculture... ."

Decline in production and productivity

The abundant agricultural production and the historical levels of productivity achieved by India declined with the large-scale interference from the state. Bajaj and Srinivas[101] note: "The abundance of food began to turn into a state of acute scarcity within decades of the onset of British rule. As the British began to dismantle the elaborate arrangements of the Indian society and began to extract unprecedented amounts of revenue from the produce of lands, vast areas began to fall out of cultivation and the productivity of lands began to decline precipitously. In the Chengalpattu region where the lands had yielded at least 2.5 tons of paddy per hectare on an average in the 1760's, and where average yields according to the British administrative records had remained around that figure up to 1788 in spite of the devastating wars of the period, productivity had declined to a mere 630 kg per hectare by 1798." With the decline in agricultural production and the resultant scarcity of food, the capacity of the people to share food with others also declined. As a result, "...it is not only the will to share food with others that came under stress during the British period, the capacity to share itself dwindled rapidly[102]."

Severe taxes

Maddison[103] notes the policy of the East India Company regarding taxes. To quote: "The main objectives of the company were to enrich its officials and finance its exports from the tax revenues of the province instead of shipping bullion to India." Note the level of land tax in Madras. "In Madras, the land tax first imposed by the East India Company was one-half the gross produce of the land." Dutt[104] noted: "... the land tax levied by the British Government is not only excessive, but what is worse, it is fluctuating and uncertain in many provinces." While in England, the land tax was between 5 and 20 per cent of the rental, "in Bengal the land tax was fixed at over 90 per cent of the rental, and in Northern India at over 80 per cent of the rental between 1793 and 1822. It is true that the British Government only followed the precedent of the previous Mahomedan rulers, who also claimed an enormous land tax. But the difference was that what the Mahomedan rulers claimed they could never fully realize; what the British rulers claimed they realized with rigour. The last Mahomedan ruler of Bengal, in the last year of his administration (1764), realised a land revenue of £817,553; within thirty years the British rulers realized a land revenue of £2,680,000 in the same Province[105]."

The authorities never thought of reducing the land taxes even in times of great difficulties. They rather used all coercive methods to collect more taxes than compared to the previous years and rejoiced when they succeeded in doing it. Warren Hastings had proudly written the following lines to the Court of Directors in 1772. This was after the death of one-third of population of Bengal, or about ten millions of people due to famine, and a third of the lands returning to waste. "Notwithstanding the loss of at least one-third of the inhabitants of the province, and the consequent decrease of the cultivation the net collections of the year 1771 exceeded even those of 1768... . It was naturally to be expected that the diminution of the revenue should have kept an equal pace with the other consequences of so great a calamity. That it did not was owing to its being violently kept up to its former standard[106]." Dharampal has found that for long periods in the late 18th and the 19th centuries, the tax on land in many areas, exceeded the total agricultural production of very fertile land. The consequences of the policy were easy to predict; in the Madras Presidency, one-third of the most fertile land went out of cultivation between the periods 1800 and 1850[107].

One of the British Indian administrators, John Shore, had recorded his observations on the issue of tax in the following words: "They have been taxed to the utmost limit; every successive province, as it has fallen into our possession, has been made a field for higher exaction; and it has always been our boast how greatly we have raised the revenue above that which the native rulers were able to extort[108]." Another Englishman, H.M. Hyndman, after detailing the proof that taxation in India was far heavier than in any other country though its population was poorer, entitled his book, 'The Bankruptcy of India.' As a result of the negative policies of the British, to borrow the words of G.K. Keatinge, a former Director of Agriculture in Bombay Presidency: "The old self-sufficing agriculture by which each tract, each village and each holding supplied its own needs is now largely a thing of the past...[109]." Madisson[110] informs that the taxes collected from India were used to expand their Empire. "The hard core of the Empire was India, with three quarters of its population. Indian taxation financed a large army under British control, which could be deployed to serve British objectives elsewhere in Asia, the Middle East and eventually in Europe." Taxes and Indian troops were used by the British to fight wars. Will Durant notes: "John Morley estimated that during the nineteenth century alone, England carried on one hundred and eleven wars in India, using for the most part Indian troops; millions of Hindus shed their blood that India might be slave. The cost of these wars for the conquest of India was met to the last penny out of the Indian taxes; the English congratulated themselves on conquering India without spending a cent[111]."

Taxes were even levied on the most essential commodity, namely salt and as a result, the common citizens suffered a lot. One of the respectful nationalist leaders of India, B.G. Tilak had painfully commented in *Kesari*: "There are no people so miserable as those of India. If a sinful man is to be punished he should be sent to India... These thoughts have been suggested by the recent order of Government on the subject of the salt duty... This inhuman action could be taken only by him who was unmindful of the utterly distressful condition of the people of India... The present is the time when such men as hold the opinion that the country conquered by the sword should be preserved also by the sword are in the ascendant... The cat is naturally meek, but when hard-pressed it is likely to turn to bay and become irresistible. Such a contingency is possible in the case of the Hindu and it is worth remembering that there is fear of a permanent possession being lost by shrinking from a little burden of taxation on the English people[112]." It must have pained him so much that at one time he said: "There are, however, some things which are yet to be taxed, so that the triumph of the English may be complete. Among such things may be mentioned the skin of the Indian people and their atmosphere[113]."

2.2.4 Trade

Sir William Joynson-Hicks, Home Minister in the Baldwin Government, expressed the intentions of the British clearly when he said: "I know it is said in the missionary meetings that we conquered India to raise the level of the Indians. That is cant. We conquered India as an outlet for the goods of Great Britain. We conquered India by the sword, and by the sword we shall hold it[114]." India's long held position as a significant exporting nation took a reverse turn during the British period. Bipan Chandra[115] writes: "The composition of India's imports and exports also underwent radical transformation during the 19th century. While prior to 1813, and ever since remote antiquity, India had primarily been an exporter of manufactures and importer of precious metals and luxury products, it gradually became, particularly after 1858, an exporter largely of agricultural raw materials and food grains and importer of manufactured products. Cotton and silk textiles and other traditional staples of export were gradually replaced by a variety of agricultural products, chief of them being raw cotton and jute, tea and coffee, opium, oil-seeds, and wheat and rice, the last two constituting nearly 17 and 26 per cent of the total exports in 1881–82 and 1904–05 respectively. Among the imports, cotton yarns and cloth, metals, machinery, sugar and oil began to predominate, cotton products alone constituting nearly 24 and 39 per cent of the total imports in 1881–82 and 1904–05 respectively."

Agarwala[116] gives figures to show as to how India had become an importer in less than two decades in the case of cotton textiles. "In 1815, the cotton goods exported from India were of the value of £100,000. In 1815, the cotton goods imported into India from England were only of the value of £26,300 but by 1832 they were over £400,000. The consequence was the decline of India's manufacture. The manufacture of silk and cotton goods had declined, and the people who used to export these goods to the markets of Europe and Asia in previous centuries now began to import them. India was reduced from the state of a manufacturing nation to that of an agricultural country." Kennedy[117] notes that domestic producers were driven out of business after 1813 due to free imports of cotton fabrics. To quote: "After 1813, imports of cotton fabrics into India rose spectacularly, from 1 million yards (1814) to 51 million (1830) to 995 million (1870), driving out many of the traditional domestic producers in the process."

Agarwala[118] quotes the evidence in the Common's Report to emphasize the process of elimination of the Indian manufacturers. "In the early years of the 19th century while the Company's trade averaged £1,882,718 annually, private trade averaged 5,451,452 per year. The process of the elimination of Indian manufactures went on, however, under the new arrangement. In 1813, Calcutta exported to London £2 million worth of cotton goods, but in 1830 instead it was importing £2 million worth of British cotton manufactures. The first import of British cotton twist into India was in 1823. In 1824, it rose to 1,21,000 lbs, and in 1828 it reached the figure of 4,000,000 lbs. Woollen goods, copper, lead, iron, glass and earthenware were also now being imported. British manufactures were imported into Calcutta on payment of a small duty of 2.5 per cent, while the import of Indian manufactures into England was discouraged by heavy duties ranging up to 400 per cent on their value."

The free trade policy of the British designed and implemented to allow free entry of goods into India had affected India's trade not just with the British, but with all other countries. Montgomery Martin had observed: "India has suffered most unjustly in her trade, not merely with England but with all other countries, by reason of the outcry for free trade on the part of England without permitting India to free trade herself[119]." Agarwala proves this statement with data. "The export to America declined from 13,633 bales in 1801 to 258 bales in 1829; to Denmark from 1457 bales to 1000, to 1500 bales after 1820; and to Portugal from 9714 bales in 1799 to 1000 bales after 1825. The export to the Arabian and Persian Gulf, which rose to between 4000 and 7000 bales between 1810 and 1820, never exceeded 2000 after 1825[120]."

The Government exported food grains resulting in the starvation of people. Bipan Chandra writes: "The nationalists believed that export of food grains was a cause of poverty and famine because India sent out not its surplus of foodgrains but the stock which was required to meet its daily needs; in reality, Indians were half-starved in order to make possible the trade in their foodstuffs[121]." Jawaharlal Nehru had observed that trade by the British was nothing but loot. To quote Nehru[122]: "It was pure loot. The 'Pagoda Tree' was shaken again and again till the most terrible famines ravaged Bengal. This process was called trade later on but that made little difference. Government was this so-called trade, and trade was plunder. There are few instances in history of anything like it. And it must be remembered that this lasted, under various names and under different forms, not for a few years but for generations... It is significant that one of the Hindustani words which has become part of the English language is 'loot.'"

The above points explain that all the critical sectors of the economy were seriously damaged by the British, first through the East India Company and later under their direct sovereign rule. Added to these, enormous resources were continuously drained out of the country for a long period, depriving the economy of the funds required for consumption and investments.

2.2.5 Economic Drain

Dadabahi Naoroji, a member of the British Parliament, a founder of the Indian National Congress and above all a nationalist economist, used all kinds of decent adjectives to describe the draining of resources. "Unrighteous, despotic, plundering, unnatural, destructive, were some of the adjectives he applied to the British policy which, in his opinion, was leading to the draining of 'the life-blood' of India and its wealth[123]." Naoroji cited the "drain as marking the difference between the rulers of India in the past and the British, for under the former there was no drain of wealth from the country. The wealth of the people remained within the country and was spent inside it. Individual citizens might suffer but the country as a whole did not lose; the loss of one citizen became the gain of another. The British, on the other hand, took wealth out of the country and spent it abroad[124]." The drain was not small. While delivering a lecture in 1872 at Poona on Indian trade and industry, Justice Ranade observed that "of the national income of India more than one-third was taken away be the British in some form or other[125]."

Dadabhai took lot of pains to calculate the economic drain of India, meticulously gathering details from the government sources. He devoted a major part of his later life on this single issue, educating different sections and compelling the authorities to stop the drain. He calculated the drain during 1835 to 1872, giving allowances for their 'profits' and 'interest on investments', even though he says, "strictly speaking £200,000,000 should be considered as a drain from the very produce of the country...[126]." "Allowing for the railway interest as a mere matter of business, and analyzing the deficit of imports or drain to England, as only about £453,000,000." Table 2.9 shows the yearly average of the drain.[127]

Table 2.9 Economic Drain (1835–1872)

(in £)

Years	Yearly Average
1835 to 1839	5,347,000
1840 to 1844	5,930,000
1845 to 1849	7,760,000
1850 to 1854	7,458,000
1855 to 1859	7,730,000
1860 to 1864	17,300,000
1865 to 1869	24,600,000
1870 to 1872	27,400,000

Source: Naoroji, Dadabhai, *Poverty and Un-British Rule in India*, 2nd Ed., Ministry of Information and Broadcasting, Government of India, New Delhi, 1966, p. 31.

What were the elements of drain? Dadabhai answered: "The drain consists of two elements—first, that arising from the remittances by European officials of their savings, and for their expenditure in England for their various wants both there and in India; from pensions and salaries paid in England; and from Government expenditure in England and India. And the second, that arising from similar remittances by non-official Europeans. As the drain prevents India from making any capital, the British by bringing back the capital which they have drained from India itself, secure almost a monopoly of all trade and important industries, and thereby further exploit and drain India, the source of the evil being the official drain[128]." The opinions of various people on the types of drain include the "extortions of the government", "appropriations of revenues by the company" and "private fortunes" by officials[129].

Later, Dutt[130] showed that one half of the net revenues 'flows annually out of India', and mentioned that the moisture of India blesses and fertilizes other lands. Dutt had estimated the annual drain at over a million and a half sterling. "The taxes raised from thirty millions of people were, after deduction of expenses and allowances, not to be spent in the country and for the benefit of the country, but to be sent to England as profits of the Company. An annual remittance of over a million and a half sterling was to be made from a subject country to the shareholders in England. A stream of gold was to flow perennially from the revenues of a poor nation to add to the wealth of the richest nation on the face of the earth[131]." Using the imports and exports figures compiled by the Governor, Dutt noted: "... the country sent out about ten times what it imported[132]."

High amounts of drain carried on for a long period would impoverish any country. "This annual drain of 3,000,000 (Pounds) on British India," wrote Montgomery Martin in 1838, "amounted in thirty years, at 12 per cent (the usual Indian rate) compound interest to the enormous sum of (Pound) 723,997,917 sterling; or, at a low rate, as (Pound) 2,000,000 for fifty years, to (Pound) 8,400,000,000 sterling! So constant and accumulating a drain even on England would soon impoverish her; how severe then must be its effects on India, where the wages of a labourer is from two pence to three pence a day?[133]." The British official himself had accepted that this drain that was going on for half a century would ultimately affect India. "For half a century we have gone on draining from two to three and sometimes four million pounds sterling a year from India, which has been remitted to Great Britain to meet the deficiencies of commercial speculations, to pay the interest of debts, to support the home establishment, and to invest on England's soil the accumulated wealth of those whose lives have been spent in Hindustan. I do not think it possible for human ingenuity to avert entirely the evil effects of a continued drain of three or four million pounds a year from a distant country like India, and which is never returned to it in any shape[134]."

What was the implication of the drain? Dadabhai[135] noted: "The grinding extortion of the English Government has effected the impoverishment of the country and people to an extent almost unparalleled." The result was that the lives of Indians had become miserable and they had started to make appeals to government for their needs, as the very fabric of the society was destroyed. Frederick John Shore[136] expressed the views of the people through the following sentences. To quote: "But because the Indians are in the present day so far behind us in arts and sciences, we are not justified in concluding that they are not capable of improvement were circumstances favourable to them. Complaints are made that whatever is to be done, an appeal is made to Government—a road, a school, a charitable institution everything must be done by Government! How can it be otherwise? In England, where so much wealth is possessed by the community, diffused over all classes, and where there are local authorities to superintend them, the greatest improvements are planned and executed by private individuals; but in India, where the Government grasps at everything and leaves the people only a bare subsistence, having destroyed almost every local authority which formerly existed, and where the interests, that is, the immediate interests, of the rulers are very different from those of the governed, the people have a right to expect that some small part of what is taken from them shall be expended on their benefit."

Saville Marriot, one of the Commissioner's of Revenue in Deccan, had mentioned in 1836 that the drain was severe and widespread and it would be difficult for people to bear such a large-scale drain. "It will be difficult to satisfy the mind that any country could bear such a drain upon its resources without sustaining very serious injury. And the writer entertains the fullest conviction that investigation would effectively establish the truth of the proposition as applicable to India. He has himself most painfully witnessed it in those parts of the country with which he was connected, and he has every reason to believe that the same evil exists, with but slight modification, throughout our eastern Empire[137]." The drain had affected the whole country and people were getting poorer. Sir John Lawrence, testifying as late as 1864 about the situation, noted: "India is, on the whole, a very poor country; the mass of the population enjoy only a scanty subsistence[138]." And Lord Mayo, in 1871, noted in his speech in the Legislative Council: "I admit the comparative poverty of this country, as compared with many other countries of the same magnitude and importance, and I am convinced of the impolicy and injustice of imposing burdens upon this people which may be called either crushing or oppressive[139]."

Quoting official details and Englishmen, Dadabhai showed the per capita income of Indians and the British, and underlined the wide disparity between them. For the year 1867–68, he calculated the total income of India for a population of 170 millions as 3.4 billion rupees, that is, per capita income of 20 rupees per annum[140]. He gave comparative figures for other countries to show the pitiable condition of Indians. During that time, the gross earnings per inhabitant in England was £41, in the UK £35.2, in the US £27.2 and in India £2[141]. In 1905, Dadabhai declared that nearly 34 million sterling or ` 51.5 crores worth of Indian produce was being drained out of India annually[142].

Apart from the company and the government, the officials also were draining out the resources, legally and illegally. When Robert Clive came to India as a clerk he was penniless. Within 20 years he became a very wealthy person. "He (Robert Clive), accepted "presents" amounting to £1,170,000 from Hindu rulers dependent upon his favour and his guns; pocketed from them, in addition, an annual tribute of £140,000; took to opium, was investigated and exonerated by Parliament, and killed himself[143]." He justified his own conduct shamelessly before the House of Commons Committee which enquired into the condition of the East India Company from 1772 to 1777. "I never sought to conceal it, but declared publicly in my letters to the Secret Committee of the India Directors that the Nabob's generosity had made my fortune easy, and that the Company's welfare was now my only motive for staying in India... What pretence could the Company have to expect, that I, after having risked my life so often in their service, should deny myself the only opportunity ever offered of acquiring a fortune without prejudice to them who it is evident would not have had more for my having had less[144]." He even patted himself for taking so less a fortune from India. "When I think," he said, "of the marvellous riches of that country, and the comparatively small part which I took away, I am astonished at my own moderation[145]."

Jawaharlal Nehru wrote that those parts of India which had remained longer under British rule were the poorest. Bengal was very rich and flourishing, but after about 200 years of British rule, it was a miserable mass of poverty-stricken, starving and dying people. While referring to the drain of wealth from India, Shore, who was Bengal's administrator in the thirties, wrote: "The halcyon days of India are over; she has been drained of a large proportion of the wealth she once possessed; and her energies have been cramped by a sordid system of misrule to which the interests of millions have been sacrificed for the benefit of the few[146]." Dutt noted that against this background it would be very difficult for any country to even maintain itself. " It will hardly be asserted that any country, however, opulent could long maintain itself, much less flourish, when it received no material supplies, and when a balance against it, of above one-third of its whole yearly value, was yearly incurred[147]." Such a drain had reduced India to a land of famines and had resulted in the impoverishment of the prosperous nation. "So great an Economic Drain out of the resources of a land would impoverish the most prosperous countries on earth; it has reduced India to a land of famines more frequent, more widespread, and more fatal, than any known before in the history of India, or of the world[148]." As a result, the economic drain had "impoverished an industrious, peaceful, and once prosperous nation[149]."

2.2.6 Was the Industrial Revolution Based on Indian Resources?

Was the Industrial Revolution financed by the wealth taken out of India? There are experts who present arguments to show that the industrial revolution was indeed based on Indian resources. Naoroji showed that "the British rule had not in reality led to any investment of foreign capital in India. India was, throughout, because of the drain, an exporter of capital[150]." Will Durant[151] noted: "As early as 1783 Edmund Burke predicted that the annual drain of Indian resources to England without equivalent return would eventually destroy India. From Plassey to Waterloo, fifty-seven years, the drain of India's wealth to England is computed by Brooks Adams at two-and-a-half to five billion dollars. He adds, what Macaulay suggested long ago, that it was this stolen wealth from India which supplied England with free capital for the development of mechanical inventions, and so made possible the Industrial Revolution. In 1901, Dutt estimated that one-half of the net revenues of India flowed annually out of the country, never to return. In 1906, Mr. Hyndman reckoned the drain at $40,000,000 a year. A.J. Wilson valued it at one-tenth of the total annual production of India. Montgomery Martin, estimating the drain at $15,000,000 a year in 1838, calculated that these annual sums, retained and gathering interest in India, would amount in half a century to $40,000,000,000. Though it may seem merely spectacular to juggle such figures, it is highly probable that the total wealth drained from India since 1757, if it had all been left and invested in India, would now amount, at a low rate of interest, to $400,000,000,000. Allow for money reinvested in India, and a sum remains easily equivalent to the difference between the poorest and the richest nations in the world."

William Digby, the British parliamentarian, had openly admitted: "England's industrial supremacy owes its origin to the vast hoards of Bengal and Karnataka being made available for her use. Before Plassey was fought and won, and before the stream of treasure began to flow to England, our industries were at very low ebb[152]." In fact scholars quote reports on the de-industrialisation of India from the British Indian officials themselves. Williamson[153] notes that "the first official report of Indian De-industrialisation seems to have come from Sir William Bentick, Governor-General of India from 1833 to 1835, whose powerful and enduring image of the effect of British mill cloth on the Indian cotton industry was quoted by Karl Marx in *Das Kapital*: "*The* misery hardly finds a parallel in the history of commerce. The bones of cotton-weavers are bleaching the plains of India." Frank[154] noted: "Industrial revolution is attributed to England. But England was a very late entry to the club of wealthy nations. The European nations and the US enter the map of world economy only from the 16th century onwards. That these nations were able to do it even then was not due to their increased production, but to colonialism, plunder and loot of the innocent native populations in different parts of the world." Based on the analysis provided by the noted economist Amiya Bagchi, Williamson[155] shows that the percentage of total population of Gangetic Bihar dependent on different industrial occupations had decreased from 21.6 per cent during 1809–1813 to 8.5 per cent in 1901. It means loss of 61 per cent industrial occupations in about 90 years.

2.2.7 India Made a Debtor Nation for the First Time in History

India was called the 'milch cow of the empire'. The British were not satisfied with the flow of money to them and so invented newer methods of taking money out. Dutt[156] had mentioned this in the following words: "... as the flow of the money from India was not sufficient to pay the dividends, there was an increasing debt—called the Public Debt of India—adding to the burdens of the taxpayers who had to pay the interest. This is the saddest episode in the sad financial history of India." Will Durant noted: "By 1858 the crimes of the Company so smelled to heaven that the British Government took over the captured and plundered territories as a colony of the Crown; a little island took over half a continent. England paid the Company handsomely, and added the purchase price to the public debt of India, to be redeemed, principal and interest (originally at 10½%), out of the taxes put upon the Hindu people. All the debts on the Company's books, together with the accrued interest on these debts, were added to the public obligations of India, to be redeemed out of the taxes put upon the Hindu people. Exploitation was dressed now in all the forms of Law—i.e. the rules laid down by the victors for the vanquished. Hypocrisy was added to brutality, while the robbery went on[157]."

Indians were made to pay for the wars outside India and for these purposes, huge amounts of money went out of the country. "During the nineteenth century India paid $450,000,000 for wars fought for *England outside of India* with Indian troops. She contributed $500,000,000 to the war chest of the Allies, $700,000,000 in subscriptions to war loans, 800,000 soldiers, and 400,000 labourers to defend the British Empire outside of India during the Great War. In 1922, 64% of the total revenue of India was devoted to this army of fratricides: Hindus compelled to kill Hindus in Burma until Burma consented to come under British rule[158]." As a result of the activities of the British, the national debt of India rose to $3,500,000,000 in 1929[159].

2.2.8 Economy Shattered to Pieces

The destruction of all the vital sectors of the economy and a severe and most inhuman drain of resources had completely shattered the Indian economy. Added to this, India was made to pay for the wars that the British waged in different soils and for expansion of the British empire. Consequently, India was made a debtor nation for the first time in its long history of prosperity and affluence. We have to note here that India did not borrow money from the British any time to become a debtor. The combined effect of all the activities by the foreign power had resulted in the steepest decline in the GDP and the collapse of the superior economic system that prevailed since the ancient periods.

One of the most significant aspects of the economic collapse from a long term perspective was the loss of balance between agriculture and industry. Chandra[160] noted this: "One of the most momentous consequences of the establishment of British supremacy in India was the disruption of the centuries' old 'union between agriculture and manufacturing industry' as a result of the progressive decline and destruction of the Indian town handicrafts and village artisan industries." As a result, at the end of the British rule, the percentage of labour force dependent on the village economy was 75 per cent for a share of 54 per cent of the national income after tax. 17 per cent of the labour force was working as landless labourers and scavengers with a share of just 4 per cent of national income[161]. Bimal Jalan[162] notes that the share of workforce in agriculture and industry was 75.7 per cent and 11.9 per cent respectively in 1951. The disruption by the British had proved to be a fatal attack on the economic and social fabric of this once great economic power, from which she is yet to recover completely.

Let us see the performance of the Indian economy through the popular measure that is used to study and compare the performance of the economies in the contemporary periods, namely the growth rate. Table 2.10 provides the rate of growth of GDP of India, the UK, and the world during 1500–1820 to 1913–1950.

Table 2.10 Rate of Growth of GDP of India, UK and the World (1500–1820 to 1913–1950)

(annual average compound growth rates)

	1500–1820	1820–1870	1870–1913	1913–1950
India	0.19	0.38	0.97	0.23
United Kingdom	0.80	2.05	1.90	1.19
World	0.32	0.93	2.11	1.85

Source: Maddison, Angus, *The World Economy—A Millennial Perspective*, 1st Indian Ed., Overseas Press (India) Private Limited, New Delhi, 2003, p. 262.

Table 2.10 shows that the rate of annual average compound growth rate of GDP of the UK was higher than the rate of growth of the world during 1500–1820 to 1820–1870, whereas the rate of growth of India was consistently lower. The rate of growth of India during 1500–1820 was 59.38 per cent of the growth rate of the world, during 1820–1870 it was 40.86 per cent, during 1870–1913, 45.97 per cent and during 1913–1950, just 12.43 per cent. One could notice that the rate of growth of India, when compared with the rate of growth of the world, had drastically come down during the above period, from 1500–1820 (59.38 per cent) to 1913–1950 (12.43 per cent) showing a decreased performance over these years. During 1500–1820, the rate of growth of the GDP of the UK was 250 per cent of the world growth, and during 1820–1870 it was 220 per cent.

Figure 2.6 presents the annual average compound growth rates of GDP of India and the UK along with that of the world during 1500–1820 to 1913–1950.

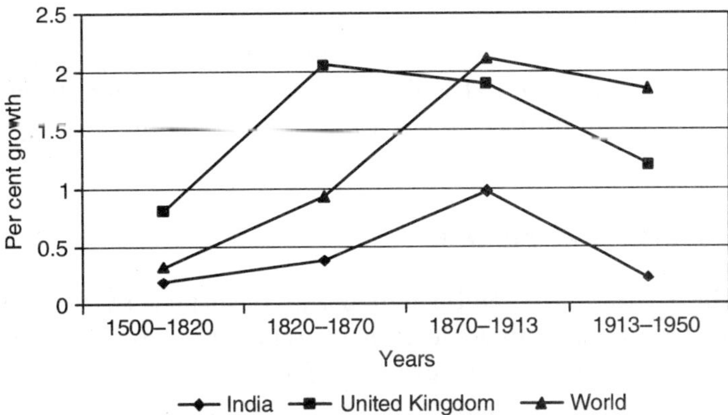

Figure 2.6 Rate of growth of GDP of India, UK and the world (1500–1820 to 1913–1950). *Note:* The years in the figure are not as per scale.

Let us see in Table 2.11 the growth rate of GDP per capita between the two countries and the world.

Table 2.11 Rate of Growth of GDP Per Capita of India, UK and the World (1500–1820 to 1913–1950)

(annual average compound growth rates)

	1500–1820	1820–1870	1870–1913	1913–1950
India	–0.01	0.00	0.54	–0.22
UK	0.27	1.26	1.01	0.92
World	0.05	0.53	1.30	0.91

Source: Maddison, Angus, *The World Economy—A Millennial Perspective*, 1st Indian Ed., Overseas Press (India) Private Limited, New Delhi, 2003, p. 265.

It is significant to note here that there was negative growth in India during 1500–1820 and zero growth during 1820–1870. So for more than three centuries till 1820, there was negative growth and thereafter, there was no growth for another fifty years. It is to be noted here that India's growth rate had turned negative for the first time in the known history during the above period. In the subsequent years, while there was 0.54 per cent growth for 43 years, the next 37 years saw –0.22 per cent growth. India's growth rate was negative for most part of the first half of the twentieth century during the British rule. It is important to note that while the economy was being drained, the per capita growth was negative for most of the time during the British period. At the same time, during 1700–1820 to 1820–1913, the annual average compound growth rate for Britain had increased by 282 per cent. Maddison notes that the "per capita income in Britain almost doubled from 1500 to 1700[163]" and "between 1820 and 1913, British per capita income grew faster than at any time in the past—three times as fast as in 1700–1820[164]."

2.2.9 Poverty and Famine

During the British rule, India which was described by Robert Clive as a "country of inexhaustible riches", when he saw it for the first time, became a country of poverty and famine. Naoroji published his first essay on Indian economy in 1867, and from then on for forty years he had continued to analyse nearly every aspect of Indian economy in his articles and speeches. His two long essays titled, "*Poverty of India*" and later, the publication of "*Poverty and Un-British Rule in India*" startled the minds of all educated Indians. Gandhiji wrote later: "My first acquaintance with the extent of Indian poverty was through Dadabhai's book[165]." Dadabhai quoted a letter between the English officials to explain the extent of poverty of the farmers. To quote from the letter: "Mr. John Bruce Norton, in his letter to Mr. Robert Lowe in 1854, on the condition of ryots in Madras, quotes the words of Mr. Bourdillon, who was one of the ablest revenue officers in the Madras Civil Service, and a member of the commission on public works: "Now, it may certainly be said of almost the whole of the ryots, paying even the highest of these sums, and even of many holding to a much larger amount, that they are always in poverty and generally in debt[166]." It is pitiable to even imagine as to how the Indian farmer who produced abundant foods and shared his foods willingly with all others had become debt-ridden and himself had to suffer from poverty during the English rule. See as to how the Englishman himself described the position: "A ryot of this class, of course, lives from hand to mouth. He rarely sees money ... His dwelling is a hut of mud-walls and thatched roof—far ruder, smaller, and more dilapidated than those of the better classes of ryots above spoken of, and still more destitute, if possible, of any thing that can be called furniture. His food, and that of his family, is partly thin porridge made of the meal of grain boiled in water, and partly boiled rice, with a little condiment; and generally, the only vessels for cooking and eating from, are of the coarsest earthenware, much inferior in grain to a good tile or brick in England, and unglazed. Brass vessels, though not wholly unknown among this class, are rare[167]."

Maddison[168] notes: "The class of landless agricultural labourers grew in size under British rule." The numbers grew, and what was their condition? Norton's letter quoted by Naoroji explained the condition of agricultural labourers also. To borrow from the letter: "As respects food, houses, and clothing, they are in a worse condition than the class of poor ryots above spoken of. It appears from the foregoing details that the condition of the agricultural labourer in this country is very poor... In fact, almost the whole of his earnings must necessarily be consumed in a spare allowance of coarse and unvaried food, and a bare sufficiency of clothing. The wretched hut he lives in can hardly be valued at all. As to anything in the way of education or mental culture, he is utterly destitute of it[169]."

Poverty and famine started visiting India often during the British rule. "Under British rule, the Indian population remained subject to recurrent famines and epidemic diseases[170]." Dutt[171] wrote on the extent of poverty and its effects in the following words: "The poverty of the Indian population at the present day is unparalleled in any civilized country; the famines which have desolated India within the last quarter of the nineteenth century are unexampled in their extent and intensity in the history of ancient or modern times. By a moderated calculation, the famines of 1877 and 1878, of 1889 and 1892, of 1897 and 1900, have carried off fifteen millions of people. The population of a faired-sized European country has been swept away from India within twenty-five years. A population equal to half of that of England has perished in India within a period which men and women still in middle age, can remember."

Will Durant[172] gave the reasons for poverty and famine in so many words. "Sir William Hunter estimated that 40,000,000 of the people of India were seldom or never able to satisfy their hunger. In 1901, 272,000 died of plague introduced from abroad, in 1902, 500,000 died of plague; in 1903, 800,000; in 1904, 1,000,000. We can now understand why there are famines in India. Their cause, in plain terms, is not the absence of food, but the inability of the people to pay for it. It was hoped the railways would solve the problem...the fact that the worst famines have come since the building of the railways...behind all these, as the fundamental source of the terrible famines in India, lies such merciless exploitation, such unbalanced exploitation of goods, and such brutal collection of high taxes in the very midst of famine..."

The poverty had made Indians weak and susceptible to illness. The poor health conditions led themselves to be regularly absent from work. Durant had made a note of this: "In the cities 34% of them are absent from work, on any day, from illness to injury. They are too poor to afford foods rich in mineral salts; they are too poor to buy fresh vegetables, much less to buy meat. The water supply, which is usually the first obligation of a government, is in primitive condition, after a century or more of British rule; dysentery and malaria have been eliminated from Panama and Cuba, but they flourish in British India. Once the Hindu was known to be among the cleanest of the clean; and even today he bathes every morning, and washes every morning the simple garment that he wears; but the increase of poverty has made social sanitation impossible. Until 1918 the total expenditure on public health, of both the central and provincial governments combined, was only $5,000,000 a year, for 240,000,000 people—an appropriation of two cents per capita[173]." As a result, the official data showed that the average years of life expectation at birth in 1833 was 21. Even during 1941–51 it was just 32[174]. In 1921, the infant mortality rate in Bombay was 666 per 1000 and in one room tenants there were 828 per 1000[175].

2.2.10 Education—The Beautiful Tree Perished

The British replaced the time-tested Indian education system and in its place introduced a new and an alien system. In his minute on Indian education prepared in 1835, Macaulay* ridiculed the traditional system of providing free education without any charges and noted: "Nothing is more certain than that it never can in any part of the world be necessary to pay men for doing what they think pleasant and profitable. India is no exception to this rule. The people of India do not require to be paid for eating rice when they are hungry, or for wearing woolen cloth in the cold season." At the same time he had also noted that it would not be possible for them to provide education to all. To quote: "... it is impossible for us, with our limited means, to attempt to educate the body of the people."†

* Macaulay's Minute on Indian Education, dated 2nd February, 1835.

† Ibid.

Durant[176] had observed in 1930: "When the British came there was, throughout India, a system of communal schools, managed by the village communities. The agents of the East India Company destroyed these village communities, and took no steps to replace the schools; even today, after a century of effort to restore them, they stand at only 66% of their number a hundred years ago. There are now in India 730,000 villages, and only 162,015 primary schools. Only 7% of the boys and 1½% of the girls receive schooling, i.e. 4% of the whole. Such schools as the Government has established are not free, but exact a tuition fee which, though small to a Western purse, looms large to a family always hovering on the edge of starvation." The expenditure of the government on education was less. "The government spends every year on education eight cents a head; it spends on the army eighty-three cents a head[177]." Noting the attitude of the Government towards education, he remarked: "Instead of encouraging education, the Government encouraged drink. When the British came, India was a sober nation. "The temperance of the people," said Warren Hastings, "is demonstrated in the simplicity of their food and their total abstinence from spirituous liquors and other substances of intoxication." With the first trading posts established by the British, saloons were opened for the sale of rum, and the East India Company made handsome profits from the trade[178].

The literacy levels declined over the years, and by 1891, official sources showed that the literacy rate was just 6.1 per cent. It touched 15.1 per cent in 1941[179]. This must be the reason why Mahatma Gandhi openly remarked in the British soil in 1931: "I say without fear of my figures being challenged successfully, that today India is more illiterate than it was fifty years or a hundred years ago, and so is Burma, because the British administrators, when they came to India, instead of taking hold of things as they were, began to root them out. They scratched the soil and began to look at the root, and left the root like that, and the beautiful tree perished[180]."

As a result, the native education system that functioned on the basis of higher principles collapsed. The system that was responsible for making the economy prosperous, even while preparing citizens for a principled life was made to die. Macualay* had stated the intention of the British to introduce a new education system in the following words: "We must at present do our best to form a class who may be interpreters between us and the millions

* Macaulay's Minute on Indian Education, dated 2nd February, 1835.

whom we govern; a class of persons, Indian in blood and colour, but English in taste, in opinions, in morals and in intellect."

2.2.11 Fatal Attack on the Economic Spirit of India

During the reign of the British, Indian economy underwent dramatic changes. The industries were wiped out; agriculture was destroyed; the economy was drained; millions died due to famine and among those who survived many suffered from hunger; the prosperity and peace, nurtured and maintained through hundreds of years of achievements suffered the most dangerous attacks, and above all, the spirit of the people of the age-old nation, who were respected by all those who came to know of them, was almost killed. The higher principles upon which the economic system had been built and functioned was fatally attacked and the intimate arrangements that existed between the economy and the society were broken. The principle of *dharma* that governed every aspect of Indian life, including the economic activities, was no longer the guiding principle in the British India. The Indians were compelled to follow an 'un-Indian' attitude, and were taught to believe in an 'anti-Indian' approach in some of the vital activities, including the economic ones. India that remained the most prosperous economic power since the ancient days had to lose her superior status and was reduced to a poor and illiterate nation. As a consequence, the longest survived and perhaps the most beneficial economic system known to mankind was defaced and almost destroyed beyond immediate recovery.

The attitude of the British towards India and their perception of the natives towards British rule was articulated by Shore when he testified to the House of Commons in 1857: "The fundamental principle of the English had been to make the whole Indian nation subservient, in every possible way, to the interests and benefits of themselves. They have been taxed to the utmost limit; every successive province, as it has fallen into our possession, has been made a field for higher exaction; and it has always been our boast how greatly we have raised the revenue above that which the native rulers were able to extort. The Indians have been excluded from every honour, dignity, or office which the lowest Englishman could be prevailed upon to accept... The summary is that the British Indian Government has been practically one of the most extortionate and oppressive that ever existed in India—one under which injustice has been and may be committed both by the Government and big individuals, provided the latter be rich, to an almost unlimited extent, and under which redress from injury is almost unattainable; the consequence of which is that we are abhorred by the people, who would hail with joy and instantly join the standard of any 'power' whom they thought string enough to occasion our downfall[181]."

Durant[182] had used strong words to narrate the attacks on the Indian economic system by the British. He wrote in 1930: "British rule in India is the most sordid and criminal exploitation of one nation by another in all recorded history. I propose to show that England has year by year been bleeding India to the point of death, and that self-government of India by the Hindus could not within any reasonable probability, have worse results than the present form of alien domination. This evidently was not a minor civilization, produced by inferior people. It ranks with the highest civilizations of history, and some, like Keyserling, would place it at the head and summit of all. The British conquest of India was the invasion and destruction of a high civilization by a trading company utterly without scruple or principle, careless of art, greedy of gain, overrunning with fire and sword a country temporarily disordered and helpless, bribing and murdering, annexing and stealing, and beginning that career of illegal and "legal" plunder which has now gone on ruthlessly for one hundred and seventy-three years, and goes on at this moment while in our secure comfort we write and read. Those who have seen the unspeakable poverty and physiological weakness of the Hindus today will hardly believe that it was the wealth of eighteenth century India which attracted the commercial pirates of England and France." It was not just the economic loss; "India also suffered non-economic losses, such as the moral loss, the loss of wisdom, experience and capacity and the stunting and emasculation of the entire people[183]." The net effect of all these changes was so distressing that it compelled even a great optimist like Mahatma Gandhi to say that India had lost her self-confidence. To quote Gandhiji: "The foreign system, under which India is governed today, has reduced India to pauperism and emasculation. We have lost self-confidence[184]."

2.3 INDIAN ECONOMY AFTER INDEPENDENCE

After years of struggle, during which thousands of people had sacrificed their lives and property, India attained independence on August 15, 1947. At that time, India was a poor country—a country with widespread poverty, illiteracy and underdevelopment. The Indian economy was in a very bad shape.

Uma Kapila[185] presents the position of the country at the time of independence in the following sentences: "Indian economy at the time of independence was overwhelmingly rural and agricultural in character with nearly 85 per cent of the population living in villages and deriving their livelihood from agricultural and related pursuits using traditional, low productivity techniques. The backwardness of Indian economy is reflected in its unbalanced occupational structure with 70 per cent of working population engaged in agriculture. Even with this large proportion of population engaged in agriculture, the country was not self-sufficient in food and raw materials for industry. The average availability of food was not only deficient in quantity and quality but also precarious as exhibited in recurrent famines. Illiteracy was as high as 84 per cent; majority of children (60 per cent) in the 6–11 age groups did not attend school. Mass communicable diseases were widespread and in the absence of a good public health service, mortality rates were very high (27 per thousand). Thus the economy was faced with the problems of mass poverty, ignorance and diseases which were aggravated by the unequal distribution of resources between groups and regions."

What was the industrial scenario at that time? The industrial sector at the time of independence was in a state of extreme underdevelopment due to the following reasons: (i) the policy of exploitation and destruction by the British for over two hundred years; (ii) the total arrogance of the government resulting in the death of native industries; (iii) weak infrastructure; (iv) focus on export orientation against the interests of the country; and (v) lack of skilled manpower, as the native arrangements were destroyed, and Indians were not encouraged to acquire the necessary skills.

During the previous two hundred years, the British did not make investments with the objective of developing the economy from a long term point of view. The thriftiest of people in the world did not have much left to save and savings were very low. With the result, capital formation suffered. With little money to save and very little to invest, the production levels were low. The standard of living was very poor with 45 per cent of people living in poverty during 1951[186]. Life expectancy was just 32.1 years in 1950–51[187].

Figure 2.7 illustrates the shares of India and China in the world GDP from 0 CE to 1950, and the shares of the UK and the US from 1500 to 1950[188].

Figure 2.7 shows the decline of the share of India drastically since the 1700s. As a result, the share of India in the global GDP came down to 4.2 per cent in 1950. China also shows a steep fall during the above period. UK, that first appeared in the GDP map in the sixteenth century, reached its peak in 1870, and then slowed down to remain above India and China in 1950. The figure also

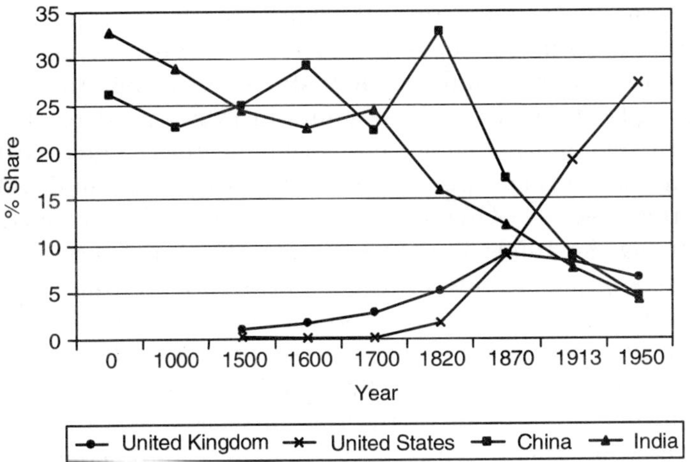

Figure 2.7 Share of India, China, UK and USA in world GDP (0 CE to 1950).
Note: The years in the figure are not as per scale.

shows the dramatic rise of the US since the later part of the nineteenth century to reach the number one status in 1913.

After independence, when the country got the freedom to frame its own policies, the ruling sections of India that decided the policies of the nation thought that only the western approaches would help India towards progress. It was unfortunate that no attempts were made to discuss an India-centered approach, after Gandhiji's untimely death in 1948. With the result, the policymakers opted for a system that was developed in the West, based on their world views and experiences. In the 1950s, the then ruling party passed a resolution for a 'socialistic pattern' of society, largely based on the then Soviet model. For more than three decades the dominant economic ideology of the successive governments was largely socialistic in approach. It is relevant to note here that the socialistic model was adopted as the most suitable one for the country without any serious discussion or debate at the national level. So the nation that had the most prosperous economic system for the longest number of years in the human history had to imitate an alien model introduced under totally different circumstances in a distant world.

It is very sad that the crucial policies concerning the economy were not taken on the basis of ground realities and historical experiences. As a result, the critical sectors of the economy, including the local industries and businesses, were not fully encouraged to flourish. So the Indian economy had to depend on the bureaucratic and the political set-up, popularly called the '*neta-babu raj*'. But in spite of the basic distortions in policy making, Indian economy started growing. Indian society had started engaging itself in different vocations, in adherence to its traditional spirit. Resultantly, the income began to increase slowly, savings started to multiply and the national economy started growing. Meanwhile the Governments stepped up investments in infrastructure and started concentrating on the basic and social sectors. The institutional financing mechanisms were established to help in the development of different sectors. One major development that started taking place during the 1950s and the subsequent decades was the entry of new groups of people into different industrial, trading and services activities in different places across the country. People belonging to different sections, from agricultural and agri-dependent backgrounds, started entering new areas in search of better opportunities. Consequently, the Indian society took the lead ahead of the governments and sowed the seeds for a new economy without anybody noticing it. The crucial step for many of the most prosperous industrial and business centres of today was taken by the so-called ordinary people in those initial years, making use of the limited freedom available to them. Studies on different industrial and business centres show that the people of India had started making their initial and decisive steps even during the earlier decades. Due to these initiatives, most of the places witnessed a dramatic shift in development with the economic activities increasing manifold. It is important to note here that people from most of the centres took the crucial steps without waiting for initiatives from the governments.

2.3.1 Growth during 1950s to 1980s

It is generally assumed that India's growth rates during the initial periods after independence was poor. But it is not really so. During the 1950s to 1980s, the rate of growth of the economy was 3.5 per cent, while the per capita growth was 1.3 per cent. The rate of growth of GDP (annual average compound growth rates) of India during 1952–78 was 4.02 per cent, compared to the growth rate 4.27 per cent for Europe. Maddison shows that it was higher than the growth rate of 3.46 per cent for the US[189]. It only shows the capacity of the Indian society to move forward even when conditions are not fully favourable to them. This stands testimony to the fervour with which Indians work, without expecting any support from the governments. Economist Deepak Nayyar notes that the economic growth had begun in the early 1950s, and not decades later as is generally believed. Quoting the growth rate of 3.5 per cent during 1950–51 to 1979–80, he says "... the turning point in the 1950s was much more significant ...[190]." There are economists who believe that the momentum for growth started in the 1980s. Nayyar disagrees with their view and says: "... the proportionate change in growth rates, both aggregate and sectoral, was much larger circa 1950 than it was circa 1980[191]." He notes further: "It is clear that the pace of economic growth during the period from 1950 to 1980 constituted a radical departure from the colonial past[192]." Generally, the economists used to criticize the lesser rate of growth during the first three decades. Nayyar answers for them: "Obviously this growth was impressive with reference to the near stagnation during the colonial era. It was also much better than the performance of the now industrialized countries at comparable stages of their development[193]." It becomes clear that the economic growth had started right after the independence, keeping the policymakers and the elite sections of the society unaware of what was happening. But at the same time it is important for us to realize that India would have achieved better performances, had the policymakers understood the Indian native systems, and not curtailed them through unsuitable policies.

2.4 INDIAN ECONOMY DURING THE RECENT DECADES

USSR had to abandon communism in the late 1980s due to the large scale failure of its model in the country, and there was a general opinion amongst the popular economists that the western model of capitalism was the only alternative for countries to achieve growth and progress. By then, the failure of the socialist model to capture the full benefits of independence in the previous decades had resulted in a change of thinking among the Indian policy-makers. There was a serious difficulty in the foreign exchange front in 1990. The Government that came to power in 1991 through a popular mandate had decided that the only alternative for the earlier policy regime was the adoption of the 'only other model' considered suitable by almost all those who mattered in policy making. Hence, for the second time after Independence, another western model was officially accepted without detailed discussions and debate on a larger scale at the national level.

But the complete U turn from a Soviet-inspired socialistic to a US inspired market model was not exactly what India needed. India wanted a model that would make her grow in all respects, giving maximum benefit to the different sections of the society. But what she got was a model planned in the West for other countries, based on their understanding of the economies and societies. We have to remember that the US inspired model is the one that is designed to maintain their supremacy in the international arena. Three points have to be noted here. Firstly, the policies that they follow and the policies that they recommend to others are different. Secondly, they recommend one standard set of policy measures to all the countries of the world, irrespective of the background and stage of development, and thirdly, their world views are based on their backgrounds, theories and approach to life.

As a result of the new policy framework, a different set of policies for liberalisation, privatisation and globalization based on the western prescriptions were announced. Recommendations for liberalizing and globalizing various sectors were suggested as 'reforms' and many of them were implemented in the course of time. It is true that the Indian economy was waiting for policy changes for a long time. But the policy changes introduced were not fully in tune with the ground realities and the ethos of this country. But in spite of it, as usual, different sections that were capable of taking advantage of the new situation began utilizing the opportunities. With more freedom in the liberalized scenario, certain sections of the economy started making use of the opportunities and resultantly the economy began to show a fast growth.

2.4.1 Economic Growth in Recent Decades

Indian economy has been growing at a faster speed in the recent decades. Virmani[194] notes that during 1980–81 to 2002–03, economic growth averaged 5.7 per cent per annum. This rate is 2.2 per cent higher than the rate during 1951–52 to 1979–80. He calls this as "the 'Bharathiya rate of growth', to distinguish it from the 3.5 per cent average rate of growth during the first phase of development, a rate that has come to be associated in most people's minds as the 'Hindu rate of growth', but is more accurately the growth during "Indian-socialist phase." While the growth rate during 1980–90 was 5.5 per cent, it reached 6 per cent between 1990 and 2000. During 1978–95, the annual average compound growth rate of India was much better than that of Europe and the USA. While the rate for India was 4.63 per cent, it was 1.74 per cent for Europe and 2.47 per cent for USA[195]. India's growth rate during this period was also better than the world average, though China grew at a higher rate of 7.49 per cent. During the recent decades, India's per capita income has also been growing steadily. While the growth rate of per capita during 1980–1990 was 3.5 per cent, it reached 4.3 per cent during 1990–2000. The rate averaged 7.3 per cent per annum for the period 2003–04 to 2007–08[196].

Table 2.12 shows the GDP growth at factor cost during the recent years, 2005–06 to 2010–11.

Table 2.12 GDP Growth Rates of India (2005–06 to 2010–11)
(at factor cost at constant prices)

(Percentage)

2005–06	2006–07	2007–08	2008–09	2009–10	2010–11
9.5	9.6	9.3	6.8(P)	8.0(Q)	8.5(R)

P—Provisional estimates; Q—Quick estimates; R—Revised estimates.

Source: Handbook of Statistics on Indian Economy 2010–11, RBI, p. 412.

Table 2.12 shows that the economy was growing at a fast pace during 2005–06 to 2007–08. After a slower growth in 2008–09 due to the global crisis, it has picked up its momentum in 2009–10. As a result the average GDP growth rate for 10 years during 2000–01 to 2009–10 touched 7.3 per cent [197]. The economy improved its performance in 2010–11 showing a growth rate of 8.5 per cent. The recent years show a faster growth in the industrial and service sectors. The performance of the corporate sector has been good. Many Indian companies are going abroad to set up factories and offices and a number of them have been taking over foreign companies. Different types of outsourcing works for foreign companies are taking place in India. The predominant sector of the economy, the under-noticed and the unrecognized family-based non-corporate sector, officially classified as 'un-organised sector' with the contempt of a colonial mindset, remains the backbone of our country, contributing enormously to the growth of our economy. More than two thousand self-made industrial and business clusters, functioning throughout the country, are contributing significantly to the growth of the economy. Some of them have become international names due to their superior quality products and have been earning good foreign exchange. The knowledge sectors are growing fast and Indians are widely recognized for their competence and professional skills throughout the world. Many foreign companies that were employing Indians in their territories have started coming to India to set up their research centres, plants and subsidiaries.

2.4.2 India in the Top League

Now India has come to occupy an important position, a significant one, in the world economy. India is ranked as the fourth largest economic power in the world on the basis of Gross National Income (in terms of Purchasing Power Parity) by the World Bank.[198] Table 2.13 presents the list of top five countries in terms of economic contribution in trillions of dollars during 2010.

Table 2.13 List of Top Five Economies in the World (2010)
(PPP Gross National Income, $ trillions, 2010)

World	75.80
United States	14.56
China	10.13
Japan	4.43
India	4.17
Germany	3.11

Source: World Development Report 2012, World Bank, pp. 392–393.

2.4.3 Share of India and Other Major Countries in World Gross Domestic Product (GDP)

The latest data by the International Monetary Fund for 2010 reveals that India's share of GDP is 5.5 per cent.[199] Figure 2.8 presents the share of India and the major contributors to the world economy, based on the figures provided by the International Monetary Fund.

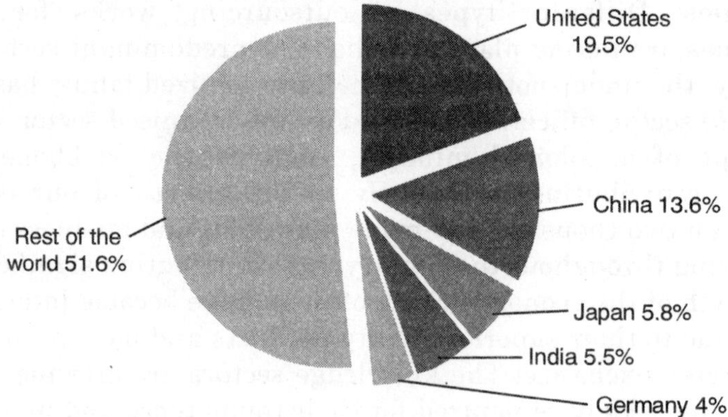

Figure 2.8 Share of India in world economy (2010).

The figure shows that India's share of global economic contribution stands at 5.5 per cent, compared to Japan with 5.8 per cent, China with 13.6 per cent and U.S with 19.5 per cent shares respectively. India's share of world GDP in 1950 was 4.2 per cent. It declined further to 3.1 per cent in 1973, and then started climbing up and reached 5.4 per cent in 2001[200]. Subsequently, the share crossed 6 per cent, before new exchange rate was incorporated by the International Monetary Fund to measure the GDP. The share of India in the exports of goods and services in the world touched 1.9 per cent during 2010[201]*.

* Table A. Classification by World Economic Outlook Groups and their Shares in Aggregate GDP, Exports of Goods and Services, and Population, 2010.

Figure 2.9 presents the positions of top five economically powerful nations in the world, based on the shares in the world GDP as provided by the International Monetary Fund.

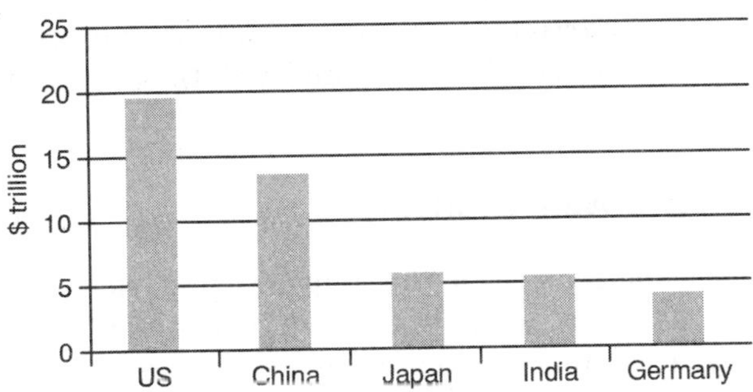

Figure 2.9 Top five economies on PPP basis (2010).

With the growth rates going up, the world has started taking a serious note of India. Though there are critical areas of concern such as agriculture, the mood is very upbeat. In every international gathering India has become the centre of the discussion. All the western economists, institutions, consulting and research bodies that used to ignore India all these years have begun to appreciate and adore India. In the World Economic Forum 2006 meeting at Davos, there was an "India Everywhere" campaign. The multilateral bodies that used to 'advise' India, have begun to appreciate India and their officials have begun to openly admire the 'Indian model'.

There is no doubt that India has arrived on the scene. Nobody can ignore India hereafter in any global discussion. India is not just only an emerging economic power, but, also a powerful society with lots of skills and potential. It has the largest younger population in the world. The society is largely peaceful and has the capacity to function on its own, without being too dependent on outside mechanisms. A great future awaits her. But it is to be remembered here that the Indian policymakers have been continuously neglecting certain vital areas, in their urgency to 'copy' the other countries and hence, our potential is yet to be realized completely. The agricultural sector has not been given the attention that it deserves in any civilized society and so it remains largely neglected. A lot of efforts are yet to be taken in social sectors, employment and infrastructure. Recent estimates note that around 25 per cent of the people or even more are still living below poverty line. The 66th round of NSS Survey on employment and unemployment situation in India 2009–10 reveals that there is a decline in the overall job creation indicating 'jobless growth'. It show that the growth rate of employment has decreased during the five-year period ended 2009–10 compared to the previous five year[202]. So the present performance is not a complete one. Moreover, the successes so far seem to be only partial as there is a lot of potential remaining untapped, even though the economic growth in recent years has been impressive.

2.4.4 Society-driven Economy

What could be the reason for this impressive performance in recent years? How could a country, whose economic systems totally destroyed by a colonial power, come back to render a world-class performance in less than sixty years? This is an enigma that we have to understand. India has grown and is growing after independence, despite obstructions, presumably due to the inherent strengths of the society. The former Ambassador of the US to India John Kenneth Galbraith*, an economist himself, had noted: "I wanted to emphasise the point, which would be widely accepted, that the success of India did not depend on the government. It depended on the energy, ingenuity and other qualifications of the Indian people. And the Indian quality to put ideas into practice. I was urging an obvious point that the progress of India did not depend on the government, as important as that might be, but was enormously dependent on the initiative, individual and group of the Indian people. I feel the same way now (as I did some forty years ago) but I would even emphasise it more. We've seen many years of Indian progress, and that is attributable to the energy and genius of the Indian people and the Indian culture." The people of India have been shaped by a unique set of social and behavioural systems driven by the age-old culture that mandates family life, hard work, savings orientation, entrepreneurship and a self-dependent mindset. It is this background that drives India to higher levels; it is not the bookish theories or policy prescriptions based on outside experiments. Even the government and state agencies seem to play only a limited role. The forces behind India's development seem to be more internal than external.

It is unfortunate that when the Indian Government and the policymakers opt for economic models and take policy decisions, they do not take the ground realities into consideration. With the result they always go for adopting outside models. The well-known media personality and a keen observer of India, Mark Tully[203]

* Galbraith, John K., interview in *Outlook,* August 20, 2001.

notes: "India has followed western economic thinking too. When socialism was in fashion, Nehru rejected Mahatma Gandhi's plea for development from the villages upward and concentrated on trying to create an industrialized nation through centralized planning. Now that the West has rejected socialism, the Indian elite talk of liberalizing the economy, making consumerism the engine of growth and allowing the wealth created to 'trickle down' to the poor. The irony is that, during the years when Rajiv Gandhi was liberalizing the economy, the growth in employment declined—and that's the growth rate that matters most in India." Aping the west is probably the most important reason as to why there is no all-round development, though the economy has been growing. We are in a situation in which even while some of the sectors are doing extremely well, there are large-scale failures in certain crucial areas. One should be very happy to see India emerging as an economic power. But at the same time one has to take into consideration the 'failure zones' of India's economy. Only then the meaningful corrections are possible.

2.4.5 Growth Started with Independence

Over the years, the changes in economic thinking of policymakers have influenced the Indian economic models in different directions. In the first three decades beginning from the 1950s, the socialistic orientation has resulted in a state-dependent system, popularly known as the 'license-permit raj' that placed restrictions on the growth of enterprises. As a result, free competition was not allowed inside the country. The 1980s saw restrictive policies being relaxed, as a result of which growth accelerated. The 1990s witnessed policies in the direction of globalization, which led to the opening up of economy in different directions. This paved the way for entry of foreign companies and investments in different sectors. While this resulted in providing opportunities for many sectors, certain major sectors have to face serious difficulties. Indian corporate sector had to face challenges and many of them started going out in search of better opportunities. Indians began to spend more money due to the consumer boom and increased incomes in the hands of young population. Thus the economic system has been witnessing fast changes in the recent periods.

While a group of experts presents the view that the 1980s signalled a shift in the economic growth, others note that the shift happened in the 1990s. Deepak Nayyar[204] states clearly that India's progress cannot be explained through the 'caricature perceptions' of growth that are generally used. Nayyar writes:

"The story of economic development in India is often distorted by beliefs in fashion or caricatures of perceptions which shape conventional wisdom ... this is misleading, not only in analyzing the past but also in contemplating the future. If we consider India during the 20th century as a whole, the turning point in economic growth was circa 1951. If we consider India since independence, the turning point in economic growth was circa 1980. And ... that the turning point in the early 1950s was much more significant than the structural break in the early 1980. In any case, 1991 was not a watershed. Thus, it is not possible to attribute the turnaround in India's growth performance to economic liberalization. Economic growth in India was respectable during 1950–80. It was a radical departure from the colonial past. And it was no worse than the growth performance of most countries during that period. But it was simply not enough in relation to India's needs. Economic growth in India was impressive during the period 1980–2005. Indeed it was much better than in most countries. But even this was not enough. The moral of the story is clear. Caricature perceptions about the economic growth in India since independence are not correct. In the first phase, from 1950 to 1980, India was not the lumbering elephant that it is often made out to be. In the second phase, from 1980 to 2005, India was not quite the running tiger that some believe it has become."

2.4.6 Unique Indian Models

From the ancient periods, the Indian approach to economics and society seems to be unique. The ancient economic model of India was a superior one that showed an outstanding performance for the longest period in the history of the world. Moreover, it was based on the noble ideals and higher principles of mankind, with a spiritual orientation to different activities. The Indian model was definitely a unique one; or otherwise how could India have developed into, and remained, a 'model nation' with complete prosperity and social peace, along with pioneering achievements in diverse areas of life? India's economic superiority was achieved through her own efforts, without exploiting other nations at any time in the course of her long history. It was always through superior products and quality services. After studying the Indian economy of the past, one is tempted to ask a few questions. When did all this development start? How could India achieve such high levels of prosperity even during 0 CE and many centuries earlier? How was it that the economic prosperity was maintained for such a long period since the ancient days? How was it that there was an all-round development, with achievements of a remarkable order? Is there any other country in the world that was prosperous and peaceful at the same time for so many centuries? Is there any other country that taught contentment amidst plenty?

Unfortunately, the entry of the British changed the body and soul of India, and as a result India became a poor country. But immediately after independence, people engaged themselves in different activities in the 'most possible economical ways.' Even in 1950–51, the Gross Domestic Savings was 8.6 per cent of GDP. Out of this, the contribution of the household sector was 66 per cent, while the organized sectors contributed the balance. We have to remember that during this period, 45 per cent of the population was living in poverty and the literacy level was just 17 per cent[205]. After five years, in 1955–56, the Gross Domestic Savings was 12.3 per cent, with the household sector contributing nearly 75 per cent of the share. As a result, the Gross Domestic Capital Formation was 8.4 per cent of GDP in 1950–51. In 1951–52, the institutional source of finance to agriculture was just 7.3 per cent, while the non-institutional credit was 92.7 per cent[206]. This shows the capacity of the Indians to mobilize funds on their own for capital formation without depending on the state. In 1955–56 capital formation reached 12.6 per cent[207]. The savings and capital formation rate have been steadily increasing since then. The people of India, irrespective of region and language, started saving more money and investing funds, the two foremost economic activities, as soon as the country became politically independent. How did this happen? Even while the government was imitating the western nations for suitable policies to lead the country towards development, how come the ordinary people, largely living in villages, with nearly five sixth of them deprived of education, engage in serious economic activities in the most intelligent ways. Looking back after six decades, it becomes clear that it is the 'economic sense' of the people that had laid the foundations for the present status. This is not to undermine the role of the state, for it has its own place. But at the same time we have to recognize the genius of the Indian mind who had already started implementing the vision to build a better future at the first available opportunity, while the policymakers were searching for solutions. It seems that it is the hidden spirit of India that is driving the Indian economy constantly towards progress, despite the official pronouncements and policies, to reach the stage at which we are today.

What are the forces that drive the economic spirit of India after independence? We can at least understand the superior performance in the earlier periods, when the native systems established over years of experience were freely functioning. But what is driving the contemporary India whose energies lay suppressed for centuries earlier? What is the model of the country that is fast emerging as one of the top two prospective powers in the world, even after a near total decimation under the colonial rule, and in spite of the policies that are based on different world views for six decades? When the developed economies are facing serious crises and an uncertain future, what makes India to move continuously forward?

REFERENCES

[1] Encyclopedia Britannica online, http://www.britannica.com.

[2] Maddison, Angus, *The World Economy—A Millennial Perspective*, 1st Indian Ed., Overseas Press (India) Private Limited, New Delhi by arrangement with Organization for Economic Cooperation and Development, 2003.

[3] Jean-Francois Jarrige, quoted in Michel Danino, '*Indian History and Civilisation: Recent Discoveries and their Significance*', Paper presented at the National Symposium on Philosophy and Practice of Education for India, organized by Sri Aurobindo Samiti at Kolkata, November 2004, p. 4.

[4] Randhawa, M.S., *A History of Agriculture in India*, quoted in Pereira, Winin, *Tending the Earth*, Earthcare Books, Bombay, 1993, p. 187.

[5] Pereira, Winin, *Tending the Earth*, Earthcare Books, Bombay, 1993.

[6] Ibid., p. 187.

[7] Quoted in Daya Krishna, *India's Planned Poverty*, Bharatiya Agro Economic Research Centre, Delhi, 1989, p. 34.

[8] Quoted in Bajaj, Jitendra and Srininvas, M.D., *Timeless India Resurgent India*, Centre for Policy Studies, Chennai, 2001, p. 44.

[9] Quoted in Dharampal, *Science and Technology in the Eighteenth Century*, Other India Press, Goa, 2000, p. 194.

[10] Ibid, p. 184.

[11] Pereira, Winin, op.cit., p. 22.

[12] Ibid.

[13] Ibid.

[14] Thiruvalluvar, *Thirukkural,* couplet 732.

[15] Quoted in Bajaj, Jitendra and Srinivas, M.D., op.cit., p. 44.

[16] Ibid.

[17] Bajaj, Jitendra (ed.), *Food for All*, Centre for Policy Studies, Chennai, 2001, p. xv.

[18] Quoted in Bajaj, Jitendra and Srinivas, M.D., op.cit., p. 50.

[19] Ibid.

[20] Bajaj, Jitendra (ed.), op.cit., pp. xv–xvi.

[21] Chhabra, B.C., quoted in Daya Krishna, *Golden Age to Globalisation—7000 Years of Indian Economy*, Swadeshi Jagran Prakashan, New Delhi, 2002, p. 25.

[22] Basham, A.L., *The Wonder that was India*, Rupa & Co., New Delhi, 2001, p. 216.

[23] Rangarajan, L.N., *Kautilya—The Arthasastra*, Penguin Books India Private Limited, New Delhi, 1992, pp. 305–306.

[24] Mookerji, Radha Kumud, *Ancient Indian Education,* Motilal Banarsidas, Delhi, 4th ed., 1969, p. 364.

[25] Agarwala, P.N., *A Comprehensive History of Business in India—from 3000 BC to 2000 AD*, Tata McGraw-Hill Publishing Company Limited, New Delhi, 2001, p. 304.

[26] Ibid., p. 356.

[27] Kennedy, Paul S., *The Rise and Fall of the Great Powers—Economic Change and Military Conflict from 1500–2000*, Fontana Press, London, 1988, p. 190.

[28] Mukund, Kanakalatha, *The Trading World of the Tamil Merchant—Evolution of Merchant Capitalism in the Coromandel*, Orient Longman Limited, Hyderabad, 1999, p. 1.

[29] Agarwala, P.N., op.cit., p. 257.

[30] Ibid., p. 259.

[31] Ibid., p. 261.

[32] Chakravarty, Ranabir, *Trade in Early India*, Oxford University Press, New Delhi, 2001, p. 6.

[33] Rangarajan, L.N., op.cit., p. 75.

[34] Agarwala, P.N., op.cit., p. 262.

[35] Frank, Andre Gunder, *Reorient: Global Economy in the Asian Age*, Vistaar Publications, New Delhi, 1998, pp. 85–88.

[36] Frank, Andre Gunder, op.cit, p. 85.

[37] Khanna, Vikramaditya S., "*The Economic History of Corporate Form in Ancient India*", 1997, p. 3. http://ssrn.com/.

[38] *Pride of India*, Samskrita Bharati, New Delhi, 2006, p. 70.

[39] Mookerji, Radha Kumud, op.cit., p. 575.

[40] *Pride of India*, op.cit., p. 71.

[41] Mookerji, Radha Kumud, op.cit., p. 347.

[42] Ibid., p. 353.

[43] Makkhan Lal with Rajendra Dixit, *Educating to Confuse and Disrupt*, 1st ed., India First Foundation, New Delhi, 2005, p. 64.

[44] Ibid., p. 50.

[45] Dharampal, *The Beautiful Tree*, 2nd ed., Keerthi Publishing House Pvt. Ltd., and AVP Printers and Publishers Pvt. Ltd., Coimbatore, 1995, pp. 42–43.

[46] Ibid., p. 12.

[47] Makkhan Lal with Rajendra Dixit, op.cit., p. 51.

[48] Dharampal, 1995, op.cit., p. 14.

[49] Ibid., p. 6.

[50] Ibid., p. 27.

[51] Quoted in Makkhan Lal with Rajendra Dixit, op.cit., p. 83.

[52] Georges Ifrah, *Histoire Universelle des Chiffres*, Vol. 2, Robert Laffont, Paris, 1994, p. 3.

[53] Shashi Tharoor, 'Why Indian science scores', *The Hindu*, June 8, 2003.

[54] Ibid.

[55] *Pride of India*, op.cit., p. 148.

[56] *Pride of India*, op.cit., p. 112.

[57] Rangarajan, L.N., op.cit., (from 1.19.35, 36), p. 177.

[58] Thiruvalluvar, op.cit., couplet 759.

[59] Bajaj, J., (ed.), op.cit., p. xvi.

[60] Ibid.

[61] Bajaj, J. and Srinivas, M.D., 2001, op.cit., p. 36.

[62] Basham, A.L., op.cit., p. 216.

[63] Thiruvalluvar, op.cit., couplet 760.

[64] Jain, V.K., '*Trading Community and Merchant Corporations*', in Chakravarty, Ranabir, op.cit., pp. 360–361.

[65] Khanna, Vikramaditya S., op.cit., p. 6.

[66] Ibid., p. 11.

[67] Quoted in Naoroji, Dadabhai, *Poverty and Un-British Rule in India*, 2nd ed., Ministry of Information and Broadcasting, Government of India, New Delhi, 1966, p. 518.

[68] Basham, A.L., op.cit., pp. 216–217.

[69] Jain, V.K., '*Trading Community and Merchant Corporations*', in Chakravarty, Ranabir, op.cit., p. 362.

[70] Basham, A.L., op.cit., p. 9.

[71] Ibid., pp. 8–9.

[72] Naoroji, Dadabhai quoted in Naoroji, Dadabhai, op.cit., p. iii.

[73] Frank, Andre Gunder, op.cit., p. 127.

[74] Sunderland quoted in Will Durant, *The Case for India,* Simon and Schuster, New York, 1930, pp. 8–9.

[75] Maddison, Angus, op.cit., p. 89.

[76] Ibid., p. 92.

[77] Ibid., p. 105.

[78] Ibid., p. 104.

[79] Agarwala, P.N., op.cit., p. 286.

[80] Ibid.

[81] Quoted in Dutt, Romesh, *The Economic History of India—Under Early British Rule,* Vol. I, 2nd ed., Kegal Paul, Trench, Trubner, Great Britain, 1906, pp. 412–413.

[82] Maddison, Angus, op.cit., p. 115.

[83] Quoted in Chandra, Bipan, *The Rise and Growth of Economic Nationalism in India,* Revised & Abridged edition, Anamika Publishers & Distributors (P) Ltd, New Delhi, 2004, p. 34.

[84] Quoted in Chandra, Bipan, op.cit., p. 104.

[85] Kennedy, Paul, op.cit., per capita levels of industrialization, 1750–1900 (relative to U.K. in 1900=100), p. 190.

[86] Agarwala, P.N., op.cit., p. 304.

[87] Ibid., p. 359.

[88] Ibid., p. 304.

[89] Bajaj, J. and Srinivas, M.D., op.cit., p. 71.

[90] Agarwala, P.N., op.cit., p. 359.

[91] Bajaj, J. and Srinivas, M.D., op.cit., p. 52.

[92] Dutt, Romesh, op.cit., p. x.

[93] Ibid.

[94] Dutt, Romesh, op.cit., pp. 26–27.

[95] Chandra, Bipan, op.cit., p. 34.

[96] Chandra, Bipan, op.cit., p. 35.

[97] Dutt, Romesh, op.cit., p. x.

[98] Ibid.

[99] Ibid., p. xi.

[100] Maddison, Angus., op.cit., p. 114.

[101] Bajaj, Jitendra and Srinivas, M.D., *Annam Bahu Kurvitha*, Centre for Policy Studies, Madras, 1996, p. 200.

[102] Ibid.

[103] Maddison, Angus, op.cit., p. 109.

[104] Dutt, Romesh, op.cit., p. xi.

[105] Ibid.

[106] Quoted in Dutt, Romesh., Vol. I, op.cit., p. 53.

[107] Dharampal, 2000, op.cit., p. xi.

[108] Dutt, Romesh, Vol. I, op.cit., p. 411.

[109] Pereira, Winin, op.cit., p. 24.

[110] Maddison, Angus, op.cit., p. 97.

[111] Will Durant, op.cit., pp. 14–15.

[112] Quoted in Chandra, Bipan, op.cit., p. 265.

[113] Quoted in Chandra, Bipan, op.cit., p. 245.

[114] Quoted in Will Durant, op.cit., pp. 163–64.

[115] Chandra, Bipan, op.cit., pp. 71–72.

[116] Agarwala, P.N., op.cit., p. 356.

[117] Kennedy, Paul S., op.cit., p. 191.

[118] *Evidence in the Commons Report of 1830, 1830–31 and 1831*, Digest quoted in Agarwala, P.N., op.cit., p. 358.

[119] Quoted in Agarwala, P.N., op.cit., p. 304.

[120] Agarwala, P.N., op.cit., p. 358.

[121] Chandra, Bipan, op.cit., p. 81.

[122] Nehru, Jawaharlal, *Discovery of India*, Penguin, New Delhi, 2004, p. 322.

[123] Quoted in Chandra, Bipan, op.cit., p. 305.

[124] Naoroji, Dadabahi, op.cit., p. vii.

[125] Chandra, Bipan, op.cit., p. 305.

[126] Naoroji, Dadabahi, op.cit., pp. 30–31.

[127] Ibid., p. 31.

[128] Ibid., p. 36.

[129] Ibid., p. 35.

[130] Dutt, Romesh, *The Economic History of India—In the Victorian Age*, Vol. II, 2nd ed., Kegal Paul, Trench, Trubner, Great Britain, 1906, p. xiv.

[131] Dutt, Romesh, Vol. I, op.cit., p. 39.

[132] Ibid., p. 47.

[133] Quoted in Dutt, Romesh, Vol. I, op.cit., pp. 409–10.

[134] Dutt, Romesh, op.cit., Vol. I, p. 410.

[135] Quoted in Naoroji, Dadabhai, op.cit., p. 37.

[136] Shore's opinion quoted in Naoroji, Dadabhai, op.cit., p. 37.

[137] Marriot quoted in Naoroji, Dadabhai, op.cit., p. 40.

[138] Lawrence quoted in Naoroji, Dadabhai, op.cit., p. 45.

[139] Mayo quoted in Naoroji, Dadabhai, op.cit., p. 45.

[140] Naoroji, Dadabhai, op.cit., p. 11.

[141] Chandra, Bipan, op.cit., p. 33.

[142] Quoted in Chandra, Bipan, op.cit., p. 308.

[143] Will Durant, op.cit., p. 10.

[144] Quoted in Dutt, Romesh, op.cit., Vol. I, p. 33.

[145] Quoted in Will Durant op.cit., p. 10.

[146] Dutt, Romesh, Vol. I, op.cit., pp. 411–412.

[147] Ibid. pp. 47–48.

[148] Ibid., p. 420.

[149] Ibid., p. 409.

[150] Naoroji, Dadabhai, op.cit., p. vii.

[151] Will Durant, op.cit., pp. 41–42.

[152] William Digby quoted in Daya Krishna, 2002, op.cit., p. 58.

[153] Williamson, Jeffrey, 'De-industrialisation and Underdevelopment: A Comparative Assessment around the Periphery 1750–1939', Paper prepared for the Harvard Economic History workshop, Harvard University, December 2004, p. 4.

[154] Frank, Andre Gunder, 'Asian-based World Economy 1400–1800: A Horizontally Integrative Macro-history', University of Amsterdam, 12 November 1995.

[155] Williamson, Jeffrey, op.cit., p. 43.

[156] Dutt, Romesh, Vol. I, op.cit., p. 408.

[157] Will Durant, op.cit., pp. 12–13.

[158] Ibid., p. 24–25.

[159] Ibid., p. 23.

[160] Chandra, Bipan, op.cit., p. 34.

[161] Maddison, Angus, op.cit., p. 111.

[162] Bimal Jalan quoted in Daya Krishna, 2002, op.cit., p. 68.

[163] Maddison, Angus, op.cit., p. 91.

[164] Ibid., p. 97.

[165] Quoted in Naoroji, Dadabhai, op.cit., p. I.

[166] Quoted in Naoroji, Dadabhai, op.cit., p. 42.

[167] Ibid.

[168] Maddison, Angus, op.cit., p. 115.

[169] Quoted in Naoroji, Dadabhai, op.cit., p. 42.

[170] Maddison, Angus, op.cit., p. 115.

[171] Dutt, Romesh, Vol. I, op.cit., p. viii.

[172] Will Durant, op.cit., pp. 51–53.

[173] Ibid., p. 51.

[174] Maddison, Angus, op.cit., p. 33.

[175] Quoted in Will Durant, op.cit., p. 54.

[176] Will Durant, op.cit., p. 44.

[177] Ibid., p. 45.

[178] Ibid., p. 47.

[179] Quoted in Tomilson, B.R., *The Economy of Modern India, 1860–1970*, 1st South Asian paperback ed., Cambridge University Press, U.K., 1998, p. 4.

[180] Quoted in Dharampal, 1995, op.cit., p. vi.

[181] Shore quoted in Will Durant, op.cit., pp. 16–17.

[182] Will Durant, op.cit., pp. 6–7.

[183] Naoroji, Dadabhai, op.cit., p. vii.

[184] Quoted in Will Durant, op.cit., p. 99.

[185] Uma Kapila (ed.), *Indian Economy since Independence*, 14th ed., 2002–03, Academic Foundation, New Delhi, 2002, p. 26.

[186] Rakesh Mohan, 'Fiscal Correction for Economic Growth' in Uma Kapila, op.cit., p. 87.

[187] Ibid.

[188] Based on data from Maddison, Angus, op.cit., p. 263.

[189] Maddison as quoted in Uma Kapila, op.cit., p. 88.

[190] Nayyar, Deepak, 'Economic Growth in Independent India—Lumbering Elephant or Running Tiger?', *Economic and Political Weekly*, Vol. XLI, No. 15, 2006, p. 1454.

[191] Ibid.

[192] Nayyar, Deepak, op.cit., p. 1455.

[193] Ibid.

[194] Virmani, Arvind, *Propelling India from Socialist Stagnation to Global Power—Vol. I: Growth Process*, Academic Foundation, New Delhi, 2006, p. 46.

[195] Maddison quoted in Uma Kapila, op.cit., p. 88.

[196] *Economic Survey 2008–09*, Ministry of Finance, Govt. of India, p. 1.

[197] *Annual Report, 2010–11*, Reserve Bank of India, p. 168.

[198] *World Development Report 2012, Gender Equality and Development*, World Bank, Washington, pp. 392–393.

[199] *World Economic Outlook, September 2011: Slowing Growth, Rising Risks*, International Monetary Fund, Washington, p. 167.

[200] Maddison, Angus, *The World History* (Two-in-One Edition), Indian Edition, Academic Foundation, New Delhi in arrangement with the Organization for Economic Co-operation and Development, 2007, p. 641.

[201] *World Economic Outlook*, September 2011: International Monetary Fund, op. cit., p. 167.

[202] *Employment and Unemployment Situation in India 2009–10, NSS 66th round,* Ministry of Statistics and Programme Implementation, Government of India, New Delhi, 2011.

[203] Mark Tully, *No Full Stops in India,* Penguin Publishers, New Delhi, 1991, p. 8.

[204] Nayyar, Deepak, op.cit., p. 1457.

[205] Mohan, Rakesh in Uma Kapila, (ed.), op.cit., p. 87.

[206] Uma Kapila, *Understanding the Problems of Indian Economy,* 4th ed. 2003–04, Academic Foundation, New Delhi, 2003, p. 272.

[207] *Economic Survey,* 2009–10, Government of India, p. A11.

3

Other Economic Models

Countries across the world follow different economic models. During the previous five centuries in which they have emerged as visible economic entities, the economic models of the West have changed many times. These changes are basically necessitated by the turn of events in different periods. In this connection, it is interesting to note that the economic models of the eastern nations have a different set of characteristics. The specific model of each country, whether it belongs to the East or the West, seems to have different features, though similarities do exist within the broad frameworks.

3.1 POPULAR WESTERN MODELS

From the end of fifteenth century, almost all the native economic systems in different parts of the world were subjected to disturbances and destructions by the colonizers and invaders. Hence, only the dominant western models of the contemporary era are discussed here. But there are groups of people, most of them natives, who still follow their traditional lifestyles, and economic systems in different parts of the world including the West.

The feudal system that was prevailing in Europe witnessed its end in the fourteenth century. The dominant economic system that prevailed from the sixteenth to eighteenth century was called 'mercantilism.' According to this theory, the bullion had to be increased by the countries, as the stock of accumulated gold represented the prosperity of nations. Mercantilism believed that the global volume of trade was 'fixed'. Hence every country tried to have a positive balance of trade through which they could maximize their bullion stock. But not all countries had the ability to have a positive balance of trade. Hence, different methods, including piracy, were also employed to increase the bullion stocks. Since the volume of trade was considered to be fixed, the mercantilists viewed the economic system as a 'zero sum game', meaning one country could benefit only at the cost of the other. Thus, there was severe competition between countries for markets. Imports were discouraged through protectionist policies and tariffs, and exports were encouraged. Governments intervened in international trade to help exports and restrict imports.

Mercantilism motivated countries to search for new markets and the competition for markets resulted in violence and wars such as the Anglo-Dutch and Franco-Dutch wars. Merchants were encouraged to go to new areas in search of the markets. This resulted in voyages across the world in different directions. The search for sea routes to India landed Columbus in the discovery of the "new lands." It was the Portuguese navigator Vasco de Gama who finally reached the western shores of India. The Europeans went on to occupy many of the countries in Americas, Africa, Asia and other parts of the world in the subsequent periods. Mercantilism encouraged and resulted in European imperialism over the rest of the world.

Though mercantilism of the early periods, as developed during the beginning of the sixteenth century, was noted for bullionism, later it believed in the development of domestic manufacturing industries and a total ban on export of raw materials. One important point to be mentioned here during this period is the treatment meted out to the working class. Labourers and farmers had to live a subsistent life as it was thought that extra income, education and leisure time would lead them to laziness, which would ultimately harm the economy. Mercantilist policies were promoted and developed by the merchants and government servants. Merchants benefited from this system through government patronage, monopolies and low wages to labourers. Governments benefited from more resources through trade and tariffs. So basically, this ideology was promoted and nurtured by imperialist nations and rent-seeking merchants. Mercantilism reached its peak during the seventeenth century.

It began to lose its hold in the eighteenth century, as economists started questioning the theory amidst wide discontents. Adam Smith published "*Wealth of Nations*" in 1776, arguing for a capitalistic model. As a result, the support for mercantilist ideology declined and the relevant regulations had to be slowly removed. Hence, the mercantilist system that dominated the western economy for more than two centuries had to lose its place.

3.1.1 Capitalism

The capitalistic model advocated by Adam Smith believed in the private ownership of enterprises in a country. This model was based on the principle of '*laissez-faire*'. Accordingly, the governments are not expected to interfere in the affairs of business. This theory believed that the means of production be privately owned and operated for profit through markets. Smith advocated this model based on the economic and social situation prevailing in Europe at that time. It was articulated as a corrective model to the mercantilist system that was not beneficial to a large majority of the people. It was believed that the capitalist system with many operators in the economy would be a better alternative. Subsequently, economists like David Ricardo and John Maynard Keynes had made significant contributions towards capitalistic school of thought over the years. The eighteenth and nineteenth centuries were dominated by the classical economists. Since the later decades of the nineteenth century, neoclassical economic thoughts emerged. These theories believe that all economic decisions are aimed at self-satisfaction. The neoclassical theories make extensive use of mathematical models to explain and demonstrate their points of view. Meanwhile, the Second World War led to the establishment of the Bretton Woods system and as a result, two important multilateral agencies, namely the International Monetary Fund and the World Bank came into existence. Gold standard was discontinued and the American dollar became the international currency, with the US agreeing for a fixed parity between gold and dollar. But later the US withdrew from this system and as a result, it was abandoned in the early 1970s.

Washington consensus

Since then, the US began to increasingly dominate the international economic scene. A set of policy prescriptions known as the "Washington Consensus" formed the core of the initiatives to be adopted as the step towards the capitalist model in the 1980s. "One size fits for all" approach was prescribed for the economic problems of different countries. After the failure of communism in the late 1980s in USSR, the US-driven capitalist ideology was promoted as the only suitable model for all the countries to progress. The failure of economies in different parts of the world, from Mexico in 1982, to ASEAN in 1997, and to Russia in 1998, and Latin America in the present decade has led to serious questions being raised about this model. Over the last few years, there have been serious criticisms against the model. Palley[1] notes: "The Washington Consensus, with its emphasis on export-led growth, has failed. It is time for a new development policy agenda that focuses on domestic demand-led growth." He continues further to explain the effect of these policies. To quote: "Proclivity to crisis is one fundamental problem of the Washington Consensus. A second fundamental problem is its failure to deliver economic growth. World growth in the period 1990–96 was slower than the period 1980–89, which in turn was slower than the period 1965–80. A third fundamental problem is the tendency of the Washington Consensus policy configuration to worsen income distribution, be it in the industrialized or developing worlds. Thus, not only has growth slowed during the period of Washington Consensus ascendancy, but there has also been an increase in income inequality within and between countries[2]."

Schumacher on market

The noted economist E.F. Schumacher[3] had warned much earlier that the concept of market itself has serious limitations. He wrote: "In a sense, the market is the institutionalization of individualism and non-responsibility. Neither buyer nor seller is responsible for anything but himself. It would be 'uneconomic' for a wealthy seller to reduce his prices to poor customers merely because they are in need, or for a wealthy buyer to pay an extra price merely because the supplier is poor. Equally it would be 'uneconomic' for a buyer to give preference to home-produced goods if imported goods are cheaper. He does not, and is not expected to, accept responsibility for the country's balance of payments." He had noted that the economic thinking based on the primacy of the market takes the sacredness out of life. "In the marketplace, for practical reasons, innumerable qualitative distinctions which are of vital importance for man and society are suppressed; they are not allowed to surface. Thus the reign of quantity celebrates its greatest triumphs in 'The Market'. Everything is equated with everything else. To equate things means to give them a price and thus to make them exchangeable. To the extent that economic thinking is based on the market, it takes the sacredness out of life, because there can be nothing sacred in something that has a price. Not surprisingly, therefore, if economic thinking pervades the whole society, even simple non-economic values like beauty, health, or cleanliness can survive only if they prove to be 'economic'[4].

Criticisms on neoclassical approach

The contemporary approach based on the neoclassical theories and quantitative techniques is seriously questioned, as they do not take into consideration the other relevant factors. Hoff and Stiglitz[5] note: "We were always told that the neoclassical model was "just a benchmark"—a tool for thinking through complicated problems—but now there is increasing recognition that its implications are likely to be misleading in realistic settings where there are diffused externalities." Fukuyama[6] writes that the difficulty with neoclassical economics is that it emphasizes only the market, leaving the role of society and culture in economic life. To quote: "We can think of neoclassical economics as being, say, eighty per cent correct; it has uncovered important truths about the nature of money and markets because its fundamental model of rational, self-interested human behaviour is correct about eighty per cent of the time. But there is a missing twenty per cent of human behaviour about which neoclassical economics can give only a poor account. As Adam Smith well understood, economic life is deeply embedded in social life, and it cannot be understood apart from the customs, morals, and habits of the society in which it occurs. In short, it cannot be divorced from culture."

Fukuyama[7] notes that the neoclassical economics has moved away from certain key foundations of classical economics and is not in a position to explain 'many aspects of the economic life'. To quote: "The problem with neoclassical economics is that it has forgotten certain key foundations on which classical economics was based. Adam Smith, the premier classical economists, believed that people are driven by a selfish desire to "better their condition", but he would never have subscribed to the notion that economic activity could be reduced to rational utility maximization. Indeed, his other major work besides *The Wealth of Nations* was *The Theory of Moral Sentiments,* which portrays economic motivation as highly complex and embedded in broader social habits and mores. The very change in the name of the discipline from "political economy" to "economics" between the eighteenth and late nineteenth centuries reflects the narrowing model of human behaviour at its core. Current economic discourse needs to recover some of the richness of classical, as opposed to neoclassical economics, by taking account of how culture shapes all aspects of human behaviour, including economic behaviour, in a number of critical ways. Not only is the neoclassical economic perspective insufficient to explain political life with its dominant emotions of indignation, pride, and shame, but it is not sufficient to explain many aspects of economic life either. Not all economic actions arise out of what are traditionally thought of as economic motives."

David Korten, a former member of the faculty of the Harvard Graduate School of Business who had founded *People-centred Development Forum*, shows that the modern capitalist system is far removed from the model advocated by Adam Smith. Grouping three categories of people, namely the economic rationalists (mostly neoclassical economists), market liberals and the members of corporate class together, and calling them as corporate libertarians, Korten[8] notes: "The proponents of the corporate libertarianism regularly pay homage to Adam Smith as their intellectual patron saint. His writing remains the intellectual foundation on which the whole structure of the deductive reasoning of the economic rationalists has been built. It is a tragic irony that although the economic rationalists now call upon that structure to give intellectual legitimacy to the ideology of corporate libertarianism, Smith's epic work *The Wealth of Nations*, first published in 1776, actually presented a radical condemnation of business monopolies sustained and protected by the state." On Adam Smith's vision of efficient market, Korten writes: "It is a market that has little in common with a globalized economy dominated by massive corporations without local or national allegiance, managed by professionals who are removed from real owners by layers of investment institutions and holding companies[9]."

Fukuyama[10] further says that the higher non-utilitarian goals pursued by people in their lives are not captured by neoclassical assumptions. "Every one of the terms of the neoclassical premise that human beings are rational utility-maximizing individuals is subject to significant qualification or exception. Take the assertion that people pursue utility. The most basic definition of utility is the narrow one associated with the nineteenth-century utilitarian, Jeremy Bentham: that utility is the pursuit of pleasure or the avoidance of pain. Such a definition is straightforward and corresponds to a commonsense understanding of economic motivation: people want to be able to consume the largest possible quantity of the good things of life. But there are numerous occasions when people pursue goals other than utility. They have been known to run into burning houses to save others, die in battle, or throw away lucrative careers so that they can commune with nature somewhere in the mountains. People do not simply vote their pocketbooks: they also have ideas that certain things are just or unjust, and they make important choices accordingly. There would not be nearly as many wars if the latter were fought simply over economic resources; unfortunately, they usually involve non-utilitarian goals like recognition, religion, justice, prestige, and honour."

Limitations of market fundamentalism

The market fundamentalist ideology, as advocated by the contemporary economists with a total freedom to the markets, has come in for serious criticisms. George Soros[11] notes that market fundamentalism has emerged as a threat to open society in the present context. To quote Soros: "Market fundamentalists believe in individual freedom, which is a cornerstone of open society, but they exaggerate the merits of the market mechanism. They believe that efficient markets assure the best allocation of resources and that any intervention, whether it comes from the state or from international institutions, is detrimental. Since market fundamentalism has become so influential, it today constitutes a greater threat to a global open society than communism or socialism, because those ideologies have been thoroughly discredited." In any country, nation-states have to play a regulatory role and shoulder social responsibilities in the overall interests of the society. But the market ideology does not give any scope for the nation-state or any other institution to intervene. In such a situation, the system cannot deliver goods to the overall well-being of the society. So the system gets flawed. Soros[12] writes on this: "The system itself is deeply flawed. Economic and political arrangements are out of kilter. The development of a global economy has not been matched by the development of a global society. The basic unit for political and social life remains the nation-state. The nation-state has been able to render certain social services to citizens; its ability to do so is impaired by the difficulties of taxing capital and the pressures of competition in international markets." It is thus becoming clear that the contemporary market economic system has serious in-built limitations. This is the reason why many conscious economists, market analysts and social scientists are questioning the usefulness of the model. Soros[13] asserts: "I am convinced that the market system, like every other human arrangement, is inherently flawed."

Moreover, the market ideology makes the problems of human beings more difficult. Korten[14] notes: "In the quest for economic growth, free-market ideology has been embraced around the world with the fervor of a fundamentalist religious faith. Money is its sole measure of value, and its practice is advancing policies that are deepening social and environmental disintegration everywhere. The economics profession serves as its priesthood. It champions values that demean the human spirit, it assumes an imaginary world divorced from reality, and it is restructuring our institutions of governance in ways that make our most fundamental problems more difficult to resolve."

Obsession with growth rates

Even the yardsticks used to measure the economic performance have come in for criticism. Growth rate, for example, is one measure used everywhere to see the economic performance of countries. But growth rate by itself does not improve the overall well-being of the citizens. Hamilton[15] wrote: "Despite high and sustained levels of economic growth in the West over a period of 50 years—growth that has seen average real incomes increase several times over—the mass of people are no more satisfied with their lives now than they were then. If growth is intended to give us better lives, and there can be no other purpose, it has failed." But all the countries are obsessed with growth rates. As observed by Hamilton, "Growth fetishism is not confined to advanced countries. Developing countries are also obsessed—perhaps the last and most potent legacy of colonialism. They have little choice[16]."

Inadequacy of national income as a measure

It is not just the growth rate, even the system of national accounts is also being questioned. In this connection it is interesting to note that even the originators of the national accounts system had forewarned the limitations of the system and advised the authorities not to use it to infer the welfare of the nation from these figures. "Even the originators of the system of national accounts that now rules our lives were acutely conscious of its limitations. John Maynard Keynes, John Hicks and Simon Kuznets first developed the system of national accounting because their governments needed better ways of managing their economies in the face of dramatic swings in the business cycle between the world wars. These economists repeatedly warned against using measures such as GNP as indicators of prosperity. Kuznets, the originator of the system of uniform national accounts in the United States, had actually warned the Congress in 1934: "The welfare of a nation can scarcely be inferred from a measurement of national income..." Unfortunately, Kuznets watched in dismay as his warnings were ignored and economists and policymakers grew accustomed to equating prosperity with growth in national income. By 1962, he wrote that the construction and use of the system of national accounting must be rethought: "Distinctions must be kept in mind between quantity and quality of growth, between its costs and returns, and between the short and the long run... Goals for 'more' growth should specify more growth of what and for what, the warnings went unheeded[17]." The system continues even today with all the countries using a set of common measures to judge the position and performances of economies.

Domination of financial markets

The modern capitalist system depends heavily on the financial markets. Such a heavy dependence of the economies on the volatile financial markets is not good. During the recent years, there have been instances where the economies of different countries had to suffer for the problems in the financial markets. In this connection, it is relevant to know the opinion of George Soros, himself a well-known player in the financial markets. Soros[18] writes: "The global capitalist system is based on the belief that financial markets, left to their own devices, tend towards equilibrium. They are supposed to move like a pendulum: they may be dislocated by external forces, so-called exogenous shocks, but they will seek to return to the equilibrium position. This belief is false. Financial markets are given to excesses and if a boom/bust sequence progresses beyond a certain point, it will never revert to where it came from. Instead of acting like a pendulum, financial markets have recently acted more like a wrecking ball, knocking over one economy after another." In spite of warnings from many concerned experts, including economists, financial markets are allowed to dominate the economic systems.

US economic system in trouble

The fundamental problems of economies during the last few years have raised further doubts about the strength of this model. No nation is happily placed, whether it is rich or poor. The richest nation in the world, namely the US has some of the most serious problems to tackle. A noted financial analyst who had worked with the IMF and World Bank warned earlier: "The US economy, rightly described as the world's engine of economic growth, is now beginning to falter under the immense debt burden of its corporate and consumer sectors. The rest of the world has grown reliant on exporting to the United States and, up, until now, has allowed the United States to pay much of its imports on credit. However, record bankruptcies and accounting fraud at the highest level of corporate America raise serious doubts about the creditworthiness of the United States. The trading partners of the United States now face the choice of continuing to invest their dollars surpluses in US dollar-denominated assets despite very compelling reasons to doubt the security of such investments, or else converting their dollar surpluses into their own currencies, which would cause their currencies to appreciate, and their exports and economic growth rates to decline. Neither choice is appealing, particularly considering the economic fragility of most of those countries and the huge amounts required to finance the US current account deficit—currently US $50 million an hour, or 5 per cent of gross domestic product (GDP) per annum[19]."

The US economy is importing more than its exports. Paul Krugman[20] reported in 2006: "Last year, America spent 57% more than it earned on world markets. That is, our imports were 57% larger than our exports." But how do they do this? Krugman[21] continues: "How did we manage to live so far beyond our means? By running up debts to Japan, China, and Middle-Eastern oil producers. We're as addicted to imported money as we are to imported oil." The US has been borrowing continuously from the international markets that it has become the largest debtor in the world today. But in spite of its heavy borrowings its problems persist; in fact, they are increasing. Even the basic problems of its citizens are not met. Take health care, for example. *Human Development Report 2005* noted that the "US public health indicators are marred by deep inequalities...[22]." What about the record of the club of rich countries in the world? When we take child poverty, a crucial measure of economic progress for any country, the situation is really bad. *Human Development Report* notes: "For 17 of the 24 OECD countries in the 1990's, research by the United Nations Children's Fund shows a rise in child poverty, defined as living in a family with an income below 50 per cent of the national median. This means that 40–50 million children are growing up in poverty in the world's richest countries. Two OECD members—Mexico and United States—have the dubious distinction of having the child poverty rates of more than 20 per cent[23]."

The troubles of the US economy have increased further since 2008 after the global economic crisis. In fact, the global crisis was preceded by a serious financial and economic crisis in the country. The bailouts and other steps initiated by the US Government after the crisis did not help much to improve the performance of their economy. Their economic problems have ultimately led to the downgrading of the sovereign rating. The hardships faced by the common people have forced them to come out openly in groups and question the economic policies in force. 'Occupy Wall Street' protests are symptoms of this phenomenon. Experts note that the problems of the US economy are more fundamental and hence advocate a wholesale change in thinking for a new beginning. For example, Korten notes: "Our economic system has failed in every dimension: financial, environmental, and social. And the current financial collapse provides an incontestable demonstration that it has failed even on its own terms. Spending trillions of dollars in an effort to restore this system to its previous condition is a reckless waste of time and resources and may be the greatest misuse of federal government credit in history. The more intelligent course is to acknowledge the failure and to set about redesigning our economic system from the bottom up to align with the realities and opportunities of the twenty-first century[24]."

Inequalities in world economies

As for the world economy as a whole, there are serious inequalities. *Human Development Report* states: "Measured more systematically by the *Gini* coefficient, the most widely used yardstick for inequality, the overall pattern of distribution for the whole world is more unequal than for any country except Namibia. On a scale where 0 is perfect equality and 100 is total inequality, the *Gini* coefficient for the world is 67[25]." It is distressing to see that after so many years of progress and development, the world has become more unequal. The disparities between and within nations have been widening. World Bank data for different periods reveal that "...whereas between 1960 and 1980 average income (measured as Gross National Product per head of population) in the industrial market economies fluctuated between 16 and 18 times more than the average level in the 'low and middle-income' economies, by the late 1990s this ratio had risen to 22–23:1[26]." Few rich individuals have more income than millions of poor people. *Human Development Report* mentions: "The world's richest 500 individuals have a combined income greater than that of the poorest 416 million. Beyond these extremes, the 2.5 billion people living on less than $2 a day—40 per cent of the world's population—account for 5 per cent of global income. The richest 10 per cent, almost all of whom live in high-income countries, account for 54 per cent[27]." With the result, we have a situation of very high incomes for a few, and extreme poverty for a vast number of people.

Globalization as a problem

The contemporary policies of globalization as advocated by the US and the multilateral agencies are viewed as the root cause of major problems in economies. In this connection it is pertinent to note the words of Stiglitz[28]: "Globalization today is not working for many of the world's poor. It is not working for much of the environment. It is not working for the stability of the global economy." As a result, it is being questioned and challenged. Stiglitz[29] says: 'Today, Globalization is being challenged around the world. There is discontent with globalization, and rightfully so. Globalization can be a force for good: the globalization of ideas about democracy and of civil society have changed the way people think, while global political movements have led to debt relief and the treaty on landmines. Globalization has helped hundreds of millions of people attain higher standards of living, beyond what they, or most economists, thought imaginable but a short while ago. The globalization of the economy has benefited countries that took advantage of it by seeking new markets for their exports and by welcoming foreign investment. Even so, the countries that have benefited the most have been those that took charge of their own destiny and recognized the role government can play in development rather than relying on the notion of a self-regulated market that would fix its own problems. But for millions of people globalization has not worked. Many have actually been made worse off, as they have seen their jobs destroyed and their lives become more insecure. They have felt increasingly powerless against forces beyond their control. They have seen their democracies undermined, their cultures eroded."

Stiglitz[30] warns that if the present economic system continues, it will create more poverty and instability. To quote: "If globalization continues to be conducted in the way that it has been in the past, if we continue to fail to learn from our mistakes, globalization will not only not succeed in promoting development but will continue to create poverty and instability. Without reform, the backlash that has already started will mount and discontent with globalization will grow."

Global economic crisis and Euro debt crisis

The economies of different countries across the world started facing difficulties since the second half of 2008. What started off earlier as the sub-prime crisis in the US housing mortgage markets began to affect their entire financial system. Mega corporations in the investment and insurance sectors such as Merryl Lynch, Lehman Brothers, Goldman Sachs and AIG that were dominating the global financial system had to be either supported by the government or faced closure. Their banking system found it difficult to face the pressure with many of the companies in trouble. Subsequently, the manufacturing sector was also affected with the major automobile companies such as the General Motors in serious difficulties. Soon the financial crisis turned into an economic crisis affecting the country as a whole.

Meanwhile, the crisis spread fast to the UK, other countries in Europe, Japan and other parts of the world. The effect was severe in some of the countries such as the UK, with serious problems to some of the big corporations. Ireland officially announced that the country had become bankrupt. To arrest the failures of corporations and the collapse of economies, different governments announced policy measures. As a result, huge bailout plans offering financial assistance to companies were implemented. Steps were taken to increase spending and help the affected sections of the society.

The crisis has exposed the vulnerability of the western economic model. The economies of some of the western countries have started shrinking since then. Their governments are still not fully clear as what kind of policies would lead them to permanent recovery and how long it would take to revive their economies. The *laissez-affaire* ideology fine-tuned further with the market fundamentalism has clearly failed. The capitalist system that considered the presence of the state as an anathema in economics all these years is now completely dependent on the state support for survival. In the process, serious doubts are being raised against the United States continuing as the most powerful economy in the years to come.

Meanwhile before the difficulties created by the global economic crisis could subside, the European economies have had to face sovereign debt crisis since the early 2010. The crisis affected Greece initially and soon other European nations such as Portugal, Italy, Ireland and Spain had to face problems. Many of the governments find it difficult to mobilize funds. Their sovereign ratings have declined. The states face the ire of their citizens as the austerity measures initiated by the governments result in hardships and reduced benefits to them. The debt situation in the Euro area has been deteriorating, leading to severe conflicts among the European nations and difficulties for the common man.

Failure of western economic theories

Western economics has usually been identified with modernity. Harvard economist Marglin[31] notes: "Economics is intimately connected to modernity; the fundamental assumptions of economics are ... simply the tacit assumptions of modernity. The centerpiece in both is the rational, calculating, self-interested individual with unlimited wants for whom society is the nation-state." But in reality, even the western societies cannot be considered totally modern. Hence, the conclusions of the modern economic theories cannot be taken as final. To quote Marglin[32]: "The assumptions of economics are only half-truths about people, even in the culture that gave birth to economics. None of us, even the most sophisticated economist, is completely modern. Modernity—economics—contends with pre- and non-modern in all of us, which is why the conclusions of economics are contestable even within the west."

The western approaches of the earlier periods had failed to provide solutions to the problems of their citizens and so they started advocating the market-centric ideology during the contemporary period. They claimed that their latest theories are superior to all the other theories and practices in the world. But the global economic crisis and the continued inability of the western countries to address their own difficulties have finally led to accepting the failure of their theories. Experts from within the western world admit that their much-advocated theories are proving to be a failure. Paul Krugman[33], the winner of the Nobel Prize in economics for 2008, notes: "much of the past 30 years of macroeconomics was spectacularly useless at best, and positively harmful at worst."

3.1.2 Communism

Communist model is based on the ideology advocated by Karl Marx and Frederick Engels in their seminal work titled '*Das Kapital*' in 1867. Written as a response to the consequences of the ill-effects of the industrial revolution in the West and based on their world view at that time, the idea of communism was considered as the alternative to the then prevailing capitalistic system. This model believed that there are two classes of people—those who own the means of production like land and factories called '*bourgeoise*', and those who belong to the working class called '*proletariat*'. Communism believed that capitalism results in exploitation, as the owners get more benefit at the cost of the labour of the working class. Hence, it emphasized all powers to the working class and came out with the call, 'workers of the world unite'. It advocated the economic enterprises to be state owned, as it is against all forms of private ownership. Hence, in this system, it is the responsibility of the state to run the economy, provide employment and protect the welfare of the people. A totalitarian government, controlled and run by the communist party, takes all decisions in the overall interests of people. In such a system, individual tastes and preferences of the people do not matter; different opinions on matters of public interest are generally not allowed. The first communist government was established in the then Soviet Russia in 1917 under the leadership of Lenin.

Inspired by this ideology, communist parties came to power in different countries over the subsequent years. Under the leadership of the then USSR, the communist countries functioned as a separate block and provided an alternative economic ideological base to the western capitalism. With its alternate views, communism inspired many people and different movements across the countries. This resulted in the setting up of the communist parties and trade union movements in different countries. There was a period in which 'cold war' for political supremacy got going between the capitalist and socialist blocks of countries in the world. Different nations were behind either one of these two blocks. The rest of the countries were called non-aligned and third world countries. After seven decades of experiment, communism failed in the late 1980s in Soviet Russia. As a result, economic policies based on *'perestroika'* (restructuring) and *'glasnost'* (openness) were initiated and subsequently, the Soviet Union itself got disintegrated into many smaller countries.

After the failure of communism in the Soviet Union, the communist model is almost dead, even though there are a few countries that still have communist governments. Even though the die-hard supporters of the system would still say that it was largely the experiments that failed, the truth of the matter is that the model has failed to live up to the expectations of the people. Hence, there is largely a uni-polar world with only the capitalistic model in front of the people to look for. It is important to note here that though China is still called communist, its economic polices are not based on communism. Remnants of communism exist only in their totalitarian approach; otherwise their economic model is not communistic. Ever since they came to power in 1949, their brand of communism was different from that of the then USSR. Later, in 1978, they abandoned communism and went towards a new model called "Market Socialism". It is interesting to note that the top leaders of the contemporary Chinese Communist Party have gone to the extent of distancing themselves from the Cultural Revolution, which was one of their main agendas earlier.

At this juncture, it is inevitable to note that even during its peak days, the communist model that was practised in different countries was not the same. Hence, we can say that there existed different models of communism. Even in India, the communist parties that were against private capital earlier now invite foreign investments. Hence, we can say the communist model as advocated by Marx no longer exists. Even the communist models that existed earlier were the localized versions of the basic ideology. During the last two decades, the fundamental philosophy of communism has changed to such an extent that it now gives a major role to the market.

Viewed objectively, it is evident that both the capitalistic and communist models are based on the western experiences and world views. Both of them do not seem to have a holistic view of life that is necessary for the long-term functioning of the society. Soros[34] writes: "Marxism claimed to have a scientific basis; so does market fundamentalism. The scientific basis of both the ideologies was established in the nineteenth century when science still promised to deliver the ultimate truth. We have learned a great deal since then both about the limitations of scientific method and the imperfections of the market mechanism. Both Marxist and laissez-faire ideologies have been thoroughly discredited. The laissez-faire ideology was the first to be dismissed, as a consequence of the Great Depression and the rise of Keynesian economics. Marxism lingered on in spite of the excesses of Stalin's rule, but, following the collapse of the Soviet system, it is now in almost total eclipse."

3.2 OTHER MODELS

The mainstream theorists believe that these two dominant models are the only alternatives that exist for mankind. They do not realize that many of the countries that followed each of these two models had in fact been following their own localized versions of the above models, and not always the original ones as advocated by the authors. In different countries, the local factors have played a decisive role in deciding the shape, size and content of these models. For example, the economic models of USSR and China were different even though both the countries were practising communism. Similarly the models of the US and Japan were different even though both of them were following capitalism. When we look at different countries a little carefully, we see a number of other models, apart from the dominant ones, in vogue. For example, the Indian Government practised a mixed economic model with a socialistic orientation for a period. The advocates of this model claimed that this model combined the virtues of both communism and capitalism. In this model, while private ownership was allowed in certain areas, government ownership was advocated in the other areas.

Even in the West, certain people belonging to different cultures and ethnic groups practise their own economic models. For example, those who belong to the Amish sect in the US do not follow the consumption model of the US. They do not use televisions, telephones, cars and even electricity. They lead a very simple life. Whenever a new idea comes by them, they usually contemplate as to whether it would allow them to continue their simple life, and only after they are satisfied about it, will they allow the idea to pass; otherwise they reject it. Even today, most of them prefer to lead a rural life engaging in agriculture. There are groups of people in different countries who are not satisfied with the free market economic model, and hence, try to evolve new models. For example, there are different groups in the US, Europe and Japan that have floated their own local currencies and use them for their day-to-day transactions within their areas. These people do not believe in their national currencies. In the Netherlands, even their central bank has recognized a local currency called "raam".

Even though only the two dominant models are discussed by the contemporary mainstream economists, there are different types of models as well in a number of places. Many of these models may not qualify to be separate models in every sense of the term as we understand, yet they are different in varying degrees.

Asian economic models

In this connection it is significant to note the performance of Asian countries during the previous centuries. Arguing for an Asia-based world economy during 1400–1800, Frank[35] mentions: "Using GNP estimates by Bairoch, still in 1750 Asia had a GNP of $120 billion [in 1960 US dollars] while all the "West," meaning Europe and the Americas [but also including Russia and Japan because of how Bairoch grouped his estimates] had a GNP before the industrial revolution of only $35 billion. Still a century later in 1860, the respective amounts were $165 billion and $115 billion … ."

The details provided in the earlier chapter revealed that Asia accounted for more than three-fourths of the global GDP more than 2000 years ago. The predominance of Asia continued in the subsequent centuries and during 1750, Asia with a share of 66 per cent of world population was contributing 80 per cent share of global production. Frank[36] notes: "… two-thirds of the world's people in Asia produced four fifths of total world output, while one-fifth of world population in Europe produced only part of the remaining one-fifth share of world production to which Africans and Americans also contributed." He notes that Asia's dominance was due to its productivity, competitiveness, technology and economic institutions[37]. He says that Asia was much more productive than the Europe and America even in the eighteenth century. "… in 1750 and in 1800 Asian production was much greater, and it was more productive and competitive than anything the Europeans and the Americans were able to muster, even with the help of the gold and silver they brought from the Americas and Africa[38]." Based on details from different sources, Frank asserts: "… all available estimates of world and regional population, production, and income, as well as the discussion … on world trade, confirm that Asia and various of its regional economies were far more productive and competitive and had far and away more weight and influence in the global economy than any or all of the "West" put together until at least 1800[39]." Thus Asia, primarily led by India and China, dominated the world economy since 0 CE to the beginning of the nineteenth century.

Asia lost its supremacy thereafter due to the colonial economic policies. The continuous dominance of Asia since the ancient periods reveals that Asia must have had very successful models. A historic study of the Asian countries shows that the basic undercurrents of the Indian civilization dominated the Asian continent for centuries. The teachings of the Chinese sage Confucius also emphasized the core Indian family values and moral behaviour. Hu Shih, former Ambassador of China to USA had noted: "India conquered and dominated China culturally for 20 centuries without ever having to send a single soldier across her border." Writing in the context of Burma, Schumacher had noted earlier that Buddhist economics was very much there, as people were practising a different set of lifestyles based on the teachings of Buddha. The basic cultural and social beliefs in the Asian countries were largely based on the Indian philosophies. Hence, there are reasons to infer that the overall economic ideology of Asia might have most probably had its roots in the Indian concepts of family system, hard work, higher savings and enterprise.

But "Asia's rightful and historically documented place has been denied by the dominance of excessively Eurocentric perspectives on early modern and recent world economic history and social science[40]." On the entry of Europe into the world economy, Frank[41] says: "... Alas however, Adam Smith—writing still before the industrial revolution in Europe—was the last major [western] social scientist to appreciate that Europe was a johnny come lately in the development of the wealth of nations. Moreover, he also did not regard the "greatest events in the history" to have been any European gift to mankind, of civilization, capitalism or anything else." Hence, Frank[42] states categorically: "So it is wrong to attribute the birth of capitalism to the European nations. It is even more wrong to assume that the economic development began with the "rise of the West."

The combined evidences provided by Maddison and Frank show that Asia was the largest contributor to the world economy for more than 1850 years, with India and China as the two powerful economies of the world. Based on the data available before us, we could say that the economic models of the Asian countries have always remained performance-oriented, till they were seriously disturbed by the outside forces. Even now, after a few centuries of disturbances and difficulties, and a different set of problems, both India and China are emerging as economic powers. What must be the reason? Also Japan is presently the third largest economic power of the world. Of the top four economic powers, except the US, all the other three are from Asia. Japan had been contributing to the global economy since 0 CE, long before the present western powers appeared to show their faces in the global GDP map. The Asian countries still hold family values and generate many times more savings than the rich nations of the West.

The Asian region has been growing faster than the other parts of the world during the recent periods. Already the share of Asia was estimated to have crossed one-third of the global GDP. International Monetary Fund[43] had mentioned earlier that the Asian region was leading the world growth with a contribution of about 45 per cent. The GDP growth of Asia during 2008 and 2009 was 5.2 per cent and 3.5 per cent respectively, compared to the rates of 0.5 per cent and –3.2 per cent for the advanced economies[44]. Hence, the International Monetary Fund[45] praises the Asian countries for their performance during and after the economic global crisis with the following words: "Asia's track record during the crisis and the recovery has been enviable. Growth remains strong, although it is moderating with emerging capacity constraints and weaker external demand." It also underlines the role of the Asian economies at the global level by saying "Asia, a bright spot in world economy[46]."

Thus, the Asian economies seem to possess more sustainable systems than the short-lived models of the West. In this connection, it is worth noting that the Developing Asia* is emerging as the 'economic driver of the world'. The GDP growth rates of Developing Asia during 2009 and 2010 were 7.2 per cent and 9.5 per cent, respectively[47]. Its share of global GDP was 22.9 per cent, while its reserves were 33.8 per cent during 2010[48]. Hence, the Asian region has been driving the global economy with higher rates of growth, after remaining in the back seat for a few centuries. Asia, led by India and China, remained strong during the recent economic crisis that affected different parts of the world. Writing on the quick recovery of the emerging Asian economies, while their western counterparts were still finding it difficult to stage a comeback after the crisis, *The Economist* wrote: "If anything, the crisis has reinforced the shift of economic power from the West to the East[49]." By all estimates, it is expected that the Asian region comprising

* Developing Asia consists of the economies of China and India (*World Economic Outlook April 2010*, International Monetary Fund).

India and China will have the highest rates of growth in the world during the coming years. The International Monetary Fund notes: "Emerging Asia is forecast to continue to post strong growth of about 8 per cent, propelled by China and India.[50]"

Table 3.1 presents the growth rates of Asia, Developing Asia, advanced economies and the World during 2010 to 2012.

Table 3.1 Growth Rates of Asia, Developing Asia, Advanced Economies and the World (2010–2012)

(Percentage changes)

	2010	2011[a]	2012[a]
Asia	8.2	6.2	6.6
Developing Asia	9.5	8.2	8.0
Advanced Economies	3.1	1.6	1.9
World	5.1	4.0	4.0

[a] Projections

Source: *World Economic Outlook, September 2011*, International Monetory Fund, p. 2 and p. 85.

What could be the reasons for the past performance and the rise of Asia during the recent periods? One possible and immediate answer could be the cultural background. If it is so, then can it be said that Asia's performance was basically due to the common cultural set up of the countries in the continent? Taking this point further, can we interpret that India is the fountain-head of all the achievements, as it was from here that the basic cultural thoughts went to different countries in Asia?

3.3 UNIVERSALITY OF WESTERN MODELS

While sharing their observations on the earlier reform experiences, Hoff and Stiglitz[51] mention that, "There is a plethora of economic models, with differing predictions concerning the outcome of various policies. If economists cannot resolve some of these differences (and in many cases we do not have the evidence needed to decisively test between competing models, while in other cases it would seem that ideological presuppositions have prevailed over a close look at empirical evidence or coherent theorizing), how is an untrained worker to judge other than by "reduced-form observations" concerning consequences?" Continuing further on the theme, they admit that "While our understanding of market economies has been enormously enhanced—markets no longer sit on the pedestal to which they were at one time assigned—our appreciation of the importance of non-economic forces (in particular, political forces) in the reform process had also increased. But our understanding of these processes is far from complete. We are at least at the stage at which we know that we do not know. That is, perhaps, a good way to begin the new century[52]."

Why is it that even the reputed economists are coming to such conclusions? Adelman[53] writes: "No area of economics has experienced as many abrupt changes in its leading paradigm since World War II as has economic development. The twists and turns in development economics have had profound implications for development policy. Specifically, the dominant development model had determined policy prescriptions concerning the desirable role of government in the economy, the degree of government intervention, the form and direction of intervention, and the nature of government-market interactions." The economist continues: "The fundamental reason for the many sudden changes in the dominant paradigm in development economics has been the (inherently misguided) search for a single-cause, and hence a single-remedy, theory of development. The specific form of argumentation has been structured by the KISS principle and has remained fundamentally the same: underdevelopment is due to constraint X; loosen X and development will be the inevitable result. The identification of the missing factor X has varied significantly over time, responding to empirical-historical learning from prior failures and successes, as well as to the other sources of paradigm change enumerated above. The universal remedy for underdevelopment, thought to be both necessary and sufficient for inducing self-sustained economic development, has varied over time, and so have recommendations for the optimal forms of state-market interactions and primary policy levers.

Alas, the search for a single open-sesame factor has been fundamentally misguided because it is based on a simplistic view of the mechanism of development and of the system in which it takes place. Unfortunately for the X theory ..., history demonstrates that the process of economic development is highly nonlinear and multifaceted. Nevertheless, like chemists' futile search for the philosopher's stone, the naïve search for the X-factor has guided theoretical and empirical research in economic development during the past half-century. As a discipline, we seem unable to admit that the X-factor does not exist; that development policy requires a more complex understanding of social systems, combining economic, social, cultural, and political institutions and their changing interactions over time; that interventions may have to be multi-pronged; that what is good for one phase of the development process may be bad for the next phase; that there are certain irreversibilities in the development process that create path dependence; and, as a result of all this, that policy prescriptions for a given country at a given time must be anchored in an understanding of its situation at that point, in time and of how it got there, not only recently but on a historical timescale. Thus, although there are certain regularities and preferred time sequences in the development process, universal institutional and policy prescriptions are likely to be incorrect[54]."

From the above observations of the learned economists we come to understand a few important points. First, there are a "plethora of economic models". Second, the dominant development models determine the policy prescriptions. Third, universal policy prescriptions are likely to be incorrect. Fourth, there are non-economic forces that influence the economic models and fifth, a proper understanding of these forces is not adequate. What is the reason for this difficulty to understand the different factors? When we analyze the economic preferences and decisions of people, we come to know that each individual is a different economic entity. So, strictly speaking, there could be as many economic models as there are individuals. Different societies have their own ways of life and so each society is different, as it represents its own beliefs and preferences evolved out of its own experiences and backgrounds. In family-based societies, each household is an economic unit, whose decisions are influenced and shaped by the members of the households based on their beliefs, preferences, priorities and tastes. In close-knit communities, the community norms and systems influence many of the economic decisions of households. The culture and habits of the people in different societies have a major influence on the economic decisions.

3.3.1 Weber on Capitalism

Earlier the eighteenth century German sociologist Max Weber thought that capitalism would prosper only in those countries where Christian protestant values dominated. But the later events proved him wrong. Fukuyama[55] says: "To this day, Weber's work continues to engender controversy, with some taking for granted the underlying truth of his hypothesis and others contesting virtually every assertion in his book. There are many empirical anomalies in the correlation between protestantism and capitalism—for example, the vigorous commercial development of the Catholic northern Italian city-states in the fourteenth and fifteenth centuries, or the failure of the Calvinist Afrikaners to develop a thriving capitalist culture until the last quarter of the twentieth century."

3.3.2 Buddhist Economics

Later, Schumacher[56] had noted that religion played an important role in the economic system. Arguing for a Buddhist economic system, Schumacher wrote: "No one seems to think that a Buddhist way of life would call for Buddhist economics, just as the modern materialistic way of life has brought forth modern economics." He said that the Buddhist economics was different from that of the modern economics. He wrote: "The keynote of Buddhist economics, therefore, is simplicity and non-violence. From an economist's point of view, the marvel of the Buddhist way of life is the utter rationality of its pattern—amazingly small means leading to extraordinary satisfactory results. For the modern economist, this is very difficult to understand. He is used to measuring the 'standard of living' by the amount of annual consumption, assuming all the time that a man who consumes more is 'better off' than a man who consumes less. A Buddhist economist would consider this approach excessively irrational: since consumption is merely a means to human well-being, the aim should be to obtain the maximum well-being with the minimum of consumption[57]." "Modern economics, on the other hand, considers consumption to be the sole end and purpose of all economic activity, taking the factors of production—land, labour, and capital—as the means[58]."

Even in the use of natural resources, he noted the difference in the approach of the modern and Buddhist economic systems. "Another striking difference between modern economics and Buddhist economics arises over the use of natural resources. Bertrand de Jouvenel, the eminent French political philosopher, has characterized 'western man' in words which may be taken as a fair description of the modern economist: 'He tends to count nothing as an expenditure, other than human effort; he does not seem to mind how much mineral matter he wastes and, far worse, how much living matter he destroys. He does not seem to realize at all that human life is a dependent part of an ecosystem of many different forms of life. As the world is ruled from towns where men are cut off from any form of life other than human, the feeling of belonging to an ecosystem is not revived. This results in a harsh and improvident treatment of things upon which we ultimately depend such as water and trees[59]."

Schumacher[60] further said that the efforts needed to lead a life of optimal consumption pattern are smaller than the efforts needed to sustain the drive for maximum consumption. "It is easy to see that the effort needed to sustain a way of life which seeks to attain the optimal pattern of consumption is likely to be much smaller than the effort needed to sustain a drive for maximum consumption. We need not be surprised, therefore, that the pressure and strain of living is very much less in, say, Burma than it is in the United States, in spite of the fact that the amount of labour-saving machinery used in the former country is only a minute fraction of the amount used in the latter." We can understand the significance of these words when we see the consumption-driven life of the West. To sustain the consumption levels, a lot of efforts are made by the governments and the corporate system. For example, credit cards are liberally given to people to enable them to spend. In the process, people become debtors and insolvents.

There are studies that show how culture has influenced the economic development of different countries. Fukuyama[61] explains as to how the Buddhist culture has helped Japan to grow. He writes: "Doubtlessly other aspects of Japanese culture have played a significant role in Japan's economic success. An important one concerns the special character of Japanese Buddhism. As Robert Bellah and others have shown, the doctrines of the Buddhist monks Baigan Ishida and Shosan Suzuki in the early Tokugawa period sanctified mundane economic activity and promulgated a commercial ethic in a manner comparable to early puritanism in England, Holland, and America. There was, in other words, the Japanese counterpart to the protestant work ethic, formulated at around the same time as its European version. This phenomenon is closely related to the Zen tradition of perfectionism in everyday, secular activities—swordsmanship, archery, carpentry, silk weaving, and the like—that comes about through inner meditation rather than explicit technique."

3.3.3 Impact of Culture on Economic Development

Discussing in the context of economic modernization, Hayami[62] notes that systems created in different cultural backgrounds could bring about successful results leading to economic development. To quote: "The problem is not which system—the western or the Japanese—is superior. What is important is to recognize that both systems, created under different cultural traditions were successful in getting modern industrial technology to bring about high productivity and affluent living." He further states that economic development is possible by developing systems suited to different cultures.

Hayami[63] shows that culture is an important factor in economic modernization. But he notes that the value system consistent with modernization is not limited to only one culture as claimed earlier by Weber. He says that religions and traditional philosophies in East Asia such as Confucianism, Buddhism and Islam can also provide relevant morality for modern economic development. To quote: "Indeed, the traditional culture or value system is an important basis of economic modernization. However, it does not appear that the value system consistent with modernization is limited to specific culture (such as Protestant ethic). The success of industrialization in Japan, Korea, and Taiwan might reflect the possibility that religions and philosophies in East Asia, such as Confucianism, can also provide relevant morality for modern economic development. Further, rapid economic advance by Indonesia, Malaysia and Thailand lends some support to the hypothesis that the principle of human organization with modernization is latent in Islam and Buddhism also."

Drucker[64] had noted that even when systems were designed by adapting the borrowed technologies and institutions, there should be interactions with the local cultures. To quote: 'The task required ... is not simply to adapt borrowed technology and institutions to traditionally given culture and value systems ... . The design of an economic system endowed with economic efficiency and social legitimacy necessarily involves dialectic interactions among technology, institution, and culture... ." Hayami notes that economic modernization is possible in different cultural and religious contexts. But unfortunately, there are not many detailed studies in different cultural contexts to explain the relationship between culture and economic development. David S. Landes[65] said: "If we learn anything from the history of economic development, it is that culture makes all the difference ... Yet culture, in the sense of the inner values and attitudes that guide a population, frightens scholars."

3.3.4 Impact of History on Economic Development

Citing examples, experts note that historical factors also play a role in shaping the economic development of different countries. "Like Germany and northern Italy, but unlike southern Italy, France, and China, Japan was never ruled in its pre-modern period by a powerful, centralized government with a large, intrusive bureaucracy. Although Japan boasts an unbroken dynastic tradition, Japanese emperors have always been weak and were never in a position to subdue, as in France, the country's feudal aristocracy. Decentralized political power permitted considerable scope for private economic activity. Just prior to the Meiji Restoration, for example, many of the local 'Han' governments into which Japan had been divided in Tokugawa times sponsored their own industries, and a number of these 'Han' industries became the basis for the major industrial enterprises after 1868[66]."

3.3.5 Economic Systems Consistent with Different Cultural Traditions

Evidences show that economic development is possible through different systems and traditions. So there could be different paths to economic developments, as opposed to the 'standardized' ones. In this context, it is useful to recall the words of Drucker[67]: "The historical fact that Japan, Korea, Taiwan and Thailand, among others, succeeded in getting on the track of sustained economic development, each based on their own unique system and tradition, strongly suggests the possibility that many low-income economies today will be able to achieve modern development in the future, not along a monolithic path, but along multiple paths according to their different traditions." Yujiro Hayami[68] notes that even low-income countries would be able to find their own unique economic systems based on their cultural and social traditions. "Thus, similar to Japan, which was successful in developing a unique system for effective utilization of modern industrial technology, Thailand, ... has been on the track of catching up with advanced economies by developing a unique system consistent with its cultural tradition. The same applies to several other Asian economies, such as Indonesia and Malaysia. ... Is there any strong reason to doubt that low-income economies suffering from poverty and stagnation today will be able to find their own unique systems consistent with modern economic development within their cultural and social traditions?"

3.3.6 Economy of Permanence

There are economists who argued for an 'economy of permanence'. They note that only an economy of permanence could be the solution to the different problems. Schumacher[69] had underlined this: "From an economic point of view, the central concept of wisdom is permanence. We must study the economics of permanence. Nothing makes economic sense unless its continuance for a long time can be projected without running into absurdities. There can be 'growth' towards a limited objective, but there cannot be unlimited, generalized growth." These economists note that only the economic systems based on the values of permanence would be sustainable. The noted Gandhian economist Joseph C. Kumarappa wrote a book titled '*Economy of Permanence*' based on the higher ideals of economics in 1945. In his book Kumarappa[70] mentioned that the Indian civilization had survived so long because it was based on the values of permanence. "The old civilizations of Egypt, Babylon, Greece and Rome are no more to tell their tale. They have vanished after a few centuries of brief, glamorous splendour because the standards on which they were built were predominantly self-centred and transient, their whole organization and system were poisoned by the institution of slavery and extortion of tributes from subject races... Their civilization is no longer a living force. In striking contrast to these, the equally old or even older civilizations of China and India, which were founded on altruistic and objective values, testify even to this day, their vitality and other attributes of permanence and non-violence in their civilization."

He had also indicated that the modern world might ridicule such a system. But there is nothing to be apologetic about it, as our forefathers had purposely laid this kind of foundation with great vision and farsightedness for a sustainable system. To use the words of Kumarappa[71]: "Modern worldly wiseacres may throw cheap gibes at the other worldliness and the religious trends of the orient. There is nothing to be apologetic in this, which after all distinguished a progressive human being from a prowling beast. The enduring qualities of these civilizations are pointers to the great farsighted standards of value our forefathers had made use of, in laying the foundations of a lasting society." India and China, for the most part of the earlier two millennia, were the most prosperous economies, with a sustainability that cannot be captured by the modern mind. In this context Kumarappa[72] noted that if India wanted to build a similar economy of permanence, then it must be on the same principles. "If we are to continue to build on their lines of permanence and non-violence, our standards too must be altruistic and objective and not those that serve merely the needs of moment. Especially at the present juncture, while political organizations are in the melting pot and so much thought is being put into the plans for the future, we have to be on our guard."

3.4 CONCLUSION

Soros[73] warns those who are still trying to draw conclusions from communism and market fundamentalism and notes that both these extremes are wrong. To quote: "Unfortunately we are once again in danger of drawing the wrong conclusions from the lessons of history. This time the danger comes not from communism but from market fundamentalism. Communism abolished the market mechanism and imposed collective control over all economic activities. Market fundamentalism seeks to abolish collective decision-making and to impose the supremacy of market values over all political and social values. Both extremes are wrong. What we need is a correct balance between politics and markets, between rule-making and playing by the rules." Korten notes that both the neo-Marxian as well as neoclassical economists have advanced experiments that did not have a clear vision. To quote Korten[74]: "Both advanced social experiments on a massive scale that embodied a partial vision of society, with disastrous consequences."

Experiences show that the western models have failed to deliver the desired results. The economic positions of different countries reveal wide disparities between and within nations. According to the *Human Development Report 2005*, "Income inequalities between countries account for the bulk of global income inequality. About two-thirds of overall inequality can be traced to this source. Inequality within countries accounts for the balance[75]." Disparities and problems are on the rise with every passing day. While the consumption levels in the western countries are increasing at an alarming rate, there is a growing majority of poor people elsewhere. Environment is being destroyed at a faster rate leading to global warming and threatening the very survival of the human race.

Experts now agree that factors such as culture, tradition, social and historical backgrounds influence the economic systems. Hence, there could be different economic models, as the lives of human beings are largely conditioned by their cultures, societies, ways of life and historical experiences. In such a situation, the western models cannot be universally applicable as the conditions are different in different places. India, being a continuing civilization with a very long history, and possessing the longest period of economic superiority, certainly must have had her own model, even though we Indians have never realized it. China, with a long history of civilization and economic prosperity, must have had her own model, before the outside influences and later communism consumed her potential. Similarly, the earlier civilizations that existed in different parts of the world for hundreds of years and more must have had their own models. The prosperous civilizations of the earlier days in Americas must have had their own models. Even the present model of emerging India is not a complete market model. In this connection, it is useful to note what Stiglitz[76] had noted on the capital control policies of India and China. To quote: "It is no accident that the two large developing countries spared the ravages of the global economic crisis—India and China—both had capital controls. While developing world countries with liberalized capital markets actually saw their incomes decline, India grew at a rate in excess of 5 per cent and China at close to 8 per cent." On the success of India and China, Saul[77] goes to the extent of saying: "They have done well out of economic modernization by not following the economic principles of globalization."

It is very unfortunate that we try to understand the economic models of different countries, particularly an ancient nation such as India, through the two popular "isms", born very much later in the West. Even the study of the world economic systems begins only from the last few centuries coinciding with the rise of the west. It is as if no economic system had existed earlier, even in prosperous civilizations such as India and China. Frank[78] notes: "The preponderance of Asian economic agents in Asia and of Asia itself in the world economy has been masked not only by the attention devoted to "the rise of the West" in the world, but also by the undue focus on European economic and political penetration of Asia." Without fundamentally strong economic models how could the ancient civilizations have survived and prospered for so many years continuously?

REFERENCES

[1] Palley, Thomas I., 'A New Development Paradigm: Domestic Demand-Led Growth—Why It Is Needed & How to Make It Happen', *Foreign Policy in Focus Discussion Paper*, September 2002, http:// www.fpif.org/.

[2] Ibid.

[3] Schumacher, E.F., *Small is Beautiful—A Study of Economics as if People Mattered,* Vintage, London, 1993, p. 30.

[4] Ibid., pp. 30–31.

[5] Hoff, Karla and Stiglitz, Joseph E., 'Modern Economic Theory and Development' in 'Meier, Gerald M. and Stiglitz, Joseph E. (Eds.), *Frontiers of Development Economics—The Future in Perspective*, World Bank and Oxford University Press Inc., New York, 2002, p. 427.

[6] Fukuyama, Francis, *Trust*, Free Press Paperbacks, New York, 1996, p. 13.

[7] Ibid., pp. 17–18.

[8] Korten, David C., *When Corporations Rule the World*, The Other India Press, Goa, 1998, p. 74.

[9] Ibid., p. 78.

[10] Fukuyama, Francis, op.cit., p. 19.

[11] Soros, George, *Open Society—Reforming Global Capitalism,* 1st Indian ed., Viva Books Private Limited, New Delhi, 2004, p. xxiv.

[12] Ibid., p. 168.

[13] Soros, George, *The Crisis of Global Capitalism,* Public Affairs, New York, 1998, p. 28.

[14] Korten, David C., op.cit., p. 69.

[15] Hamilton, Clive, *Growth Fetish,* South Asian Edition, Allen & Unwin, Australia, 2004, p. 3.

[16] Ibid., p. 5.

[17] Ibid., p. 13.

[18] Soros, George, 1998, op.cit., p. xvi.

[19] Duncan, Richard, *The Dollar Crisis—Causes, Consequences, Cures,* John Wiley and Sons (Asia) Pte Ltd., Singapore, 2005, p. x.

[20] Krugman, Paul, 'Debt and Denial', *The Hindu,* February 14, 2006, p. 11.

[21] Ibid.

[22] *Human Development Report 2005,* Oxford University Press, New Delhi, 2005, p. 58.

[23] Ibid., p. 69.

[24] Korten, David C., *Agenda for a New Economy,* Tata McGraw-Hill Publishing Company Limited, New Delhi, 2009, p. 3.

[25] *Human Development Report 2005,* op.cit., p. 38.

[26] World Bank data quoted in Shutt, Harry, *A New Democracy—Alternatives to a Bankrupt World Order,* Zed Books, London, 2001, p. 86.

[27] Ibid., p. 4.

[28] Stiglitz, Joseph E., *Globalization and its Discontents,* Penguin Books, New Delhi, 2002, p. 215.

[29] Ibid., p. 248.

[30] Ibid.

[31] Marglin, Stephen A., *The Dismal Science: How Thinking Like an Economist Undermines Community,* Oxford University Press, New Delhi, 2009, p. 36.

[32] Ibid., p. 38.

[33] Krugman, Paul quoted in 'What went wrong with Economics', *The Economist,* July 16, 2009.

[34] Soros, George, 1998, op.cit., p. 127.

[35] Frank, Andre Gunder, 'Asian-based World Economy 1400–1800: A Horizontally Integrative Macro-history', University of Amsterdam, November 12, 1995, op. cit.

[36] Frank, Andre Gunder, *Re Orient: Global Economy in the Asian Age*, Vistaar Publications, New Delhi, 1998, pp. 172–173.

[37] Ibid., p. 174.

[38] Ibid., p. 172.

[39] Ibid., p. 174.

[40] Frank, Andre Gunder, 1995, op.cit.

[41] Ibid.

[42] Ibid.

[43] International Monetary Fund, *Finance and Development*, June 2006, Vol. 43, No. 2, www.imf.org.

[44] International Monetary Fund, *World Economic Outlook April 2010*, IMF, Washington, p. 49.

[45] International Monetary Fund, *World Economic Outlook September 2011*, op.cit., p. 84.

[46] Ibid., p. 85.

[47] Ibid., p. 2.

[48] *World Economic Outlook:* Database quoted in the *Report on Currency and Finance 2008–09*, Reserve Bank of India, p. 91.

[49] 'On the Rebound', *The Economist*, August 15, 2009.

[50] International Monetary Fund, *World Economic Outlook September 2011*, op.cit., p. 8.

[51] Hoff, Karla and Stiglitz, Joseph E., in Meier, Gerald M., and Stiglitz, Joseph E. (Eds.), op.cit., p. 425.

[52] Ibid., p. 428.

[53] Adelman, Irma, 'Fallacies in Development Theory and Their Implications for Policy, in Meier, Gerald M. and Stiglitz, Joseph E. (Eds.), op.cit., p. 103.

[54] Ibid., pp. 104–105.

[55] Fukuyama, Francis, op.cit., p. 44.

[56] Schumacher, E.F., op.cit., p. 38.

[57] Ibid., pp. 41–42.

[58] Ibid., p. 42.

[59] Ibid., pp. 43–44.

[60] Ibid., pp. 42–43.

[61] Fukuyama, Francis, op.cit., pp. 182–183.

[62] Hayami, Yujiro, *Development Economics—From the Poverty to the Wealth of Nations,* Clarendon Press, Oxford University Press Inc., New York, 1998, p. 280.

[63] Ibid.

[64] Drucker, Peter F., *Managing in the Next Society*, Butterworth–Heinemann, Oxford, Reprinted, 2003, p. 282.

[65] Landes, David S., quoted in Meir, Gerald M., 'The Old Generation of Development Economists and the New', in Meier, Gerald M. and Stiglitz, Joseph E. (Eds.), op.cit., p. 30.

[66] Hayami, Yujiro, op.cit., p. 182.

[67] Drucker, Peter F., op.cit., p. 282.

[68] Hayami Yujiro, op.cit., p. 282.

[69] Schumacher, E.F., op.cit., p. 20.

[70] Kumarappa, J.C., *Economy of Permanence*, 6th ed., Sarva Seva Sangh Prakashan, Varanasi, 1997, p. 40.

[71] Ibid., pp. 40–41.

[72] Ibid., p. 41.

[73] Soros, George, 2004, op.cit., p. xxvii.

[74] Korten, David C., op.cit., p. 80.

[75] *Human Development Report 2005*, op.cit., p. 38.

[76] Stiglitz, Joseph E., op.cit., p. 125.

[77] Saul, John Ralston, *The Collapse of Globalism* quoted in D. Murali, EDIMENSON, 'Globalisation is now officially dead', *The Hindu Business Line,* February 4, 2006, p. 10.

[78] Frank, Andre Gunder, 1998, op.cit., p. 166.

4

Basic Features of Different Economic Models

Are the features of different economic models one and the same? Or are they different for different models? If they are different, then to what extent do they exhibit differences? This chapter presents the basic features of the Indian and western economic models. For the presentation on western models, only the contemporary capitalistic models are taken. The communist models are not taken up for discussion as the ideology is widely accepted to have failed, though some may entertain contrary views.

4.1 FEATURES OF THE INDIAN ECONOMIC MODEL

What are the basic features of the Indian economic models? How different are they to the western models? Let us first see the basic characteristics of the Indian models. India being a vast country, nurturing diverse systems of life, one could notice certain differences in economic behaviour within the country. Hence the common features of Indian models are presented.

4.1.1 Family Base

The Indian society is family based. The smallest social, economic and cultural unit of India is the family. While writing on the family system in ancient India, Basham[1] says: "The family, rather than the individual, was looked on as the unit of the social system; thus the population of a given region was generally estimated in families rather than in heads. The bonds of family were such that relationships within the group were often blurred or lost sight of; for instance a son might commonly refer to all his father's wives indiscriminately as his mothers, and the distinction between brother and paternal cousin was not always made clearly—even today the same word is used for both." It is the families that drive the economy of India. There were nearly 192 million households in India in 2001.* About two-thirds of India's national income comes from the family-based sectors. The economic activities in different sectors are mostly in the hands of families.

There is no individualism as such in India. Generally, no one thinks and acts like an individual. Everyone belongs to a family. Everyone is a part of a family with duties and responsibilities. Each family is a part and parcel of a community of close-knit relatives. The relationship gets extended beyond the blood relatives to friends and others in villages, towns and cities. Everyone thinks, acts and lives not just for himself or herself, but also for all others in the family. *Arthashastra* notes that the *Dharma* of the head of the family is to sacrifice his own pleasures for the sake of the family members. It is the general norm in the Indian families that parents sacrifice their lives for children and later, when the children grow up, they take care of their elders. With the result, everyone lives for others at one point in time or other. It is not just the case with parents and children. When the father is no more, or he is retired from active life, then it is the responsibility of the elder son in the family to look after the rest of the family. In such cases a lot of sacrifice is involved and the elder ones take it as their duty and generally do not consider it as a sacrifice. There are families in which the elder sisters sacrifice their lives for the younger ones and the rest of the family. It is the general system in Indian households that the elderly brothers marry only after marrying off their younger sisters. With such systems in practice, all important decisions are family decisions, with the elders playing the lead role. Even if the father or mother or an elder brother or elder sister or grandfather or grandmother takes a decision individually, it is deemed to have been taken in the interests of the family. It is the family that runs through each of them and their decisions.

Everyone who starts a venture does it not just for himself, but for the family as a whole. With the result, all businesses are family businesses. Siblings, children and grandchildren inherit them. In fact, in most instances, the idea of venturing into businesses is because of a desire to leave some fortune behind to the children. So when a person promotes a venture, the entire family contributes to its savings. The parents, grandparents, siblings and even in-laws

---

* Census of India, 2001 mentions that totally there were 191,963,935 households in India. http://www.censusindia.net.

contribute funds to the venture. Other close relatives, community men and friends also make their contributions in many instances. In a number of industrial and business centres, most of the initial capital was supplied through own savings and family contributions. Contributions from relatives, friends and community are the other major sources of funds.

Whenever there is an urgency or a need for funds for social, cultural and economic necessities, it is the families that help. The family is the basis of all economic activities including business. The economic decisions are almost always influenced by family considerations. Even a wealthy industrialist normally consults his wife, and his parents and children, whenever necessary, before making important economic decisions for the family. This is true to a great extent even in business. The senior-most members of the family, father or mother or wife or all of them are always consulted or at least informed of all economic decisions. In many companies, the chairman of the company is usually the elderly father or grandfather, because the Indian economic system, including the corporate system, would prefer to conduct its affairs under the watchful and experienced eyes of the senior most people in the family.

The family system enables the members to share their contribution to the success of business in all possible ways. In different businesses, many times housewives also contribute a share of work apart from their household responsibilities. Similarly, children help their parents during their free time. Writing on the success of Patels in England, Patel and Rutten[2] describe the participation of family members in business in the following words: "It is observed that in many cases both husband and wife run the shop in rotation. Some of them are not very fluent in the English language though their clients are mostly whites, blacks, and non-Gujaratis. However, they manage to communicate with their customers pleasantly with limited command over English language. When their children grow up they also start helping their parents, particularly the sons."

The institution of strong families with close-knit communities is the unique feature of the Indian civilization. This institution is very old and matured. It is a product of age-old experience. Every activity in India—economic, social and cultural—revolves around families. It is the family set-up that provides the foundation for what the economists now call as 'social capital'. The social capital provides a strong base to the economic development, apart from maintaining peace and order in the society. In this system, everyone plays one's part for the overall benefit of the family and the community around them. No one questions the other unnecessarily, as everyone has a place and a role in the family. Even today, in many places across the country, we see non-corporate businesses in the hands of the joint families, in which the business is conducted by the families of brothers, sons and even grandsons together. Even though the system of joint family has suffered due to the changing times, and nuclear families are increasing due to a variety of reasons, the family system is functioning successfully to a great extent contributing to the economic progress of the country.

4.1.2 High Level of Savings

The Indian society is savings-oriented. Traditionally Indians are known for their savings. People save everywhere and in every possible way. They save without knowing that they are saving. It is a part of Indian culture and a way of life. Whether one is rich or poor, savings will be there. The father saves for the family and many a times the mother saves without the other family members even knowing about it, in small sums. Spending more than what is necessary is considered a sin in the traditional Indian system. Spending is generally not in commensurate with the incomes but is mostly dependent on the needs. Right from their youth, Indians are taught to minimize their needs and so spending becomes unnecessary beyond a limit.

Even a person, who does not have enough money to satisfy all his present requirements, tries to save for tomorrow by sacrificing something today. As a result, savings take place. The savings are in different forms. It is not always in the form of gold and bank deposits, even though they are the important avenues. There are different avenues that include many indigenous ones. With the result it is difficult and almost impossible for the government authorities to calculate the exact quantum of savings.

Composition of savings

The official rate of saving for the financial year 2009–10 was 33.7 per cent of GDP. It is one of the high rates in the world. The saving rates of the different sectors of the economy, namely the household, private corporate and government sectors, for the different decades beginning from the 1950s are given in Table 4.1.

Table 4.1 Saving Rates in Different Sectors of Economy (1950–51 to 2009–10) (as percentage of GDP at current market prices)

Items/Year	1950–51	1960–61	1970–71	1980–81	1990–91	2000–01#	2009–10*
Gross domestic savings	8.6	11.2	14.2	18.5	22.8	23.7	33.7
Household sector	5.7	6.5	9.5	12.9	18.4	21.6	23.5
Private corporate sector	0.9	1.6	1.5	1.6	2.7	3.9	8.1
Public sector	2.0	3.1	3.3	4.00	1.8	–1.8	2.1
Household sector savings to gross domestic savings (%)	66	58	67	70	81	91	67

#Provisional estimates *Quick estimates

Note: Household sector savings to gross domestic savings percentages are calculations by the author based on the above figures.

Source: *Economic Survey 2010–11*, A-10.

We could see that the saving rate of the economy has doubled from the 1950s to the 1980s, from about 9 per cent to more than 18 per cent, and has further increased to 33.7 per cent in 2009–10. Such a high increase in savings has been achieved through the efforts of the household and other sectors. The contribution of the household sector has always remained high and in 2000–01, it contributed more than 90 per cent to the total domestic savings of India. Its share in 2009–10 was 67 per cent. Here, the family owned enterprises involved in business are also included under households. The savings rates of the households are without considering their investments in gold, as the authorities treat them as a consumption item. There are other indigenous methods of savings which are not taken into account for calculating the savings rates, as the relevant figures are not available.

Composition of household savings

It may be useful to note that at present the share of financial savings is slightly more in the household sector as compared to the physical savings. In the category of financial savings, the largest saving avenues remain to be the bank deposits, life insurance funds and provident and pension funds. Table 4.2 provides the percentage shares of different financial assets of the household sector (Gross) from 2008–09 to 2010–11.

Table 4.2 Financial Saving of the Household Sector (2008–09 to 2010–11)

(per cent to total financial saving)

Item/year	2008–09	2009–10	2010–11
Currency	12.7	9.8	13.3
Bank deposits	60.7	47.2	47.3
(i) With commercial banks	52.8	41.7	42.0
(ii) With non-banking companies	2.0	1.9	2.9
(iii) With cooperative banks and societies	4.7	3.6	2.5
(iv) Trade debt (Net)	1.2	–0.1	–0.1
Shares and debentures	–0.7	4.6	–0.4
(i) Private corporate business	1.0	1.3	1.2
(ii) Banking	0.0	0.1	0.1
(iii) Bonds of public sector undertakings	0.1	0.1	0.1
(iv) Mutual funds (including UTI)	–1.4	3.3	–1.8
Claims on government	–3.8	4.3	6.5
Life insurance funds	21.0	22.6	24.2
Provident and pension funds	10.1	11.5	9.1

Note: 2008–09 and 2009–10 data are provisional; 2010–11 data are preliminary estimates.
Source: Annual Report 2010–11, Reserve Bank of India, p. 173.

Table 4.2 shows the preference of the Indian public towards bank deposits, life insurance funds and provident and pension funds. Bank deposits continue remain the top priority of the Indian people, though its share has come down during the last three years. It is interesting to note that the Bank Deposits and Life Insurance Funds have a combined share of about seventy per cent or more in the total financial savings during the above period. The table shows the overall preference of the public towards secured investments. This only indicates that the Indian citizens are cautious by nature, primarily due to their family orientation. Claims on government that used to attract a higher proportion of funds during the earlier periods have come down in the recent years. The proportion of funds invested in shares and debentures of private sector companies remains very little, hovering around one per cent during the above period. It shows that the investments in shares and debentures of companies are not in the priority list of the Indian public, though the stock markets are becoming popular in recent years among a few sections of the society.

Gold as savings

India is one of the largest buyers of gold in the world. More than 90 per cent of this goes into jewellery making. In the past, the Indian demand was more than 20 per cent of global consumption[3].

But the domestic production of gold is very negligible. McKinsey[4] Report 2005 notes that the amount invested in gold was much larger than the aggregate capital raised from the stock market. It says that Indians possess $200 billion of gold, equal to nearly half of the country's bank deposits, and during the previous year bought $10 billion worth of gold which was nearly twice the amount of foreign direct investment in India. It was reported that Indians purchased 963 tons of gold during 2010. It is estimated there is a gold stock worth 18000 tons in India. Vaidyanathan[5] notes: "If we include gold alone in the savings, then the savings rate would be higher by another two percentage points." Gold is considered not just as an investment in India; it is also treated as insurance and a social security for the large majority of people.

Indigenous avenues

There are different indigenous savings mechanisms that play an important part in savings. Chit funds, for example, are a popular mechanism of savings in Tamil Nadu. It helps people at different levels to save money. There are chits that involve savings of ₹ 100 every month to ₹ 100,000 and more. In certain areas of Tamil Nadu, when people need funds to promote a venture they mobilize their relatives and friends and organize a chit so that it would help them with the funds. Periodically, which may vary from one month to three months, the members of the chit have to assemble and it usually turns out to be a get-together of all members with their families for lunch. This meeting is held in the houses of the chit members by rotation. Every member has to host one meeting during the tenure of the chit. So these are all not just savings and fund raising mechanisms but are also occasions for family get-togethers. All these mechanisms are not only indigenous; they are relationship-based and are not state dependent. In all these cases, it is the society that comes out with initiatives like these, based on their conveniences and needs. Hence there is no doubt that the savings of India will be much more than the official rate, when we take all types of savings into consideration. Vaidyanathan[6] says: "If we consider only the disposable income of households, the saving rate as a percentage of that will be more than 40."

As savings is considered a basic duty, everyone and every family save as much as possible. It is this savings that forms the basis for all economic activities and it is the one single factor that helps in the promotion of all entrepreneurial ventures. It is mainly due to these savings that the economy has grown after independence. Empirical and research studies in different business and industrial clusters indicate that savings are the basis of industrial and business development in all these centres.* The *Economic Census 2005* reveals that almost 90 per cent of the enterprises in the unorganized sector are self-financed in nature[7].

Capital formation

Encouraged by savings, capital formation has remained as a core economic activity of Indians even in their difficult times. This could be understood from the data relating to capital formation after Independence. Even in 1950–51, capital formation was 8.4 per cent of GDP. Since then capital formation has been consistently growing. Table 4.3 shows the rate of gross domestic capital formation in India from the 1950s.

Table 4.3 Capital Formation (1950–51 to 2009–10)

(as percentage of GDP at current market prices)

Items/Year	1950–51	1960–61	1970–71	1980–81	1990–91	2000–01	2009–10
Gross domestic capital formation	8.4	14.0	15.1	19.9	26.0	24.3	36.5

Note: 2009–10 data is based on quick estimates.
Source: *Economic Survey 2009–10*, p. A-11.

Table 4.3 shows a steady increase in capital formation since 1950–51 and a high level of increase in the recent periods. Savings of the household sector plays a crucial role in capital formation. Vaidyanathan[8] notes that capital formation by household sector has remained more than 40 per cent during the last three decades. Moreover, the household sector also contributes significantly to the private as well as government sectors for their capital formation. The private corporate sector has shown consistently a higher share in capital formation compared to savings, indicating flow of funds from the household sector through intermediation of banking institutions and capital markets. The government also takes a huge portion of household savings to carry on its capital formation activities. Capital formation in the household sector which was of the order of 90 per cent in the 1950s, is now around 30 per cent. This is because a substantial portion of household savings are taken away by the government and private corporate sectors for their capital formation. Investments from Foreign Direct Investments and Foreign Institutional Investments only play a supplementary role in the total Indian investments. Moreover, foreign investments

* Discussed in Chapter 6.

are confined only to selected sectors. In almost all the clusters, the entire capital formation has taken place through the efforts of the local societies. In many of these places even bank finance is only secondary. So the predominant role has always been played by local investments primarily facilitated by the high level of domestic savings.

4.1.3 Self-employment as the Base

Self-employment is the base of the Indian economy. Traditionally, it is considered a virtue to do something on one's own. Until a few years back, going for jobs and working under somebody was considered low in status among many Indian communities. Even today, doing something on one's own or getting engaged in the family business is considered as one's duty and a superior way of life in certain communities. The 62nd round of the National Sample Survey Organization (NSSO) report on the employment situation in the country in 2005–06 reveals that even now Indian prefers self-employment. The survey shows that 57 per cent of the males and about 62 per cent of females belonging to working classes in rural parts of the country are self-employed. The corresponding figures for urban India are 42 for males and 44 for females[9]. The concept of self-employment is unique to the Indian system and we do not find a parallel to this in the contemporary western world.

Vidura Neethi, given by Sage Vidura more than 5000 years ago, states that 'Self-employment is the best status in life'. It seems that since ancient times self-employment had been given the highest status compared to all other forms of activity and that must be the reason why it was emphasized by a reputed sage of the earlier times. When we consider the negative effects of the modern economic ideologies, namely capitalism and communism on the society in the long run, self-employment seems to be the best form of organization. It is neither communism nor capitalism, but seems to combine the best of both these economic ideologies. It is a form of capitalism that cannot dominate and control markets to the disadvantage of the society. It is also a form of socialism where everyone has a job and none remains unemployed. In the self-employment system, one works for oneself and not for any other person and so there are no chances for exploitation. It is a responsibility-based economic system compared to the rights-based systems of modern ideologies. To understand the importance of self-employment in India, we have to see the employment position in the organized sector, namely the public and the private sectors, and the self-employment sector.

Employment in the public sector

Table 4.4 gives the number of persons employed in the government and semi-government organizations during 1991 to 2008.

Table 4.4 Employment in the Public Sector (1991–2008)

(lakh persons as on March 31)

	1991	2001	2008
Central Government	34.11	32.61	27.39
State Governments	71.12	74.25	71.71
Quasi-Governments	62.22	61.92	57.96
Local bodies	23.13	22.61	19.68
Total	**190.58**	**191.38**	**176.74**

Source: *Economic Survey 2009–10*, p. A-52.

Table 4.4 shows that the total employment provided by the government sector was only 176.74 lakh during 2008. Studies of the employment position show that the employment opportunities in the public sector have been declining since the mid-1990s.

Employment in the private sector

Table 4.5 provides the employment data for the private sector during 1991 to 2008.

Table 4.5 shows that the organized private sector employed a total of 98.38 lakh persons during the year ended March 31, 2008. Even though there has been an increase in private sector employment since the 1990s, it is not very significant when compared to the total workforce in the country. When the number of persons employed in both the government and the private sectors are taken together, we find that these sectors have provided additional employment to less than eight lakh persons only during the entire period. As of end of March 2007, both these sectors were giving employment to 275.12 lakh persons only. Their combined share in the total employment of the country is around 8 per cent.

Table 4.5 Employment in the Private Sector (1991–2008)

(lakh persons as on March 31)

	1991	2001	2008
Agriculture, hunting etc.	8.91	9.31	9.92
Manufacturing	44.81	50.13	49.70
Wholesale and retail trade	3.00	3.39	2.72
Finance, insurance, real estate, etc.	2.54	3.70	10.96
Community, social and personal services	14.85	17.34	21.73
Total	**76.77**	**86.52**	**98.38**

Source: *Economic Survey, 2009–10*, p. A-52.

Employment in the self-employment sector

Self-employment sector provides the maximum employment opportunities to Indians. Project OASIS Report, 1999 submitted to the Government of India states that the share of this sector in the total workforce (based on 1991 census figures) was 53 per cent[10]. Table 4.6 provides the details.

Table 4.6 Share of Different Categories of Workers

	Number of workers (in millions)	Percentage
Regular salaried employees	47	15.2
Casual/contract workers	97	31
Self-employed	166	53
Total	**310**	

Source: Project OASIS Report, Government of India, 1999.

The Report shows that of the working population, 15.2 per cent (47 million) are regular salaried employees while over 53 per cent (166 million) are self-employed and 31 per cent (97 million) are casual/contract workers. In this context it is worthwhile to note that the share of workers in the self-employed category was only 6.6 per cent in the US, as against the share of private waged and salaried workers who constitute 78.5 per cent.*

Significance of self-employment sector

Self-employment contributes 30 per cent to the GDP of India. This sector pays significantly higher taxes in relation to their share in the income. It contributes more than 45 per cent share in income tax. Its share of income tax to its GDP was 3.3 per cent in 1993–94 compared to 2.2 per cent for all categories[11]. Its contribution to savings is estimated at about 70 per cent, the highest in the country. Apart from its financial contributions, this sector plays a crucial role in the functioning of our economy and its growth. The self-employed sector is a self-made sector that does not depend on the governments. The government does not spend much for this sector. Moreover, this sector is the breeding ground for future enterprises. The major clusters of today were once the initiatives of a few entrepreneurs from this category. In this respect it is most appropriate to say that this sector has played a dominant role by laying the foundation for the present economic position of our country.

This is one sector that clearly distinguishes the Indian economic system from the other systems. It is a unique sector that solves

* Share of different categories of workers in US in 2000, US Bureau of Census.

many of the ills of the modern economic systems. But it is unfortunate that this sector which plays such a significant role, contributing nearly one third to the economy, does not get the recognition it rightfully deserves.

4.1.4 Highly Entrepreneurial

The people of India, by nature, are hard-working and entrepreneurial. Since the desire to be independent and an urge to stand on one's own legs is widely prevalent in the society, many Indians possess the latent desire to achieve and excel. Moreover, the desire to leave something better for their children and future generations constantly compels people to save money and engage themselves in some entrepreneurial activity or other, however small the venture may be. With the result, a lot of entrepreneurial activities begin to take shape. Even though a tendency to take up jobs is increasing especially among the English educated sections of the society in the recent years, still the entrepreneurial spirit among the people of the country continues to remain to a large extent. Based on surveys across different countries, Babson College, USA and London Business School, UK have jointly commenced a research initiative namely, Global Entrepreneurship Monitor project, aimed at assessing the level of entrepreneurial activities. *Global Entrepreneurship Monitor** (GEM) 2002 noted that India was the second most entrepreneurially active nation in the world with 17.9 per cent of the population engaged in various entrepreneurial activities[12]. While China had 12.3 per cent of people engaged in entrepreneurial activities, in the US it was more than 10.5 per cent[13]. GEM also studied the start-up activities as against the entrepreneurial activities by existing firms. While globally start-ups outnumbered the firm entrepreneurship by a ratio of 5 to 1, the ratio for India touched 10[14].

Since people in every locality are mostly known to each other due to the close personal and community relationships, the entry of one person into a business or industry influences others to follow suit. The success of one person encourages others to enter the same business or industry. Many times the successful person himself inducts his close relatives and acquaintances into the business. As a result, people constantly undertake different kinds of entrepreneurial activities. The high level of entrepreneurial inclination can be understood when we see the number and variety

* The results are based on the Total Entrepreneurial Activity (TEA) Index across 37 countries. www.gemconsortium.org.

of enterprises functioning at different levels. Taking the unorganized sector, the *Economic Census 2005* reveals that there are 41.83 million establishments in the country engaged in different economic activities, other than crop production and plantation[15]. The third *All India Census of Small Scale Industries* had earlier noted that the total number of units in the SSI sector was more than 105 million[16]. The growth of corporate sector in India during the past decades is well known. So entrepreneurship is not confined to just one sector, but seems to be spread across different sectors. Moreover, entrepreneurship seems to prevail across different social groups among the unorganized sector and SSIs. The *Economic Census 1998* figures reveal that 44.8 per cent of the unorganized enterprises are owned by SC/ST/OBCs. This encompasses manufacturing, construction, trade, hotel/restaurant, transport, finance and other services[17].

Similarly, the All India Census of SSIs notes that more than 56.2 per cent of the total units are owned by communities categorized under the SC/ST/OBC groups[18]. The total number of units managed by women are around 9.5 per cent[19]. Entrepreneurial activities take place even in highly disadvantageous situations. Dharavi in Mumbai is known to the outside world as the largest slum in the country. But "the annual turnover from Dharavi's myriad enterprises is anywhere between ` 1,500 crores and ` 3,000 crores. According to official sources, there are 4,902 industrial units in Dharavi, of which textiles form 1,036, pottery 932, leather 567, plastic processing 478 and *Jari* stitching 498[20]." India Brand Equity Foundation notes that "with more than 85 million businesses, India is one of the most entrepreneurial countries in the world[21]." Different studies reveal a clear attitude towards entrepreneurship in different parts of the country. Even in the high risk business of finance, ordinary people dare to venture to far off states, where the people are as alien to them as their language, to establish business and emerge successful in a few years.

One has to see to believe the kind of diverse entrepreneurial activities taking place in different places and the amazing entrepreneurial abilities of Indians. In Rajkot, for example, entrepreneurs are engaged in a wide variety of engineering activities. Similarly, in Tirupur people own different types of ancillary units involving different processes. One cannot presume the backgrounds of these entrepreneurs from their present positions. They have reached the present levels only due to their high entrepreneurial skills.

4.1.5 Non-corporate Sector as the Core

The non-corporate sector includes those non-company entities that belong to non-agricultural and non-government (departmental and non-departmental enterprises) activities. It excludes company forms of organizations in private sector as well as public sector. It consists of partnership/proprietorship forms of organizations and other self-employed persons. Cooperative forms of organizations are also part of this group. Vaidyanathan notes that the non-corporate sector has the largest share in our national income, manufacturing activities, services, savings, investment, both direct and indirect taxes, credit market, employment and forex earnings. It is often referred to as "un-organized" or "informal" or "residual" sector. These terminologies are based on concepts pertaining to the western experiences[22]. Hence, terming them as "un-organized" is most inappropriate as they are well-organized from the economic and organizational points of view. Moreover, they are not the residual segment of the economy. They are very much part of the formal system of laws/rules/regulations[23].

Table 4.7 presents the share of the unorganized sector in net domestic product for 1993–94 and 2002–03[24].

Table 4.7 Share of Unorganized Segment in Net Domestic Product by Economic Activity (1993–94 and 2002–03)

(at current prices)

Industry	1993–94	2002–03
Agriculture, forestry and fishing	96.5	95.9
Manufacturing	36.6	36.6
Construction	51.1	62.8
Trade, hotels and restaurants	88.8	74.2
Transport, storage and communication	42.7	62.9
Financing, insurance, real estate and business services	50.7	39.6
Community, social and personal services	19.0	17.3
Net domestic product at factor cost	63.1	56.7

Source: Statement 76.3, Statement of NAS 2005, *Central Statistical Organization*, Government of India, p. 108.

The table shows that the share of the unorganized segment in the net domestic product of the country is almost 57 per cent in 2002–03. It is important to note that the share of this sector is high in the fastest growing economic activities such as trade, construction and transport. Vaidyanathan writes that the non-corporate sector consisting of partnership/proprietorship firms has the largest share in our national income with nearly 38 per cent of contribution, followed by agricultural and government sectors. The Indian corporate sector contributes only 14 per cent of the national income[25]. We have to remember here that there is no proper valuation of the family-based non-corporate sector and there is lot of underestimation. For example, it is argued that in activities covered under the organized sector of manufacturing, the non-corporate portion is estimated to the tune of 3 per cent[26]. Hence, in reality the contribution of this sector may be more than what the data indicates. Earlier, Harriss-White[27] had noted that "the informal economy was ... estimated as comprising 60 per cent of net domestic product, 68 per cent of income, 60 per cent of savings, 31 per cent of agricultural exports, and even 41 per cent of manufactured exports." The share of non-corporate sector in total savings and capital formation is very significant.

It is important to note that the non-corporate sector plays a major role in the industrial and service sectors. The non-corporate sector constitutes a large portion of the following eight activities, namely unregistered manufacturing, construction, wholesale and retail trade, hotels and restaurants, transport other than railways, storage, real-estate ownership of dwellings and business services, and other services[28]. Table 4.7 shows that in activities like trade (wholesale and retail), transport (other than railways), construction, and hotels and restaurants, the share of the non-corporate sector in the national income is more than 60 per cent. National Sample Survey Organization (NSSO) data reveals that during 2000–01, there were 170.2 lakh units in the unorganized manufacturing sector employing 370.8 lakh workers[29]. Contribution of this sector to rural employment is very high. Quoting Annual Survey of Industries of Government of India, Chadha mentions that around mid-1990s, nearly 90 per cent of rural manufacturing employment was in the unorganized segment alone[30].

Share of non-corporate sector in services

Services sector is the largest sector in the economy accounting for 65.6 per cent of the GDP. Moreover, this sector has been contributing significantly to the growth of Indian economy during the past two decades. It is considered to be the main driver of GDP growth. The growth in the services sector during the past two decades has been much higher than that of manufacturing and agricultural sectors. The Reserve Bank of India underlines the importance of the services sector to the Indian economy in the following words: "The high growth in the services sector has been underpinning the buoyancy in India's growth. This sector exhibited an average growth of above 10 per cent during the five years preceding 2008–09 and its share and relative contribution in GDP amounted to above 60 per cent and 70 per cent respectively during this period. The contribution of services exports in the overall value-added accelerated sharply from 6.9 per cent in 2000–01 to 15.1 per cent during 2008–09. Despite the decelerating growth during 2008–09 and 2009–10 against the backdrop of knock-on effects of the global economic crisis, the services sector continued to grow at a higher pace than the overall growth in the Indian economy. The resilience displayed by the services sector during the recent crisis cushioned the economy from the worsening growth witnessed by most of the advanced and emerging market economies[31]."

Table 4.8 presents the growth rates of the three major sectors of the Indian economy during the last three years.

Table 4.8 Growth Rates of the Three Major Sectors (2008–09 to 2010–11)

	2008–09	2009–10#	2010–11*
Agriculture and allied	–0.1	0.4	6.6
Industry	4.0	8.3	7.8
Services	9.5	9.7	9.2
Total	6.8	8.0	8.5

#Quick estimates *Revised estimates

Source: Annual Report 2010–11, Reserve Bank of India, p. 168.

Vaidyanathan notes that the role of the non-corporate sector is very significant in seven of the service sector activities, namely construction, trade, hotels and restaurants, non-railway transport, storage, real estate, ownership of dwelling and business services and other services[32]. The contribution of these activities to the Net Domestic Product (NDP) of the country has been consistently high during the previous four decades. "The share of these seven major services in the NDP for different years has consistently gone up from 30 per cent in 1960–61 to 41 per cent in 2000–01, showing an increase in the role of these activities in the economy during the period, but more particularly in the 1990s[33]." Of these, five sectors, namely trade, hotels and restaurants, transport, construction, storage and communication, financing, insurance, real estate and business services and community, social and personal services constitute the dominant parts of the service sector. These activities are conducted by the proprietorship and partnership type of organizations with the active involvement from the members of family and close circles. In this context, "It is important to understand that corresponding proportions in developed market economies are less than 10 per cent. In other words, developed markets are significantly corporatized in such activities as trade, construction, hotels and restaurants, transport, etc.[34]."

Contribution of non-corporate sector to economic growth

The sectors that are responsible for the growth of the Indian economy during the last decade and more are the services and industrial sectors. In the last decade, the average annual growth rate of the service sector was more than 8 per cent, while the growth rate of the industrial sector was around 5 per cent. It is important to note that eight major activities in the non-corporate sector have grown by more than 14 per cent CAGR between 1993–94 and 2001–02[35]. So the contribution of non corporate sector is one of the important reasons for the growth in the economy since the 1990s. It is interesting to see that the entities in the non-corporate sector are not listed in any of the stock exchanges; they are not even companies. They are mostly proprietorship and partnership firms. But it is they who dominate the fastest growing activities of the economy.

It is a reality that we do not give the non-corporate sector the importance that it deserves. We are all under the impression that it is the corporate sector that dominates our economy. This is not true. This is not to undermine the role of the corporate sector, which has its own place and importance. But this is only meant to state the obvious. The share of the non-corporate sector to the national income is nearly 57 per cent, as compared to the corporate sector's contribution of 14 per cent. The share of corporate sector in domestic savings as a percentage of GDP is about 8 per cent, whereas the share of non-corporate sector is nearly 24 per cent. So, it is the non-corporate sector that plays the most dominant and vital role in India's economy. Vaidyanathan asserts: "Hence, the proposition that the corporate sector is critical to our economy is not borne out by facts. But it is repeated ad nauseam, since such is the case in the UK and the US, and one begins to think that this is so for all countries[36]."

4.1.6 Community Orientation and Social Capital

It is the families and communities that constitute the society in India. In the Indian system, families get extended to close-knit relatives who then lead on to wider circles. Thus, there are reasons to assume that Indians have one of the largest circle of relatives in the whole world. Apart from these relationships, there are others such as friends, colleagues, neighbours, and acquaintances that also form part of the close circles depending on their proximity. The Indian society has always treated even strangers as guests. Even today, in some parts of the country, a stranger can enter the kitchen of a house during meal time without prior permission from any one in the house to partake in their food. The members of the household will have no questions as it is an accepted custom that any one who is hungry is free to enter any house for food. Earlier, even when people from foreign lands came here to escape from sufferings in their homelands, India accepted them as part of her land and provided them with all the necessary support, including lands. Indians abide by their custom of "*Atithi Devo Bhava*", which means that a guest is equal to God. The ancient sages advised people to treat everyone in different parts of the world as relatives. So by tradition, Indians treat everyone with warmth and affection and are used to accommodate and live with different groups. It is this tradition that helps India to live as a single nation, in spite of her diversities and differences.

At the basic level, each family owns its members and takes responsibility to maintain them and provide necessary support. Though the system of living with parents and elders is becoming difficult in many cases due to the modern lifestyles necessitated by occupations in different places, the basic concept of family is continued to be maintained to a large extent. Due to the close relationships and cultural traditions, the social orientation continues to remain as the basic foundation of life. Hence, people try to live like a well-knit society—big or small—and not just as families alone.

As a result, the burden of the government in maintaining the society is greatly reduced. Compared to many of the nations in the world, and especially the western nations, the expenditure incurred to run and maintain the society is very less. Whether one takes into consideration the social security system, or the old-age homes, or the administrative and judicial infrastructure, the expenditures are very less as the Indian society is largely self-functioning.

Sociologists underline that a nation could be maintained successfully only when people are able to live with each other as groups. The German sociologist, Durkheim[37] had earlier noted: "A nation can be maintained only if, between the State and the individual, there is interposed a whole series of secondary groups near enough to the individuals to attract them strongly in their sphere of action and drag them, in this way, into the general torrent of social life... Occupational groups are suited to fill this role, and that is their destiny..." Community orientation creates trust among the members of the society. Fukuyama[38] notes that trust has an economic value. To quote: "The ability to associate depends, in turn, on the degree to which communities share norms and values and are able to subordinate individual interests to those of larger groups. Out of such shared values comes trust, and trust, as we will see, has a large and measurable economic value." Trust results in 'social capital.'

Aiyer[39] explains social capital in the following words. "From time immemorial, groups of people have created strong communities, based on commonly observed rules and mutual self-help. These social links discourage deviant behaviour through ostracism and other social penalties, create a climate of trust in which agreements are honoured and grievances redressed, and facilitate collective action against threats from outsiders and risks from natural disasters. This is social capital. Unlike financial or human capital, it cannot be owned by individuals, only by social groups. Being less tangible than financial or human capital, it is difficult to measure and so has been ignored in the past. Yet it is an invaluable asset."

He also mentions the significance of social capital for the economic development of nations. To continue: "But neither human nor financial capital can adequately explain why some nations succeed and others fail. A third element, called social capital, has long been emphasized by sociologists, and is now increasingly recognized by economists. Sociologists like Robert Putnam have demonstrated that enormous economic benefits flow from social capital. Contrasting the huge economic success of northern Italy with the relative failure of the southern part, he finds that the mafias have eroded social capital and hence, economic development in the south. High levels of trust greatly reduce risks and costs, and so encourage enterprise, and innovation while reducing the costs of redress. So social capital ultimately translates into financial capital[40]."

Some of the modern experts note that the caste-based community system in India helps in the development of the economic and business systems. For example, Gurucharan Das[41] notes: "In the nineteenth century, British colonialists used to blame our caste system for everything wrong in India. Now I have a different perspective. Instead of morally judging caste, I seek to understand its impact on competitiveness. I have come to believe that being endowed with commercial castes is a source of advantage in the global economy. *Bania* traders know how to accumulate and manage capital. They have the financial resources and, more important, financial acumen. They have an austere lifestyle and the propensity to take calculated risks. They have proven their flexibility of mind as they have graduated from trading to industry. These constitute significant strengths. Joel Kotkin demonstrates these strengths in the case of Palanpuri *Jains*, who have used their caste and family networks in wresting half the global market for uncut diamonds from the Jews."

It is learnt that in the earlier periods, the society was categorized into four broad groups namely *Brahmins, Kshatriyas, Vaisyas* and *Sudras,* based on the occupations of people. There are no commonly accepted and definite views as to how and from when the system of different castes or *'jaatis'* came into practice. One of the serious problems of the contemporary Indian society is the arrangement of certain groups of people into backward classes and scheduled classes. Such kind of arrangement has resulted in the evil practice of treating people belonging to a few castes as untouchables, which calls for an immediate and complete removal. Fortunately, there is a large scale awareness regarding this issue and efforts are going on for many years to remove such practices. The study of the economic development of contemporary India indicates the role of many castes or *jaatis* in different businesses, trades and industries. When castes are viewed from the point of view of political parties, many times one incurs a wrong picture. Many political parties view castes from a narrow political approach. So there are occasions for ill feelings and hatred. But when the castes are seen from the economic point of view, a totally different picture emerges.

Due to historical reasons, different castes were, and even today to a large extent are, concentrated in different regions and places. Due to their common origin, the characteristics that they share and the locational proximity, each of these castes have a natural bondage. This bondage, which is there among all the communities, extends beyond families and touches all aspects of their lives, including the economic activities. With the result, we see a higher presence of different castes in many of the businesses, industries and services at different levels throughout the country. In fact one could notice this even beyond the borders of the country. Business and trade was traditionally in the hands of the *Bania* castes. A study conducted in the 1990s noted that "Fifteen out of the twenty largest industrial houses in 1997 were derived from the *Vaishya* or *Bania* trading castes. Eight of them were *Marwaris*[42]." Even today we see a dominant presence of many of these *bania* castes in certain trades and business. But in the last few decades, we see people from the agricultural communities, with many of them belonging to the so-called backward castes, emerging as prosperous industrial and trading communities. In fact, it is interesting to note that these new industrial and business communities are taking India to the international markets by making highly competitive products.

Experts emphasize that all kinds of positive social relationships, however small they may be, result in trust, and create social capital which is a very important asset for an economy. Since communities are social arrangements based on mutual relationships, they provide the foundations for social and economic activities. India, with her universal outlook and larger community orientation, has natural advantages in this regard. It is important to mention here the quality of Indians to adjust with persons from different backgrounds and be engaged in economic activities. Thus, one could see people from different states of India doing business in many of the industrial and business centres without any difficulty.

4.1.7 Faith and Relationship

Indian society is based on relationships and faith. As the society is organized into families and larger communities, relationships play the dominant role. In the traditional arrangements, the activities of the entire villages or localities were so arranged as to involve different groups of people together. The developments in the society during the past few decades have resulted in a lot of changes to the earlier arrangements. In certain communities even today the activities are so arranged as to help each other and maintain social order, even while growing economically. For example, a study of the fisherman community living along the northern part of the east coast in Tamil Nadu revealed interesting facts[43] (see Box 4.1).

Box 4.1 Communities—Social capital, faith and relationships

The community living along the northern part of coastal areas in Tamil Nadu is called '*Pattinavars*'. They are a close-knit community. In each of these villages, there is a head, called '*Nattar*', who is selected by people on the basis of background and reputation. The head, along with a few other representatives chosen by the village, are responsible for all the village affairs, whether they are economical, social or otherwise. Each family contributes its share of revenue by way of a share of the catch towards the common funds. On a fixed day the larger village council meets every month to take all the necessary decisions. All matters, including finance, are routinely discussed. The head and his team submit the accounts and get acceptance for future plans.

There was an interesting incident a few years back in one of these villages. The accounts for a small sum were missing. The *Nattar* and his team could not figure out the reason for the missing sum in spite of their best efforts. Immediately the *Nattar* resigned from his responsibility. The entire village expressed their full faith and wanted him to lead the village. But he did not agree, taking full responsibility for the mistake, and relinquished his responsibility in favour of another person.

Though the fishermen, who do not have boats, work for those who own them, there are no employer-employee relationships; the benefits are only shared. When the bread winner is not able to go for fishing due to ill health, the village supports his family. When someone loses his boat, the village takes up the responsibility to help him. All disputes, within and between villages are settled by themselves, and as a result law enforcement by the state or outside agencies is not necessary.

Womenfolk enjoy a lot of respect in their society. While men catch fish, the businesses are handled by them. There are no divorces. In certain villages, before the fishermen go out into the seas in the early morning, they touch the feet of their mothers to get their blessings; if they are not available, then they touch the feet of their wives, as they see their sea-goddess in women.

Relationships involve faith. So economic transactions among people known to each other are based on faith. Faith-based transactions are easy, fast and reduce transaction costs. Further they do not involve or depend on the state machinery. Relationship-based transactions are facilitated due to the close-knit relationships in the society and the consequent social capital. The social capital is largely due to the friendly and fraternal relationships among people of different groups across the country. Much of the economic transactions that Indians regularly carry out on a daily basis, generally, depend only on faith. It is not just the non-monetary activities, or activities involving small sums of money. Even the bigger financial transactions involving larger amounts of money are undertaken on faith and goodwill. In the village system, it is common to see money transactions taking place without the knowledge of a third party. In certain areas of Tamil Nadu, people give loans in the presence of their village deity. But with no one to see, people do not cheat. Similarly, it is common to see people entering oral agreements for purchase and sale of assets. They do not go back on their words later. This is still happening today even in the modern business settings in different centres. Even though the traditional arrangements based completely on faith and relationships are beginning to wane in different places, there is still a large scale presence of faith-based transactions across the country at all levels.

Earlier, it was a common practice for people in different places to give their savings or surplus funds to respected persons in the village or locality. Even though this practice was almost a general norm in the earlier decades, one could see this still being followed in different places. *McKinsey Special Edition 2005* mentions that "just 40 per cent of households have signed up as borrowers or depositors with banks in India[44]." One major reason for the banking habits of Indians remaining low even when there is a consistently higher savings rate is their traditional faith-based modes of savings and borrowings. As such, different indigenous methods of financing are functioning in India due to the faith-based relationships in the society. Raising of funds or borrowing by a good person is still possible in many places due to relationships. In certain areas of Gujarat, whenever a *Patel* of good nature and integrity expresses his requirement for funds to promote a new venture, all those who believed him would contribute towards initial capital. In fact, when people deposit their funds in non-banking finance companies, they see the reputation of the persons behind the concerns and accordingly, take the investment decisions. A study of the unorganized finance sector in the textile cluster of Karur showed that almost all the financial transactions were taking place only on faith and goodwill[45]. It was learnt that the financiers normally did not demand documents or pledge of assets before giving funds, as funds were given only on the reputation of the borrower or the recommender.

4.1.8 Society-driven and Not State-dependent

Indian economic system is largely driven by the society. Indians have been living as independent communities without leaning on the state since the ancient days. While writing on the village communities in ancient India, Basham[46] quotes an instance from a *Jataka* story to explain the self-dependent attitude of the people. "One day they stood in the middle of the village to transact village business, and they ... (decided to) do good works; so they would get up betimes, and go out with knives, axes and crowbars. With their crowbars they rolled away the stones on the four highways; they cut down the trees which caught the axles of their carts; they levelled the irregularities (of the roads); they built an embankment and dug tanks; they made a village hall; they showed charity and kept the (Buddhist) commandments." It shows the spirit of the Indian society to take up public works voluntarily without waiting for the state.

Such an independent spirit, without waiting for the state or its mechanisms, pervades the Indian society since the ancient days.

It is mostly the society that generates savings, facilitates capital formation and engages in different entrepreneurial activities. Table 4.9 presents the domestic credit provided by the banking sector in India, China, US and the world.

Table 4.9 Credit-GDP Ratio of the Banking Sector in India, China, US and the World (1970 to 2001–06)

(per cent to GDP)

Country	1970	1981–85*	1986–90*	1991–95*	1996–00*	2001–06*
China	–	60.2	81.2	92.6	109.2	138.6
India	9.2	18.3	20.1	19.9	21.2	33.5@
US	118.0	126.5	150.4	163.6	195.3	216.1
World	88.4	108.3	132.6	142.8	155.4	163.3

* Average

@ Pertains to the average of 2001–07 period.

Source: *Report on Currency and Finance 2006–08,* Reserve Bank of India, 2008, p. 244.

Table 4.9 shows that the credit-GDP ratio of the banking sector during 2001–06 was only 33.5 per cent to GDP in India, compared to 138.6 per cent in China and 216.1 per cent in the US. The growth of the self-employed sector and almost all of the industrial and business clusters are entirely due to the initiatives and efforts of the society. In most of the clusters, the government initiative and support is very minimum or almost nil. In fact, it is the society in different centres across the country that creates the necessary facilities such as schools and colleges and social infrastructure required for the citizens. Due to this attitude of the society, the dependence on the state is minimal and the consequent burdens of the governments are less. Moreover, as the Indian society is largely self-financing, the expenditure of the state on social support systems is very less compared to the western countries.

4.1.9 Driven by Norms and Values

Evidences indicate that efforts to direct the economic and business systems based on certain basic norms and values were prevalent in India since the ancient days. Sages and scriptures regularly advised traders and merchants to conduct their affairs based on principles. For example, the *Arthashastra* mentioned the following principles for fair trading[47].

1. Both locally produced and imported goods shall be sold for the benefit of the public. {2.16.5}
2. When there is an excess supply of a commodity, a buffer stock shall be built up by paying a price higher than the prevailing market price. When the market price reaches the support level, the buying price shall be changed according to the situation. {2.16.2, 3}
3. When there is a glut of a commodity, its sale shall be canalized (through state controlled outlets) and merchants shall sell only from the accumulated stock, until it is exhausted, on a daily wage basis (with no profit margin for them). {4.2.33–35}
4. Surplus stocks unaccounted for in the hands of merchants shall be sold for the benefit of the public. {4.2.26, 27}
5. Even a large profit shall be foregone if it is likely to cause harm to the public. {2.16.6}
6. No artificial scarcity shall be created by accumulation of commodities constantly in demand; these shall (be made available at all times and) not be subjected to restrictions on when they may be sold. {2.16.7}

One can see a set of basic minimum disciplines in all business transactions across the country even today. Of course, there could be deviations, due to changing times and attitudes. But largely the system functions on the basis of a set of norms and values. One can observe even higher values in the close-knit non-corporate sector in several clusters. In the case of the *ghee* industry in Tamil Nadu, it was learnt that in most of the instances traders refused to open the second outlet, when another one promoted by their men was already functioning in a particular centre[48]. Even though no one stops the other traders from opening a second or third outlet, it is not done so as a matter of principle. Even in the modern corporate sector, one could notice certain basic norms being observed in vital matters. For example, takeover rules permit everyone who is capable of taking over the probable companies to attempt for it. But why is it that in India there are not many takeovers, especially the hostile ones, when compared to the western countries? Indian system, by tradition, restrains people to takeover a company promoted by someone else, even though the rules and funds permit such eventualities.

4.2 FEATURES OF WESTERN MODELS

Having seen the basic features of the Indian economic models, we shall now turn our attention towards the basic features of the western models. This is important as the western countries are rich, modern and developed. The rest of the world wants to emulate and copy the West as they are considered to be the models for all other economies of the world.

4.2.1 Individualism

Individualism forms the basis of life in most of the western countries. An increasing majority of the westerners do not prefer family or social commitments. The 'Self' is placed before everything else in life. Self-interest is the guiding principle. Self-growth is the aim and self-gratification is the end of life. In the process, the larger responsibilities at the family and society levels are not given due importance. With the result, the families break down and there is lesser chance of people living as close-knit communities. Hence, the local communities fail to live as groups. There is loss of social capital, the invisible thread that unites people for common purposes, everywhere. When there is a decline in social capital, there is decline of social order and peace. This sets in motion a series of chain reactions whereby decline of social order results in the loss of a peaceful life which in turn leads to various economic problems.

Commenting on the rise of individualism in the US, Fukuyama[49] writes: "... the United States has been changing, rather dramatically, over the past couple of generations with respect to its art of association. In many ways, American society is becoming as individualistic as Americans have always believed it was; the inherent tendency of rights-based liberalism to expand and multiply those rights against the authority of virtually all existing communities has been pushed towards its logical conclusion. The decline of trust and sociability in the United States is also evident in any number of changes in American society; the rise of violent crime and civil litigation; the breakdown of family structure; the decline of a wide range of intermediate social structures like neighbourhoods, churches, unions, clubs, and charities; and the general sense among Americans of a lack of shared values and community with those around them."

He narrates on the decline of family life and community system in the US. "Family life, which constitutes the smallest and most basic form of association, has deteriorated markedly since the 1960's with a sharp increase in rates of divorce and single-parent families. Beyond the family, too, there has been a steady breakdown of older communities like neighborhoods, churches, and workplaces. At the same time, there has been a vast increase in the general level of distrust, as measured by the wariness that Americans have for their fellow citizens due to the rise of crime, or in the massive increases in litigation as a means of settling disputes. In recent years the state, often in the guise of the court system, has supported a rapidly expanding set of individual rights that have undermined the ability of larger communities to set standards for the behaviour of their members. Thus, the United States today presents a contradictory picture of a society living off a great fund of previously accumulated social capital that gives it a rich and dynamic associational life, while at the same time manifesting extremes of distrust and social individualism that tend to isolate and atomize its members. This type of individualism always existed in a potential form, yet through most of America's existence it had been kept in check by strong communal currents[50]."

It was reported that in the US, every second marriage resulted in divorce, despite the short periods of married lives. Divorce rates have been increasing in many other western countries over the last few decades. This results in the break up of families. With the result, there is an increasing number of divorcees, single-mothers, single-fathers and so on. When a family breaks up, it has a drastic effect on many people in different ways. Apart from the parties concerned, the most affected are the children of the divorcing parties. The children with single parents lose the chance of living in happy families with both the parents taking care of them. As a result, they grow up under immense emotional pressure without having the warmth of their family support. When they grow up, they carry their emotional burdens with them. This emotional imbalance creates a lot of disturbance from their childhood. As a result, a good number of them deviate from normal life and get attracted to abnormal activities, thus becoming juvenile delinquents. Strong repercussions can be seen even in schools and colleges, where many a times there are reports of different forms of violent incidents, including gun-attacks, killing their peers, classmates and teachers.

Studies show that more than 40 per cent of the children born in the US are born to un-wed mothers. In a number of cases, the fathers of these children are not known at all. What kind of future do these children have? How will the un-wed young mothers take care of these children and provide them with the necessary comforts they require? In many cases, the un-wed mothers themselves are young and just school-going girls. This is a serious impact of individualism. In some countries of the West, there is an increasing tendency in the recent years, among men and women, to 'live together' without getting married or entering into any bondage whatsoever. The result is the loss of families and close-knit societies. Interestingly, as a consequence, the governments have been giving concessions and tax-breaks to compel people to remain married. But how can tax-breaks make people live as husbands and wives, when there are no higher instincts to create and live as families?

What is the impact of individualism and decline of families and communities for western economies? Writing in the context of the US, Fukuyama notes: "This decline of sociability has important implications for American democracy, perhaps even more so than for the economy. Already the United States pays significantly more than other industrialized countries for police protection and keeps more than 1 per cent of its total population in prison. The United States also pays substantially more than the Europe or Japan does to its lawyers, so that its citizens can sue one another. Both of these costs, which amount to a measurable percentage of gross domestic product annually, constitute a direct tax imposed by the breakdown of trust in the society. In the future, the economic effects may be more far-reaching; the ability of Americans to start and work within a wide variety of new organizations may begin to deteriorate as its very diversity lowers trust and creates new barriers to cooperation. In addition to its physical capital, the United States has been living off a fund of social capital. Just as its savings rate has been too low to replace physical plant and infrastructure adequately, so its replenishment of social capital has lagged in recent decades. The accumulation of social capital, however, is a complicated and in many ways, mysterious cultural process. While governments can enact policies that have the effect of depleting social capital, they have great difficulties understanding how to build it up again[51]."

The break-up of the family system is affecting the western countries in different ways. Many of their citizens do not want to produce children, as they do not want families and the responsibilities associated with the family system. Many men and women prefer to lead a life of 'arrangement' rather than being bound by marriage. With the result, the population has been fast declining in many developed countries. Though desperate attempts are made by the governments to see that the population does not go down, they are helpless. The replacement rate, necessary to keep the population going steadily, has been continuously falling. Many of these countries have already begun to feel the difficulties of a reduced population. Due to the large-scale absence of the family system, the people in the western countries depend heavily on the social security system operated by the governments. The US has had ideas of privatizing this system but is faced with stern opposition, as people do not believe in depending on the private-run system for their livelihood. They are of the views that the failure of the system would land them in the streets, as there are no other social arrangements to protect them. But the governments find it difficult to run the system as the costs are increasing every year. Data compiled by the Organization for Economic Cooperation and Development (OECD) shows that the social expenditure is already taking anywhere between about one-fifth to one-third of GDPs in different countries. Table 4.10 provides the data relating to public social expenditure for selected OECD countries[52].

Table 4.10 Public Social Expenditure in OECD Countries (1990–2007)

(as a percentage of GDP)

Countries	1990	2000	2004	2007
France	24.9	27.7	29.0	28.4
Germany	21.7	26.6	27.2	25.2
UK	16.8	18.6	20.5	20.5
USA	13.5	14.5	15.9	16.2
OECD total	17.6	18.9	19.9	19.2

Source: *OECD Fact Book 2010, www.oecd.org.*

In fact, the social security expenditure is the single largest expenditure to many nations in the west. This amount cannot be cut or even reduced by any government as that would land their societies in trouble. At present, there is another problem to this system. The system runs on the basis of the contributions provided by the adult workforce as a share of their earnings. Since the working population has been declining and the replacement rates are not adequate, the contributions necessary from the workforce to keep the system running have been coming down. Governments that are already burdened with a large outgo towards social security find this situation too difficult to bear. Where will they go for funds when they cannot be generated by the current workforce? With the result, many of these countries have already started wooing the retired people to resume work, and a few of the countries either have increased the retirement age or are seriously considering doing it. But this can only be a temporary solution.

The governments have begun to understand that what they need is the family and social systems. But it is difficult to create such systems as they cannot be legislated; they have to be created by society through culture and higher values. Fukuyama says: "Today, having abandoned the promise of social engineering, virtually all serious observers understand that liberal, political and economic institutions depend on a healthy and dynamic civil society for their vitality. "Civil society"—a complex welter of intermediate institutions, including businesses, voluntary associations, educational institutions, clubs, unions, media, charities, and churches—builds, in turn, on the family, the primary instrument by which people are socialized into their culture and given the skills that allow them to live in broader society and through which the values and knowledge of that society are transmitted across the generations. A strong and stable family structure and durable social institutions cannot be legislated into existence the way a government can create a central bank or an army. A thriving civil society depends on people's habits, customs, and ethics—attributes that can be shaped only indirectly through conscious political action and must otherwise be nourished through an increased awareness and respect for culture[53]."

But how to create the family and social systems, when people are living under the illusion of individualism, is a million dollar question. The large-scale absence of families and social institutions, with the erosion of culture and loss of higher values, are resulting in a lot of social and economic difficulties in those countries. Lack of savings, unrestrained consumerism, exploitation of resources, high transaction costs and absence of a meaningful life are some of the major difficulties. It is unfortunate that the overall system encourages these individualistic tendencies for its benefits, at the cost of families and sustainable communities.

4.2.2 Consumerism and the Decline of Savings

The individualistic lifestyles lead to unrestrained consumption behaviour and the result is consumerism. When individualism is the way of life, people spend money in whatever way they want. Since there is no discipline imposed by families and societies, everyone spends as much as he or she wants. Moreover, in individualistic societies, there is no compulsion to save money as one is not expected to take care of parents, grandparents or other family members. With the result, all the money that one earns remains in the hands of the earner and is spent for oneself. In the market driven economies, the markets continuously create new desires and luxuries become necessities. Everyone, including a newborn child is looked upon as a customer. Every occasion is viewed as an opportunity to boost sales. When the markets begin to dominate, they become very powerful. They begin to create new lifestyles and dictate desires. In such a scenario, the market becomes the most important entity; as a result, the governments and other social institutions gradually lose their authority. Human beings become mere instruments in the hands of the all powerful markets and those who control them.

Market is a faceless entity dominated by mega corporations who are only worried about their profits. Maximizing the bottom lines is the only objective of the companies. To increase their bottom lines, companies create new demands, make newer products, destroy the environment indiscriminately and spoil the health of the consumers. People are expected to consume more and buy continuously. Even when people do not have money, institutions lend money; credit card companies issue cards so that people can buy. The credit card culture has affected the lives of people in such a way that they borrow their future incomes to spend during the current year. In certain countries of the West, there is more number of credit cards than the number of people in the country. The credit card usage is so widespread and indiscriminate that many college students become insolvents even before they complete their graduation. In the race to compete in the credit card market, companies give cards to students on the day of their admission into colleges in anticipation of their future incomes after completion of their courses. Young boys and girls with lots of money at their disposal, without any efforts to earn them, spend them the way they are driven by the markets, as there is little restraint on their behaviour.

In the last few years, consumerism has reached very high levels. People spend money on all luxury items, including the unnecessary ones. In this connection it may be pertinent to refer to the data presented in the United Nations Development Report reflecting the priorities of the richer world[54]. Table 4.11 provides the data.

Table 4.11 Priorities of the Richer Countries

Global priority	$US Billions
Cosmetics in the United States	8
Ice cream in Europe	11
Perfumes in Europe and the United States	12
Pet foods in Europe and the United States	17
Business entertainment in Japan	35
Cigarettes in Europe	50
Alcoholic drinks in Europe	105
Narcotics drugs in the world	400

Source: United Nations Development Report 1998, p. 37.

The amounts mentioned for many of the luxury items given in Table 4.11 are unbelievable, especially for the smaller populations in the West.

The same report has presented the following data provided in Table 4.12 to show how little was necessary to achieve universal access to basic social services in all developing countries.

Table 4.12 Amount Needed for Universal Basic Needs

Global priority	$US Billions
Basic education for all	6
Water and sanitation for all	9
Reproductive health for all women	12
Basic health and nutrition	13

In this connection, it would be useful to note the observations of the *Human Development Report 2005*. It says: "Using a global income distribution data base, we estimate a cost of $300 billion for lifting 1 billion people living on less than $1 day threshold. That amount represents 1.6 per cent of the income of the richest 10 per cent of the world's population[55]."

Is it not a shame that the richer nations and the richest sections of the world spend so much money on unwanted and unhealthy items, when a small share of this amount would be enough to provide the basic human requirements? But the richer sections would not be able to attempt anything in the right direction as they have become addicted to consumerist impulsions. But with this kind of spending, are they happy? No. On the basis of surveys conducted in the US, Hamilton[56] writes: "In the United States, where consistent surveys have been conducted since 1946, real incomes have increased by 400 per cent, yet there has been no increase in reported levels of well-being. Indeed, the proportion of Americans reporting themselves to be 'very happy' declined from 35 per cent in 1957 to 30 per cent in 1988, while the percentage who said they agreed with the statement that they were 'pretty well-satisfied with (their) financial situation' fell from 42 to 30 per cent. This is astonishing: despite a trebling of real incomes during the period, fewer Americans in the 1990s are satisfied with their incomes than was the case in the 1950s."

When people spend all the money that they earn and even more, how will there be savings in the society? With the result, saving rates are less in the western countries. In fact, the savings have been declining significantly in the last few years due to the consumerist tendencies. Table 4.13 presents the household saving rates of the selected rich countries during 2000 to 2009.

Table 4.13 Household Net Saving Rates in Rich Countries (as a percentage of household disposable income)

Net savings	2000	2005	2007	2009
Canada	4.8	2.2	2.9	4.7
Germany	9.2	10.5	10.8	11.1
Japan	8.8	3.9	2.5	—
United Kingdom	0.1	–1.2	–3.2	1.2
Euro area	8.3	8.4	8.2	9.6
United States	3.0	1.5	2.1	6.2

Source: *OECD Fact Book* 2011, www.oecd.org.

Table 4.13 shows that the saving rates are low for all the countries, when compared to India. In fact, the saving rates have remained lower than 10 per cent for all the countries, except Germany. Moreover, the rates have either been falling or have showed marginal increases for different countries between 2000 and 2009. The saving rates are very poor for the UK. It is significant to note that the saving rates of the UK have remained negative for two years during the above period. Krugman[57] reported in 2006 that in the US, "last year the personal savings rate fell below zero for the first time in 1933." The consumerist societies make their citizens paupers. Social Justice Policy Group, commissioned by the Leader of Her Majesty's Opposition in the UK, to make policy recommendations to the Conservative Party on issues of social justice, came out with its interim report in 2006. Discussing about indebtedness in their country, the report notes that lending to individuals has grown rapidly over the recent years. In July 2004, such lending passed the £1 trillion mark, equivalent to an average debt per household of £40,000; by September, it was £1.25 trillion. The report also notes that the ratio of debt to income has been increasing at a fast pace. While the ratio was less than 50 per cent in the 1970s, it has risen to 140 per cent by 2005. It also mentions that the total number of credit cards in the country was 72 million, against an adult population of 46 million[58].

When citizens do not have savings, how will the governments have funds in their coffers? Ultimately, the citizens and the governments perennially suffer from want of funds. The US is estimated to borrow more than $2 billion every day in the financial markets. Its current account deficit reached 6 per cent of its GDP during 2006, and remains at more than 3 per cent even now. With the result, the US has already become the biggest borrower in the world. This situation has arisen mainly because spending has become a compulsory habit in the country. When they have money, the system encourages them to spend. When they do not have money, the system compels them to spend. The western economic system thrives so much on spending that even when the economy is down, they feel that people should spend more to revive it. Reflecting this thinking, in one of its issues earlier *The Economist* wrote: "SHOPPING: it's long been one of America's favourite pastimes, but more recently it has taken centre stage in the battle to prevent the world's biggest economy from sliding into recession[59]."

Thus, the contemporary western economic system is based on the principle of spending. In their system, spending is considered as virtue, and economists, policy makers and the whole establishment encourage people to spend. Their economics believes that savings is unnecessary. Unfortuantely, they do not even realize that the dictionary meaning of the word 'economy' is thrift. As a result, they have spoiled the people from saving and now the governments find it difficult to generate money. So they resort to borrowing. But how long will the governments be able to borrow continuously?

4.2.3 State Dependence

All forms of familial and social support mechanisms which are natural to mankind are being destroyed in the name of individualism. When the tendencies for all natural relationships are destroyed, people fail to function as groups in the common interest. In such a situation, the governments, with all their limitations, have to intervene in the functioning of the society as otherwise the societies will not function properly. In this connection, it is useful to see what Fukuyama has written on this aspect. "A liberal state is ultimately a limited state, with government activity strictly bounded by a sphere of individual liberty. If such a society is not to become anarchic or otherwise ungovernable, then it must be capable of self-government at levels of social organization below the state. Such a system depends ultimately not just on law but on the self-restraint of individuals. If they are not tolerant and respectful of each other or do not abide by the laws they set for themselves, they will require a strong and coercive state to keep each other in line. If they cannot cohere for common purposes, then they will need an intrusive state to provide the organization they cannot provide themselves[60]."

The societies are becoming increasingly dependent on the state mechanisms for their functioning. The dependence of the people on the state is so high that they constantly need the support of the state for even day to day matters. As a result, the governments need to strengthen all the instruments of state involved in administration, judiciary and distribution of welfare. The costs incurred towards creating and maintaining institutions for all these purposes are enormous. Speaking on the issue of cost to the nation due to family breakdowns in Britain, it was reported that "the cost to the country is now well over £20 billion per annum, a significant proportion of which is paid in benefits to lone parents[61]." While the people are dependent on state mechanisms for their living, the markets have made people increasingly dependent on them for decision-making. Resultantly, we see people with a totally dependent attitude, without the ability to function independently as groups for their common as well as personal good.

But the governments cannot provide all the necessary assistance and facilities continuously to the satisfaction of all concerned. It is not that the governments do not want to do; but in fact, they are not capable. Governments cannot give what an affectionate family can give; and governments cannot provide what a compassionate civil society can provide. Governments cannot provide social peace, if the society is not at peace with itself. Governments cannot provide social security to all its citizens for a long time, when there is no family mechanism to take care of people. A distant, faceless and an institutionalized mechanism of state, however good its intentions may be, cannot create the natural relationships necessary for a meaningful life among people.

Presently, the single-most burdensome issue for the western economies is the social security expenditure. Many of the countries find it difficult to run the system as the expenditures are increasing every year. But they cannot discontinue the system. With the result they somehow manage the system with all the difficulties knowing fully well that they have to face serious problems in the coming years. The only alternative is to create and establish the family system, which seems to be not possible in the present situation. Meanwhile the recent economic crisis has added a new dimension to the concept of state support. Even big corporations that are in trouble are seeking the support of governments for funds. In many cases, the governments are compelled to give away lots of public money to rescue these companies.

4.2.4 Market as the Core

While communism is against giving any significant role to the market, the western capitalism gives the central role to it. Apart from the individuals and the state, the third most important entity in the West is the market. The market has become so powerful that the other two entities often lose their power in front of it. With the result, the market has come to dominate all aspects of life. As long as markets were functioning within certain boundaries there were no serious problems. But with the emergence of mega corporations functioning across different continents, they have begun to dominate even the sovereign governments. In such a scenario, the domestic institutions lose their significance.

In recent years, there are instances where the mega corporations have become so powerful that they interfere with the functioning of the local systems for their benefits. In the process, they do not hesitate to interfere in the functioning of the governmental and economic systems. Consequently, there is large-scale disruption to the societies. The market is only worried about profits. It is not bothered about any other issues. In its greed to earn more and more profits, market destroys environment; destabilizes economies and interferes with the cultural and social systems of citizens. During the last few years the financial markets have become very powerful in the economic systems. The transactions in the international financial markets are more than 90 times the actual movements of goods and services throughout the world. Much of the financial transactions are for speculative purposes.

In this connection, it is relevant to quote the words of George Soros[62] who said: "It is dangerous, ..., to place excessive reliance on the market mechanism. Markets are designed to facilitate the free exchange of goods and services among willing participants, but they are not, on their own, capable of taking care of collective needs such as law and order or the maintenance of the market mechanism itself. Nor are they competent to ensure social justice."

4.2.5 Contract-based Relationships

When individualism dominates life, relationships are created only when they are needed by one or more parties. In such a system, relationship is only a burden to be tolerated for the time being in return for some other thing. While even strangers are to be treated like one's own kith and kin in Indian culture, every other person is considered an intruder in one's private life in the West. Hence, relationships tend to become contract-based, however close the relationships may be, depending on the pleasures and benefits of the contracting parties.

In economic matters, contractual relationship is the general norm. All economic relationships begin and end with contracts. As a result, the transaction costs become very high. But it cannot be avoided as there are very little personal relationships, more so in economic matters. In India, we see crores of rupees changing hands everyday without any agreements, and a number of businesses running for years with only oral agreements with regard to investments and sharing of profits and losses. A phone call or a small chit is enough for transfer of lakhs of rupees. In many places it is common to see transactions taking place between two people without the notice of any third party. Funds support by relatives, friends and acquaintances is a regular part of business in India. But such systems are almost totally absent in the West.

In contract-based relationships there is no scope for personal discretion. Both the parties have to follow the contracts. Even in genuine circumstances, the parties have no scope for any relaxation of the provisions of the contract. Therefore, there are chances for hardships. So the cost becomes generally high in contract-based transactions.

4.2.6 Need for Formal Rules and Regulations in Transactions

Since relationships are contract-based, clearly spelt out rules and regulations with penalty for deviations are a necessity. Hence, rules and regulations are framed for all relationships, including personal. In economic transactions, they are much more important, as any deviation may result in loss of some benefit to one or more of the contracting parties. So the rule book, the institutions that govern the rules and the systems associated with their functioning become critical. Each and every aspect of life is governed by externally imposed rules and regulations. Life is conditioned to function only when there are rules and regulations.

4.2.7 Unsustainable Foundations

The western capitalist model has not fulfilled the needs of their own population. With all their rhetoric, their system has not contributed to the overall welfare of the majority of the citizens. Hamilton[63] notes: "Despite high and sustained levels of economic growth in the West over a period of 50 years—growth that has seen average real incomes increase several times over—the mass of people are no more satisfied with their lives now than they were then. If growth is intended to give us better lives, and there can be no other purpose, it has failed." After more than six decades of post-world war economic growth, even the group of rich countries has serious problems to handle. Unemployment stands at 8.6 per cent of the labour force during 2010 in OECD countries[64]. These countries pay as much as $1 billion subsidy a day to their agricultural sector and even more to keep their place in the world economy. They also resort to every kind of arm-twisting tactics to maintain their position in the global economy.

The self-employed population in the rich countries is low. Details show that it has also been declining for many countries over the years. Table 4.14 presents the self-employment rates in the developed countries of the west for selected years from 1990 to 2010.

Table 4.14 Self-employed Rates in OECD Countries

(as a percentage of total employment)

Countries	1990	2000	2005	2010
France	13.2	9.3	9.1	—
Germany	—	11.0	12.4	11.6
UK	15.1	12.8	12.9	13.9
USA	8.8	7.4	7.5	7.0
EU 27 total	—	18.3	17.3	—
OECD total	—	17.7	16.8	—

Source: OECD Fact Book 2011, www.oecd.org.

Table 4.14 shows that the self-employment rates in the developed parts of the world are low. The rate is only 7.0 per cent in the US in 2010. The poor rates of self-employment are due to the economic models that encourage only big corporations at the cost of small initiatives at the local levels.

Even within the rich countries, growth rates for all groups of citizens are uneven. It is not even linked to productivity. In a study, two Northwestern University economists noted that the normal link between productivity and real earnings was broken in the US[65]. They show that between 1997 and 2001, the top 10 per cent of the US wage and salary earners had received 49 per cent of the growth, while the top 1 per cent alone had received 24 per cent. But at the same time, the bottom 50 per cent had received less than 13 per cent. Why is this so? Where are these developments leading to? Disparities within groups of people, even in the social sectors, have only widened in the last few years. Krugman[66] writes: "For lower income working Americans, lack of health insurance is quickly becoming the new normal..." Quoting survey results released by the Commonwealth Fund, Krugman continues: "The survey found that 41 per cent of non-elderly American adults with income between $20,000 and $40,000 a year were without health insurance for all or part of 2005. That's up from 28 per cent as recently as 2001". The richest nation in the world was unable to assure health security to a significant majority of the people till recently, in spite of their advanced technologies and modern health care systems.

The western economic model is also badly affecting the lives of citizens across the world. *Human Development Report 2005* had earlier noted: "The US Department of Agriculture estimates that the country's 20,000 cotton farmers will receive government payments of $4.7 billion in 2005—an amount equivalent to the market value of the crop and more than the US aid to Sub-Saharan Africa[67]." This is the strategy of the richest nation to keep their agriculture out of competition from the poorest farmers in the world. What are the consequences of these payments? Cotton prices fell in the poor countries, and "in Benin alone the fall in cotton prices in 2001–02 was linked to an increase in poverty from 37 per cent to 59 per cent[68]." As a result of the lopsided policies followed by the western economies, the poorer countries of the world are subjected to inhuman suffering. For example, "... Sub-Saharan Africa had almost 100 million more people living in poverty in 2001 than in 1990[69]." The lives of people living in Africa, Latin America and many other countries across the world are constantly under threat due to the unscientific economic models of the west.

In the name of free trade, the economies of the poor and the developing countries are disturbed; their natural and mineral wealth is exploited and they are not allowed to lead a life of their own based on their lifestyles and preferences. In the earlier centuries it was colonialism; in the present period it is the modern capitalism. The result is that we have an uneven world which is increasingly becoming unsafe for mankind. Earlier, when communism had failed under its own weight, experts had claimed that the western capitalist model would provide alternative solutions to the global economic system. Now where is the western capitalism taking the world? It is becoming clearer that the foundations of the modern capitalistic order are unsustainable, as they are heavily shaking.

The recent developments in the US and the European region show that their ideas and approaches are not conducive for sustaining their own economic systems. On the one hand, more families are getting bankrupt, while on the other, countries accumulate high levels of debt. Table 4.15 presents the indebtedness and leverage in the richer western world.

Table 4.15 Indebtedness and Leverage in Western Economies

(as per cent of 2011 GDP)

	United States	**United Kingdom**	**Euro Area**	**Greece**
Government gross debt	100	81	89	166
Households gross debt	92	101	70	71
Total economy gross external liabilities	151	607	169	202

Source: Global Financial Stability Report, International Monetary Fund, September 2011, p. 5.

4.3 DIFFERENT APPROACHES AND DIFFERENT MODELS

A study of the features of the Indian models along with the western models presents a contrasting picture. The basic characteristics of the western models seem to be totally different from the Indian models. This is basically due to the differences in the orientation and outlook of citizens in two different parts of the world. While 'self-interest' is the basis of the western economic system, the Indian approach has always been 'above the self.' Moreover, while the foundations of the Indian systems seem to rest on solid grounds, the western systems are shaking with weak foundations. In such a scenario, it is difficult, even to compare both the models on the same set of yardsticks. It seems unnecessary and may even be counterproductive to copy the western models as the Indian models are more comprehensive and rooted to the soil.

REFERENCES

[1] Basham, A.L., *The Wonder that was India,* Rupa & Co., New Delhi, 2001, p. 155.

[2] Patel, Parvin J. and Rutten, Mario, 'Patels of Central Gujarat in Greater London', *Economic and Political Weekly,* Vol. 34, Nos. 16 and 17, 1999, pp. 952–954.

[3] Vaidyanathan, R., 'Gold, Savings and P&P Sector: Foolish Governments, Smart Women', *The Hindu Business Line,* September 9, 2004.

[4] Farrel, Diana and Lund, Susan, Reforming India's Financial System, 2005 Special Edition *McKinsey Quarterly,* p. 105.

[5] Vaidyanathan, R., 'The Least Acknowledged Big Savers', *The Hindu Business Line,* July 15, 2004.

[6] Vaidyanathan, R., 'End Consumption, Nurture Savings', *The Hindu Business Line,* May 5, 2005.

[7] *Economic Census 2005,* Table 2.8, Government of India, New Delhi.

[8] Vaidyanathan, R., 'Capital Formation and P&P Sector—The Inconsistencies and Adjustments', *The Hindu Business Line,* August 26, 2004.

[9] National Sample Survey Organization quoted in *The Financial Express,* January 29, 2008.

[10] *Project OASIS Report,* submitted to the Ministry of Social Justice and Empowerment, Government of India, New Delhi, 1999.

[11] Vaidyanathan, R., 'Bias Against the Self-employed', *The Hindu Business Line*, February 24, 2005.

[12] *Global Entrepreneurship Monitor 2002 Summary Report, November 2002*, Babson College, Ewing Marion Kauffman Foundation and London Business School.

[13] Ibid.

[14] Ramadorai, S., Speech at the Ahmedabad Management Association quoting GEM Report, April 22, 2003.

[15] *Economic Census 2005,* op.cit.

[16] *Final Results: Third All India Census of Small Scale Industries 2001–02,* Ministry of Small Scale Industries, Government of India, New Delhi, 2004.

[17] *Economic Census*, op.cit.

[18] *Final Results: Third All India Census of Small Scale Industries 2001–02*, op.cit.

[19] Ibid.

[20] Meena Menon, 'Dharavi Residents Wary of New Project', *The Hindu*, 8.8.2004.

[21] India Brand Equity Foundation, 'Hinterland India: The Real Source of India's Entrepreneurship', in www.ibef.org quoting *Global Entrepreneurship Monitor Report 2003.*

[22] Vaidyanathan, R., 'Understanding the Unorganized Sector', *The Hindu Business Line*, June 3, 2004.

[23] Ibid.

[24] From Statement 76.3—Share of Unorganized Segment in Net Domestic Product by Economic Activity, Statement of NAS 2005, 1993–94 to 2002–03/2003–04, Central Statistical Organization, Government of India, 2005, p. 108.

[25] Vaidyanathan, R., 'Success of Unorganized Services', *The Hindu Business Line,* July 1, 2004.

[26] Ibid.

[27] Harriss-White, Barbara, 'India's Informal Economy: Facing the Twenty-first Century', in Kaushik Basu (Ed.), *India's Emerging Economy—Performance and Prospects in the 1990s and Beyond*. Oxford University Press, New Delhi, 2005.

[28] Vaidyanathan, R., 'Understanding the Unorganized Sector', op.cit.

[29] National Sample Survey Organization quoted in Chadha, G.K., *Rural Industry in India, Policy Perspectives, Past Performance*

and Future Options, South Asia Advisory Team, International Labour Organization, New Delhi, 2003, p. 181.

[30] Chadha, G.K., *Rural Industry in India, Policy Perspectives, Past Performance and Future Options,* South Asia Advisory Team, International Labour Organization, New Delhi, 2003, p. 61.

[31] *Report on Currency and Finance 2008–09*, RBI, Mumbai, pp. 287–288.

[32] Vaidyanathan, R., 'Success of Unorganized Services', op.cit.

[33] Ibid.

[34] Ibid.

[35] Vaidyanathan, R., 'Capital Formation and P&P Sector—The Inconsistencies and Adjustments', op.cit.

[36] Vaidyanathan, R., 'Stock Market: Barometer of Economy?', *The Hindu Business Line,* March 24, 2005.

[37] Durkheim, Emile, *The Division of Labor in Society,* The Free Press, New York, 1997, p. liv.

[38] Fukuyama, Francis, *Trust,* Free Press Paperbacks, New York, 1996, p. 10.

[39] Swaminathan S. Aiyar, 'Social Capital—An Idea Whose Time Has Come', *The Times of India,* May 28, 2000.

[40] Swaminathan S. Aiyar, 'Harness the Caste System', *The Times of India,* June 4, 2000.

[41] Gurucharan, Das, *India Unbound—From Independence to the Global Information Age,* Penguin Books, New Delhi, 2002, p. 150.

[42] Gurucharan, Das, *Seminar,* 482, October 1999.

[43] Kanagasabapathi, P., 'A Study of *Pattinavar* Community', unpublished report, Swadeshi Academic Council, Coimbatore, 2005.

[44] *McKinsey Special Edition*, 2005, op.cit., p. 105.

[45] Kanagasabapathi, P., *A Study on Unorganized Finance Sector in India,* Swadeshi Academic Council, Coimbatore, 2002.

[46] Basham, A.L., op.cit., p. 190.

[47] Rangarajan, L.N., *Kautilya—The Arthashastra,* Penguin Books, New Delhi, 1992, p. 336.

[48] Kanagasabapathi, P. and Ramanathan, A.R., 'A Study on Butter and Ghee Industry in Kangayam with special reference

to Sozhiya Chetty community', unpublished report, P.S.G. Institute of Management, Coimbatore, March 2006.

[49] Fukuyama, op.cit., p. 10.

[50] Ibid., p. 51.

[51] Ibid., p. 11.

[52] *OECD Fact Book 2011,* 'Economic, Environmental and Social Statistics—Macro Economic Trends', Organization for Economic Cooperation and Development. www.oecd.org.

[53] Fukuyama, op.cit., pp. 4–5.

[54] *The State of Human Development, United National Development Report 1998*, p. 37. http://hdr.undp.org.

[55] *Human Development Report 2005*, Oxford University Press, New Delhi, p. 4.

[56] Hamilton, Clive, *Growth Fetish*, South Asian ed., Allen and Unwin, Australia, 2004, p. 30.

[57] Krugman, Paul, 'Debt and Denial', *The Hindu,* February 14, 2006, p. 11.

[58] 'The State of the Nation Report—Indebtedness', Social Justice Policy Group, London, December 2006, p. 11. www.povertydebate.com.

[59] 'Spend, Spend, Spend', *The Economist,* August 31, 2001.

[60] Fukuyama, op.cit., p. 357.

[61] 'Breakdown Britain—Interim Report on the State of the Nation', Social Justice Policy Group, London, December 2006, p. 33. www.povertydebate.com.

[62] Soros, George, *Open Society—Reforming Global Capitalism*, 1st Indian ed., Viva Books Private Limited, New Delhi, 2004, p. 6.

[63] Hamilton, Clive, op.cit., p. 3.

[64] 'Unemployment Rates: Total', *OECD Fact Book 2011.*

[65] Dew-Becker, Ian and Gordon, J. Robert, 'Where Did the Productivity Growth Go?—Inflation Dynamics and the Distribution of Income', *National Bureau of Economic* Research, Working Paper No. 11842, December 2005. www.nber.org

[66] Krugman, Paul, *The Hindu,* May 2, 2006, p. 9.

[67] *Human Development Report 2005*, op.cit., p. 131.

[68] Ibid.

[69] Ibid., p. 34.

5

Types of Business Models

Business is the most important component of the economy. It is crucial to the survival and growth of economies. Are business models in different countries the same? Or are they different? While writing on the Japanese and American corporations, Fukuyama[1] notes: "The Japanese corporation is frequently described as family-like. The assertion that "a good foreman looks at his workers as a father does his children," usually elicits strong assent in Japanese opinion surveys. The Japanese are more likely than Americans to say their work supervisor "looks after you personally in matters not connected with work," by eighty-seven to fifty per cent. In fact, the moral bonds that arise among employees at a company frequently take precedence over their actual families. Quite typically, workers voluntarily attend company-sponsored weekend retreats rather than spend the time with their family, or they go out in the evenings drinking with work associates rather than stay at home with their wife and children. Their willingness to sacrifice the interests of the family for the sake of the firm is taken as a sign of loyalty; reluctance to do so would be seen as a moral failing. And as in a real family, it is very hard to opt out of the relationship: if one's corporate 'father' is seen as too overbearing, one usually does not have the option of disowning him by quitting and working somewhere else." Why is this difference? Is this due to differences between the West and the East? Let us see the background of the western and the eastern business models to get an idea. Later, we will see whether the business models are universal or not.

5.1 WESTERN BUSINESS MODELS

Business models are shaped and influenced by the economic systems. While the capitalistic system allows the entrepreneurs to choose the type of models that suit them, the state directs and dominates the business in the communist system. Within these two broad economic systems, there seems to be different kinds of business models. For example, if we take the capitalist economies of the triad group (comprising the US, Japan and the EU), we observe many differences in their business models. All the countries in the group follow capitalistic ideology. Yet the business models in many of these countries are different.

America is a nation where individualism and aggressive business manners dominate. In the traditional Japanese systems, a consensual family style of management remained the preferred model. In Japan, individualism and aggressiveness are generally not tolerated beyond a limit. People who showed self-assertive tendencies were described as *aku ga tsuyoi* (ah-kuu gah t'sue-yoe-ee), or people who are strong, or even harsh, in tastes. Such difference are not just because these countries belong to different continents in which people of different cultural and social backgrounds live. There are differences even between the models of the US and European Union, though people who share a common cultural background live in both these geographical areas. It is important to note here that even within the EU, where only the borders divide nations, the business models differ. This shows that business models are not based on economic systems alone, but are rather influenced by other factors too.

5.2 EASTERN BUSINESS MODELS

The eastern business models seem to be different from that of the western models. For example, the two richest countries of the world, the US and Japan, have distinct approaches in their business models, though both of them practise capitalist ideology. It is important to note here that both these economies have achieved supremacy by following different business models. Even among the countries in the East, we see differences in business models, although there are similarities between many of them in different respects. The Japanese-American author Fukuyama has shown that cultural differences between countries influence business models. Writing on China and Japan, Fukuyama[2] notes: "A further element of Japanese culture that permitted an added element of flexibility in business relationships, was the long-standing Japanese tradition that actual power holders do not have to correspond to the nominal power holders. This again constitutes a major point of difference between Japanese and Chinese culture. In Japan, frequently the real holder of power is an anonymous person behind the scenes, who is content to exercise rule indirectly."

Fukuyama presents that even the position of families in different countries influences business systems. Though both China and Japan are family-oriented societies, the position of families in these two countries is different. Hence their corporate models vary. Fukuyama[3] notes: "While Japanese firms are frequently said to be "family-like," Chinese companies are literally families. The Japanese corporation has an authority structure and sense of moral obligation among its members that is similar to what prevails in a family, but it also has elements of voluntarism, unconstrained by kinship considerations that make it much more like a western voluntary association than like a Chinese family or lineage. The very different position of the family in Japanese society when compared to China was reinforced by Japanese Confucianism as well."

There seems to be many differences in business practices among eastern countries in different functional areas. Table 5.1 presents the authority and control systems in Japan, Korea and Taiwan[4].

Table 5.1 Authority and Control Systems in Japan, Korea and Taiwan

S. No.	Characteristics	Kaisa	Chaebol	Jia
1.	Owner's personal authority	Low	High	High
2.	Family managers	Few	Many	Many
3.	Centralisation	Medium	High	High
4.	Middle manager's empowerment	High	Average	Low
5.	Formal hierarchy	High	Medium	Low
6.	Team autonomy	High	Low	Limited
7.	Group morale	High	Low	Low
8.	Omniscient boss	Low	High	High
9.	Managerial style	Facilitative	Authoritarian	Paternalistic

Note: Kaisa, Chaebol and Jia are the business organizations in Japan, Korea and Taiwan respectively.

Source: Negendhi, A.R., 'Management and Economic Development' quoted in Shirur, Srinivas, 2005, pp. 33–34.

Table 5.1 shows that there are many differences in the business systems of Japan, Korea and Taiwan. In the eastern world, the Indian businesses have unique systems and special features that are discussed in the following chapters.

5.3 UNIVERSALITY OF MODELS

A brief introduction to the business models of the western and eastern countries shows that there does not seem to be a uniform model in all the countries. There are differences in business models between the eastern and the western nations; there are also differences within the West and the East. Similarly, irrespective of the economic ideologies, there are differences among nations practising a particular ideology. For example, the capitalistic America does not have the same business model followed in the capitalistic France. Similarly, the communist China does not prefer the same business model as practised in communist Cuba.

Analysts present that even the global corporations do not follow uniform global models. Rugman[5] notes: "Everyone thinks of McDonalds, Coca Cola, and IBM as global players and then assumes that they have global strategies. Yet each of these three firms has been careful to avoid a simplistic global strategy and takes pains to understand its local markets. Their top management teams are not global, but either home- or host-country based. McDonalds is a global brand name, but its products are not homogeneous. In India, there are vegetarian instead of beef burgers. In Asia, there are spicier foods than in North America. In Russia, McDonalds had to reconstruct the entire supply chain to provide inputs of good enough quality. Its managers are local and, indeed, follow a generalized fast-food production formula. But they are essentially operating as independent franchises, paying percentage royalties with a great degree of independence as to how they operate the business."

Fukuyama[6] notes that stable families, strong communities and mutual trust also influence businesses. To quote: "Small businesses in American inner cities are seldom owned by African-Americans; they tend to be controlled by other ethnic groups, like the Jews earlier in this century and Koreans today. One reason is an absence of strong community and mutual trust among the contemporary African-American 'underclass'. Korean businesses are organized around stable families and benefit from rotating credit associations within the broader ethnic community; inner-city African-American families are weak and credit associations virtually non-existent."

The developments in the past few years indicate that even the religious beliefs and teachings influence the business models. For example, Permal, the $10 billion US-based fund of hedge funds group, had launched the first *shariah*-compliant Islamic hedge fund in 2003[7]. Muslim investors do not invest in hedge funds because *shariah* law does not allow them in hedging or shorting portfolios. Hence, the *shariah*-compliant hedge fund was developed to use the '*salam sale*' contract to create a short position in the market. This is a technical contract by which the fund will profit from a fall in the shares without having to short the stock itself. *Global Financial Stability Report* had noted that "Islamic bonds have played an increasingly important role in Malaysia's financial market. Over the past 10 years, the issuance of Islamic bonds in Malaysia has been growing at a compound rate of 31 per cent, outgrowing the issuance of bonds in total, which were growing at the rate of 13 per cent over the same period[8]." The report continues: "Islamic bonds (*Sukuk*) must comply to the *Shariah* principles. The *Shariah* principles are Islamic laws and rules that govern religious, cultural, social, political, and economic aspects of Islamic societies. An important financial aspect of *Shariah* principles is the prohibition of interest (*riba*) on borrowing. Therefore, a fixed or predetermined rate of return is prohibited, whereas the earning of profits or returns from underlying assets is encouraged[9]." The issuers of Islamic bonds in Malaysia include the governments, government agencies, private corporations, International Bank for Reconstruction and Development and International Finance Corporation. Even in India, an investment company announced a portfolio scheme for the investors belonging to the *Jain* community a few years back. As the *Jainese* system advises against drinking and meat-eating, the scheme was designed to invest funds based on their beliefs. Dow Jones & Company announced the launch of 'Dharma Index' in 2008 to track the stocks of companies that observe the values of dharma-based religions such as Hinduism and Buddhism[10].

Thus, different factors seem to influence business models. Basically, business models evolve in different societies based on their economic systems. But, there are other factors such as cultural, social and community systems that play an important role in the making of business models. Even within a country where people from different backgrounds live, their attitudes and approaches to businesses differ. Hence, there could be differences in business models within countries with diverse backgrounds and beliefs. In India, where different communities and societies practise distinct cultural and social systems, there could be different business models. Studies in two major clusters in western Tamil Nadu revealed that even the circumstances and the practical requirements shape the business models. Sankagiri, engaged in transports and Thiruchengode engaged in rigs are separate clusters, well known throughout the country in their respective fields of operations. They are run by the people from the same backgrounds and they are close to each other, within a distance of about 20 kilometres. Yet the business organizations in both the centres are different[11]. While in Sankagiri the preferred form of organization is proprietorship, Thiruchengode has more partnership firms. Hence, the business models even within a region have variations. So the notion, that the business models across various countries in the world are uniform, does not seem to be correct.

REFERENCES

[1] Fukuyama, Francis, *Trust*, Free Press Paperbacks, New York, 1996, p. 189.

[2] Ibid., p. 181.

[3] Ibid.

[4] Negendhi, A.R., 'Management and Economic Development' quoted in Shirur, Srinivas, *Strategic Alternatives for Family Business Houses*, Deep and Deep Publications Pvt. Ltd., New Delhi, 2005, pp. 33–34.

[5] Rugman, Alan, *The End of Globalisation*, AMACOM, New York, 2001, p. 170.

[6] Fukuyama, Francis, op.cit., p. 10.

[7] Rigby, Elizabeth, *The Financial Times*, November, 17, 2003.

[8] International Monetary Fund, 'Islamic Bonds in Malaysia' in *Global Financial Stability Report—Market development and issues*, Washington, 2005, p. 126.

[9] Ibid.

[10] Daniel Burke, 'Dow Jones Unveils Dharma Index', Religion News Service, January 16, 2008. http://pewforum.org/news.

[11] Kanagasabapathi, P., and Arun Kumar, M.N., 'A Study on Namakkal Transport Industry', unpublished report, P.S.G. Institute of Management, Coimbatore, April 2006. Kanagasabapathi, P., and Arun Kumar, M.N., 'A Study on Sankagiri Transport Industry and Thiruchengode Rig Industry', unpublished report, P.S.G. Institute of Management, Coimbatore, April, 2005.

6

INDIAN BUSINESS MODELS

As we have seen earlier in Chapters 2–4, the Indian economic models are unique, shaped by long periods of experience and strong fundamentals. India is a land of diversities with people of different backgrounds influenced by different landscapes, climatic conditions and resources. The Indian system gives scope for people to lead lives in their own ways recognizing and respecting diversities. Against this background, the study of Indian business systems is expected to provide interesting insights into the evolution and functioning of business models. This chapter begins with a brief description of business in ancient India, proceeds to present an overview of business during the British period, and then outlines the course of business in independent India. Later, the presentation takes us to the structure and models of Indian business during the present period.

6.1 BUSINESS IN ANCIENT INDIA

As India is an ancient nation with a proud economic background, businesses must have existed and flourished since the earlier times. It is relevant to remember that India was well-known in the international business since the ancient times. Agarwala[1] writes: "Commerce played a great role in making India the universal exporting centre of the economic world in ancient times." He notes that there were commercial cities and trade centres dominated by the merchant class more than five thousand years ago. To quote: "Commercial cities like Harappa and Mohenjodaro were founded in the fourth and third millennium BC. Trade centres had also come up in western India in the fourth and third millennium BC resulting in the domination of Indian society by merchants; these commercial people were instrumental in bringing about the first mercantile revolution. India thus became a great exporting country[2]."

Apart from the individual and family-based businesses, different forms of organizations seemed to have functioned since the earlier times. Khanna[3] notes: "The earliest Indian writings do make references to organizational forms. The *Rig Veda* makes reference to the *pani* (akin to a partnership amongst traders for trade caravans) and the *Mahabharata* to the *sreni*." Evidences indicate that these forms of organizations were known to have existed at least about 2800 years ago. Based on sources, Khanna[4] writes: "... if one uses the most recent dating for the earliest written materials (1500 BC to 1000 BC) then by 1000 BC to 800 BC the *sreni* and *pani* were known to Indians." He notes further that 'the *sreni* predates the earliest Roman prototype corporations by centuries' and it is 'considerably more complex and detailed than the Roman entities'[5].

It is important to note that the ancient *sreni* and the modern corporate form of organization exhibit similarities, though they are separated by many centuries. Table 6.1 compares the select characteristics of the modern US corporate and the ancient Indian *sreni* forms of organizations.

Table 6.1 Comparison between the Modern US Corporate and the Ancient Indian *Sreni* Forms of Organizations

Characteristics	Modern US corporation	Ancient Indian *sreni*
Separate entity	Yes	Yes
Centralized management	Yes	Yes
Transferability of interest	Yes	Probably Yes
Limited liability	Yes (though recently)	Probably Not
Agent has power to bind entity?	Yes	Yes
Management elected?	Yes	Yes (though at times appears hereditary)
Can management be removed?	Yes	Yes
Liability insulation	Yes	Yes (less detailed than the US)
Formation is easy	Yes	Yes
Register with the state	Yes	Yes
State approval needed	Yes (though weak)	Yes
Entry is easy	Yes	Some conditions, but no caste bars
Sharing of assets and liabilities	Terms of agreement	Terms of agreement with additional rules
Exit is easy	Yes	Yes, but with obligations potentially
Board/Committee independence	Yes	Probably Yes
Other board qualifications	Yes	Yes (less detailed than the US)
Open debate in meetings and shareholder resolutions	Yes, with some limits	Yes, with some limits (but less than in the US)
Transparency is valuable and disclosure encouraged	Yes	Probably yes (less detailed than the US)

Source: Khanna Vikramaditya, S., The Economic History of Corporate Form in Ancient India, 1997, p. 26.

Table 6.1 shows that the ancient Indian *sreni* form of organization possessed characteristics similar to the modern US corporations. It only shows the capacity of ancient Indians to establish different types of enterprises suited to the growth of businesses much ahead of the times. Besides business, the corporate form of organization was used for other purposes also in the ancient days. "Not only was the corporate form used for business enterprises in Ancient India, but also for political and social purposes and went by variety of names—*gana, samgha, sabha, sreni* and others too[6]."

During the period of Indus Civilization from about 4000 BCE* to 1900 BCE, there was trade within and outside the country. Khanna mentions that even during this period, "... it does appear that some of the basic pre-conditions for the development of organizational forms were present....[7]." Around 700 BCE, two Indian religions, namely Buddhism and Jainism were founded. Different sources suggest that during this period, "the *sreni* were numerous, in varied fields, and indeed could be mobile from one place to another. The *sreni* were clearly important in the society as they were often invited for official state functions. They were also actively involved in trading, production (crafts), and rudimentary banking services by this time. Their importance is further highlighted by the fact that the *Bhandagarika* (an arbitrator for inter-*sreni* disputes) became established as a government official[8]." Later during the times of the Mauryan Empire, the state played an important role in regulating the economic activities and "the *sreni* were a large and growing sector of Indian life[9]."

The Gupta Empire roughly dating from 240 to 550 CE is referred to as "India's Golden Age." Efficient administration, scientific and technological developments and contacts of the rulers with the other countries helped the growth of the economy and resulted in a vibrant domestic and foreign trade during this period. "Some estimate that there were at least 150 *sreni* by this time[10]." It is reported that the written sources during this period provide detailed accounts of *sreni*, "... the importance and enforceability of *sreni dharma*, the mobility of the *sreni*, the multi-profession *sreni*, and the expansion of the *sreni* into various other aspects of life[11]." During the post-Gupta period, a number of kingdoms ruled parts of India for around 400 years, and there were wars resulting in the general decline of trade. Around 1000 CE, different parts of North India was subjected to Islamic invasions and about two centuries later South India was invaded. During that time onwards, there were frequent wars within the country to obtain control of different regions. As a result the business suffered and the *sreni* form of organization continued to weaken.

---

* BCE—Before Common Era.

Agarwala[12] notes that "During the period of Delhi Sultanate, which extended from the closing years of the twelfth century to the founding of the Mughal Empire in 1526, the economic activities in cities continued to flourish despite the decay of the ancient self-governing village assemblies. Ibn Battutah, during his travels from 1333 to 1346, found great cities with rich markets in the Upper Gangetic valley, in Malwa and Gujarat, in the Deccan and in Bengal as well as in the Malabar region in the extreme south. He found the ports of Quilon and Calicut in Malabar comparable with Alexandria in Egypt, Sudak in the Crimea and Zaytun in China in terms of their magnificence and the quantum of trade handled by them."

6.2 BUSINESS DURING THE BRITISH DOMINATION

At the time of the establishment of the English East India Company (EIC), Asia was dominating the world trade with India playing a leading role. Robins[13] writes: "When the London-based Company was established in 1600, Europe continued to live in the economic shadow of Asia, with England operating as one of its more marginal kingdoms. Spices and other luxury goods had been imported from Asia into Europe for thousands of years, carried across the Middle East. It was a trade dominated by local merchants, with Europeans in a dependent position at the end of the chain." In 1618, the English Company negotiated its first trade agreement with the Mughal Empire. The entry of the Company into India had resulted in violent changes in the business situation. Josiah Child who was elected as the Company governor (chairman) in 1681 "wanted the company to become a sovereign power in India, forcing the Mughal Empire to trade with it on terms of equality[14]." During 1686 to 1689, Child launched war with the Mughal Empire. This war proved to be the beginning of what has come to be known as the Anglo-Mughal wars.

From the beginning, the Company engaged in corrupt practices, and used different methods through which it extracted undue benefits. "The foundations for the Company's operations in Mughal India were laid out in the succession of imperial decrees (*firman*), which defined the company's privileges granted by the emperor. From the 1650s, the Company had won the ability to export goods from Hugli, the main port of Bengal, duty-free in return for an annual payment of ₹ 3000. But it was only in 1717 that the Company managed to win imperial backing for this position through the famous *firman* of Emperor Farrukhsiyar. As part of this decree, the Company's president at Calcutta was given unprecedented authority to issue passes (*dastaks*), which would then exempt shipments from paying duty. Like many multinationals operating today, the Company had been awarded a tax status that favoured it over local traders[15]."

The Company also used the merchant class in Bengal, the richest province of India, to fish in the troubled waters and later ditched them after their victory at Plassey in 1757. "In Bengal, all those merchant collaborators, without whose complicity the British victory at Plassey would have been impossible, lost their merchant privileges, and therefore, business powers, within barely a few years of the British success[16]." The possession of Bengal and the subsequent developments have made the Company the richest in the world. It is estimated that between 1757 and 1780, £38,400,000 worth of funds went for the Company in terms of goods transferred back to Britain on an unrequited basis[17]. In the following years after the Plassey victory, the Company used its position to control the foreign and internal trade in Bengal. As a result, there was a transformation of the character of Indian business as well within a few decades after this period. The businesses at different levels suffered as the British made inroads into the domestic markets. "The large urban merchants through whom the European companies previously used to procure Indian goods for their own countries and other markets now became the distributors of imported products brought in by the European, chiefly British, traders[18]."

The uprising against the Company rule in the form of First War of Independence in 1857 ultimately paved the way for its subsequent collapse. The British government nationalised it through the India Act of 1858, before it was dissolved in 1874. The course of Indian economy and business, and even the world economy, witnessed turbulent changes during the existence of the Company. As a result, this period witnessed the collapse of the centuries-old structure of Indian business systems leading to severe economic and social problems reversing the flow of wealth from West to the East. Robins[19] notes: "Colonial rule was certainly the outcome of the Company's adventurism in Asia. But it was the hunt for personal and corporate profit that had drawn the Company inexorably on. The results of this enduring dynamic were world-shattering. By the time of its demise, the Company had changed the course of economic history, reversing the centuries-old flow of wealth from West to East."

The colonial government that followed placed limits on the growth of business. There were many difficulties and the finance for business was scarce. Of the many private banks, only one was in

Indian hands. The Indian industrialists had to depend on conventional sources of finance such as family and community networks and indigenous bankers. During the last three decades of the nineteenth century, textile mills promoted by Indians as joint stock companies came into being in different parts of the country. But all other industries were controlled by the British. "Almost until the end of the nineteenth century, the only industry in which the Indian entrepreneurship had expressed itself was cotton textiles, where European presence was extremely limited. On the other hand, jute textiles, coal mining, steam shipping, inland navigation, and tea and coffee plantations remained almost European preserves[20]."

In the final decades of nineteenth century, chambers of commerce representing the native businesses at local levels came into being, as against those promoted exclusively by the westerners earlier. Subsequently, the rise of nationalistic aspirations combined with the need for economic independence brought forth the need for *Swadeshi* economic ideology. Tripathi and Jumani[21] note: "The growing sense of identity in Indian business interests, particularly the industrialists, and the rising nationalist tendencies in society as a whole provided a great deal of impetus to the idea of *swadeshi*-economic autonomy."

As a result, many new ventures in the manufacturing sector were promoted during the initial decades of the twentieth century, particularly in Bengal. Tata Iron and Steel Company was registered in 1907, with the entire capital being raised in India within three weeks of the issue of prospectus. This was after Dorabji Tata returned without success from London, where he had gone to raise funds in the market for his project.

Later World War I created new opportunities for businesses and as a result, more people became involved in setting up new enterprises. Consequently, the Indian business was becoming visible. Later industries started coming up during the inter-war period, but the industrial development was localized to a few cities and lopsided. The Indian business interests could not gain supremacy, however much they tried. Out of the 57 largest groups in 1939, only 19 were Indians[22]. The English companies were dominating the businesses in most of the sectors.

6.3 BUSINESS IN INDEPENDENT INDIA

India, at the time of independence, was predominantly an agricultural economy. Industry was known only to a few sections of the society. It was in this scenario that the new policies of free India witnessed the division of the industrial sector into two categories, namely the public sector and the private sector. Business historians note that these policy pronouncements did not create much difficulty in the minds of the Indian businessmen. "The obvious constraints for the free enterprise system, inherent in these policy pronouncements, did not cause much concern in the Indian business world[23]." Using the new-found opportunities, private industry started growing, displacing the British expatriates who were in a commanding position till 1947. Meanwhile, the 'license-permit *raj*' created difficulties for the growth of industry and business, while the number of foreign companies was declining during this period. But in spite of the difficulties, the growth continued with the entry of new groups of people into business. Tripathi and Jumani[24] capture the situation during those times: "Despite the growing tendency towards business splits and myriad restrictions on the functioning of the private sector, the Indian business class registered substantial expansion after independence. Not only did the number of persons opting for business as a profession increasingly go up, the new entrants into the profession came from a more varied background than was the case at the time of independence. Caste and conventional social divisions were already losing much of their hold on occupational choices even before independence. In free India, the process gained momentum, as prospects of economic gain and self-fulfilment became the principal determinants of the choice of career. All socio-cultural barriers against entry into business seem to have collapsed as attractive business opportunities unfolded themselves."

The changes in the outlook of the governments since the mid-1980s and the liberalization process initiated since the beginning of the 1990s, heralded new developments in the industrial and business scenario of the country. Knowledge-based industries threw up many successful businessmen from among the educated class, even while new entrepreneurs were emerging in different industries from ordinary backgrounds. Business was becoming global and many business centres were gaining attention at the international level. Companies began to recruit people with professional qualifications in large numbers. Many Indian businessmen started going outside the boundaries of the country to capitalize on the emerging opportunities. The new era witnessed the entry of an increasing number of foreign business interests in different sectors. While this situation created opportunities for new challenges and is making the 'India brand' known to the outside world, the domestic business sector has to face difficulties leading to decreasing opportunities for certain sections. As a result, the structure and models of the Indian business sector are witnessing changes.

6.4 BUSINESS MODELS DURING THE PRESENT PERIOD

The business models of the contemporary period are broadly discussed under three broad headings namely non-corporate sector, clusters and corporate sector.*

6.4.1 Non-corporate Sector

The non-corporate sector plays a crucial role in the Indian businesses. It is the single largest sector in the Indian economic and business systems. Here it is discussed under three broad headings, namely unorganized sector, small scale industries (SSI) sector, and micro, small and medium enterprises (MSME) sector.

Unorganized sector

There are millions of enterprises in the unorganized sector in India. Final results of the Economic Census 2005 reveal that there were 41.83 million establishments in the country with 100.90 million persons working in them. Table 6.2 presents the number of establishments in different states and union territories.

Table 6.2 State-wise Distribution of Establishments

Sl. No.	State name	No. of establishments
1	Jammu & Kashmir	324,908
2	Himachal Pradesh	267,773
3	Punjab	1,071,666
4	Chandigarh	64,805
5	Uttarakhand	325,157
6	Haryana	833,898
7	Delhi	757,743
8	Rajasthan	1,961,465
9	Uttar Pradesh	4,020,610
10	Bihar	1,224,652
11	Sikkim	19,362
12	Arunachal Pradesh	28,734
13	Nagaland	35,578
14	Manipur	104,732
15	Mizoram	47,730
16	Tripura	189,423

(Contd.)

* Generally the business sector could be discussed under two broad categories, namely the non-corporate and the corporate sectors. Since clusters play a pivotal role in the Indian businesses, they are discussed separately with findings based on field studies conducted in different business centres.

Table 6.2 State-wise Distribution of Establishments (Contd.)

Sl. No.	State name	No. of establishments
17	Meghalaya	83,207
18	Assam	983,693
19	West Bengal	4,204,740
20	Jharkhand	491,372
21	Orissa	1,830,298
22	Chhattisgarh	637,305
23	Madhya Pradesh	1,735,262
24	Gujarat	2,426,022
25	Daman & Diu	10,178
26	D. & N. Haveli	8,530
27	Maharashtra	4,225,312
28	Andhra Pradesh	3.996,982
29	Karnataka	2,538,874
30	Goa	73,515
31	Lakshadweep	3,182
32	Kerala	2,803,828
33	Tamil Nadu	4,433,391
34	Puduchery	49,574
35	A. & N. Islands	13,488
	All States	**41,826,989**

Source: *Economic Census 2005*, Government of India.

It is significant to note that each of the three states namely, Tamil Nadu, Maharashtra and West Bengal has more than 10 per cent of the total establishments in the country.

Table 6.3 presents the distribution details of these establishments by location and type.

The table shows that out of the total establishments, 25.54 million (61 per cent) were located in rural areas and the remaining 16.3 million (39 per cent) in urban areas. 35.75 million (85.5 per cent) establishments were engaged in non-agricultural activities while the remaining 6.08 million (14.5 per cent) were engaged in agricultural activities other than crop production and plantation. Thus, the agricultural and non-agricultural establishments were found to be in the ratio of around 1:6. About 64.4 per cent (26.9 million) establishments were own-account establishments without any hired worker. The remaining units numbering around 14.9 million constituted the establishments where at least one person worked almost on a regular basis. Of the total number of persons working in all these establishments, 52.07 million persons (51.6 per cent) were working in rural establishments and the rest in urban establishments. A further study of other Census details shows that about 89.99 million

Table 6.3 Distribution of Establishments by Location and Type–All India (Figures in absolute number)

Sl. No.	Type of establishment	Rural		Urban		Combined
		Number	%	Number	%	
(1)	(2)	(3)	(4)	(5)	(6)	(7)
1	**Establishments**					
	Agricultural	5,708,999 (22.36)	93.90	370,984 (2.28)	6.10	6,079,983 (14.54)
	Non-agricultural	19,827,067 (77.64)	55.46	15,919,939 (97.72)	44.54	35,747,006 (85.46)
	Total	25,536,066 (100.00)	61.05	16,290,923 (100.00)	38.95	41,826,989 (100.00)
2	**Own account establishments**					
	Agricultural	4,848,014 (26.77)	94.46	284,205 (3.22)	5.54	5,132,219 (19.05)
	Non-agricultural	13,262,173 (73.23)	60.81	8,545,656 (96.78)	39.19	21,807,829 (80.95)
	Total	18,110,187 (100.00)	67.22	8,829,861 (100.00)	32.78	26,940,048 (100.00)
3	**Establishments with hired workers**					
	Agricultural	860,985 (11.59)	90.84	86,779 (1.16)	9.16	947,764 (6.37)
	Non-agricultural	6,564,894 (88.41)	47.10	7,374,283 (98.84)	52.90	13,939,177 (93.63)
	Total	7,425,879 (100.00)	49.88	7,461,062 (100.00)	50.12	14,886,941 (100.00)
4	**Establishments with special characteristics**					
	Without premises	5,051,156 (19.78)	66.98	2,489,894 (15.28)	33.02	7,541,050 (18.03)
	Without power	20,137,203 (78.86)	63.44	11,607,406 (71.25)	36.56	31,744,609 (75.90)
	Perennial	23,650,226 (92.61)	59.71	15,960,315 (97.97)	40.29	39,610,541 (94.70)
	Under private ownership	23,774,245 (93.10)	60.02	15,835,792 (97.21)	39.98	39,610,037 (94.70)

Note: Figures in brackets show the percentage of establishments to all establishments in the respective areas.

Source: *Economic Census 2005*, Government of India.

workers were working in non-agricultural establishments, while around 10.9 million persons were working in agricultural establishments. Hired labour of around 54.38 million formed the major proportion (54 per cent) of the total employment. The number of establishments and the number of persons working in this sector shows that this sector plays a significant role in Indian businesses. It is important to note that the number of people working as hired labour in this sector is almost two times the number of people employed in both the government and organized private sectors.

These establishments have grown at the rate of 4.69 per cent per annum during 1998–2005. Among them the manufacturing sector was the largest employer providing employment to 25.5 million (25.25 per cent) persons. This was followed by 25.1 million persons (24.91 per cent) in retail trading and 9.2 million (9.13 per cent) in farming of animals. The average employment per establishment was 2.41 persons. The distribution of establishments by the size class of employment revealed that around 95 per cent of establishments were having 1 to 5 workers. The maximum growth rate of establishments during 1998–2005 was observed in the state of Mizoram followed by Tripura, Kerala and Tamil Nadu.

Small scale industries sector

Small scale industries play a significant role in the Indian business sector. The Ministry of Small Scale Industries of the Government of India has published its *Third Census of the Small Scale Industries* in 2004. The census relates to the reference year 2001–02. Apart from studying the registered SSI units, the ministry has for the first time conducted a sample survey of the unregistered SSI sector in about 19,278 villages/urban blocks. According to the survey, the SSI sector has 10.52 million units in both the registered and unregistered categories. Of this, rural units comprise 55 per cent[25]. About 42.26 per cent of the total units were small scale industries and the rest were small scale service and business enterprises. The share of ancillary units among small scale industries was at 2.98 per cent[26]. There were 44,25,587 tiny units among the SSIs[27]. The total fixed investment of this sector was ₹ 1,54,348 crores and the total gross output ₹ 2,82,269 crores. They were providing employment to 2,49,32,763 persons and there were 50,606 exporting units with exports worth ₹ 14,199 crores[28]. About 44 per cent of the units were in the services sector, followed by 40 per cent of the units in manufacturing and allied activities and 16 per cent of units in repairing and maintenance activities[29]. The service sector has emerged as the dominant component in the total SSI sector with a share of 44 per cent of the units[30]. It was found that the number of activities pursued in the SSI sector was 672[31]. The total number of products/services produced/rendered in this sector was 6003[32]. About 95.8 per cent of the units in the total SSI sector were found to be of the proprietary type of ownership. The number of women enterprises was 10,63,721 (10.11 per cent)[33]. Uttar Pradesh, Andhra Pradesh, Maharashtra, Madhya Pradesh and Tamil Nadu are the top five states having a total share of 47.22 per cent in terms of number of units[34]. Most of the units are run by the ordinary sections of people in our country. About 56.8 per cent of them are managed by the scheduled castes, scheduled tribes and other backward castes. The SSI sector seems to be the most egalitarian one, with opportunities for all sections of people. The contribution of the SSI sector businesses to production, employment and exports is very important in the Indian economy and business.

SSI sector has been continuously growing over the years and as the latest data reveals there were 29.81 million units in India giving employment to 69.54 million people during the year 2009–10. Table 6.4 provides the performance details of SSIs during 2005–06 to 2009–10[35].

Table 6.4 Performance of Small Scale Industries (2005–06 to 2009–10)

Item/Year	2005–06	2006–07	2007–08	2008–09	2009–10*
Units (million nos.)	12.34	26.10	27.28	28.52	29.81
Production (₹ crores)	4,97,842	7,09,398	7,90,759	8,80,805	9,82,919
Employment (million nos.)	29.49	59.46	62.63	65.94	69.54
Exports (₹ crores)	1,50,242	1,82,538	2,02,017	n.a	n.a

* Provisional n.a.: not available

Source: Ministry of Micro, Small and Medium Enterprises, Government of India quoted in the *Handbook of Statistics on the Indian Economy*, 2010–11, Reserve Bank of India, p. 89.

Micro, small and medium enterprises sector

During 2007, the Ministry of Small Scale Industries and the Ministry of Agro and Rural Industries at the central level were merged to form the Ministry of Micro, Small and Medium Enterprises (MSMEs). The Ministry is engaged in helping the state governments in the development of the MSME sector. The Ministry notes that the MSME sector plays an important role in the Indian economy contributing 8.72 per cent to the GDP during 2008–09. It elaborates the contribution of the sector further: "The micro, small and medium enterprises sector contributes significantly to the manufacturing output, employment and exports of the country. It is estimated that in terms of value, the sector accounts for about 45 per cent of the manufacturing output and 40 per cent of the total exports of the country. The sector is estimated to employ about 59 million persons in over 26 million units throughout the country. Further this sector has consistently registered a higher growth rate than the rest of the industrial sector. There are over 6000 products ranging from traditional to high tech items, which are being manufactured by the MSMEs in India. It is well known that the MSME sector provides the maximum opportunities for both self-employments and jobs after agriculture sector[35]." Table 6.5 presents the performance of the MSME sector from 2006–07 to 2009–10.

Table 6.5 MSMEs Performance: Units, Investments, Production, Employment and Exports

Year	Total MSMEs (lakh nos.)	Fixed Investments (₹, crore)	Production (₹, crore)	Employment (lakh persons)	Exports (₹, crore)
2006–07	261.01	5,00,578	7,09,398	594.61	1,82,538
2007–08#	272.79	5,58,190	7,90,759	626.34	2,02,017
2008–09#	285.16	6,21,753	8,80,805	659.35	—
2009–10#	298.08	6,93,835	9,82,919	695.38	—

Projected

Source: *Annual Report 2010–11*, Ministry of Micro, Small and Medium Enterprises, pp.15–16.

It is important to note that this sector has registered an average rate of growth of around 4.5 per cent during the recent three-year period, while the employment opportunities provided by it is increasing at the rate of about 5.3 per cent. The fourth All India Census of MSMEs conducted with the reference period 2006–07 reveals interesting information. The size of the registered MSME sector is estimated to have 15,63,974 units across the country. The proportion of micro, small and medium enterprises in the sector is 94.94 per cent, 4.89 per cent and 0.17 per cent, respectively. Manufacturing enterprises account for 67.10 per cent of the units in the sector, while the share of the service enterprises is 32.90 per cent. A little more than 45 per cent of the enterprises are functioning in the rural areas, while about 55 per cent are functioning from the urban areas[36].

Features of non-corporate sector businesses

Let us see the basic features of the non-corporate businesses briefly.

1. **Proprietary and partnership firms:** The non-corporate sector is dominated by the proprietorship units. Most of the units are proprietary in nature. In the unorganized sector, almost all the units are proprietary in nature, while the rest are partnership organizations. In the SSI segment, 1,00,84,250 (95.8 per cent) are proprietary, 2,02,852 (1.9 per cent) are partnership and 71,437 (0.68 per cent) are private companies. Cooperatives number 14,569 (0.14 per cent) and the rest numbering 1,48,082 (1.41 per cent) come under the 'Others' category. Here we see a predominant share of 95.8 per cent of the units functioning as the proprietary units. The next preferred form of organization is partnership firms with nearly 2 per cent share. Hence, 97.7 per cent of the total units in the SSI sector function as proprietary and partnership firms.

In case of the MSME sector, 90.81 per cent are proprietary enterprises, 4.01 per cent partnership, 2.78 per cent private companies, 0.54 per cent public limited companies, 0.30 per cent cooperatives and 2.30 per cent others.

2. **Self-made and least dependent on state and institutions:** Most of the business organizations are proprietary units. They are all promoted by the initiatives of enterprising people and are all self-made. A small segment of the units belong to the partnership category. In all these units the promoters take upon themselves the complete responsibility of all the activities. Hence, almost the entire non-corporate sector units are promoted by people through their own efforts.

In most of the cases, the promoters of these units are ordinary people. Many of them do not have much formal education. A majority of them are not exposed to outside situations. They do not depend on the state or state mechanisms for their businesses. Many of them, especially the ones that belong to the unregistered sector, do not even go to the banks and financial institutions for loans. They try to manage the funds themselves through close and local sources. They try to be very sincere in repayment of funds. In the SSI sector, the units with outstanding loans was only 4.55 per cent[37]. Even most of this is due to the difficulties these units face in the changed circumstances where they have to fight with the bigger and mechanized units, and a change in the market conditions. Their dependence on critical resources seems to be very less. When one looks at the source of power for these units, 40 per cent of them do not use power at all. While 46.8 per cent of the units use electricity, only 5.66 per cent use oil[38]. Even their consumption of electricity and oil is less.

3. **Generation of huge savings:** The non-corporate sector generates a high proportion of savings in the country. Vaidyanathan[39] estimated that "... around 40 per cent of the savings is attributable to the non-corporate sector . . ." Moreover, savings by the non-corporate sector has been increasing over the last few decades. On the importance of this sector to wealth creation, he notes: ". . . non-corporate sector is a significant wealth creator in our economy and also a major engine of growth in the 1990s."

Table 6.6 presents the rates of gross domestic savings in GDP and the share of the household sector in gross domestic savings for selected years from 1980–81 to 2009–10.

Table 6.6 Savings by the Household Sector (1980–81 to 2009–10)

	1980–81	1990–91	2000–01	2009–10
Percentage of gross domestic savings in GDP	18.5	22.8	23.7	33.7
Percentage of household sector savings in gross domestic savings	70	81	91	67

Note: Percentage calculations of the household sector savings in gross domestic savings are by the author.

Source: Percentage of Gross Domestic Savings in GDP from *Economic Survey 2010–11*, A-10.

Table 6.6 shows that the household sector has been consistently contributing a major part of the savings to the Indian economy. The contribution of the non-corporate sector to this should be significant. Non-corporate sector saves money through different methods, with many of them being indigenous. Chadha[40] notes that own savings play a vital role in rural industries even for adopting technological improvements. Own savings contribute 87.25 per cent of finance for new designs, 78.57 per cent for new products, 69.23 per cent for new raw materials and 51.56 per cent for improved machinery.

4. **Capital formation through own efforts:** The rates of savings and capital formation (investments) as a percentage of GDP during 2006–07 to 2009–10 are given in Table 6.7.

Table 6.7 Savings and Investments (2006–07 to 2009–10)

(as percentage of GDP at current market prices)

	2006–07	2007–08	2008–09#	2009–10*
Gross domestic savings	34.61	36.85	32.21	33.70
Gross capital formation (investments)	35.67	38.14	34.52	36.48
Savings-investment gap	–1.06	–1.29	–2.31	–2.78

#Provisional estimates *Quick estimates

Note: Savings-investment gap is the difference between the rate of savings and the rate of investment.

Source: Annual Report 2010–11, SEBI, p. 4.

In the case of the non-corporate sector, much of the capital is raised by the promoters through their own and local sources. Many of them go to the banks and financial institutions mainly for additional funds. Some of them, especially the smaller units, also access funds through different schemes promoted by the governments. The rates of capital formation by the family-based non-corporate enterprises have generally remained higher than the other sectors. Table 6.8 provides the sector-wise capital formation figures for the latest periods.

Table 6.8 Gross Domestic Capital Formation (2006–07 to 2009–10)

(as percentage of GDP at current market prices)

Item	2006–07	2007–08	2008–09#	2009–10*
Household sector	11.9	10.8	13.1	11.7
Public sector	8.3	8.9	9.5	9.2
Private corporate sector	14.5	17.3	11.5	13.2
Gross domestic capital formation	35.7	38.1	34.5	36.5

#Preliminary estimates *Quick estimates

Source: *Economic Survey* 2010–11, p. 8.

Table 6.8 shows that the household sector has been contributing a higher share to the capital formation, after the private corporate sector. The government remained generally a small saver since the late 1990s, though there are continuous improvements from 2003–04. The private corporate sector is able to contribute more to capital formation by accessing the savings of the household sector through banking institutions and capital markets. It is to be remembered that a substantial share of the household savings is taken away by the government and private corporate sectors for their capital formation. But even then, around one-third of the capital formation in the economy is due to the household sector, in spite of the share coming down during the last few years[41].

5. **Less investments, more benefits:** Generally, the non-corporate sector seems to give more benefits to the amount invested. For every one lakh rupees of investment, the SSI sector gives employment to 1.62 persons. In the case of unregistered SSI sector, it is even more with 3 persons[42]. *Economic Census 1998* notes that the unorganized sector enterprises employ an average of 2.35 workers each[43]. When we take fixed investment per unit, it is only ₹ 1.47 lakhs, while the gross output per unit is ₹ 2.68 lakhs[44]. Non-corporate sector units make the maximum use of the locally available resources and skills for their products and services. It is important to note that with all kinds of limitations, the non-corporate sector makes the optimum use of available resources. It is a remarkable achievement that the units in the SSI sector are engaged in a number of products and services exceeding 6000. Moreover, there were 50,606 units engaged in exports[45].

Experts argue that productivity ethics are much stronger in the unorganized sector than in the organized sectors. Chakraborty[46] notes: "... simple living is associated with non-centralized functioning; non-centralized functioning ensures small and autonomous work-groups; unity, cohesion and the sense of belonging are more natural to such groups; hence, in principle, they are more humanely productive. This is why we still observe the productivity ethic to be much stronger in the pristine and unorganized, rural and household sectors of India than in the upstart, organized urban sector."

6.4.2 Clusters

Clusters occupy a significant place in the non-corporate sector. They play a crucial role in the development of the Indian businesses. Their contribution to the national income, employment, exports and innovation is very significant. The United Nations Industrial Development Organization (UNIDO) had noted earlier that "In India, it is estimated that there are approximately 350 small scale industries clusters and around 2000 rural and artisan based clusters contributing to almost 60 per cent of the manufactured exports and 40 per cent of the employment in the manufacturing industry[47]."

The Ministry of Small Scale Industries, Government of India, has estimated that there are 2042 clusters, of which 1223 are in the registered sector in 26 states, and another 819 in the unregistered sector in 25 states/union territories[48]. These clusters cover 521 different products and have a share of 32.68 per cent and 37.85 per cent in the total estimated number of registered and unregistered units functioning in the country[49]. The estimated number of cluster-based enterprises in the registered SSI sector constitutes 32.68 per cent of the total, fixed investment 18.95 per cent, gross output 16.99 per cent and employment 27.66 per cent[50]. In the unregistered SSI sector, the share of clusters in the total number of units is 37.85 per cent, in fixed investments 22.45 per cent, in gross output 21.04 per cent and in employment 34.63 per cent[51]. There are totally 15,35,357 units in the clusters contributing to a gross output of ₹ 42,169 crores in the SSI sector. Uttar Pradesh has the largest number of clusters with a total of 288, with 3,08,266 registered and unregistered units[52]. There are certain clusters that are engaged in the same or similar activities throughout the country. For example, there are 155 furniture and fixture, wooden, NEC clusters with 100 or more units in 22 states from Jammu & Kashmir to Tamil Nadu and Gujarat to Mizoram with 36,166 units in the registered SSI sector alone[53].

Chief characteristics of clusters

Clusters have unique characteristics that have to be comprehended in order to get an idea of their system and functioning.

1. **Promoted and run by ordinary persons:** Almost all of these clusters are promoted and developed by the so-called ordinary persons of India. The initial units in all these clusters were promoted by one or more entrepreneurial people. Later, the number of units grew due to the influence of the promoters of the earlier units and the success of the initial ventures. With the promotion of more and more units, clusters were established. Almost all the promoters in most of the clusters are ordinary local people with less or least formal education and lesser amount of funds required for investments. For example, in the Sankagiri* transport cluster of Tamil Nadu with the second largest lorry traffic in the country, 90 per cent of as truck-owners had entered the transport business either as drivers or as cleaners[54]. The present position of the cluster is entirely due to the efforts of these ordinary people. A study of the ancillary units engaged in eight different activities supporting the knitwear industry of Tirupur showed that 92 per cent of the entrepreneurs are from agricultural backgrounds[55]. Among the exporters of Karur, 73 per cent were found to be directly from agricultural backgrounds, while a sizable share of the remaining were engaged in small businesses along with agriculture[56].

(a) *Ordinary villagers create employment to foreigners in their lands:* Though it may be surprising, many of these people from ordinary backgrounds dominate the international trade and some of them create employment opportunities for foreigners in their lands. The following lines explain the role of Gujaratis from ordinary backgrounds doing successful business in foreign countries. "For Indian diamond merchants, many of whom are the descendants of farmers from Palanpur and Kathiawar in Gujarat, the whole world has become their beat. The diamond-paved city of Antwerp is a second home to them, as is the bustling diamond district of New York. Hong Kong, China, Vietnam, Russia, Sri Lanka and Canada are all extensions of their factories and workplaces and their glittering crafts are found in retail emporia around the world. In order to support this industry, the *Palanpuries* and few of the *Patel* community had to ensure a constant flow of rough diamonds. They chose to migrate to Antwerp, as it was the world capital for the rough trade. In the last four decades slowly and gradually they have grown to a group of nearly 300 families who form one of the highly respected immigrants to reside in Belgium. They are the most

* Sankagiri is also spelt as Sankari in English.

affluent society. Most of them are self-employed, and have in the recent years created local employment by employing secretaries, accountants, as sorters, and supported auxiliary industries[57]." True to the Indian traditions of basic humility, many of them consider themselves as only ordinary people, even after achieving success in the national and international markets.

(b) *From ordinary peasants to exporters:* In this connection it may be useful to note as to how people from the poorer peasant classes have become successful exporters in Tirupur, defying the conventional western theories. Chari[58] writes on this: "... What is most important about the agrarian question in the environs of Tirupur is that it does not conform to the notion that diversifying rich peasants are the most likely "carrier class" of agrarian transition and industrialization in India. The *Gounder* peasantry of western Tamil Nadu has taken a non-linear route in that it was undergoing a process of class differentiation throughout the first half of the twentieth century, and it was certain young men from the poorer end of this differentiating peasantry who would become Tiruppur's fraternal capital. What is to be made of this anomaly to orthodox Marxist expectations?"

2. **Less of formal education, more of practical knowledge:** Most of the entrepreneurs who promoted these clusters and emerged highly successful, have little or less formal education. Chari notes that among the Tirupur exporters from the *Gounder* community, who were earlier workers, the level of education for 25 per cent of them is primary or less than that, while 66 per cent of them have secondary education or even less. Among the domestic players, belonging to *Gounder* ex-worker category, 42 per cent of them are educated up to middle level or even less, while 76 per cent have secondary education or less[59]. A study conducted among a sample of 35 diamond exporters from Surat and Ahmedabad revealed that only two of them have completed more than higher secondary school level of education. It also showed that while 40 per cent of them have less than fifth standard education, 26 per cent of them are uneducated[60]. In a study of the printing industry in Sivakasi, a majority of the entrepreneurs have expressed that it was only experience and not education that had helped them in their business[61]. Seventy-three per cent of the rig-owners of Thiruchengode revealed that lack of formal education was not a hindrance to them in their business[62]. It is surprising to hear these words from highly successful people who have businesses

across the country in various states. It only shows their entrepreneurship and confidence to manage their businesses. Rajkot entrepreneurs who make superior engineering products claimed that hardly 10 per cent of them have even a minimum level of formal education*. It was learnt that the shop floor was their training institutes. In fact, the real educational institutions for the cluster entrepreneurs seem to be their places of work.

Illiterates and less educated as innovators: Empirical and research studies in a number of naturally evolved clusters in different states show that in spite of the level of formal education being less or low, the entrepreneurs exhibit enormous common sense and business acumen, and have acquired a lot of technical and management skills over the years. Of those who won awards from the National Innovation Foundation, set up by the Department of Science and Technology of the Government of India in 2003, 30 per cent were not even fully literate[63]. Due to the high level of skills that the entrepreneurs possess, they have acquired the capacity to succeed not only in the local and domestic markets, but also in the highly competitive western markets dominated by multinational companies run by professionals with degrees from the much demanded business schools.

3. **Superior levels of entrepreneurship:** The clusters are dominated by people who have a very high level of entrepreneurship. The traditional notion that one should do something on one's own to progress in life motivates people to enter and take up new ventures. India, being a relationship-based society, enables people to watch their own relatives and friends doing business and try to emulate them. The traditional saving habits, hard-working nature and close relationships motivate them to enter new ventures. The failure of agriculture in different regions across the country over the years and the resultant need to maintain and increase the status seemed to have accelerated the entrepreneurial process in many clusters. As a result, every year witnesses the arrival of new entrepreneurs in many of these clusters; so much so that one tends to feel that entrepreneurship has become a natural habit of these people in clusters.

Nothing is difficult for these entrepreneurs as they create opportunities out of impossibilities. The people of Saurashtra, for example, severely affected by drought, moved out to cities like Surat, in search of jobs and many have landed themselves in the diamond industry. Today they have ended up dominating it. It is

* Harishbhai Joshi, Rajkot, interview, 26.12.2006.

mainly due to their efforts that we have attained a distinguished position in the world market, for more than 90 per cent of the total diamonds polished in the world goes out of India. Similarly, many successful clusters in different states such as Jamnagar, Sivakasi, Tirupur and Namakkal were developed by those people who were badly affected due to the large scale failure of agriculture in these areas. Presently, these are the dominant clusters in their areas of operations in India. The background of the transport owners in Sankagiri is striking. Ninety per cent of them come from agriculture-dependent families. Of these, 20 per cent of them were earlier engaged in cattle breeding[64]. Through hard work and dedication, they have transformed Sankagiri into a vibrant business centre. Today they own the largest number of *Taurus* vehicles in the country, apart from owning other types of vehicles. As a result, more than 70 per cent of the Sankagiri population is presently engaged in activities related to transports. The same is the story in many of the clusters across the country.

(a) *Entrepreneurs build clusters:* Morvi in the state of Gujarat, well-known for wall clocks, is a town brimming with diverse activities such as manufacture of sanitary-ware, ceramic tiles, telephone instruments, calculators and diamond-cutting. There were more than 300 units engaged in the manufacture of wall clocks and ancillaries; about 150 ceramic factories; about 200 clay tile factories; about 90 sanitary-ware units; more than 1000 diamond-cutting units; 3 units for making telephone instruments and 2 units engaged in making calculators.* It was estimated earlier that about two lakh wall clocks were being made everyday in this town, the highest number in Asia. The well-known brands such as *Ajanta* and *Samay* are the biggest players. *Samay* has the most modern manufacturing unit in Morvi. Besides wall clocks, they also make computers and time-pieces. The Chairman of *Samay* U. Patel proudly noted that it all started by reverse engineering when one Patel had earlier dismantled a foreign wall clock and reassembled it.† What surprises everyone is that this town was destroyed by the floods in the *Macchu* river in 1979. As a result, 1200 persons had lost their lives and crores worth of property was lost. The town was, however, rebuilt entirely by the community through their superior levels of entrepreneurship. Today Morvi is known throughout the country and abroad for their products.

---

*Jaswani, P.A. to MLA, Morvi, interview, 28th December 2002.

† U. Patel, Chairman, Samay, interview, 26th December, 2002.

The people of these clusters, in spite of severe handicaps and innumerable difficulties, have exhibited an extraordinary amount of entrepreneurship and in the process, have made themselves and the nation richer. In the case of Jamnagar brassware cluster, people could not continue with agriculture as the water became salty, due to their proximity to the sea. As a result they promoted brass units by importing 90 per cent of the raw material from outside the country. India Brand Equity Foundation has noted that 'hinterland India' is the real source of entrepreneurship[65]. Without any help or support, these people—majority of whom come from very ordinary backgrounds—have emerged as successful entrepreneurs. Most of them did not have a strong background and many of them did not have sufficient funds and yet, they have become highly successful.

(b) *Entrepreneurship is dynamic, not restricted to one business:* It was noticed in a number of clusters such as Rajkot, Coimbatore, Sivakasi and Thiruchengode that the entrepreneurs initially started with one activity and later diversified into different areas, sometimes even unrelated ones. Today, Rajkot makes all kinds of engineering products. Coimbatore is known for foundries, pump manufacturing, auto ancillaries, textiles and wet grinders. It is also emerging in other areas such as Information Technology and related services, education, packaging and medical services. The seeds for the industrial developments were originally sown when there was a need for foundry items from the then British-promoted textile mills.* Today, Coimbatore leads the country in pump manufacturing. Sivakasi initially started with match industry. Later, it diversified into fireworks and then printing, which was a forward integration. Thiruchengode started with rigs, and then it moved onto powerlooms and is now involved in different activities such as textile mills and paper manufacturing.

4. **Relationship-based business and faith-based transactions:** India is a relationship-based society. From time immemorial, Indians were taught to treat even the strangers as their own brothers and sisters. As a result, different sections of people from a wide variety of backgrounds live in the society with mutual respect towards each other. Hence, a superior sense of fraternity exists in

---

* Gandhikumar, ex-president, CODISSIA, Coimbatore, interview, 31st August 2006.

the whole society. Clusters being comparatively smaller places with known faces and frequent interactions, relationships become almost natural and easy. In such an atmosphere, most of the transactions take place on the basis of faith. Faith-based transactions find an important place in all businesses, including the high risk finance. In a study of non-corporate finance sector in Karur, it was found that almost the entire financial transactions revolved around goodwill and faith. In fact, the loans were given only on the recommendations of relatives, friends and business contacts[66].

Most of the clusters are dominated by one or more communities. The enterprising community or communities that live in and around the clusters, naturally dominate the cluster, as entrepreneurship itself is to a great extent influenced by the communities. With the result, we see clusters dominated by a specific community or a few communities. While we see the Jamnagar brassware industry in Gujarat dominated by *Patels*, we notice the Sivakasi fireworks industry in Tamil Nadu dominated by *Nadars*. This community relationship extends beyond the narrow limits of specific cluster areas and reaches out to other areas in a state and other states in the country and even to other countries. For example, *Patels* are engaged in the diamond industry in different centres of Gujarat and abroad. The *Nadars* are engaged in retail trade across the entire Tamil Nadu and control a major share of retail trade in the state. They are also found in a few important cities of India, where a sizeable section of Tamil population live. Close community relationships, in this way, play a major role in clusters.

Relationships with all—extending beyond narrow community limits: But the relationships are not restricted to the communities that dominate the clusters. In all these clusters, relationships naturally extend beyond specific communities to all sections of people. Due to this basic characteristic of the society, the businesses get organized on the basis of relationships. A close-knit relationship exists among people of all communities, irrespective of their caste, region and religion. There are businessmen from all parts of the country in the Tirupur cluster today. In many of the clusters, there are *Marwari* businessmen doing business with people of all backgrounds. A study on the Dindigul leather cluster in Tamil Nadu showed a close relationship among entrepreneurs belonging to the three major religious communities in India[67]. It was observed that in the Ramanagara silk industry in Karnataka, once the biggest cocoon market in Asia, intimate personal and business relationships exist among people belonging to the two major religious communities. Moreover, most of these clusters possess higher norms that are strictly followed irrespective of personal relationships. While writing on the Kanpur saddlery cluster, Dwivedi[68] quotes: "Norms function in the cluster irrespective of the personal relationship that entrepreneurs have with each other and have an implication in providing stability to the entire cluster. We reported earlier that there are no legal contracts held among businessmen in this cluster. This practice seems to be based on normative behaviour rather than a matter of having personal experience with the other party. Even in case of new ties, a contract is not demanded because it is simply not considered a way to do business."

5. **Built on self-endeavour and not state dependent:** Almost all these clusters are built by the entrepreneurs themselves through their own initiatives and efforts. Generally, a venture that begins with the enterprise and initiative of one or two entrepreneurs, spearheads the formation of clusters. Sivakasi was a dry area about 90 years back. All the crops failed then. Two enterprising visionaries Ayya Nadar and Shanmuga Nadar, people from very ordinary backgrounds, decided to initiate new ventures and promoted the first match unit in 1923. To achieve their objective, they went to Calcutta (now Kolkata), to learn the trade of making matches, on the encouragement and financial support provided by Chinna Nadar of Trichy.* As a result, Sivakasi contributed 80 per cent of India's safety matches, 90 per cent of fireworks and 60 per cent of offset printing solutions[69]. Its printing industry, which was initially started to cater to the needs of the local match and firework industries, has grown to such an extent that even cheque books of foreign countries are printed there[70]. Thus, in every place, what was begun by just one or two entrepreneurs who ventured into an industry have now become clusters. Many of these clusters have become important at the national and international levels.

(a) *Clusters are spontaneous initiatives of the local entrepreneurs:* In almost all the clusters, the government investment was either negligible or completely nil, especially in the beginning. In many of these places there was not even an initiative by the government for initial support. Almost all the clusters were developed by the local entrepreneurs, largely without the support of the state or state mechanisms. In this connection, it would be appropriate to mention that the United Nations Industrial Development Organization (UNIDO) had observed that most of the clusters in India were

* S.A.P. Arumugaselvan, Kaliswari Fireworks, Sivakasi, interview, 10th August, 2006.

developed by the entrepreneurs through their own initiatives. In the words of Chadha[71]: "A recent UNIDO survey of 138 industrial clusters in India shows that only 13 of these clusters were induced by government policy while the remaining 125 grew spontaneously at the initiative of entrepreneurs themselves." It was observed that many of the few initiatives promoted by the governments did not succeed. Quoting the National Council of Applied Economic Research Survey, the report of the expert committee on small entreprises has noted that "industrial estates developed by the government suffer the consequences of ignoring the overriding importance of agglomeration economies in inducing investment by small and medium scale enterprises[72]."

(b) *Clusters step in, where states fail:* Once the clusters develop, the entrepreneurs establish schools, colleges and other common facilities such as marriage-halls required for their community. In almost all the clusters, one could notice educational institutions established by the local communities. As a result, clusters develop into full-fledged centres. People from these clusters create almost all the facilities they require through their own efforts; they do not wait for the state or depend on it to fulfil their needs. Just a few years back, the two major industrial cities of western Tamil Nadu, namely Coimbatore and Tirupur, saw the local societies, led by the industrial and business community, promoting NGOs to develop their cities. *Siruthuli* in Coimbatore is concentrating its efforts on preserving water resources, while *Valam* of Tirupur is engaged in public infrastructure development. Within a limited period of time, both of them took up and completed projects which were very important for the society, but remained neglected by the governments for a long time. There are different types of innovative initiatives at the individual levels to improve the facilities in clusters. For example, a successful businessman in Tirupur, A.M. Karthikeyan, constructs houses with his own funds for employees in the highly crammed city of Tirupur. This helps employees from outside the area, many of whom come from distant places, to own a house in the high cost city. The employees are given facilities to repay the cost of the house over a period of years in installments.

6. **Generation of savings and mobilization of funds from close and local sources:** Generation of savings is a part of life in India. The savings get mobilized through different methods and are

channelized to form part of the initial capital and the working capital for different ventures in clusters. Savings are usually in the range of a high order in many clusters. Chari[73] notes that the exporters from the *Gounder* ex-worker category in Tirupur could save up to 85 per cent, while the domestic manufacturers from three different backgrounds had saved between 45 per cent and 52 per cent. Apart from the entrepreneurs concerned, savings of the family plays an important role in businesses. Chari notes that family sources and savings from prior earnings are the major sources of initial capital in Tirupur. He also shows that the sources of capital were the most diversified, spanning farm, family and non-farm work, and to a lesser extent from chit funds, marriage dowries, and land sales. Studies in different clusters in Tamil Nadu and Gujarat confirm that savings and family sources are the most important sources of capital. It was noticed in Surat and Ahmedabad, that almost 46 per cent of the diamond exporters received more than 30 per cent of their initial capital from relatives[74].

It was observed in western Tamil Nadu that the ladies of families from agricultural backgrounds, save money out of their own land-based and home-based activities, and contribute to the promotion of businesses. Studies show that even dowry has played an important role as a source of capital for businesses in some centres in western Tamil Nadu. In the Sankagiri transport cluster, it was observed that even for working capital, only 3 per cent of the owners sourced funds from banks[75]. The rest of the businessmen managed their funds through different sources*. In many clusters, local finance plays an important role as a source of funds, especially for subsequent needs and working capital. A study of Karur showed that out of the estimated funds of ₹ 2400 crores required for the local industry in 2001, the local financiers supplied two-thirds of the funds, even though there were more than fifty branches of banks including the headquarters of two nationalized banks[76]. There are a number of native arrangements and mechanisms that help people mobilize funds. In the context of Tirupur, it was noted: "A large and diverse market in private and informal credit exists to make the whole production a complex function. Non-bank sources of credit in Tirupur include private finance companies, rotating credit unions called chit funds, moneylenders, and forms of mutual assistance between friends, family or kin[77]."

No foreign investments, all local savings: As a result, the dependence of businessmen on banking institutions and formal

* The sample for this study consisted of 30 truck owners.

sources is very less, especially at the initial stages. An important point to be noted here is, that the funds coming as investments are mostly savings and surplus from agricultural sector and other informal activities. In none of these clusters, there is a foreign investment. All these clusters have grown only due to domestic investments, most of them generated locally around them. The entrepreneurs of these clusters have proved that they can grow very fast with local capital to emerge as successful players at the national and international levels, and hence, the argument of foreign capital is totally not applicable to them.

7. **High levels of cooperation and competition:** Due to the close relationships that exist in clusters, there is a good level of understanding and cooperation among businessmen. In many cases, this cooperation extends beyond business and reaches out to the families. Due to this cooperation, business becomes easy and grows faster. In the non-corporate finance business in Karur, financiers usually exchange details related to the creditworthiness of the borrowers.* Thus, a borrower with unsatisfactory credentials, would find it almost impossible to borrow from any financier in the locality, as information regarding his poor financial record would be shared amongst all financiers. Such valuable information prevents the other financiers from risking their funds. What is to be noted here is, that information regarding the potential defaulter is shared not only among associates, but also with the competitors to caution them against possible defaults. Generally, cooperation extends beyond close circles and embraces others in the cluster, crossing all borders of relationships. In all the clusters, a higher number of businessmen have noted a better level of understanding and cooperation among their peers irrespective of their community and backgrounds.

Cooperation co-exists with competition. The urge to compete is developed by looking at others who perform well. Generally, people tend to relate themselves to those whom they know better, such as relatives, peers and friends. This kind of identity motivates people in the same group to work harder and achieve greater successes. This is a 'creative competition' as it results in increase in production, new initiatives and increased profits. This creative competition exists in almost all clusters, resulting in the increase of business activities. But at the same time, it was noted in different instances, that competition does not generally prevent businessmen from cooperating with each other as all of them know that mutual understanding and help are necessary to run the business smoothly.

* Sivasamy, Karur, interview, 30th July, 2002.

8. **Improvements and innovation:** Many of the clusters are the breeding grounds for continuous improvements and are the laboratories for innovations. In fact, some of these clusters were born out of the creative genius of the ordinary Indians. The seeds for the Rajkot diesel industry were sown in the 1950s, when an ordinary *Patel* removed all the parts of an engine manufactured by a foreign company and successfully re-assembled it. Once the local entrepreneurs understood the mechanism, they made better engines at a cheaper cost. This compelled Leicester, the UK-based company, to approach the Rajkot manufacturers to make diesel engines in its brand name, to which, however, the locals refused. Many people entered the industry and over the years, Rajkot became the premier centre in the manufacture of diesel engines in Asia. There were about 65 diesel engine units in 2002, manufacturing around 1.5 lakh units annually, under well-known brand names such as *Standard Agro* and *Field Marshal*. The Rajkot entrepreneurs are so capable that they make different types of engineering products at competitive rates. As a result, Rajkot supplies diesel engines, machines and machinery items to all parts of the country and outside. Also it was estimated that one million rings were forged in Rajkot. These rings are supplied to many companies including the US automobile giant, General Motors. The entrepreneurs proudly claim that within six months of the launch of a new four wheeler, anywhere in the world, they would be ready to supply its spare parts. SKF, the global leader in bearings, openly acknowledged that the bearings made in Rajkot were superior in quality and precision than the bearings made in any other part of the world.*

Continuous improvements are constantly made by these people even without most of them realizing it. Many of the innovations are the results of the 'thinking minds' existing among these entrepreneurs. The story of the wet grinder industry in Coimbatore is simple. Traditionally, people used to rotate the grinding stone with their hands to grind food materials. One entrepreneur thought, 'Why not we make the grinding stone rotate, instead of people rotating it with their hands?' He worked on it and the wet grinder industry was born. Today there are hundreds of units engaged in the manufacture of wet grinders in Coimbatore. These grinders are sent to different parts of the country and are even exported. There are instances in which improvements and innovations have resulted in taking on the multi-nationals, leading to the capture of the markets from them† (see Box 6.1).

* Harishbhai Joshi, Rajkot, interview, 26.12.2002.

† P. Sundaram, Director, P.S.A. Industries (India) Private Limited, Tirupur, interview, 12.9.2006.

Box 6.1 Entrepreneurs from ordinary backgrounds take on multinationals through superior skills

Sundaram comes from a small village about 8 km from Tirupur. After third standard, he joined his uncle's workshop at the age of ten. His entrepreneurial spirit compelled him to promote his own unit at the age of twenty one. Initially, into manufacturing of small engineering items, he started manufacturing calendaring machines in 1991. When the business was going well, he happened to see a demonstration of a newly-introduced compacting machine by a foreign company. These machines are used in the hosiery industry to remove the shrinkages in fabrics. Immediately he realized that he could make better machines at a cheaper cost.

Sundaram entered this industry in 1995 and struggled all along spending more than sixteen hours a day for his venture. In the process, he sought the help of academic and research institutions for clearing doubts; he approached banks for funds. Unfortunately, he could not get help for any of his needs. With the initial money provided by his mother earned out of selling milk, and funds from local financiers, he came out with his first machine in 1998. The price of his Nova brand machine was one third of the price of the US based company then controlling the market. His foreign competitors were astonished to see the machine from this 'engineering genius'. As a result, they had to reduce their original prices immediately.

Sundaram made regular improvements and innovations to the machine. For example, in the process area component heating, he introduced oil heating, instead of the usual water heating. His major international competitor had to adopt this method subsequently. Currently, P.S.A. Industries Private Limited promoted by him, is the major player in India leaving his competitors way behind. Today he has enquiries for his machines from different parts of the world, including Europe.

He has proved that lack of formal education is neither a criterion nor a hindrance to his innovative abilities. In fact in his quest for innovation, some of the highly educated technical experts at reputed institutions and scientists that he met were unable to provide any clues to his difficulties and ultimately he had to rely on his own brain to make the machine.

In the case of the *Ram Gharia* community in Gujarat and Punjab, it was noticed that they possess in-born technical skills. Many of the entrepreneurs of Gujarat and Punjab attributed their successes to the 'engineering brains' of *Ram Gharias*. Most of the *Ram Gharias* have not had their formal education. Yet, they are endowed with high levels of technical knowledge which even many of the best engineering graduates do not seem to have. As a result of the innovative and creative brains, continuous innovations and improvements occur naturally in many of the clusters.

9. **Global business centres:** Most of the clusters are state level and regional level centres in their areas of operation. A good many of them are national level players too. Some of them are internationally known and in the last few years more numbers of them are emerging as global centres due to their expertise and

quality products. It is difficult to record all of them here. Tirupur is internationally acclaimed for its knitwear products and its exports for the fiscal year 2010–11 was ₹ 12,500 crores[78]. The woollen garments of Ludhiana are sold in different countries. Moreover it is the largest centre for bicycles and spares in the world. Karur is emerging as a popular name for its textile made-ups and furnishing items across different continents. Surat is synonymous with diamonds that its name is known throughout the world, with a turn over of ₹ 70,000 crores. Many a times we do not know that in the products of some of the centres a major portion of the manufacture is exported. For example, about 90 per cent of the hand tools exported out of India five years back were from Jalandhar. Jalandhar was also known for a long time as supplier of the best willows to the Australian cricketers, among others. Basti Nau in Jalandhar is one of the biggest sports lanes in the world, frequented by sports personalities from different countries. In the knowledge sectors, cities such as Bangalore, Pune and Hyderabad have emerged as global centres. Bangalore has more IT professionals than the Silicon Valley. Different *Fortune 500* companies have already set up their R&D centres and offices in Bangalore. Cities such as Pune are emerging as educational centres with students from different countries enrolling themselves for studies. As a result, India is emerging as a global centre in various manufacturing and service activities.

10. **Drivers of economic development:** The economic development of different regions and states is driven by clusters. The economically advanced states of India such as Gujarat, Tamil Nadu and Punjab have well performing clusters. One major reason for the success of Gujarat as an economically prosperous state is the high performance of its clusters such as Surat, Rajkot, Jamnagar, and Morvi. Similarly, the performance and growth of successful clusters such as Sivakasi, Tirupur, Karur and Coimbatore is helping Tamil Nadu in its emergence as an advanced industrial state in the country. Today most of the western Tamil Nadu and parts of southern Tamil Nadu are economically advanced, only due to the success of clusters. Ludhiana, Jalandhar and Batala are among the most important clusters in Punjab.

In this connection, the story of Gujarat diamond clusters would be revealing. In 1962 when China invaded India, the local economy was suffering. The Gold Control Act had pushed the small diamond dealers to market their polished diamonds abroad as an alternative market. A group of *Palanpuri* Gujarati diamond dealers convinced the Government of India, then starving of foreign exchange, to allow rough diamonds to be imported. They explained that by keeping

India as a manufacturing and polishing centre, these goods could be re-exported after having considerable value added to them. The diamond dealers did not ask for any aid from the government such as subsides, or duty concessions. As a result, the subsequent years saw the industry grow without any burden on the economy, and without any noise, chemical, air or water pollution. Power consumption was extremely low compared to the ratio of value added. Most importantly, the semi-literate and the un-educated workforce was converted into efficient artisans and highly paid people. Today the international diamond trade is dominated by Gujarat and her people[79].

6.4.3 Corporate Sector

The modern corporate system developed in India in the nineteenth century. Following the British system, the British Indian Government passed the Companies Act in 1850. In 1857, the Companies Act introducing limited liability was enacted. By 1860, the number of companies floated had risen to 60[80]. The first stock exchange in Asia started its operations in Bombay in 1875. The growth of the companies during the decade of the 1880s is presented in Table 6.9.

Table 6.9 Growth of Companies in the 1880s

Years	Companies at work	Paid-up capital (in ₹ 000's)	% Change over previous year
1881–2	505	156,817	–
1882–3	547	170,959	9
1883–4	649	187,506	9.8
1884–5	694	206,358	10
1885–6	806	210,015	2
1886–7	886	213,804	12
1887–8	910	223,261	4
1888–9	895	229,295	3

Source: Agarwala, P.N., A Comprehensive History of Business in India—from 3000 BC to 2000 AD, Tata-McGraw-Hill Publishing Company Limited, New Delhi, 2001, p. 451.

Table 6.9 shows the fast growth of the companies in the 1880s. In just one decade, the companies have grown by nearly 80 per cent. Table 6.10 illustrates the growth of joint stock enterprises over a period of three decades at the turn of the nineteenth century.

Table 6.10 Growth of Companies (1882 to 1913–14)

Years	No of companies	Paid-up capital (in ₹ 000's)
1882	505	157,000
1892	950	266,000
1900	1340	347,000
1909–90	2216	610,000
1913–14	2744	766,000

Source: Agarwala, P.N., *A Comprehensive History of Business in India—from 3000* BC *to 2000* AD, Tata-McGraw-Hill Publishing Company Limited, New Delhi, 2001, p. 462.

Table 6.10 shows that in little more than thirty years, the number of companies had grown by 543 per cent. During these periods, the British interests dominated the Indian industry.

Seeds of swadeshi *initiatives*

Agarwala[81] mentions: "The years 1900 to 1915 may be reckoned as roughly the period when capitalism in India started its transition from the phase of mercantile capitalism to that of industrial capitalism." Maddison[82] notes that "Indian firms in industry, insurance and banking were given a boost from 1905 onwards by the *swadeshi* movement, which was a nationalist boycott of British goods in favour of Indian enterprise." Dutta[83] shows that "According to the 1911 census report, 60 per cent of industry at the time was owned and managed by non-Indians." The share of the Europeans was more than 80 per cent in plantations and engineering industries. 1913 marked the start of the period which saw the passing of the Indian Companies Act modelled on the British Act of 1908. It governed corporate businesses till 1936. It was later amended considerably in 1956. Maddison[84] writes that "during the First World War, lack of British imports strengthened the hold of Indian firms on the home markets for textiles and steel. After the War, under nationalist pressure, the government started to favour Indian enterprise in its purchase of stores and it agreed to create a tariff commission in 1921 which started to raise tariffs for protective reasons."

Managing agencies

Even then a listing of top 50 business groups in 1939 showed that 32 of the managing agency firms were owned by the British. The overall dominance of the British continued in various forms. Maddison[85] continues: "Many of the most lucrative, commercial, financial, business and plantation jobs in the modern sector were occupied by foreigners. Long after the East India Company's legally enforced monopoly privileges were ended, the British continued to exercise effective dominance through their control of the banking sector and the system of "managing agencies". These agencies, originally set up by former employees of the East India Company, were used to both manage industrial enterprise and to handle most of India's international trade." Moreover, "Indian industrial efficiency was hampered by the British administration's neglect of technical education, and the reluctance of British firms and managing agencies to provide training or managerial experience to Indians. Even in the Bombay textile industry, where most of the capital was Indian, 28 per cent of the managerial and supervisory staff were British in 1925 (42 per cent in 1895) and the British component was even bigger in more complex industries[86]."

Second World War and after

During the Second World War and after, the corporate sector began to grow at a faster rate. In 1946 and 1947, the number of newly floated companies came to 2484 and 4510 respectively, with a corres-ponding rise of ₹ 350 million, and ₹ 560 million in the paid-up capital[87]. The number of companies in 1948 increased to 22,675 with a paid-up capital of ₹ 5700 million as against 11,114 companies in 1939 with a paid up capital of only ₹ 2900 million[88]. In 1956, the number of companies stood at 29,874 with a paid-up capital of ₹ 10,240 million[89]. As many as 600 industrial concerns were either controlled or managed by 36 managing agency firms in 1951[90]. The leading Indian managing agency houses comprised the Tatas, Birlas, Dalmias, Singhanias, Thapars and Goenkas[91]. In this connection, Agarwala[92] mentions that the edifice of the Indian joint stock enterprise grew out of indigenous systems of banking and trade. In Madras and Coimbatore, the *Chettiars* represented an important banking community.

Growth of corporate sector in recent decades

The business and the corporate sectors were not adequately encouraged after independence, due to the socialistic policies of the successive governments for more than three decades. The corporate sector began attracting the attention of the government from the 1980s. Restrictive policies began to be liberalized; the stronghold of the state was slowly dismantled. From 1991 onwards, policy initiatives were made to encourage and promote the corporate sector. As a result, this sector has been growing fast in the recent periods. Table 6.11 presents the total number of companies working in India as on 31.12.2010[93].

Table 6.11 Number of Indian companies at work (2010)

Category of companies		Number of companies	Total number of companies
Companies limited by shares at work	Public limited	81,926	8,72,740
	Private limited	7,90,814	

Source: *Annual Report 2009–10*, Ministry of Corporate Affairs, Government of India, p. 48.

Table 6.11 shows that there were 8,72,740 companies at work at the end of December 2010. Out of this, the non-government companies accounted for the maximum with 8,71,125 numbers, while the government companies numbered 1591. There were 2903 foreign companies as defined under Section 591 of the Companies Act, 1956. Many Indian companies have emerged as successful players in the recent decades in different fields delivering quality products and services. Some of them are able to compete successfully with the big corporations of the western nations. In certain sectors such as pharmaceuticals, Indian companies are manufacturing excellent products at highly competitive rates. More and more Indian companies have been going abroad in the recent years to establish subsidiary units, to create production facilities and to expand businesses. In the process, a good number of them are becoming multinationals.

Corporate sector performance in recent years

The performance of the corporate sector has been impressive during the recent years. But the companies had to face difficulties in 2008–09 due to the global economic crisis. Table 6.12 presents the performance of the corporate sector during 2007–08 to 2009–10.

Table 6.12 Corporate Financial Performance (2007–08 to 2009–10)

(growth rates in per cent)

	2007–08	2008–09	2009–10
Sales	18.6	17.2	11.7
Gross profit	24.9	–4.2	24.9
Net profit	26.0	–18.4	28.8
Net profit (percentage of sales)	9.8	8.1	9.4

Source: *Report on Currency and Finance 2008–09*, Reserve Bank of India, p. 286.

Table 6.12 shows that the sales and profits of companies have been growing during the recent years. The overall performance has also improved in 2009–10, after the crisis. Different studies reveal that the corporate sector has gained more confidence to meet competition and achieve success.

Stock markets

Beginning from the 1980s, stock markets have been showing continuous growth. Though there are around twenty stock exchanges in India, there are no transactions in most of the exchanges. The National Stock Exchange (NSE) and the Stock Exchange of Mumbai (BSE) completely dominate the Indian securities market. SEBI notes: "Over the years NSE and BSE have emerged as the nationwide stock exchanges of the country contributing to almost 100 per cent of total turnover. Apart from NSE and BSE, Calcutta and UPSE stock exchanges reported some transactions[94]." BSE has 7783 scrips listed for trading, while the NSE has 1456 companies listed with it[95]. The total turnover in the stock markets during 2010–11 was ₹ 46,82,437 crores in the cash segment, while it was ₹ 2,92,48,375 crores in the equity derivatives segment [96].

One of the notable developments in the recent years has been the growth of derivative markets in India. In the words of SEBI: "Exchange traded derivatives form an important segment of Indian stock markets. The derivatives market has grown substantially over the years in India. Trading in derivatives is dominated by NSE with a market share of 99 per cent in the total equity derivatives turnover. Over the years the ratio of derivatives market turnover to cash market turnover has been gradually increasing. During 2010–11, the turnover of derivatives market was 6.2 times of the cash turnover on all-India equity exchanges as compared to 4.6 times in 2009–10[97]."

The major market indicators related to the BSE and NSE for 2009–10 to 2010–11 are presented in Table 6.13.

Table 6.13 Stock Market Indicators (2009–10 to 2010–11)

Indicators	BSE		NSE	
	2009–10	2010–11	2009–10	2010–11
BSE Sensex/S&P CNX Nifty	17,528	19,445	5,249	5,834
Cash Segment Turnover (₹ crore)	13,78,809	11,05,027	41,38,023	35,77,410
P/E ratio	21.3	21.2	22.3	22.1
Market capitalisation (₹ crore)	61,65,619	68,39,083	60,09,173	67,02,616

Source: BSE and NSE quoted in *Annual Report 2010–11*, SEBI, p. 38.

Features of Indian corporate sector

An important factor to be noted here is the predominance of families in the corporate sector. Dutta[98] notes that "family firms are 99.9 per cent of all Indian companies." Families dominate even the biggest companies in the country. Eighty per cent of the 500 biggest companies are family businesses[99]. There is also a community orientation in the corporate sector. Quoting *Business Today*, Gurucharan Das[100] notes that "Fifteen out of the twenty largest industrial houses in 1997 were derived from the Vaishya or Bania trading castes. Eight of them were Marwaris." Quoting E-Square data, Dutta[101] noted that 70 per cent of India's rupee billionaires were from just three communities. Marwaris dominate the list of top billionaires with 25 representatives. In this connection, Dutta[102] mentions that "the business families in India belong to some distinct communities."

The functioning systems of the Indian corporate sector include unique methods, some of which are specific to the communities. For example, the *Marwari* businessmen followed the traditional system of bookkeeping called *parta*. It is a day-to-day trial balance calculated in an abbreviated form. It is a unique information system that gives the financial position of the company to the top management on a daily basis. Even the general financing pattern of the Indian corporate sector exhibits differences compared to the western corporate world. Earlier, Mall[103] had shown that "companies tended to rely more on retained earnings till 1983 rather than on fresh infusion of paid-up capital, which has increased considerably since then." There seems to be a lesser dependence on borrowings during the recent periods, though the proportion of borrowings as a source of funds has shown variance over the years. Table 6.14 presents details regarding the internal and external sources of funds and borrowings for non-government non-financial public limited companies for the years, 1997–98 to 2000–01 and 2001–02 to 2005–06.

Table 6.14 Sources of Funds for Corporate Sector (1997–98 to 2000–01 and 2001–02 to 2005–06)

(figures in percentages)

	1997–98 to 2000–01	2001–02 to 2005–06
Internal sources	43.1	56.1
External sources	56.9	43.9
Borrowings	28.6	13.8

Source: Report on Currency and Finance 2006–08, Reserve Bank of India, 2008, p. 260.

Securities and Exchange Board of India notes that the funds raised from the internal sources for non-government non-financial companies were 28.9 per cent of the total in 1994–95, and it touched 55.5 per cent in 2004–05, before going down to 36.9 per cent in 2007–08. The share of reserves and surplus averaged around 23 per cent during 2003–04 to 2007–08[104]. Centre for Monitoring Indian

Economy noted that the share of fresh capital raised from the capital markets as a source of funds increased from 4.5 per cent to 16.2 per cent during 2002–03 to 2007–08[105]. The share of debt in the resources raised by the corporate sector remains high. Table 6.15 presents the resources raised by the corporate sector through the issue of equity and debt, and the percentage share of debt in the resources mobilized during 2001–02 to 2009–10.

Table 6.15 Resources Raised by Corporate Sector (2001–02 to 2009–10)

(₹ crore)

Years	Equity issues	Debt issues	% share of debt in total resource mobilization
2001–02	1272	71,147	98.2
2004–05	24,388	87,272	78.2
2005–06	27,372	96,483	77.9
2006–07	32,903	1,46,471	81.7
2007–08	85,427	2,05,513	69.3
2008–09	14,721	1,89,502	94.2
2009–10	55,055	2,70,190	87.1

Source: *Handbook of Statistics in Indian Securities Market*, 2009, p. 14 and 2010, p. 69, SEBI.

The table shows that the debt capital remained the predominant source of funds raised by the corporate sector throughout the period. It may be relevant to note here that the recent periods have been witnessing many new developments in the capital markets.

Indian business models are unique

The Indian business sector is family based. It is dominated by the non-corporate sector, contributing significantly to employment, turnover and exports. Clusters play a crucial role in the economy and business of India. The development of the non-corporate sector, especially the successful clusters, breaks many myths surrounding the standard development paradigms. All these days the establishment had developed wrong notions about the non-corporate sector. Experience shows that much of the non-corporate sector does not depend on the state; rather it is the other way round, for they generate a lot of revenues and provide almost the entire employment which the government cannot provide otherwise. The government should try to understand and nourish it, instead of bringing it under unnecessary bureaucratic controls, killing its spirit and soul. The corporate sector has come a long way in the last six decades. Certain differences in the systems and approaches could be noticed between the corporate and the non-corporate sectors. For example, while the non-corporate sector depends mainly on savings, own funds and local mechanisms for capital, the corporate sector has easier avenues for external mobilization of funds. Indian corporate sector exhibits western orientations compared to the non-corporate sector. This might be due to the historical circumstances and influences. Indian corporate sector was not given the required freedom to function on its own for a very long time, initially by the British and later by the Indian governments. Since the 1990s, there has been a disproportionate influence of the western practices and theories on the Indian corporate sector. Hence, it seems that a completely native corporate model could not be allowed to evolve on its own. But at the same time, the functioning Indian models are in many ways different from that of the west, shaped as it is by the cultural, social and other influences of the country.

It is appropriate to note here that new business initiatives undertaken during the recent past are proving to be very successful models, establishing an Indian identity throughout the world. The success of the Narayana Hrudayalaya hospitals promoted by Dr. Devi Prasad Shetty is an example eagerly studied in different parts of the world. The group which started with its first hospital in 2001 in Bangalore for heart diseases, now has a chain of hospitals in different centres of India with 5000 beds catering to different ailments[106]. Its two heart hospitals, namely Narayana Hrudayalaya Heart Hospital, Bangalore and Rabindranath Tagore International Institute of Cardiac Service, Kolkata perform about 12 per cent of the heart surgeries in the country. Currently, Narayana Hrudayalaya performs the largest number of heart surgeries in the world for children. It treats patients from 73 countries for complex heart diseases. The group has launched many innovative schemes with the objective of providing health care facilities to the underprivileged sections of the society. Its micro-health insurance programme called Yeshawini, taken up in association with the Karnataka Government, covers about 30 lakh farmers and provides health cover for a monthly premium of just ₹ 10. Its tele-cardiology programme using the Indian Space Research Organization satellite facilities provides advice to thousands of patients free of cost. Narayana Hrudayalaya has proposed a hospital and research centre at Cayman Islands to provide health care facilities to the people of the western world at a cheaper cost.

The successes of Narayana Hrudayalaya experiments are based on newer ideas to reach out to all and the needy. Its high volume approach, combined with the maximum utilization of the available facilities which was never before thought of in the health care industry all these years, has enabled it to reduce the overall costs on a massive scale. As a result, Narayana Hrudayalaya charges $2000 on an average for an open heart surgery compared to $20,000 to $1,00,000 charged by the hospitals in the US, and still earns higher profits[107]. Within a short period, the Narayana Hrudayalaya model has become very successful and is being studied not just by the health care industry, but also by the international bodies such as the International Labour Organization and World Bank for attempting similar schemes in other parts of the world.

It is significant to know that the Indian companies have started building new business models during the recent periods. Prahalad and Mashelkar[108] note: "Smart Indian companies have come up with new technologies and radical business models to penetrate the country's mass markets." New models are being created by disrupting the existing ones. Prahalad and Mashelkar[109] mention: "Several Indian companies have used western technologies but created business models that have completely altered an industry's economics. For instance, IT-based software and service providers such as Satyam, Wipro, Infosys, TCS, and HCL use off-the-shelf hardware, but they deploy new talent-based business models to be globally competitive." Narrating the case of Bharti Airtel, they mention that the company is able to provide mobile phone services at very cheap rates due to its business model. To quote them again: "Thanks to its unique business model, Bharti Airtel is able to charge 1 cent per minute of talk time—compared with 2 cents in China and 8 cents in the US—making it the world's most affordable mobile telephone service. In 2009 the company had signed on approximately 100 million subscribers, and it plans to double that number by 2012. The company's ability to scale has quickly paid dividends: its operating margins increased from –2.25 per cent in 2003 to 28.3 per cent in 2008. Despite an intensely competitive market, Bharti Airtel reported revenues of $7.25 billion in 2008, and its revenues grew 43 per cent from 2004 to 2008. ... Companies in every industry worldwide are trying to emulate Bharti Airtel's formula for success[110]."

The ground realities and the new developments make the western management experts to openly admit that the Indian models have inherent strengths and there is much to learn from them. Greame Salaman[111], the noted management expert from the UK, notes that he "strongly believes that there are several inherent strengths in Indian companies that need to be exploited." Praising the Indian systems, he says: "Frankly, I think we (the west) need to learn from you."

REFERENCES

[1] Agarwala, P.N., *A Comprehensive History of Business in India—from 3000 BC to 2000 AD,* Tata-McGraw Hill Publishing Company Limited, New Delhi, 2001, p. 265.

[2] Ibid., p. 266.

[3] Khanna, Vikramaditya S., 'The Economic History of Corporate Form in Ancient India', 1997, http: //ssrn.com, p. 30.

[4] Ibid., p. 35 .

[5] Ibid., p. 25.

[6] Ibid., pp. 20–21.

[7] Ibid., p. 34.

[8] Ibid., p.36.

[9] Ibid., p. 40.

[10] Ibid., p. 48.

[11] Ibid.

[12] Agarwala, P.N., op.cit., p. 281.

[13] Robins, Nick, *The Corporation that Changed the World—How the East India Company Shaped the Modern Multinational,* Orient Longman, Hyderabad, 2006, p. 41.

[14] Ibid., p. 49.

[15] Ibid., p. 64.

[16] Tripathi, Dwijendra and Jumani, Jyoti, *The Concise Oxford History of Indian Business,* Oxford University Press, New Delhi, 2007, p. 18.

[17] Robins, Nick, op.cit., p. 79.

[18] Tripathi, Dwijendra and Jumani, Jyoti, op.cit., p. 21.

[19] Robins, Nick, op.cit., p. 7.

[20] Tripathi, Dwijendra and Jumani, Jyoti, op.cit., p. 77.

[21] Ibid., p. 78.

[22] Ibid., p. 111.

[23] Ibid., p. 149.

[24] Ibid., p. 199.

[25] *Final Results: Third All India Census of Small Scale Industries 2001–02,* Ministry of Small Scale Industries, Government of India, New Delhi, 2004, p. 1.

[26] Ibid., p. 6.

[27] Ibid., p. 1.

[28] Ibid., p. 3.

[29] Ibid., p. 50.

[30] Ibid., p. 6.

[31] Ibid., p. 54.

[32] Ibid.

[33] Ibid., p. 57.

[34] Ibid., p. 49.

[35] *Annual Report 2010–11*, Ministry of Micro, Small and Medium Enterprises, Government of India, pp. 13–14.

[36] Ibid., p. 23.

[37] *Final results: Third All India Census of Small Scale Industries 2001–02*, op.cit., p. 2.

[38] Ibid., p. 1.

[39] Vaidyanathan, R., 'The Least Acknowledged Big Savers', *The Hindu Business Line*, July 15, 2004.

[40] Chadha, G.K., *Rural Industry in India, Policy Perspectives, Past Performance and Future options,* South Asia Advisory Team, International Labour Organisation, New Delhi, 2003, p. 222.

[41] *Economic Survey 2009–10,* Government of India, New Delhi, p. 11.

[42] *Final Results: Third All India Census of Small Scale Industries 2001–02*, op.cit., p. 2.

[43] *Economic Census 1998,* Ministry of Finance, Government of India, New Delhi.

[44] *Final Results: Third All India Census of Small Scale Industries 2001–02*, op.cit., p. 2.

[45] Ibid.

[46] Chakraborty, S.K., *Ethics in Management: Vedantic Perspectives*, 3rd impression, Oxford University Press, New Delhi, 1999, p. 280.

[47] Fabio Russo, Strengthening Indian SME Clusters: UNIDO Experience, Case Study Project: US/GLO/95/144, July 1999, UNIDO. http://www.unido.org/userfiles/RussoF/Vie.3pdf.

[48] *Final Results: Third All India Census of Small Scale Industries 2001–02*, op.cit., pp. 83–85.

[49] Ibid., pp. 83 and 85.

[50] Ibid., p. 83.

[51] Ibid., p. 85.

[52] Ibid., pp. 84–85.

[53] Ibid., p. 257.

[54] Kanagasabapathi, P., and Arun Kumar, M.N., 'A Study on Sankagiri Transport and Thiruchengodu Rig Industry', unpublished report, P.S.G. Institute of Management, Coimbatore, April 2005.

[55] Kanagasabapathi, P., and Anuradha, R., 'A Study on Reasons Behind the Success of Knitwear Industry in Tirupur with Regard to the Ancillary Units', unpublished report, P.S.G. College of Technology, Coimbatore, March 2004.

[56] Kanagasabapathi, P., and Rathishree, P., 'A Study on Karur Textile Export Industry', unpublished report, P.S.G. Institute of Management, Coimbatore, April 2005.

[57] Quoted in Patel, Sharad and Kanagasabapathi, P., 'A Study on Gujarat Diamond Export Industry', unpublished report, P.S.G. Institute of Management, Coimbatore, April 2005.

[58] Chari, Sharad, *Fraternal Capital*, Permanent Black, Delhi, 2004, p. 276.

[59] Ibid., p. 293.

[60] Patel, Sharad and Kanagasabapathi, P., op.cit.

[61] Kanagasabapathi, P., and Gopalsamy, R., 'A Study on Supply Chain Practices and Performances in the Printing Industry of Sivakasi', unpublished report, P.S.G. College of Technology, Coimbatore, April 2006.

[62] Kanagasabapathi, P., and Arun Kumar, M.N., June 2005, op.cit.

[63] *Hinterland India: The Real Source of India's Entrepreneurship*, India Brand Equity Foundation, Department of Science and Technology, Government of India, www.ibef.org.

[64] Kanagasabapathi, P., and Arun Kumar, M.N., June 2005, op.cit.

[65] *Hinterland India: The Real Source of India's Entrepreneurship*, India Brand Equity Foundation, op.cit.

[66] Kanagasabapathi, P., *Unorganized Finance Sector: The Engine for Economic Growth—A Study with Reference to Karur, Tamil Nadu,* Swadeshi Academic Council, Coimbatore, 2002.

[67] Ali, Akbar M., and Kanagasabapathi, P., 'A Study on Leather Tanneries in Dindugul', unpublished report, P.S.G. College of Technology, Coimbatore, April 2004.

[68] Dwivedi, Mridula, *Nature of Trust in Small Firm Clusters: A Case Study of Kanpur Saddlery Cluster*, Paper presented at the conference on 'Clusters, Industrial Districts and Firms: The Challenge of Globalisation', Modena, Italy, 2003.

[69] Quoted in Kanagasabapathi, P., and Gopalsamy, R., op.cit.

[70] Ibid.

[71] Chadha, G.K., op.cit.

[72] From the Report of the Expert Committee on Small Enterprises quoted in Ashwani Saith *Rural Industrialization in India—Some Policy Perspectives,* South Asia Multidisciplinary Advisory Team, International Labour Organization, New Delhi, 2000, p. 71.

[73] Chari, Sharad, op.cit., p. 293.

[74] Patel, Sharad, and Kanagasabapathi, P., op.cit.

[75] Kanagasabapathi, P., and Arun Kumar, M.N., June 2005, op.cit.

[76] Kanagasabapathi, P., 2002, op.cit.

[77] Chari, Sharad, op.cit., p. 86.

[78] Tirupur Exporters Association quoted in *The Hindu*, 17 April, 2011.

[79] Quoted in Patel, Sharad, and Kanagasabapathi, P., op.cit.

[80] Agarwala, P.N., op.cit., p. 590.

[81] Ibid., p. 462.

[82] Maddison, Angus, *The World Economy—A Millennial Perspective,* First Indian Edition, Overseas Press (India) Private Limited, New Delhi by arrangement with Organisation for Economic Cooperation and Development, 2003, p. 116.

[83] Sudipt Dutta, *Family Business in India,* Response Books, New Delhi, 2007, p. 44.

[84] Maddison, Angus, op.cit., p. 116.

[85] Ibid.

[86] Ibid.

[87] Agarwala, P.N., op.cit., p. 466.

[88] Ibid.

[89] Ibid.

[90] Ibid.

[91] Ibid.

[92] Agarwala, P.N., op.cit., p. 462.

[93] Statistical Review of the Corporate Sector, *Annual Report 2009–10*, Ministry of Corporate Affairs, Government of India, p. 48. http://www.mca.gov.in/.

[94] *Annual Report 2010–11*, Securities and Exchange Board of India, p. 53.

[95] Ibid., p. 121.

[96] Ibid., p. 38.

[97] Ibid., p. 57.

[98] Sudipt Dutta, op.cit., p. 17.

[99] Ibid.

[100] 'Fifteen Industrial Houses', *Business Today* quoted in Gurucharan Das, 'The Problem', *Seminar* 482, October 1999, p. 12.

[101] Sudipt Dutta, op.cit., p. 65.

[102] Ibid., p. 64.

[103] Mall, C.P., quoted in Sudipt Dutta, op.cit., p. 131.

[104] Reserve Bank of India quoted in the *Handbook of Statistics on the Indian Securities Market 2009*, Securities and Exchange Board of India, Mumbai, p. 21.

[105] Centre for Monitoring Indian Economy, Corporate Sector, CMIE, Mumbai, February 2009, p. 259.

[106] www.narayanahospitals.com.

[107] 'The Henry Ford of Heart Surgery', *The Wall Street Journal* Asian Edition, November 25, 2009.

[108] Prahalad, C.K. and Mashelkar, R.A., 'Innovation's Holy Grail', *Harvard Business Review*, July–August 2010, p. 134.

[109] Ibid., p. 135.

[110] Ibid., p. 137.

[111] Salaman, Greame, 'India need not follow western biz model', interview, *The Hindu Business Line*, 1.10.2002.

7

BASIC FEATURES OF DIFFERENT BUSINESS MODELS

A study of the basic features of different business models will enable us to understand the differences among them. It is necessary to understand them and perceive the distinguishing factors at a time when the global business scenario is undergoing major changes. Moreover, unless the backgrounds and natures of different models are known, it might not be possible to properly plan and formulate policies in the emerging scenario. An overview of the basic differences between the different models is presented in this chapter.

7.1 BASIC FEATURES OF INDIAN BUSINESS MODELS

7.1.1 Family Orientation

The tradition of family business is age-old. Sudipt Dutta[1] notes that "Indian family businesses have a rich and continuous tradition, perhaps going back 5,000 years." As a result, family orientation is prevalent in all businesses. As far as the non-corporate sector is concerned, there is a complete family orientation. The ownership pattern of enterprises in this sector reveals that the proprietorship pattern is predominant. The required finance for initial investments is raised through the family savings, earnings of the family, support from relatives and friends, sale or pledge of assets of the family and borrowings from the local financiers using the family goodwill and against family assets. The family-tag manifests everywhere while raising of funds. A study of the financing systems in different business centres shows that most of the funds are raised through the traditional family-based mechanisms.

Family connections are used in different ways in business. When the risk is high or when more funds are required, entrepreneurs prefer the partnership method of organization. The partners may be brothers, cousins or close relatives, followed by friends. In some of the businesses, the brothers and cousins are the only partners. A study of the ghee business in Tamil Nadu, dominated by the *Sozhiya Chetty* community, revealed that in all their ventures, the uncles, brothers and the cousins are the partners[2]. This partnership extends naturally to new business ventures outside the family businesses initiated by members of the family. It was observed in one family that when the son of a brother, who had studied medicine, established a hospital, all his uncles, brothers and cousins were taken in as partners, even though each one of them were completely involved in the ghee business already[3]. Adi Godrej[4], the scion of the successful Godrej business family, notes that "... it is estimated that 95 per cent of the registered firms are family businesses."

The smooth run in the traditional family businesses took a turbulent turn during the British rule. In a number of instances, families engaged in businesses were disturbed. In the case of textiles, thousands of families belonging to weaving business were not allowed to continue in their business. They were forced to leave their traditional family businesses in search of jobs in altogether new areas for a livelihood. But in spite of the disturbances, family businesses have continued to survive and prosper. Dutta[5] notes: "The Indian family business design is based on the basic axiom of them against us. It is a matter of prestige that clansmen and the community must not be the objects of scorn of the rest of the society. The last 1,000 years, since the first Muslim invasion, have strengthened this community feeling. The Muslim invader treated the Hindu merchant with ill-concealed disdain, while the British maintained a clear distinction between the Indian businessman and his European counterpart. After Independence in 1947, government regulation and socialistic ideologies further institutionalised this solidarity. Also, the limited availability of bank finance meant that enterprise had to be financed from family and community capital. The Indian family business has retained its lead in the Indian business environment right through these 1,000 years."

Families in corporate sector

Shirur[6] mentions that of the largest 125 companies in 1947, 58 per cent were family-controlled companies under the managing agency system. *Business Today* Annual Survey 1994 noted that

75 per cent of the largest 500 companies were family-controlled companies in India[7]. Kamat[8] writes on the significance of families in the Indian corporate sector. To quote: "The family is business. As in the five decades before Indian independence, so in the 50 years of independent India, it is the business family that has dominated the country's corporate economy. If, at mid-night on August 15, 1947, as the world indifferently slept, 18 families owned almost every company in the country, at mid-day on August 15, 1997, as the global economy jealously watched, 461 of the 500 most valuable companies in the country were controlled by families. Thus, it is the business family that is the most powerful form of enterprise in corporate India even today."

Outstanding features of family businesses

Godrej[9] mentions that "Family-owned businesses play a crucial role in the economy of most countries... Worldwide, family-managed businesses employ half the world's workforce and generate well over half the world's GDP." But what is important of India's family business is their sheer domination of the business sector and the special features that they possess. There are two outstanding features that should be mentioned here. One is the tradition of surrendering one's individuality before the family. "One outstanding quality of the Indian business family is the complete surrender of individuality of the member to the general welfare of the family and its activities. This surrender of personal vanity and ambition in the larger interest of the family and, by extension, the community or *biradari,* results in a unique sense of competition rather than conflict[10]." Second is the attitude of self-denial and dedication. "The Indian businessman believes in the puritanical ethic of self-denial... It is remarkable that this cultural ethos, which has evolved over centuries, even today stands largely untouched by the Anglo-Saxon laws of the land[11]."

Families provide continuity to business

Family businesses have definite advantages. From the point of view of the society, continuity could be maintained in family businesses. Dutta[12] notes that "western research indicates that 70 per cent of firms close after the death of the founder because there is nobody to continue. In India, however, things are very different... The continuance of the business is seldom in debate among those connected with it... An Indian businessman gains in stature within the community once his succession is effected because continuity of the family business for another generation has been worked out."

Tripathi[13] points out "that almost two-thirds of today's leading business families have had a firm control over the management of the companies promoted by them for several decades, despite revolutionary changes in the business environment since Independence... That so many families have remained at the forefront and maintained their hold over these companies for such a long time, is a clear testimony to the critical position that the family continues to occupy in Indian business." In the Indian system, there is a common tendency for families to own businesses. Hence, one could even see businessmen selling their personal assets to continue their businesses, if the situation demanded. In the traditional business families, children were taught to learn the art of business from a young age so that business would come naturally to them.

Bigger family, more success?

Earlier, businesses were in the hands of joint families and all the male members of the family kept themselves involved in business. The joint family system provides many benefits to the growth of business. Gurucharan Das[14] notes: "A more unique characteristic of Indian business, at least until recently, was that it was managed as a joint family and derived a competitive advantage from this fact." He quotes Joel Kotkin to point out the critical role that the joint family system played in the international diamond business. To quote: "The famous example is of the *Palanpuri Jains* of western India, who have established commercial colonies in such diamond centres as Tel Aviv, Antwerp, Mumbai, London and New York and who today account for roughly 50 per cent of all purchases of rough diamonds in the world. Because of the inherent trust in a joint family, *Jain* diamond merchants rely on inter-ethnic ties to keep this highly scattered, specialised and intrinsically high-risk business together... It is the family and ethnic ties that give them competitive advantage and partially explain their recent gains in market share at the expense of the orthodox Jews[15]." Joint families have many advantages such as division of responsibilities, pooling of talents and sharing of risks. It was observed in a few cases that growth seemed to be faster where the brothers and cousins were more in number and all of them were equally involved in the family business. In such cases the brothers and cousins divide the functional responsibilities and concentrate in their area of operations. In the case of the promoter family of *Ajanta* clocks, it was proudly claimed that the brothers of the founder family divided the country into different geographical regions and took responsibility for each of the regions. As a result of their concentrated efforts they made their products highly successful throughout the country.* The brothers of the well-known, The Chennai Silks family in Tamil Nadu, attribute that the success of their business is entirely due to their joint family† (see Box 7.1).

Box 7.1 Success of joint families in business—The bigger, the better?

The Chennai Silks (TCS) is a well-known textile company in Tamil Nadu. They are one of the few companies that have fully integrated their business. They make yarns, weave materials, process cloth, sell them in their outlets and export. They run the business in different parts of the country. Their group turnover is around ₹1500 crores. They have diversified into jewellery business. Within a short span of time, their concern Sri Kumaran Jewellers, has made a name for itself.

What is the secret behind their steady success? The business is run by the Kulandaivelu family of eight brothers. Initially, they shared all kinds of responsibilities, depending on the situations. They rotated jobs as and when it was considered necessary. The word of the eldest brother was final in all matters. Once it was decided by the seniormost of brothers, the rest of them worked hard to implement the decision. After a steady rise, now they have divided the responsibilities on a mutual basis. Each of them is in charge of a functional area and specific projects.

All the eight of them meet once in a month regularly in their father's house. They have made it a practice to start all their meetings with discussions on personal and family matters. Family comes first and business later. Whenever a brother has any difficulty, others offer suggestions and solutions. If required, counselling is given by the rest of them. No brother would be allowed to feel that he is alone in difficulties. After making everybody comfortable, the business discussion starts. They make the plans, review their performances and take all the decisions then and there in the meetings. Thereafter, no questions are asked. Though one or more of the other brothers may sometimes have different views, the decision of the concerned brother, in charge of the particular activity is final. Each brother has the last word in his area of operation. The responsibilities to the children of the brothers are being given according to their qualifications and tastes, even through creating new avenues.

The admiring feature of this family is the expertise of the brothers in different functional areas. For example, the person in charge of Human Relations is a pleasing personality who has the knack of analyzing human beings from various angles before providing solutions in a most logical and acceptable manner. The person in charge of finance is a wizard and is extremely careful about investing each rupee of business. Similarly, the person in charge of projects is such an expert that he would be able to complete the project quickly, much to the discomfiture of the specialized project houses. It is therefore no surprise that they make the best combination of talents required to run the business very successfully. All of them unanimously agree that it was their joint efforts as one man that has made them what they are today.

* Patel, U., Chairman, Samay Co., Morvi, interview, 26.12.2002.

† Vinayakam, K., Director, SCM Textiles Ltd., Coimbatore, interview, 27.08.2006.

The joint family system of business is slowly disappearing. But even now one could notice the families of brothers jointly engaged in businesses, though many a times, their families might not be under the same roof. In some of the businesses, the relationship extends to cousins and their families living in different places. In the case of powerloom textiles, it was observed that the *Marwari* businessmen buying clothes in Tamil Nadu operate through their network of brothers and cousins staying in strategic business locations in the northern states. In the process they earn more. It was observed in a few business centres that the families of brothers, sisters and close relatives jointly promote ventures as partners, though all of them might not be working full time for the business. At the same time, we have to remember that many business families are splitting up due to differences. There are also instances of businesses picking up after family splits as each family tries to assert itself and prove its worth. The well-known case of Ambani brothers could be cited as an example in this regard.

In the last few decades newer families from different backgrounds have emerged successful in different businesses. Business is no longer the domain of a few families. It is open to all who have the entrepreneurship abilities. In spite of all the external changes that have been happening in India, the business sector continues to remain under the family system. It is to the credit of the Indian family system that it is able to withstand the economic, political and international changes and march towards prosperity. Hence, it would be no exaggeration to say that the Indian businesses are the contribution of the unique family system.

7.1.2 Dominance of the Non-corporate Sector

Non-corporate sector is the most crucial part of the Indian business system. The share of non-corporate sector to the Indian economy and business is much higher than the other sectors. In fact, the share of this sector is higher than the combined share of the other two sectors, namely the corporate sector and the government sector. Table 7.1 presents the share of the non-corporate sector to the net domestic product in selected areas during 2002–03.

Apart from its higher share of contribution to the economy and business, this sector plays a very significant role in providing employment. Moreover, the non-corporate sector businesses develop on their own without depending on the state. Out of the 10.52 million units in the SSI sector, only 4.55 per cent units have outstanding loans with institutional sources[16]. Forty per cent of these units function without making use of power[17]. The faster

Table 7.1 Share of Unorganized Segment in Net Domestic Product by Economic Activity (2002–03) (at current prices)

Industry	2002–03
Manufacturing	36.6
Construction	62.8
Trade, hotels and restaurants	74.2
Transport, storage and communication	62.9
Financing, insurance, real estate & business services	39.6
Community, social & personal services	17.3
Net domestic product at factor cost	56.7

Source: Statement 76.3, *Statement of National Account Statistics 2005*, Central Statistical Organization, Government of India.

growth of India during the last few years has been led by the growth of the non-corporate sector. The growth of this sector in many of the service activities is much faster than the growth in the activities coming under the corporate sector. The share of the non-corporate business in India's exports is also significant. It is the contribution of this sector that makes items such as gems and jewellery and textiles the largest contributories to the Indian basket of exports. India is known throughout the world for its quality products due to the non-corporate businesses of different clusters such as Tirupur, Rajkot, Surat, Ludhiana and Karur. The businessmen from many of these clusters compete with big companies from different countries and multinational enterprises and emerge successfully thereby establishing the name of the country. Many western companies, including the multinational firms, openly admire the higher quality of the non-corporate businesses.

This sector is engaged in a wide variety of manufacturing and service activities, depending on the local situations. For example, the *dabbawala* business in Mumbai is an innovative business designed and executed by a group of uneducated and undereducated people from the ordinary classes to suit the local conditions. The business plan is so designed to make it perfectly functional, while at the same time keeping it cost effective. The innovative spirit of the non-corporate business sector could be seen in many centres across the country. It is this innovative spirit that has made Rajkot the centre for manufacturing oil engines and Morvi the centre for making wall-clocks in India. Moreover, the non-corporate sector continuously produces lakhs of entrepreneurs every year making India one of the largest entrepreneurial nations in the world. It is also the breeding ground for future corporations and big businesses.

The non-corporate businesses are basically family-based enterprises having strong roots in the family and community systems. India being a diverse country with people from different backgrounds, the local entrepreneurs have devised business models that suit their conditions and systems. Overall, the non-corporate business seems to rest on the larger foundations of Indian ethos and values.

7.1.3 Generation of Funds from Own and Close Sources

In the Indian business system, most of the funds are usually generated by the promoters through savings and close sources of networks.

Generation of funds in unorganized sector

The data provided by the Government of India shows that for the establishments covered in the Economic Census 2005, most of the funds are raised by the promoters from their own sources, as can be seen in Table 7.2.

Table 7.2 shows that out of a total of 41.83 million establishments functioning in the country, 37.63 million (89.97 per cent) were found to be self-financing. This is a very high number for the ordinary sections of the society. It clearly shows that a very high percentage of the promoters self-finance their ventures to engage in different types of entrepreneurial activities. The number of establishments financed by financial and non-financial institutions were 1.41 million (3.37 per cent) and 0.62 million (1.49 per cent), respectively. A total of 0.40 million establishments (0.96 per cent) was reported to have taken assistance of other voluntary organizations including NGOs. It is only 4.21 per cent of the establishments that were found to be financed by the government sources. Hence more than 95 per cent of the establishments were financed by the promoters and non-governmental sources.

Mobilization of funds in clusters

Studies of clusters, where the larger enterprises are functioning, show that most of the funds are provided by promoters' savings, contribution from family and close sources. A study of the branded ghee business in Tamil Nadu revealed that in almost all the cases the families provided the entire funds to start businesses[18]. There

Table 7.2 Distribution of All Establishments by Major Activity Group and by Source of Finance
(Figure in absolute number)

Sl. No.	Activity	Number of establishments financed by				
		No Finance/ self-financing	Assistance from Government sources	Borrowing from financial institution	Borrowing from non-institution money lender	Others like NGO, voluntary organization, etc.
(1)	(2)	(3)	(4)	(5)	(6)	(7)
1	Farming of animals	4,989,736	81,575	130,882	61,275	25,843
2	Agriculture services	389,727	11,990	21,945	4,146	2,200
3	Fishing etc.	324,207	10,213	9,866	14,143	2,235
4	All agricultural activities	5,703,670	103,778	162,693	79,564	30,278
5	Mining and quarrying	74,556	3,074	5,254	1,387	534
6	Manufacturing	7,723,191	127,341	299,767	127,187	44,719
7	Electricity, gas and water supply	39,785	22,192	1,753	470	994
8	Construction	303,953	4,108	7,230	3,641	1,401
9	Sale, maint. and repair of motor vehicles, motorcycles	651,916	13,634	36,283	10,984	3,866
10	Wholesale trade	777,209	15,439	38,801	15,739	5,229
11	Retail trade	13,946,148	219,650	481,138	243,464	62,590
12	Hotels and restaurants	1,375,043	30,514	48,250	28,087	9,915
13	Transport, storage	1,260,059	50,479	140,887	48,038	13,091
14	Post and telecommunications	609,240	52,635	22,951	8,556	4,008
15	Financial intermediation	225,502	43,060	11,420	3,234	8,938
16	Real estate, renting and bussiness services	912,391	24,142	54,521	16,730	7,266
17	Public administration and defence; compulsory social security	283,533	264,597	11,211	1,873	12,145
18	Education	799,181	585,445	21,281	6,035	29,411
19	Health and social work	617,400	126,250	20,297	5,306	11,478
20	Other community, social and personal service activities	2,326,347	74,320	46,064	24,143	155,339
21	Other activities	1,376	146	137	12	95
22	All non-agricultural activities	31,926,830	1,657,026	1,247,245	544,886	371,019
23	All agricultural and non-agricultural activities	37,630,500	1,760,804	1,409,938	624,450	401,297

Source: *Economic Census 2005*, Government of India.

was no outside funding at all. A study conducted among 35 diamond exporters in Surat and Ahmedabad revealed that 16 of them had received more than 30 per cent of the initial capital from their relatives, while another 15 had received funds to the extent of 20 per cent to 30 per cent[19]. In Rajkot, it was revealed that entrepreneurs got funds from relatives and community men without interest and even without any time limit for repayment. Promoters mobilize funds through other sources such as informal networks, indigenous methods and local financiers also. Though the funds contributed by banks and institutional sources vary from business to business, generally they are less.

Role of ladies in financing

In this context, it is important to record the role that mothers, grandmothers, wives and sisters play by contributing funds to the businesses. While writing on the mothers of *Gounder* caste households in Coimbatore region, Chari[20] notes: "The mother of the *Gounder* household was key, not only in unwaged, reproductive labour but also in marketing household products. Moreover, she seems to have controlled family earnings to secure commodities necessary to reproduce the family. This implication that women held the purse-strings of rural *Gounder* households recurs in the gendered self-perceptions of *Gounder* men today, specifically in the ways self-made men speak of accessing family savings from their mothers." In the case of promoters of the Tirupur based *Viking* brand, one of the largest brands of hosiery items in the country, it was the maternal grandmother who helped them by pledging her jewels and lands to finance the business when they were facing difficulties in different stages.* In a few cases it was observed that dowries have played the crucial role in the promotion of ventures. In a study conducted among the *Reddiar* community businessmen in two districts of central Tamil Nadu, seven out of forty businessmen interviewed revealed that they were supported by their married sisters for making initial investments[21].

Local financiers

Apart from own and close sources, local financiers play a notable role in many of the centres. Even when bank facilities are there, businessmen prefer the local financiers to banks. This is due to different reasons such as convenience, easy availability and lack of rigid formalities and procedures. In the context of Karur, it was

* Eswaran, Promoter-brother of Viking group of companies, Tirupur, interview, 27.08.2006.

mentioned: "Borrowers in Karur clearly prefer the unorganized sector than the banks even though the interest rates are higher. Personal relationships, flexibility and timely assistance are the reasons for preferring the unorganized sector[22]." Of course, this might be a little more exceptional because in most of the cases the partners of the finance entities in Karur were relatives, friends and contacts of the businessmen. But in most of the centres, the businessmen tend to rely more on traditional networks and local financiers than on banks and institutions.

Plough back most, consume little

Moreover, it is important to note that the businessmen in clusters usually invest most of their surpluses back into the business for expansion and diversification. Purchase of assets and savings are the other priorities. Generally, the consumption expenditure is very less. Though the tendency to spend more is increasing among the younger generations especially in a few centres, they are largely restrained by the family and community norms. In the case of Palladam powerloom textile exporters, it was observed that all of them had reinvested their surpluses into the business, with 80 per cent of them investing their entire surpluses, and 13.3 per cent of them investing 80 per cent[23]. It shows that even for expansion and diversification, the businessmen mostly rely on own funds.

Lesser borrowings from banks

Even in the case of the corporate sector, Indian companies seem to rely less on borrowings from banks and financial institutions. The data provided by the Reserve Bank of India shows that the bank borrowings by the non-government, non-financial public limited companies averaged 20.4 per cent during 2003–04 to 2007–08[24]. Bank credit to the private sector has always remained lower compared to the other countries in the world. Table 7.3 presents figures of bank credit to the private sector in India, China, US and the world during 1970s to 2001–03.

Table 7.3 Bank Credit to the Private Sector: A Cross-country Survey (1970s to 2001–03)

(per cent to GDP)

Country	1970s	1981–85	1986–90	1991–95	1999–00	2001–03
China	51.7	60.2	79.6	91.1	111.8	136.6
India	18.8	27.9	30.5	28.8	29.4	35.5
US	117.4	121.7	147.6	162.5	220.6	190.6
World	80.4	88.2	110.0	120.3	139.8	131.5

Source: Report on Currency and Finance, 2003–04, Reserve Bank of India, 2004, p. 160.

Table 7.3 shows that during 2001–03, bank credit to the private sector as a per cent of GDP was only 35.5 per cent in India, whereas it was 136.6 per cent in China and 190.6 per cent in the US. It is important to note that the percentage of bank credit provided to the private sector in India is less than 19 per cent of the credit provided in the US, and is only 27 per cent of the world average. Table 7.4 provides figures for credit to private sectors for the recent years.

Table 7.4 Credit to Private Sector (2001–04)

(per cent to GDP)

Country/Year	2001	2002	2003	04
China	63	65	62	63
India	33	37	37	41
US	225	212	236	249
World	134	130	136	138

Source: Annual Report 2005–06, Reserve Bank of India, 2006, p. 37.

Table 7.4 clearly proves that credit to private sector in India is comparatively lower than the international standards. *Global Financial Stability Report 2005* reports that during 2004 private sector credit to GDP was 38.3 per cent in India, 140.5 per cent in China and 155.8 per cent in the UK[25]. These figures show that the dependency of the Indian private sector on bank credit is lesser when compared to the advanced economies in the world.

Foreign investments

Table 7.5 provides foreign direct investments as percentage of GDP of India during 1992–93 to 2004–05[26].

Table 7.5 Foreign Direct Investments (1992–93 to 2004–05)

(as percentage of GDP)

	1992–93	1993–94	1994–95	1995–96	1996–97	1997–98	1998–99	1999–00	2000–01	2001–02	2002–03	2003–04	2004–05
FDI	0.13	0.21	0.41	0.60	0.73	0.87	0.59	0.48	0.88	1.28	0.99	0.78	0.80

Source: Reserve Bank of India and Economic Survey as quoted in *Economic and Political Weekly*, March 8, 2006, p. 992.

Table 7.5 clearly reveals that the share of foreign direct investment in India during the above period has been very minimal. During the entire period, more than 99 per cent of the investments were due to the domestic funds. In none of the years, except during 2001–02, the foreign investments exceeded 1 per cent. In fact, in some of the earlier years, the saving rates were more than the rates of gross domestic investments. It is another matter that even this small foreign investment comes with a lot of conditionalities, much against the interests of the local industries and the economy.

Table 7.6 presents figures for foreign direct and portfolio investments from 1992–93 to 2010–11 in rupee and dollar terms.

Table 7.6 Foreign Investment Inflows (1992–93 to 2010–11)

Year	A. Direct investment		B. Portfolio investment		Total (A + B)	
	(₹ crore)	(US $ million)	(₹ crore)	(US $ million)	(₹ crore)	(US $ million)
1	2	3	4	5	6	7
1992–93	965	315	748	244	1713	559
1993–94	1838	586	11,188	3567	13,026	4153
1994–95	4126	1314	12,007	3824	16,133	5138
1995–96	7172	2144	9192	2748	16,364	4892
1996–97	10,015	2821	11,758	3312	21,773	6133
1997–98	13,220	3557	6794	1828	20,014	5385
1998–99	10,358	2462	–257	–61	10,101	2401
1999–00	9338	2155	13,112	3026	22,450	5181
2000–01	18,406	4029	12,609	2760	31,015	6789
2001–02	29,235	6130	9639	2021	38,874	8151
2002–03	24,367	5035	4738	979	29,105	6014
2003–04	19,860	4322	52,279	11,377	72,139	15,699
2004–05	27,188	6051	41,854	9315	69,042	15,366
2005–06	39,674	8961	55,307	12,492	94,981	21,453
2006–07	1,03,367	22,826	31,713	7003	1,35,080	29,829
2007–08	1,40,180	34,835	1,09,741	27,271	2,49,921	62,106
2008–09	1,73,741	37,838	–63,618	–13,855	1,10,123	23,983
2009–10	1,79,059	37,763	1,53,516	32,376	3,32,575	70,139
2010–11	1,38,462	30,380	1,43,435	31,471	2,81,897	61,851

Notes:
1. Data for 2009–10 and 2010–11 are provisional.
2. Data from 1995–96 onwards include acquisition of shares of Indian companies by non-residents under Section 6 of FEMA, 1999. Data on such acquisitions are included as part of FDI since January 1996.
3. Data on FDI have been revised since 2000–01 with expanded coverage to approach international best practices. Data from 2000–01 onwards are not comparable with FDI data for earlier years.
4. Negative (–) sign indicates outflow.
5. Direct investment data for 2006–07 include swap of shares of 3.1 billion.

Source: Handbook of Statistics on the Indian Economy 2010–11, Reserve Bank of India, p. 260.

Table 7.6 reveals a steady increase in foreign investments since the beginning of the 1990s. Direct investments have been gradually allowed into different sectors over the years and as a result, more foreign investments have come into selected industries. But even then, as the Reserve Bank of India notes: "Domestic saving financed more than 95 per cent of investments, and the remaining by capital flows[27]."

Inflow of funds under the portfolio investments remained higher since 2003–04, except during 2008–09 due to the slowdown caused by the global crisis. More foreign institutional investors (FIIs) have entered India during the past few years and there were 1722 FIIs registered with the Securities and Exchange Board of India at the end of March 2011[28]. The FIIs remain very active in the Indian stock markets during the recent years. The Securities and Exchange Board of India notes: "FIIs play an important role in Indian securities markets. Since 1992–93, when FIIs were allowed entry into the Indian financial markets, foreign institutional investment has increased over the years except in 2008–09. In tandem with the boom in stock markets and a better global scenario, investments by FIIs into India were quite high in last few years, particularly since 2003–04. FIIs made a record investment in the Indian equity market in 2010–11, surpassing the 2009–10 inflows[29]." It mentions particularly the higher investments during 2010–11 and notes: "The total net investment of FII was ₹1,46,438 crores in 2010–11. This was the highest net FII investments into Indian securities markets in any financial year so far[30]."

Use of money

It was observed in the non-corporate sector that the businessmen generally make the best use of every rupee they invest. An analysis by the *Economic Times Intelligence Group* noted that the Indian companies in the FMCG category 'seem to be almost thrice as efficient as global heavyweights when it comes to utilization of capital.' It showed that for every rupee invested, the Indian companies generated ₹ 4 worth of sales, whereas it was only ₹ 1.50 for multinationals[31].

7.1.4 Community Drive

Indian business is society-driven. It is the society that promotes and drives businesses. Only after the businesses prosper, do the states enter the picture. Clearly, in almost all the cases, it is the communities that take up initiatives for businesses and establish ventures. As the businesses grow, economic developments follow suit. Earlier, business used to be mostly in the hands of a few trading communities. The trading networks continued to survive the changes in the political situation for many centuries. Dutta[32] notes that "the business families in India belong to some distinct communities. Raychaudhuri and Habib observe that the same communities have continued to dominate business over the millennia. These are mostly the trader castes of the Hindu caste system." But it does not seem to mean that business was confined to only a few communities. Writing in the context of trade in western India during the eleventh to fourteenth centuries, Jain[33] mentions that "trade was the chief vocation of the *vaisyas,* but it was certainly not their monopoly. The pressure of economic circumstances and the urge for economic gains had compelled people from all sections and strata of society to take to trade from earlier times. In fact, the concept of *apaddharma*, which allowed the people of higher as well as lower *varnas* to take up trade in times of distress, made mercantile community a class in which the cult of wealth cut across the concept of castes." Quoting sources, Rudner David West[34] mentions that there was no caste basis in Indian commercial activities during the sixteenth to the nineteenth centuries.

Banias *and neo*-banias

There have been many developments during the later centuries, but the trading castes continue to have a major share of business even today. Gurucharan Das[35] notes: "Indian firms, by and large, continue to be family-run. And that, too, by the *Bania* families of the traditional trading castes. It is predominantly the *Aggarwals* and *Guptas* in the North, the *Chettiars* in the South, the *Parsees*, Gujarati *Jains* and *Banias,* Muslim *Khojas* and *Memons* in the West, and *Marwaris* in the East, and, in fact, across the country. Of these, the *Marwaris* have been the most successful." The history of post-independent India shows that non-trading castes have entered businesses in a big way and have made a name for themselves within a short time. Some of the communities from traditional agricultural backgrounds such as the *Patels* in Gujarat and the *Nadars* and *Gounders* in Tamil Nadu have proved to be very astute in diverse manufacturing and business activities at the national and even international levels. These neo-business communities have learned the art of business within a short time and are presently engaged in different types of activities. The growth and development of businesses during the last few decades, especially at the non-corporate and cluster levels, are mainly due to the efforts of these communities. Studies show that no business is difficult to these neo-business communities. Whether it is the diamond or engineering industries in Gujarat, or hosiery, transport, fireworks or rig industries of Tamil Nadu, they are all driven by the neo-business communities. While in a few cases they have learnt the businesses from trading communities, in a number of instances, they have promoted different businesses themselves.

It is important to note that a few agricultural communities that trace their original roots to the neighbouring states have proved to be very successful in different businesses as neo-*banias* by completely integrating with the local societies, enriching the local economy and society. Taking Tamil Nadu for example, the *Khamma Naidus* of Coimbatore region have proved themselves to be successful businessmen in different businesses such as textiles, foundries and pump manufacturing. The seeds for industrial development and higher education in Coimbatore were shown by them, which was later picked up by the local communities. Similarly the *Rajus* of Rajapalayam region excelled in textiles during the earlier decades. The *Reddys* of Trichy belt have proved themselves in hotels and transports.

It is significant to mention that the number of people entering business and industrial sectors from the socially disadvantaged sections of the society has been increasing over the years. The 4th All India Census of the Micro, Small and Medium Enterprises (MSME) sector reveals that 48.75 per cent of the registered enterprises in the country are owned by the socially backward classes. The Census notes that out of the total number of units estimated in the registered MSME sector, 38.28 per cent are owned by the Other Backward Castes, 7.60 per cent by the Scheduled Castes and 2.87 per cent by the Scheduled Tribes. Thus, there are 1.64 lakh enterprises owned by the entrepreneurs belonging to the Scheduled Caste and Scheduled Tribe categories[36].

In this connection, it is relevant to note that the number of entrepreneurs from Dalit communities running companies very successfully with higher turnovers is increasing. Dalit Indian Chamber of Commerce and Industry was promoted in 2005 to bring together businessmen and professionals belonging to the community with a vision to help people to 'be job givers, instead of job seekers.'

*Neo-*banias *promote new businesses*

Let us take, for example, the rig industry of Tiruchengode in Tamil Nadu. Thiruchengode, forming part of Namakkal district, has made a name for itself throughout the country for rigs. The history of this industry is informative. During the 1960s, there was a severe water scarcity in Tiruchengode. A group of persons from the farming households joined together to buy a rig for digging borewells in their lands. Then they found that others too required rigs, as the water levels were low. Seeing the demand, they formed into smaller groups, made new partnerships, purchased rigs and started digging wells for others in the neighbouring areas. Soon they realized that water level was scarce in different places including the other states. More people entered the business and they began moving to different states such as Karnataka, Andhra Pradesh, Maharashtra, Madhya Pradesh, Rajasthan and Orissa. In fact, when there was an acute scarcity of water in a few states, the rig owners from Thiruchengode went to those places and helped the governments to tide over the water crisis. This is an entirely community-driven effort without any outside advice or help. The people who sowed the seeds of the business were all ordinary persons. Is it not remarkable then that the business promoted by the ordinary persons of the society went to help the governments in their difficult times?

When the rig owners started business, they developed models that were suitable to them. They generally preferred partnerships. This was necessary for an important reason. This business required travel to long distances and absence from families for longer durations. So one needed faithful partners, as otherwise one would not be able to manage the business in distant places single-handedly. Close friends and relatives were thus chosen as partners. A study by Kanagasabapathi and Arun Kumar[37] showed that there were nearly 58 per cent of friends and 32 per cent of relatives as partners. The study also showed that 58 per cent of partners were chosen for managing the business, as against 16 per cent for investments. It is important to note here that in a majority of the cases, partners were selected for management of businesses during the leave period of the main partners from the work-sites. It is interesting to note that when investments are not the main criterion, friends are preferred as partners to relatives. Through this method of partnerships and hard work, they successfully expanded and established the rig business on a national scale. Now let us see the retail business in Tamil Nadu. The retail business was new to the *Nadar* community when they entered the business initially, as their traditional occupation was related to agriculture. But today, they dominate the retail business sector in Tamil Nadu, having set up shops throughout the state. They operate even outside the state in a few metropolitan cities.

Communities have cost advantages

Experts note that the community relationships provide certain benefits and cost advantages in business. One is trust, which is very important for business. Communities generate high levels of trust due to their close-knit relationships. Second is the lower transaction costs compared to the rates determined by the markets. As a result, efficiency is increased and costs are reduced. Hayami[38] notes: "...trust accumulated through personal interactions in the community increases efficiency and reduces costs associated with the division of labour." The World Bank has acknowledged that the community-based relationships help business to become competitive in the international markets. The *World Development Report 2001* reveals as to how the majority community of Tirupur was able to succeed in the knitted garment industry due to the transfer of capital through community networks.

The *Report* notes: "Since 1985, Tirupur has become a hotbed of economic activity in the production of knitted garments. By the 1990s, with high growth rates of exports, Tirupur was a world leader in the knitted garment industry. The success of this industry is striking. This is particularly so as the production of knitted garments is capital-intensive, and the state banking monopoly had been ineffective at targeting capital funds to efficient entrepreneurs, especially at the levels necessary to sustain Tirupur's high growth rates. What is behind this story of development? The needed capital was raised within the *Gounder* community, a caste relegated to land-based activities, relying on community and family networks. Those with capital in the *Gounder* community transfer it to others in the community through long-established informal credit institutions and rotating savings and credit associations. These networks were viewed as more reliable in transmitting information and enforcing contracts than the banking and legal systems that offered weak protection of creditor rights. The intense competition in the garment industry ensured that good money would not follow bad and that firms would pay attention to the needs of customers[39]."

Community-dominated businesses

There are instances in which almost all or a majority of families of communities belonging to specific villages or areas are in a single business. For example, the *Reddiar* community, belonging to a few villages in a southern district of Tamil Nadu, confines itself to the hotel industry. People from these villages have spread out to different areas of the state to start hotels as partnership ventures, and have later moved into the nearby states. A few of them own hotels even abroad. They identify themselves totally with the hotel industry, though in recent times, they are found to enter other businesses too. In the case of *Borah* Muslims, one could identify an orientation towards only one industry. Most of them are in the hardware business in different parts of the country and even outside. Due to the close-knit relationship within the community, new entrants are encouraged and supported by the community men.

Opportunities for all communities

As a result of the development dynamics, new communities from different backgrounds have been entering businesses in India for a long time. The entry of newer communities is more during the last few decades. Tripathi and Jumani[40] note: “In fact, it can be safely maintained that at practically every watershed of Indian industrial history—the groups and individuals, whom the conventional caste norms should have kept from indulging in business activities, plunged into the modern organized sector more readily than those who were already settled in traditional lines.” In this connection, studies in different prominent business centres give highly informative and interesting results. For example, a study of the Visakhapatnam businessmen showed that most of them were from the nearby districts, while the share of locals was minimum[41].

Though many of the businesses and business centres are dominated by one or more communities, there are not many difficulties for the new entrants from diverse backgrounds. Different studies in business centres have shown that businessmen generally do not take into account the community factor in the course of business. It is significant to note that there are many owners from the so-called scheduled castes in business centres. In the match industry dominated Sivakasi region in South India, one could observe several owners from these communities. In the Dhottabellapura silk centre in Karnataka, many *Harijans* owned weaving units. Jodhka[42] notes that independent entrepreneurship has been rising among dalits in Uttar Pradesh and Haryana regions. In the Sankagiri transport cluster, when a loyal employee belonging to the so-called scheduled caste wanted to start his own business, his employer belonging to the majority community provided him with a part of the investment. For the balance of funds, the majority community men stood guarantee to him for a loan against chit, while he contributed his savings as the rest. There are instances where people from the so-called most backward castes are engaged in business with the locally dominant communities as equal partners. All these developments indicate that though businesses are dominated by communities, the field is open to all the willing entrants. There does not seem to be serious barriers for any one from any background to engage in businesses.

Higher and similar value systems throughout the country

It is important to note that there exists a close relationship among businessmen irrespective of their backgrounds, such as caste, region and religion. Writing in the context of the Kanpur saddlery units, where two different religious communities are engaged in business, Dwivedi[43] notes: "...it can be seen that exporters and suppliers from both the communities have no reservations about working with each other. Moreover, because exporters come from two different communities and one community has almost a monopoly over the most important raw material—leather, if inter-firm trust and co-operation is to occur, it has to be across cultural identities." In this context, it is important to note that higher value systems prevail among different business communities across the country. Dutta[44] notes: "The cultural artifacts—the languages spoken, gods worshipped and the numerous other details—differ from business community to business community across the country. But the value systems are surprisingly similar."

7.1.5 Relationship, Faith and Goodwill as the Base

Indian businesses, especially at the non-corporate level, largely function on the basis of faith and goodwill. Whenever an urgent need for finance arises, the businessmen always turn to other businessmen for help. They borrow from others, either with interest or without it, depending on their relationships. Usually no security is demanded. It is completely the faith, based on personal relationships that enables the lender to lend funds. Such monetary transactions are there in almost all the places in different businesses across the country. As was noted earlier, even in the case of the finance business, faith and goodwill form the basis of much of the transactions. The financiers give more weightage to the reputation and goodwill of a person than the documents and material evidences. In different communities there are financial mechanisms to help their people promote businesses, and to rescue them when they incur losses. For example, Mittal noted that there were one lakh merchants belonging to the *Agroha biradari* of the *Agarwal* merchants in Agroha town. When one of their businesses fails, each of the remaining 99,999 businessmen would donate one rupee and a brick to help the insolvent person so that he could build his house and start business again[45]. In the Indian system, relationships extend naturally beyond specific communities, easily in business matters. It was observed in the Gujarat kite industry that people from two religious communities work with each other closely, mutually depending on each other in different centres[46].

Different kinds of relationships

The influence of relationships in business is of different types. In a number of cases the blood relatives influence people to enter business. In the case of the diamond export industry, 18 out of a sample of 35 exporters cited the influence of relatives as the motivation for entering business[47]. In fact, in all the centres, there is large scale influence of relatives in business. But then the relationships go beyond relatives and extend to friends, employees and contacts. In many of these clusters, one could notice a sizeable number of friends as partners in businesses. In such cases, all other relationships become secondary. It is common to see ex-workers joining together to promote businesses. There are instances in which the loyal and talented employees are taken up as partners, as a mark of recognition of their services to the growth of firms without any financial contribution. In a few clusters, there is the practice of the employer giving a part of the seed money without interest to his ex-employees when they promote businesses; in a few other places employees leave a part of their salary with their owners. After a few years, the employees get the accumulated amount and use it as capital to promote a venture. In many cases, when the ex-employees start businesses, their first transaction would be with their previous owners.

Even in the case of the corporate sector one could see a general camaraderie among businessmen, in spite of the intense competition and even rivalry. Normally, the differences do not degenerate into open conflicts, even though this is not always the case. There is an overall sense of explicit mutual respect among businessmen. This is perhaps the major reason for companies not generally taking over the ones promoted by others, unlike in the case of the western countries. The natural tendency of networking has helped Indians establish businesses even in distant lands. The *Patels*, for example, dominate the motel industry in the US through their network of relationships. In fact, the networks of Indians have been acknowledged in the western countries. It was mentioned that the UK-based banks, Lloyds and Midland, offer loans to Indian businessmen on the basis of guarantees offered by the community[48].

Relationship-based practices become general norms

The business practices born out of relationships become the general norms in business centres. So a minimum amount of goodwill is extended to everyone irrespective of the personal relationships. With regard to Kanpur saddlery cluster, it was mentioned: "What is remarkable about these ties is that they function without any contracts even when a new business is initiated. Thus, right from the start, a minimum amount of goodwill is extended to any party within the cluster, irrespective of the personal ties. As contracts are not used at all and this practice does not depend on personal ties, it seems to act as a sociological precondition for trust and co-operation to develop[49]." As a result, faith and goodwill form the basis of business in different centres. A study among businessmen belonging to different centres in the Gujarat kite industry revealed that the business transactions take place on the basis of trust without any documents, due to practice and inherent faith[50]. Kanagasabapathi[51] mentions: "Studies of business practices in different industrial and business centres show the prevalence of higher human values and unwritten norms in the contemporary Indian business systems, especially at the non-corporate sector levels."

7.1.6 Less Dependence on State

Traditionally, Indians live as families and communities. Since the ancient times, one could see Indians having lived as self-sustaining and independent communities. In fact, there were kingless states in ancient periods. Generally, Indians never seem to have depended totally on the state, maybe except during invasions and alien rules, when their systems were not allowed to function. The native Indian businesses and business systems were systematically destroyed by the British during their rule. The culture of doing business was stymied for more than two centuries. As a result, the high native entrepreneurial spirit of India had to lie low. After independence, there was large scale failure on the part of the policy-makers to understand and recognize the traditional entrepreneurial spirit of India, and no serious attempts were made to give the required freedom to enable people to engage in businesses. But in spite of this, a large number of people entered different ventures in the decades after independence. A few of them had started entering business even earlier. These entrepreneurs had started enterprises with their own initiatives with the amount they could mobilize, and functioned on their own without bothering about the state. In the context of Karur, Corsi[52] quotes Neelakantan to say: "The most particular aspect of industrial development of Karur is that although the authorities are now intervening to control and orientate the direction of this change, its origin was no fruit of a government strategy or of large investment in the sector." It is to be remembered that the Indian economy and business had largely remained a product of the society, until the intervention of the

British. So, basically, the Indian mind has always been a self-dependent, and not a state-dependent, one.

Success despite the state

After independence, when people realized that the rulers would no longer be able to curtail their initiatives completely, they began to initiate new ventures. Though the government policies were not exactly favourable, people took the lead and promoted enterprises. The self-dependent mind of the Indians began to assert itself without worrying about the support from the state and state mechanisms. It was this assertion that led to the large-scale developments in various sectors. The seeds for entrepreneurial activities in India in different industrial and business clusters were sown, even during the times of Nehruvian era of socialism. The people of India took to entrepreneurial activities, in spite of, and not because of the governments. Writing in the context of the Gounder Community, Chari[53] notes: "To paraphrase S. Neelakantan, an economist from western Tamil Nadu, familiar with these environs, Gounders have succeeded *despite* the state, and it is this success under inhospitable conditions that highlights the central role of the entrepreneur." This could be understood when we realize that most of the clusters were promoted by the entrepreneurs, even without the governments realizing the fact. After the 1990s when there was liberalization and the economy was opened up, people who were in a position to take advantage of the opportunities, made full use of them immediately, and different sections of the Indian businesses grew fast. As a result, they have raised India to the position of one of the fastest growing economies in the world.

Fukuyama[54] writes: "A healthy capitalist economy is one in which there will be sufficient social capital in the underlying society to permit businesses, corporations, networks, and the like to be self-organizing. In default of this self-organizing capability, the state can step in to promote key firms and sectors, but markets almost always work more efficiently when private actors are making the decisions." The independent attitude of Indians has made them to develop all the facilities that they require on their own initiatives without depending on the state. In the recent decades, the organized business sector has cultivated the power to represent its problems and put forth its demands. But most of the businesses in the non-corporate sector have not gathered enough clout to voice their grievances. While the different sectors of businesses grow with the support of the state and institutional mechanisms in developed countries, much of the Indian businesses have grown on their own.

7.1.7 Risk-bearing Nature

Indian businessmen generally tend to bear all the risks upon themselves. In the non-corporate sector, the owners shoulder all the risks, as it is their nature and necessity. In the case of proprietorship units, which are the most common forms of organization, the proprietors take all the risks on their shoulders. They contribute their savings, sell or pledge their assets, get support from relatives and friends, borrow money from local sources and start ventures. If something goes wrong, they take up all the responsibility for their investments. In the case of partnership businesses, the partners share the risks.

Many a time, the promoters of the non-corporate sector units are left to shoulder the entire burden upon themselves because the state and the institutions do not provide adequate help to them, due to lack of proper understanding of the ground realties and inadequacies of the system. With regard to finance, generally these businesses do not get adequate attention from the banks. As a result, they go to moneylenders and local financiers who charge high rates of interest. But even after paying higher rates for their funds, most of the businesses succeed due to the cost saving measures and dedication of the promoters. In the case of corporate sector, the dependence of companies on equity markets is generally low, compared to the western countries.

7.2 BASIC FEATURES OF WESTERN BUSINESS MODELS

The basic features of western business models are presented in the following pages.

7.2.1 Individualistic

The western business models are based on individualistic notions, as their economic ideology is rooted in individualism. We have seen earlier in Chapters 3 and 4, as to how the economic philosophy of the West revolves around the idea that everyone is an individual trying to maximize one's own pleasures and benefits, disregarding the cost to others and the overall system in which they operate. As a result, the pleasure or enjoyment of each one of them is supreme, however transient it may be. Hence, individual choices with regard to preferences, likes and dislikes, are predominant in every family and small group. So their business models try to attract and target different groups of people as individuals, according to their preferences and choices. The system encourages businesses to be more and more individualistic in their approaches. Even the children are their target customers. Accordingly, products are designed and advertised, and human tendencies are exploited, no matter whether they are beneficial to the user or not. There are instances when mothers had to intervene on behalf of the interests of their children, but even then the state could not do much to help them protect their wards from the narrow business interests.

Since everyone is made to think and act as an individual, desires are created by advertisements and products are sold thereafter. This is facilitated by making people believe that spending is a must and one should spend even when one does not have the resources. Banks provide all sorts of facilities to make people borrow through different schemes and new instruments. Credit cards are freely distributed in anticipation of future incomes. With the result, every one tries to borrow and participate in spending as much as possible. People are encouraged to buy more products, for luxury than for necessity. Hence, there is a huge market for luxury products. In such a system, the companies are worried only about their sales and profits. The overall interests of the individual, let alone the community and the macro systems, are not given even the minimum respect that they deserve.

This individualistic orientation gets reflected in every walk of their life and business activities. So whether it is financing or marketing, this orientation remains as the basis. It is not that the West does not have family-owned enterprises. In fact, in many of the countries, the family-owned enterprises are higher in number. Even in the US there are more number of highly successful family-owned enterprises and companies. Gurucharan Das[55] notes that in the US, which is considered as the most 'professionalized' business nation, 40 per cent of GNP is still created by family companies and more than 80 per cent of all enterprises are family-run. But their business orientation is based on individualistic notions. The businessmen are not bothered about the long term consequences of the individualistic approaches, as their sole motive is earning more and more profits.

Top management as selfish individuals

When corporations deal with the outside world, the top managements would see to it that they maximize benefits at all costs. They resort to all kinds of methods to increase their bottom lines. But when it comes to the benefits from the corporations concerned, many of the top managements would use all techniques to garner as much benefits as possible to them, without worrying about others who contribute to their growth. To earn more for themselves, they cook up accounts and boost the numbers without looking at the long-term consequences of the organizations entrusted to them as custodians. This is the lesson that we learn from the recent experiences in the US and the West. The fact that the shareholders, as the owners who have contributed capital, might have to lose their wealth is not their prime consideration. Such is the level of individualistic orientation in the business system.

Greame Salaman[56] succinctly explains the attitudes of the US Chief Executives and cautions India not to follow the West: "In the West, leaders have become 'celebrity egos', paying themselves vast amounts of money and pursuing often their own interests at the expense of the staff or the shareholder. Ten years ago, in an American organization, the CEO's salary was 28 times more than the lowest rung employee. Today, it is 500 times more. These people have just gone mad. They have been robbing companies at the expense not only of the workforce but also at the expense of the shareholder. In theory, you have a chairman and a CEO. The chairman runs the board on behalf of the investors and then ensures that the CEO runs the business on their behalf. But increasingly, in America, the CEO and the chairman are the same person. This means, the system of checks and balances can be lost. As far as Indian companies are concerned, they are much more likely to be family-owned, retain the distance between the chairman and the CEO, define leadership in terms of the long-term success of the business and growth rather than in terms of the extravagant rewards to the chief executive. Also, the notion of protection and looking after the workforce is still a dominant value in Indian businesses, which is not the case in the individualistic culture of the West. So, what I am basically saying is that we could learn from you. I don't think it is necessarily the case that you need to follow the West. I think it'll be a very good thing if you don't."

7.2.2 Dominance of the Corporate Sector

In the western economic and business systems, notably the US, the corporate sector is dominant. Though the small scale and medium scale enterprises are much more in number and operate successfully in different fields, the corporate sector dominates the system. In the words of Dugger[57]: "In the corporate economies of the contemporary West, the market is a passive institution. The active institution is the corporation... an inherently narrow and short-sighted organization. The corporation has evolved to serve the interests of whoever controls it, at the expense of whomever does not".

Writing in the mid-90s, Korten pointed out that a few agri-business corporations had made millions of farming communities to ultimately "disappear" in the US. To quote Korten[58]: "From 1935 to 1989, the number of small firms in the United States declined from 6.8 million to under 2.1 million; during the same period, US population roughly doubled. As farmers have gone out of business, so too have the local suppliers, implement dealers, and other small businesses that once supported them. Entire rural communities have disappeared. Meanwhile, the major US agri-business corporations have grown and consolidated their power. The top ten "farms" in the United States are now international agri-business corporations with names like Tyson Foods, ConAgra, Gold Kist, Continental Grain, Perdue Farms, Pilgrims Pride, and Cargill—each with annual farm products sales ranging from $310 million to $1.7 billion." There is no doubt that the corporate sector contributes significantly to their business systems. But what is disturbing is the manner of its growth and the disproportionate dominance it wields, making the economical, social and political systems highly susceptible to its interests.

With the rise in the power of mega corporations, human interests get subordinated to the larger corporate interests. Korten[59] notes: "The contemporary corporation increasingly exists as an entity apart—even from the people who compose it. Every member of the corporate class, no matter how powerful his or her position within the corporation, has become expendable—as growing numbers of top executives are learning. As corporations gain in autonomous institutional power and become more detached from people and place, the human interest and the corporate interest increasingly diverge. It is almost as though we were invaded by alien beings, intent on colonizing our planet, reducing us to serfs, and then excluding as many of us as possible." Khor[60] says: "... the large corporations have taken over a large part of the decision-making even in the developed countries, at the expense of the power of the State or political and social leaders." The enormous concentration of resources at the disposal of a small number of corporations has made them dominate the political process in the richest countries. Shutt[61] notes: "This wealth is translated into political power by means of the huge and ever expanding contributions made (quite legally) by these organizations to the functioning of political parties. This phenomenon is more conspicuous in the US, where the scale of such corporate funding is estimated to have reached around US $3 billion in the federal elections of 2000, still, be it noted, a modest sum compared to the massive pay-off corporate America receives through federal spending programmes, subsidies and tax-breaks. The stronghold which big business has thus gained over the political process and the agenda of mainstream political parties in all industrialized countries is of course further reinforced by its collective control of the press and other mass media."

The power of the western corporate sector has grown so much that they interfere in the functioning of the economic and business systems of other countries. Korten[62] says: "Corporations have emerged as the dominant governance institutions on the planet, with the largest among them reaching into virtually every country of the world and exceeding most governments in size and power. Increasingly, it is the corporate interest more than the human interest that defines the policy agendas of states and international bodies, although this reality and its implications have gone largely unnoticed and unaddressed."

7.2.3 Contract-based Transactions

Generally, all the transactions in the western countries are contract-based. As mutual faith and goodwill are fast eroding, even the family relationships have begun to be increasingly based on contracts. Consequently, all business relationships are mostly contract-based. So for every transaction, it is safe to go through a contract, no matter how much it costs. In such a system, the final cost will be more as transaction costs multiply at each level. But it is safe to go through the contracts as otherwise it might become difficult to get the work completed, due to the absence of trust in the society. There are of course exceptions to these general practices, as close-knit communities mostly transact on the basis of trust.

7.2.4 Risk-diverting Nature

Generally the western system seems to pass on and divert the risks away from the top management. In the name of sharing risks, the system allows them to pass on the burdens to other parties and the ordinary citizens. Corporations issue equity securities and raise funds. As shareholders are the co-owners, they share the risks and of course, profits of corporations. The happenings in the last few years at some of the very big companies have proved that the top executives take enormous powers into their hands using the system to their advantage without commensurate responsibility. They enjoy a lot of benefits, with huge compensations and special privileges. But when the companies collapse, the ordinary shareholders suffer disproportionately. In the case of Enron, thousands of employees and investors lost their life-savings, children's college funds and pensions, when the company collapsed. It was reported that investors lost more than $60 billion in the collapse of Enron. In this case, for the mistakes of the top management, thousands of investors suffered. Thus the corporate system is used to divert the risks away from the top management to the investors and institutions. In the case of small and medium enterprises sector, there is a higher proportion of assistance from banks and institutions compared to India, though the promoters of smaller units raise a very large part of funds through family and close sources.

7.2.5 Large-scale Absence of Ethical Orientation

Recent developments indicate that an ethical orientation to business has been absent on a large scale. In fact, the basic ethical practices have largely declined in the last few years. The failures of mega corporations such as Enron and WorldCom a few years ago have proved that their corporate practices are totally unethical. Enron Corporation, the American energy company with around 21,000 people working in it, was one of the leading electricity, natural gas, paper and communications companies in the world, with claimed revenues of $101 billion in 2000. *Fortune* had been naming Enron as 'America's Most Innovative Company' for six consecutive years. It was later revealed that its reported financial condition was sustained mostly by systematic and creatively planned accounting frauds. It filed for bankruptcy in 2001. WorldCom was the second largest long distance phone company in the US with 85,000 employees in more than 60 countries. After charges were raised that there was a $11 billion accounting scandal in the company, it went into bankruptcy protection in 2002. In 2005, the founder of the company was found guilty and convicted on grounds of fraud, conspiracy and filing false documents with regulators, and was sentenced to 25 years in prison. In the aftermath of the Enron fiasco, it came to light that different companies were shamelessly cooking up their accounts against all basic norms of human behaviour. What was more disturbing was the collusion of the big auditing firms who were supposed to 'audit' the accounts of these companies. For over a long period of time, there have been complaints against the western multinational enterprises for their approaches and business practices in different parts of the world. The recent case of 'insider trading' in the US involving a top-notch hedge found manager shows that the higher echelons of the corporate sector can go to any length to get the extra returns.

7.3 UNIQUE NATURE OF INDIAN BUSINESS MODELS

The general orientation towards business in India seems to be largely different from that of the West. Moreover, the environment and the world views of Indians and the westerners are different. As such, the business models of India exhibit differences when compared with the business models of the West. As far as the non-corporate sector is concerned, India has a very large non-corporate sector, which, in fact, dominates the Indian business system. The non-corporate business has unique features, which has few parallels in the western countries. In the case of corporate sector, one could notice differences between India and the West in different functional areas, though some of them are getting narrowed due to international influences. The production models in the West are more mechanized and capital-intensive compared to India. The technology models of the West are generally designed to suit small populations. While the financing model of the corporate sector in the USA is largely equity-based, it is not so in India. Though the stock markets are becoming popular, the Indian corporate sector relies more on own funds and debt capital. The marketing models in the West are totally brand-oriented and impersonal. Due to the individualistic lifestyles, the buying decisions are made individually in the West. But in India, families and communities discipline and restrain the buying behaviour to a large extent. So the markets for luxury goods are many times lesser in India than in the West. Hence their marketing methods differ from the Indian methods. This is the reason why the western multinationals are compelled to change their strategies in India to suit the Indian situations.

The corporate culture of the western multinational companies (MNCs) and family businesses are different. Table 7.7 presents a few differences[63].

Table 7.7 Corporate Culture in MNCs and Family Businesses

Dimensions of corporate culture	Multinational companies	Family businesses
1. Nature of desired managerial skills and capabilities	Emphasis on professional qualification and ranks	Emphasis on street smartness and demonstrated skill
2. Managerial style of planning and decision-making	Emphasis on information gathering, non-entrepreneurial decision-making	Emphasis on selective information usage, intuitive and qualitative decision-making of an entrepreneurial nature
3. Management system adopted	Emphasis on use of elegant, scientific, sophisticated and rational system	Emphasis on reliance of business sense and no frill system
4. Nature of management control	Emphasis on comprehensive, formal and written reporting	Emphasis on primary use of verbal reporting

Source: S.K. Bhattacharya (1998), *Organizational Culture: An Indian Perspective*, p. 48.

The general business models of India and the western countries have significant differences. Guy Dollet, the then CEO of Arcelor, had used the following words, when the Indian born Mittals were trying to take control of Arcelor. To quote: "Our corporate models are different. There are differences in corporate governance and culture[64]." Different experts, including those from the West, note that the cultural orientation would be the major strength of the Indian corporate sector in the coming years. While speaking on the Indian and western business systems, Salaman[65] particularly noted the role of culture in the Indian business system and said: "One of the differences is that Indian companies because of cultural aspects have some degree of immunity against some of the viruses spreading in organizations in the West."

It is this unique background and home grown talents that are taking India to higher levels. It is interesting to note that the Indian companies make much better use of capital than the multinational enterprises, run by top-notch international professionals. Economic Times Intelligence Group has shown that the growth story of Indian corporate sector "seems to be due to domestic factors rather than external ones[66]." In this background it would be useful to remember that many international observers are cautioning Indians who try to follow the western business models blindly. To quote Salaman[67], "India, at the moment, may seem like a sleepy player. But having started the process of deregulation and the core strengths of its businesses, it has the potential to follow a path of its own. As I said earlier, you need not follow the western model." On the whole, the Indian business system exhibits special characteristics that are not to be found in the western systems. Many of these characteristics are India's core strengths and it is time we understood them so that we could nurture our businesses in the most suitable style.

REFERENCES

[1] Sudipt Dutta, *Family Business in India*, Response Books, New Delhi, 1997, p. 18.

[2] Kanagasabapathi, P., and Ramanathan, A.R., 'A Study on Butter and Ghee Industry in Kangayam with special reference to Sozhiya Chetty Community,' unpublished report, P.S.G. Institute of Management, Coimbatore, March 2006.

[3] Ibid.

[4] Godrej, Adi B., 'The Family Concern', *Business Today,* January 16, 2005.

[5] Sudipt Dutta, op.cit., p. 247.

[6] Shirur, Srinivas, *Strategic Alternatives for Family Business Houses*, Deep and Deep Publication Pvt. Ltd., New Delhi, 2005, pp. 33–34.

[7] Business Today Annual Survey 1994, *Business Today*, July 22–August 6, 1994.

[8] Kamat, Vinay, Business Today Annual Survey, *Business Today,* August 22–September 6, 1997, p. 17.

[9] Godrej, Adi, op.cit., p. 19.

[10] Sudipt Dutta, op.cit., p. 19.

[11] Ibid., p. 21.

[12] Ibid., p. 121.

[13] Tripathi, Dwijendra, 'Change and Continuity', *Seminar* 482, October 1999, p. 31.

[14] Gurucharan Das, 'The Problem', *Seminar* 482, October 1999, p. 15.

[15] Ibid.

[16] *Final Results: Third All India Census of Small Scale Industries 2001–02*, op.cit., p. 2.

[17] Ibid., p. 1.

[18] Kanagasabapathi, P., and Ramanathan, A.R., op.cit.

[19] Patel, Sharad and Kanagasabapathi, P., 'A Study on Gujarat Diamond Export Industry,' unpublished report, P.S.G. Institute of Management, Coimbatore, April 2005.

[20] Chari, Sharad, *Fraternal Capital*, Permanent Black, Delhi, 2004, p. 156.

[21] Kanagasabapathi, P., and Reddy, Senthil V., 'A Study on Entrepreneurship among Reddiars', unpublished report, P.S.G. College of Technology, Coimbatore, April 2004.

[22] Kanagasabapathi, P., *Unorganized Finance Sector: The Engine for Economic growth—A Study with Reference to Karur, Tamil Nadu*, Swedeshi Academic Council, Coimbatore, 2002, p. 50.

[23] Kanagasabapathi, P., and Menakha, I., 'A Study on Powerloom Textile Export Industry of Palladam', unpublished report, P.S.G. College of Technology, Coimbatore, April 2005.

[24] Reserve Bank of India quoted in the *Handbook of Statistics on the Indian Securities Market 2009,* SEBI, Mumbai, p. 21.

[25] International Monetary Fund, *Global Financial Stability Report—Market Development and Issues,* Washington, 2005, p. 62.

[26] Reserve Bank of India and Economic Survey as quoted in Rakshit, Mihir, 'On Liberalizing Foreign Institutional Investments', *Economic and Political Weekly,* Vol. 41, No. 11, 2006, p. 992.

[27] Reserve Bank of India, *Annual Report 2008–09,* RBI, Mumbai, p. 30.

[28] *Annual Report 2010–11,* Securities and Exchange Board of India, p. 88.

[29] Ibid., pp. 74–75.

[30] Ibid., pp. 76.

[31] Economic Times Intelligence Group Analysis, 'Capital Strength—Desis Beat MNCs in Use of Money', *The Economic Times,* Chennai, 2 August, 2006.

[32] Sudipt Dutta, op.cit., p. 64.

[33] Jain, V.K., in Chakravarti, Ranabir, *Trade in Early India,* Oxfort University Press, New Delhi, 2001, pp. 347–348.

[34] Rudner, Davis West, *Caste and Capitalism in Colonial India—The Nattukkottai Chettiars,* University of California Press, Berkeley,1994, p. 47.

[35] Gurucharan Das, *Seminar,* op.cit., p. 12.

[36] *Annual Report, 2011,* Ministry of Micro, Small and Medium Enterprises, op. cit., pp 25.

[37] Kanagasabapathi, P., and Arun Kumar, M.N., 'A Study on Sankagiri Transport and Thiruchengodu Rig Industry,' unpublished report, P.S.G. Institute of Management, Coimbatore, April 2005.

[38] Hayami Yujiro, *Development Economics—From the Poverty to the Wealth of the Nation,* Clarendon Press, Oxford University Press Inc., New York, 1998, p. 246.

[39] *World Development Report 2001,* World Bank, Washington, 2001, p. 175.

[40] Tripathi, Dwijendra and Jumani, Jyoti, *The Concise Oxford History of Indian Business,* Oxford University Press, New Delhi, 2007, p. 236.

[41] Goli, Venkat Raju, and Kanagasabapathi, P., 'A Socio-Economic Study of the Entrepreneurs of Visakhapatnam', unpublished report, P.S.G. College of Technology, Coimbatore, July 2003.

[42] Jodhka, Surinder S., 'Dalits in Business: Self-employment Scheduled Castes in North West India', *Economic and Political Weekly*, Vol. XLV No. 11, March 13, 2010, p. 48.

[43] Dwivedi, Mridula, 'Nature of Trust in Small Firm Clusters: A Case Study of Kanpur Saddlery Clusters,' Paper presented at the Conference on 'Clusters Industrial Districts and Firms: The Challenge of Globalization', Modena, Italy, 2003.

[44] Sudipt Dutta, op.cit., p. 20.

[45] Ibid., p. 19.

[46] *Soaring High-Kites and Community Endeavour*, Swadeshi Academic Council, Coimbatore, 2004.

[47] Patel Sharad, and Kanagasabapathi, P., op.cit.

[48] Sudipt Dutta, op.cit., p. 232.

[49] Dwivedi, Mridula, op.cit.

[50] *Soaring High-Kites and Community Endeavour*, op.cit.

[51] Kanagasabapathi, P., 'Ethics and Values in Indian Economy and Business', *International Journal of Social Economics*, Special Issue on India, Part I, Vol. 34, Issue 9, 2007, p. 585.

[52] Corsi, Marco, 'Modernity, Modernisation, Development: The Karur Industrial District', Paper presented at the workshop on Asia-Pacific studies in Australia and Europe: A Research Agenda for the Future, Australian National University, Canberra, July 5–6, 2002.

[53] Chari, Sharad, op.cit, p. 219.

[54] Fukuyama, Francis, *Trust*, Free Press Paperbacks, New York, 1996, p. 356.

[55] Gurucharan Das, *Seminar*, op.cit., p. 12.

[56] Salaman, Greame, 'India Need not Follow Western Biz Model, interview, *The Hindu Business Line*, October 1, 2002.

[57] Dugger, William M., quoted in Korten, David C., p. 173.

[58] Korten, David C., *When Corporation Rule the World,* The Other India Press, Goa, 1998, p. 224.

[59] Korten, David C., op.cit., p. 74.

[60] Khor, Martin, *Rethinking Globalisation,* Books for Change, Bangalore, 2001, p. 11.

[61] Shutt, Harry, *A New Democracy, Alternatives to a Bankrupt World Order*, Zed Books, London, 2001, pp. 62–63.

[62] Korten, David C., op.cit., p. 54.

[63] Bhattacharya, S.K., 'Organisational Culture: An Indian Perspective', *Business World,* February 1–14, 1998, p. 48.

[64] Naravane, Vaiju, 'Arcelor Chief Backtracks on Remarks Against Mittal', *The Hindu,* February 20, 2006, p. 11.

[65] Salaman, Greame, op.cit.

[66] Economic Times Intelligence Group Study quoted in *The Economic Times,* Chennai, August 25, 2006.

[67] Salaman, Greame, op.cit.

8

Management Models

We have seen that the Indian economic and business models are different from that of the other models, especially from that of the West. What about the management models of India and the West? Are they one and the same? Or are they completely different? This chapter discusses the different management models with special emphasis on the Indian models.

8.1 MANAGEMENT MODELS OF WEST AND EAST

When we observe the lifestyle of people across various countries in the world, we could see different approaches towards life. Such differences influence the business and decision-making systems. Sharma[1] says: "This difference in approach/attitude towards life, makes a qualitative change in the mission and objectives of the business enterprises and also affects the decision-making process." Hence, there could be different management models in different countries. Moreover, as long as there are differences in economic and business systems, there would be differences in management systems also.

Experts note that the economic systems prevailing in different countries influence the management models. Prof. S.K. Chakraborty[2], who has done pioneering works relating to the Indian management systems, notes: "A survey of the managerial and administrative processes also reveals the same dominating paradigm as in economics. This is not surprising for, without organizations, economics does not realize or manifest itself. Hence managerial philosophy in organizations tends to be the lengthened shadow of the ruling economic philosophy." Many experts emphasize that culture plays a significant role in the management systems. Parthasarathy[3] asserts that "Management is predominantly culture specific." There could be little doubt that when the cultural framework plays a significant role in the economic and business systems, then it would have an important influence on the management systems also.

Basically, there are two types of thought with regard to the approaches towards life. Chakraborty[4] notes: "It is prejudicial to the real interest of Indian management not to know or to choose to ignore the two fundamentally different streams of human temperament in the world: the western (especially since the renaissance) masculine, logical, rational aggressiveness and the eastern feminine, intuitive, receptive realization." Based on these two broad approaches, there could be a number of models depending on various factors. Sharma[5] writes: "There is no single model that is applied everywhere in different countries. "Pascale and Athos in their book, *The Art of Japanese Management*, have contrasted the approach adopted by the professional managers of the western and the eastern world, in solving their problems. The principal difference between the eastern institutions and those in the West is that ours is tuned to organizational structure and formal systems to cope with those challenges. In contrast, eastern institutions, while until recently advancing more slowly in thinking about organizational forms and formal systems, paid more attention to social and spiritual means."

Let us look at the evolution, development and functioning of the western management models briefly.

8.2 WESTERN MANAGEMENT MODELS

Management theories of the West started emerging in Europe and America from the final decades of the nineteenth century. "The Classical School of Management thought and thinkers emerged from 1880s to 1930s. It was the result of unprecedented growth during the industrial revolution. Large and complex organizations created the organizational complexities, and problems of operational efficiency[6]." Practising managers such as Taylor and Henry Fayol, and social scientists such as Mayo and McGregor had contributed to the earliest management theories. Later, it was the academicians and the management consultants who have been predominantly contributing. Cole[7] writes: "Most of the contributors to the theory and practice of management nowadays are academics with strong research backgrounds, and most are from USA. Of the practitioners, almost all are practicing management consultants, indeed most also hold positions in American universities." It is relevant to note that the western management theories are of recent origin and the later ones are mostly contributed by the US academicians.

As the rest of the world was under the economic dominance and influence of the European, and later the American thinking, their management theories came to be adopted and used in other countries. After America began to dominate the global economic scene, they began popularizing their management models. They supported the establishment of management and business schools in developing countries. As a result, the US model of management appeared to be the most appropriate model for all the countries. The increasing spread and influence of the multinational corporations during the last few decades have also helped the US and the western management systems to spread out to different parts of the world. The economic and business models of the West are driven by cut-throat competition. Their management models also seem to be rooted on the same principles that govern their ideas of economics and business.

8.2.1 Flaws in the Western Models

Too much of individualism and competition has created irrepairable distortions in the system. Even the organizational loyalty, which is very important for any system to succeed, is considered incorrect. "Western thinking, by and large, prompts us to treat organizational loyalty as an anti-professional value. The truth is that today professionalism is almost a byword for loyalty towards personal mercenary aims. Yet no great achievement is ever possible, without a focus of loyalty which transcends the individual self. Besides, in the long run, life itself loses meaning if every thought and action remains centered on the little self only[8]." The top management is interested in getting the maximum benefits for themselves, even at the cost of the interests of the employees and shareholders. While commenting on the present system, Drucker[9] lamented: "Today, I believe it is socially and morally unforgivable when managers reap huge profits for themselves but fire workers. As societies, we will pay a heavy price for the contempt this generates among the middle managers and workers[9]." Unfortunately, in their greediness to show results, they throw all ethical norms to the winds, and as a result, all the other constituents of the system, namely, the employees, the government, the shareholders and the society suffer.

Several experts voice their opinions with regard to the problems associated with the western management concepts. Salaman[10] 'candidly admits that there are several flaws in the western model of managing a business.' Too much of individualism, the principle of maximization of profits at all costs, little concern for values and a narrow view of life could be some of the major flaws in the system.

"Swami Jitatmananda quotes, 'Peter Drucker admits with a rare frankness that although he has tried to see the new dimensions of modern management he has not been able to deal either with the "moral horrors" or "spiritual agonies" arising out of modern management culture'. Further, Tom Peter, the other management guru in the West, observes that 'even the best companies have management beliefs which are narrow in scope'[11]."

What is the reason for the flaws of the western models? Chakraborty[12] asserts that it is the absence of ethical principles in western management that is causing difficulties. "A survey of the managerial and administrative processes also reveals the same dominating paradigm as in economics... It is the invasion of this credo into management which causes it to leave out the ethico-moral man in managerial processes."

How suitable are the western models for other countries?

There are problems that arise in the course of transferring the western models of management to other cultures. Based on the results of a survey of cultural characteristics of the Egyptian and the UK technical education principals and senior managers, Brown and Humphreys[13] note: "The research suggests that while there are some commonalities between the two groups, there are also significant cultural differences. The nature and extent of these differences are such that it is unwise to assume that the management theories and practices developed in the West will be appropriate and applicable in Egypt. Specifically, it means that western management tools have to be adapted and reformed to fit the cultural context of the recipient nation, something which has rarely been happened." During the last few decades, the management concepts and theories of the US have been advocated for countries in different parts of the world. But those concepts were found unsuitable even in the neighbouring Canada. Quoting studies conducted in America and Canada by Berry, Parthasarathy[14] says: "... he found it inappropriate to import American socio-psychological concepts to Canada." The author continues: "... if there are difficulties in transporting theories, methods and findings from the United States to Canada, how much more likely are there to be problems when larger cultural contexts are involved? Can Japanese achievement be understood in terms of American achievement motivation theory? Can Freudian theory be used to understand father-son conflicts in Melanesia? It is obvious that there are limits to the transcultural portability of knowledge. Even research findings seem to be subject to cultural socialization effects of the researchers."

After conducting surveys of human values, Hofstede noted differences in the dimensions of the western and eastern surveys, and while commenting on the findings, stated: "... not only values and practices but even theories are products of culturally determined socialization. This should make us modest when we try to transfer, for example, western types of education and management or training packages to people in a Third World country. Not only the tools but also the categories available for thinking may be unfit for the other environment[15]."

8.2.2 Do Only the Western Models Lead to Success?

Is there a single management method suitable for all the cultures? Studies have shown that different countries could evolve their own models, depending on the realities and backgrounds, and succeed. "Mercer has time and again highlighted the strong belief in individualism and its virtues at IBM. This he calls an element of 'advanced philosophy'. There can be no quarrel with that in the USA. Yet, the Matsushita list talks of 'harmony and cooperation' and, is still rated at par on all objective parameters with that of IBM and its equivalents in the West...[16]." Comparing the value systems of Japan and China vs. America, Chakraborty[17] notes: "It is obvious that in American culture 'humility', 'gratitude', etc. are values too tender and soft. Not unexpected perhaps given the historical backdrop of the no-holds-barred conquest of the vast and wild West in the new world. Yet such tender, normative 'human' values have not prevented Matsushita from attaining the hard, positivistic 'organizational' goals: values of growth, quality, profits, etc."

Now let us turn our attention towards the Indian management models.

8.3 INDIAN MANAGEMENT MODELS

First let us see the Indian management models from the cultural point of view, as different experts have been strongly underlining the ethical orientation in the Indian management systems since the ancient days. The push for a higher orientation has become all the more important in the recent years after the large-scale failure of moral values in the western management systems. Next, let us have an idea of the functioning management models at the non-corporate and corporate levels. This is very important as an understanding of the functioning models is necessary, especially at a time when India is emerging as a powerful nation. Finally, we shall see the position of modern management education in India and the need for a practical orientation to the study of management.

8.3.1 Indian Management

Ancient Indian economy, having been very prosperous for many centuries with successful businesses, must have had good management systems. This must be the reason why management concepts were predominant in the ancient literatures and scriptures. In fact, we could see various management concepts discussed in different literatures, apart from the very well-known books such as *Bhagawad Gita, Arthashastra* and *Thirukkural.* More than two thousand years ago, Thiruvalluvar had written on what are now considered as the modern management concepts such as human relations development, norms of good governance and communication skills in different chapters. Nanda[18] asserts: "The scholars in Europe and America have to be informed that management thought in ancient India are not limited to one book, i.e. Kautilya's *Arthashastra.* This is one of the many books of knowledge in relation to management." One could see the usage of management principles in the form of sayings and proverbs in the day-to-day lives of the ordinary citizens. These proverbs could explain different management ideas in just a few words beautifully. They are available in many Indian languages. Nanda[19] notes that "In ancient India, we find a lot of definition of subjects relating to management in some way or other." Management concepts are not in anyway new to India; they are common even among the ordinary Indians since the ancient periods.

Before going into the Indian management systems, we will try to understand the basic differences between the Indian and the western systems. Sharma[20] notes: "In Indian culture, 'family' is the primary social unit of interaction and each 'individual' is a part of the family. In Western culture, 'individual' is the central unit (without any reference to family) and as 'individual', he is taken as a primary social unit. For the sake of simplicity, the terms 'collectivistic' and 'individualistic' have been used to distinguish the Indian and the western cultures. Subhash Sharma, in addition to the above terminology, has also employed 'eco-driven' and 'ego-driven' terms respectively." The western world view is limited, whereas the Indian world view is holistic. Parthasarathy[21] notes: "The western world view holds that man is a limited organism having a one time existence and is separate, autonomous, more solid and atomized (made up of a set of discrete traits, abilities, values and motives). Man is a 'sensate' being, this—worldly, hedonistic, utilitarian, empirical, secular and humanistic." He continues: "The Indian *Vedantic* world views consciousness as primary. Matter is the effect rather than cause of consciousness[22]." The world views of different societies are very important for understanding management models. "The values that are particular to our society are extremely important in the context of management, where group effort rather than an individual endeavour is more important[23]." This is because what is value for one society may not be the same for the other. Chakraborty[24] mentions: "What is a value in IBM could be the reverse in an Indian firm—to take the cue from Hiriyanna who makes this distinction at a general level in respect of *kama* or desire and says that it can easily degenerate from being a value to being the reverse."

Unfortunately, the impact of cultural dimension in the study of management is usually ignored. "The impact of this cultural dimension has been the neglect of 'self' in the study of management. Control of one's passions and senses, emotions and feelings, development of qualities like sympathy, empathy, comradeship and brotherhood, have been ignored or at best assigned an insignificant priority[25]." Hence, as Singh notes: "... the prevailing notions about what values Indian managers generally held did not accurately reflect 'existing realities[26]." As a result we have the western notions with regard to our assumptions regarding the management situation in India. "We tend to be blind to our own assumptions when we are locked inside them. One way of breaking out of this prison of perception is by contrasting our assumptions with those of other cultures[27]." We are the inheritors of a broader and a more holistic vision than the limited modern management views of the West. "Our culture provides us with 'the cosmic vision' which, translated in terms of business, amounts to accepting and owning our social responsibility towards all the stakeholders like shareholders, employees and their unions, consumers, society, government, financial institutions, suppliers, etc., and beyond, competitors, environment—physical, social, religious, cultural, educational and even the inanimate kingdom. We cannot think of harming anyone in this cosmos. In our culture, we have the concept of *Rinas*. The *Rina* concept goes far beyond the 'social responsibility' concept[28]."

The native view of looking at the whole world as a family provides inputs for Indian management philosophy. "When we are interacting with others, individuals, groups and organizations—we are dealing with members of the same *Kutumb* or family. Mutual help and support is the guiding principle in such dealings. All this provides the necessary inputs for the management philosophy[29]." This has deep implications for the multi-cultural world in which businesses are taking place across the countries. When holistic ideas begin to dominate the management field, then there would be a complete change in the management practices. Experts note that history provides the Indian businesses a leadership model, and not just a management model. "India has had a long tradition of sacro-secular symbiosis extending over thousand of years. For instance, Raja Janak is considered a symbol of this tradition and was termed a *raj-rishi*. This tradition still continues. Ashok, Akbar, Rani Ahilya Bai, Rana Pratap, Shivaji, Guru Govind Singh, Mahatma Gandhi, Swami Vivekananda and scores of others belonged to this tradition. They were all *Raj Rishis* (the term *Raja* is being used in the sense of a leader). This model of leadership is applicable in all walks of life and business leadership is no exception to it. Our business leaders have to keep this *Raj Rishi* role model before them[30]."

Can India adopt the western models?

The Indian economic and business systems are vastly different from that of the West. In such a situation, it is not advisable to adopt the western management models, unless they are found suitable and necessary to our conditions. Moreover, the Indian approach to life is different from that of the West. Against this background, "Can a society, which has spirituality as its dominating characteristic, adopt the 'management philosophy' developed in the West per se[31]." When India tries to emulate the western models she might not be able to attain authentic success. "Authentic success in Indian organizations will remain an elusive purple patch if superficial emulation of techniques springing from the western temper remains the mainstay. They will tend to be swept away by dominantly left-brained techniques[32]."

Moral dimensions of management

The moral foundations of human activities are missing in the modern management systems. This is probably because these systems were born in the societies where maximization of profits was considered the sole objective of business. Of course, in the recent years, when the mega corporations like Enron and WorldCom collapsed, voices were raised on the need for moral values in management. But no serious attempts could be made in this respect, as they do not seem to have any clue to come out of their difficulties. It is unfortunate that there was no response from the Indian side, though solutions were readily available with us. "Studied and prolonged muteness amongst both our practicing top managers and management academics about the moral dimension of management is a striking phenomenon. This is paradoxical in a culture which possesses perfect insights about human ends and means—both secular and sacred. In a land where Vivekananda had declared that 'this universe is simply a gymnasium in which the soul is taking exercise', where Tagore had taught that self-abnegation leads to the fundamental reality of self—'the reality which is the moral and spiritual basis of the realm of human values', where Gandhiji had asserted that 'altruism is the highest form of morality', where Aurobindo had proclaimed that 'virtue comes to the natural man by a struggle with his pleasure-seeking nature', it is a mystery why most of us behave the way we do. It seems as though these modern prophets never lived amongst us, or as if they were indulging in mere antiquarianism[33]."

Role of culture in management

India's achievements are mainly due to the rich cultural backgrounds. Of late, Indians are excelling in different fields as managers and professionals in India and abroad. This is due to their backgrounds and upbringing shaped by years of heritage and practices. Even when the Indians learn the western practices, most of them do not allow the practices to dominate them completely. Ramanujam[34] writes: "When Indians learn, quite expertly, modern science, business, or technology, they "compartmentalise" these interests ...; the new ways of thought and behaviour do not replace, but live along with the older "socio-cultural" ways." It is good that we do not leave our socio-cultural ways but it would be better if we follow a system in commensurate with our own ethos."

Chakraborty[35] asserts that India could achieve greatness only by following a management system based on native cultural traditions. "The need for authentic management, management that is true to cultural roots, is becoming clearer daily in both the East and the West. The United States, for instance, cannot meet Japan's great industrial challenge by copying Japanese methods. Japanese methods do not fit the American ethos. The graft will not take. America must regain its industrial excellence through methods that are compatible with its own unique character and values. Similarly, India will not realize its material potential through copying the US, Britain or Japan. India will be great only by being India. Neither a country nor a person can achieve greatness through imitation. Greatness cannot be achieved through imitation. It can only be achieved through authenticity. The Bhagavad Gita says, "Better in one's own *dharma,* though imperfect, than the *dharma* of another well performed. He who does the duty ordained by his own nature incurs no sin."

Revitalization of Indian ethos

Experts feel that there should be a revitalization of the Indian ethos, instead of trying to change the culture. "... re-spiritualization of the workplace is quite consonant with India's long heritage, despite gross aberrations from it in modern industrial organizations. For the time being, this deep-structure grain of the Indian ethos will need to be revitalized and brought into the open to the basic material needs of its teeming millions. It is not necessary to change our culture to respond to this productivity challenge ... What is necessary is to bring them back into play in life and work. Embarking on the fragmentist, hazardous and unpredictable course of changing a culture, which is very little or only superficially understood in the first place, could mean just a waste of a great deal of time and energy. Cultural change is after all not like changing a set of clothes[36]."

Contemporary Indians believe in western management

In this context, it is unfortunate to see that a large segment of the academicians have illusions about the Indian society and backgrounds. Chakraborty[37] notes: "A large and respected segment of Indian academics today declares that the notion of Indian culture is a myth. Because of the existence of so many religions in this country, along with endless diversity of local customs and deities within the fold of Hinduism itself, it is untrue as well as harmful to speak of any single homogeneous Indian culture. True enough. The visible web of Indian culture reveals many hues and textures. Besides the indigenous Vedantic, Buddhist, Jaina and Sikh traditions, Indian culture has absorbed numerous enriching strands from Islamic, Christian, and Parsi traditions. And yet even within this great diversity of outward forms of culture, e.g. crafts, music, architecture, dress, painting, food, and so on, we detect also numerous significant commonalities constituting a distinct class when compared to non-Indian cultures."

Examples could be cited to show that there is large-scale influence of culture in the Indian society, in spite of the many diversities[38]. To give a sample:

1. Showing formal respect to elders, superiors and teachers is a uniform feature of the Indian society.
2. Some kind of God-consciousness is a pervasive feature of the Indian society in all its variety.
3. The notion of marriage as a lifelong bond of mutual fidelity is a dominant characteristic across all segments of Indian citizens.
4. In no Indian home (barring that of a few pseudo-western families) is a child made to sleep alone in order to protect it from the so-called dependence on parents.

Based on these practices, Chakraborty[39] underlines: "A legion of other examples could be cited. The point to be made is that when we think of Indian culture, uniformity in many vital respects keeps pace with diversity in others." Why is this uniformity in spite of many differences among Indians? Chakraborty[40] answers: "But Indian ethos, which is essentially and at its best *Vedantic*, is quite different from, though complimentary to Indian culture. If the latter is the ornate, colourful outward superstructure, the former is the deep and unseen foundation supporting the superstructure. Just as, periodically, the superstructure is modified or extended, so has been the case with Indian culture. But never has the hidden and solid foundation of the Indian ethos been subjected to such external changes[40]."

Chakraborty[41] states that the basic characteristics of India are due to the age-old civilization. "All its principal ingredients have sprung from the Indian geographical land mass and attained perfection within this very ambience long before other cultures had begun to arrive." Hence, he notes: "So although one might or might not agree that there is no one Indian culture, it is more important to understand and accept that there is indeed one Indian ethos at the level of the *Vedantic* 'deep structure'[42]." But to what extent is the ethos of the past relevant in modern times? "This ethos had evolved and matured in remote antiquity, they argue, so how can it have any relevance to the management of modern societies, economies, and organizations? They do not seem to realize that slowly, silently, and inexorably the so-called new-wave thinking in many parts of the world is quietly moving towards embracing time-honoured, enduring, classical tenets[43]."

In spite of the realities, most of the modern Indians still believe that the western approach to management is correct. "Those who write on management in India often insist on keeping the secular world of business goals and means. This is an example of deep-seated fragmentism[44].” We try to copy everything from the West. “... India’s misfortune is that even now we seek new light and fresh confidence for everything from the West—whether it be far West of the UK-USA, or the near-west of the erstwhile USSR[45].” What is the reason for this attitude? Chakraborty[46] notes: “For, like the eminent scholar of philosophy, Prof. Bhattacharya, I myself believe that the bulk of educated Indians, even in the nineties, continue to suffer from a ‘rootless universalism.” Why is this problem? Srinivas[47] says: “Our education has not so far helped us to understand ourselves, to understand the significance of our past, the realities of our present and our mission of the future. It has tended to drive our real mind into the unconscious, and to replace it by a shadow mind that has no roots in our past and in our real present. Our old mind cannot be wholly driven underground and its imposed substitute cannot function effectively and productively. The result is that there is confusion between the two minds and a hopeless Babel in the world of ideas[47].” Aurobindo had noted that Indians disown their underlying strengths and see only the gross aberrations. “It is a poor psychological strategy to disown the underlying strengths and only lament about the gross aberrations which immediately meets the eye[48].”

India’s higher responsibility towards management thought

It could be seen that the Indian society always governed its actions with reference to higher ideals, even while engaging itself in routine activities. “Indian society developed with an unsurpassed organizing ability, stable effectiveness, practical insight into its communal coordination of the mundane life of interest and desire, *kama* and *artha*; it governed always its action by a reference at every point to the moral and religious law, the *dharma*; but it never lost sight of spiritual liberation as our highest point and the ultimate aim of the effort of Life[49].” What is the reason for this? The answer could be found in the words of Tagore: “We still know that only in ... spiritual wealth and welfare does civilization attain its end, and not in a profile production of materials, not in the competition of intemperate power with power[50]?” It is India’s obligation not just to herself but to the whole world to attempt for a transformation in the management approach. “The irrefutable commandment is that the secular and the material must be informed and invested with the sacred and spiritual... India’s obligation to herself and to the world is to relive this sacro-secular symbiosis for effective transformation in every epoch[51].” Mahatma Gandhi had mentioned: “High thinking is inconsistent with complicated material life based on high speed imposed on by Mammon worship. All the graces of life are possible only when we learn the art of living nobly[52]."

Sarkar[53] notes that the Indian civilization presents a world view that is stable and leisurely. To quote: "Broadly contrasted with the opportunist industrial order of today... where the whole energy of man is used up in making sure of mere existence, the civilization of India presents to us the spectacle of something stable and leisurely: and this is not merely by virtue of some kind of inertia, but as the result of deliberate organization based on a definite view... of the meaning and purpose of life." The learned experts argue that a management model rooted in the local culture is most suitable to India. Even the western thinkers feel that they have destroyed the originality of the native systems in their countries. For example, "Lessem, a British management writer, admits... 'it is no accident of history that spiritual and material values have been split apart in the West. Indeed, it has served to advance the cause of individualism. It is only that now we are beginning to realize the costs. Secularly based individualism detracts from the making of shared meaning[54]." Sharma notes that the core competence of India is not used to build the management structures. "Each nation or race pours all its energies to produce its own archetypal human being. One strives to attain this in the man-of-commerce, another in the conqueror, the third in the explorer, and the fourth in the statesman and so on. What has been India's striving? The *rushi*, i.e. the seer. For the benefit of the students of management, this cultural characteristic of India may be termed as our 'core competence'. Unfortunately, we have not used this competence to build our management structures. Concerned as we are with leadership at present, this core competence is to be utilized—rather this has to be the bedrock for laying the foundation of leadership[55]."

8.3.2 Functioning Management Models

Even while striving to develop models based on the superior ethos and culture of India, our immediate duty is to recognize and respect the existence and functioning of the Indian and Indianized models. It is important to understand that unique Indian models are functioning at different levels across the country, though we fail to recognize them. In this connection, it is relevant to note that these models are working at the corporate as well as the non-corporate sectors.

Whenever we think of the management models, we tend to take the corporate sector only. Even in the corporate sector, the focus is more on the multinational corporations and a few top companies. Generally, we assume that the practices adopted by them are followed by the rest of the corporate sector. Whenever studies are taken up, the normal tendency is to take a few yardsticks based on the western assumptions and apply them to a few select companies, without understanding the ground realties. But fortunately in the recent period, the idea of studying the Indian companies on a much wider scale is slowly emerging in certain quarters.

Peter Cappelli and others[56] note that senior executives at 98 of the largest India-based companies were interviewed to find out how they were driving their organizations to higher performance. In the very beginning of their paper, they mention: "In conversations with leaders at Infosys, Reliance Industries, Tata, Mahindra & Mahindra, Aventis Pharma, and many others, a picture emerged of a distinctive Indian model[57]." Comparing the leadership practices of India with that of the western countries, they write: "Far more than their western counterparts, these leaders and their organizations take a long term, internally focused view[58]." They mention that the Indian companies emphasize less on western methods of planning and analysis. To quote: "They tend to focus less on western-style planning and analysis and more on creating incentives, organizational structures, and culture that will enable an improvisational approach to strategy[59]." As the experts realize that the managerial approaches of India are superior, they advise the leaders of the western corporate world to adapt them for better performance. The authors underline: "Western leaders would do well to understand the managerial approaches that have fueled the rise of India's largest companies, and mindfully adapt them[60]."

As noted earlier, the Indian management approaches are different due to the unique nature of the Indian economic and social systems. Peter Cappelli and others mention this aspect when they point out the leadership approaches in our country. To quote: "The Indian leadership approach arose from the unique circumstances of the Indian economy and society[61]." Hence, the generally prevalent notion that the functioning of Indian corporate sector is based on the western approaches does not seem to represent the realities. See, for example, Box 8.1 for a distinct Indian management model in operation.

Box 8.1 Management models based on Indian values

With two degrees and an appointment letter as Deputy Collector, the young Bhavarlal Hiralal Jain from rural Maharashtra, decided to enter business. With ₹7000, the family's total savings of three generations from agriculture as capital, he purchased empty drums and started selling kerosene door to door. The very next day after he started his business, the Central Government announced a hike in kerosene prices. On learning this, Mr. Jain placed a board outside his shop informing his customers that kerosene would continue to be sold at the old rates until existing stocks were sold out.

What was started as Jain Brothers in 1963 became a more than ₹ 3000 crore conglomerate in the name of Jain Irrigation Systems Ltd. (JISL). JISL's core activities revolve around agriculture as his mother wanted him to do something that would satisfy not just the needs of his family, but would enable him to feed even the birds and animals. The company is into diverse activities, from making refined papain to processed foods on the one hand and PVC pipes to micro irrigation systems on the other. It has established units in different parts of the world such as the US, Switzerland and Israel.

Affectionately called 'Bhau' (elder brother) by all who know him, Mr. Jain treats all his staff members as his associates. The entire 573 acre Chairman's Office campus is smoke-free, liquor-free and vegetarian. Even tea and coffee are not taken by him or any of his associates. But Kichidy is provided to all, free of cost, during lunch time. His management approaches are based on his experiences and learning, and not text book oriented. He strongly feels that companies should function as 'socially committed organizations'. All his four sons have joint responsibility in all the activities of the company. Hierarchy in the administrative system is minimum. Any employee of the company can meet the Chairman any time without an appointment. There have been no strikes and there are no unions. At the family level, all his sons with their families live under one roof with the senior Jain.

Most of Mr. Jain's activities and experiments are centred around Jalgoan, a rain shadow region of the Deccan Plateau. The Anubhuti residential school provides education through the 'experimental learning method'. The Gandhi Research Foundation promoted in collaboration with the North Maharashtra University is collecting all the books by and on Mahatma Gandhi. He devotes a lot of time and resources for promoting alternative energies, wasteland development, planting trees, providing amenities to rural areas, naturopathy and helping the deserving people.

The non-corporate sector plays a crucial role in the Indian economy and business. Apart from its dominance in the total system, this sector is the nursery for all future companies. But unfortunately, we have never attempted to recognize the management systems of this vital sector. Studies on the management styles and practices in the non-corporate sector reveal that their management models are purely native. Studies of different economic centres, including the highly successful industrial and business centres covering different types of organizations including companies, and society-based business initiatives provide important clues to the functioning of management systems. These studies give a refreshing picture of the realistic situation. The results of the studies give a very different set of conclusions when compared to our 'generalized' notions of the management models.

Personnel management in practice

Let us take, for example, the issue of personnel management which is a very important area in modern management. In almost all the successful centres, the overall management approach towards employees is friendly, and not antagonistic. There is a personal orientation beyond the owner–labourer relationship. The entrepreneurs try to keep their employees satisfied by helping them whenever such help is required. In many instances there is a 'fraternal approach' towards the employees as far as possible. In almost all the places, the entrepreneurs prefer the known persons or persons recommended by those who are close to them. For example, in Sankagiri transport centre, 70 per cent of the drivers are recruited on the basis of guarantees provided by relatives, friends and other associates[62]. In such cases, it becomes obligatory for both the parties—the entrepreneurs and the employees—to trust and help each other for their mutual benefits. In the course of time, most of these relationships get extended into personal and family relationships.

In western Tamil Nadu, there is an industrialist who has promoted more than 10 textile spinning units, all by himself during the last twenty years. He has employed more than 10,000 people[63]. There has been no strike, and there has not been a single protest by the employees during all these years. He is not a human resource expert in the modern sense of the term and is not even a textile professional. How is he maintaining such a high level of human relations and extraordinary success in business? It is all due to his personality as a concerned and a humane employer moving closely with all the workers, irrespective of their status. He knows the names and backgrounds of all the employees and remains as a source of support to all of them in times of difficulties.

There are companies who encourage the family values among employees and recognize the Indian system of maintaining joint families through additional incentives* (see Box 8.2).

---

* N. Subramaniam, Managing Director, Habasit Iakoka Ltd., Coimbatore, interview, 10.09.2006.

Box 8.2 Nurturing family systems—Corporate style

Habasit Iakoka is a well-known textile accessory manufacturing company with headquarters in Coimbatore. Originally promoted as Iakoka Syntrans by two cousins and two of their friends, it imports and markets power transmission belts, conveyor belts, timing belts, etc. Currently, it is the largest manufacturer of synthetic sandwich spindle tapes in the world. The company is now part of the Habasit AG, Switzerland, the leading player in the field at the international level.

There are about 270 employees working in the company at Coimbatore with about 40 per cent of them being ladies. With Shri N. Subramaniam as the Managing Director and his team, groomed in the higher traditions of rural India, the management adopts innovative methods to encourage family values. The company gives an additional monthly salary to those employees who keep their elderly parents with them. The women employees who live with their parents-in-law get a still higher addition in their salary. The employees are thus encouraged to respect and take care of their parents and parents-in-law.

The company organizes a 'family day' every year to which the families of employees are invited to participate in daylong recreational and educational programmes. Further the management conducts periodic meetings with all the employees, during which the performance of the company, including its financial performance, is shared. This is not an obligation, yet this is practised to involve the employees in the development of the company. The company was given a special award of appreciation for adopting the best management practices by Habasit AG for the first time in its history, thus recognizing the Indian approaches to management.

The management of Habasit Iakoka informed that they were in fact inspired to encourage family systems through incentives by another company belonging to the same region. So these kinds of practices are going on silently without outsiders knowing about them. These are innovative methods designed to nurture the family systems in the changing circumstances.

It is employers who create more employers

In many of the places, a sizeable number of the workers or employees join work with an idea to promote their own ventures after a few years of experience. When they move out of employment, the owners themselves support the ex-workers in all possible ways. Some of them give financial support. Some of the workers leave a part of their monthly remuneration with the owners every month, such that at the time of leaving, they get a sizeable sum. As a mark of respect, in most of the instances the ex-workers get their first orders from the ex-owners. In many places in the southern and the western parts of India many entrepreneurs proudly claimed that they had already 'created' more than ten entrepreneurs. Normally, the existing entrepreneurs of different centres do not view the new entrepreneurs as their competitors. This is in sharp contrast to the modern corporate world where any new entry is viewed with suspicion. In a particular instance, one entrepreneur helped his loyal ex-worker to set up a shop just opposite his own shop as a mark of gratitude to his services. Is it not a higher ideal? Apart from the noble aspects involved, it is perhaps these attitudes that make our country one of the highest entrepreneurial nations. One can go on writing the humane aspects that we see in the Indian non-corporate sector even today. There are many instances in which the loyal employees are provided with a share of profit and a share in the business. In a few cases, the committed young men are elevated to the position of sons-in-law by the families of the owners. Thus there are numerous ways in which the employee commitment and loyalty is rewarded. The point to be noted here is that in all these cases, there are the human and the moral elements.

Similarly, we see different management styles or methods in different functional areas. These styles are not always uniform. There are differences. These differences are due to various reasons and are influenced by the realities of the situations. The ground realities are managed so well by different formulations in approaches that one gets astonished to see the ingenuity of our entrepreneurs. For example, wherever there is a need for more funds or more manpower or wherever there is higher risk involved in business, people prefer to promote their ventures as partnerships.

Sharing of wealth for social concerns

Another important point to be noted is the social consciousness and the philanthropic attitude of the industrialists and businessmen. In almost all the centres, the entrepreneurs have created enormous social infrastructure. Almost all the educational institutions in different centres have been promoted by the successful entrepreneurs or community associations. It is mostly the institutions promoted by these people that have brought education nearer to the people. The contribution of the governments to the field of education is minimum when compared to the investments by the entrepreneurial classes. Similarly, their investments for common facilities are noteworthy. The contribution of clusters to the religious and cultural activities is also significant. In short, they willingly contribute a share of their income to make their places a better one. Most of such contributions are made as part of their duty to the society, with least publicity or without any publicity at all.

Overall management abilities

An important aspect in the management systems of the non-corporate sector is the overall management approach of the entrepreneurs. These entrepreneurs have to live to the satisfaction of all the parties concerned. They are not like corporate managements who sit at the top far away from the shareholders and employees. These people are close to all the stakeholders. They have direct contact with all of them. Hence, they are closely watched by all concerned. Moreover, in the non-corporate businesses, an entrepreneur takes upon himself all the risks involved. One has to be a financial expert, a human relations man, a marketing wizard and a production specialist, all at one time. It requires all-round skills to manage the different situations and come out successfully. Hence, one has to follow an all-round or a 'holistic' management style to do business successfully in the non-corporate sector.

'Indianized' styles in corporate sector

As far as the corporate management approach is concerned, there is more of a traditional orientation in a majority of the companies. In many places, one can still notice the traditional office systems devoid of a luxurious outlook, elderly promoters attending work regularly and helping the subsequent generations in all possible ways, and in a few cases, loyal employees contributing sincerely well after retirements. But nearly all of them have adapted to the modern times, without losing the traditional value systems. It is a common feature to see the managements updating themselves with the operations and performance of the companies using latest technologies. Almost all the subsequent generations have a minimum qualification of a degree or more and have learned to use as much technology as they require for operations and management. In many cases, the heirs to the business try to acquire technical and management qualifications in the relevant fields from good institutions. Moreover, they employ persons with the required qualifications. But this segment of the corporate sector is little noticed as they are away from much of the media and limelight.

As far as the big corporations are concerned, by and large, there is an outward tendency to emulate the West. Immediately after the 1990s, there was a strong inclination towards the western models, particularly in a few sectors. All through this period, in many instances, the promoter families tried to steer the businesses without losing track of their value systems. Now there seems to be a silent rethinking with regard to adopting all that is from the West, at least in a few quarters, in the changed international economic scenario. In a number of instances, companies are also slowly beginning to inculcate the virtues of Indian practices and ancient wisdom. Courses on yoga and meditation are being given to employees. There is also a mix of the West and the Indian methods in different instances. As far as the management practices are concerned, there is an Indianized approach of the western concepts and practices. Even the multinational enterprises that operate here know that India is a 'culturally tough' nation. Hence, they Indianize their practices, as much as possible, to establish their business and succeed. These Indianized approaches seemed to have worked better in different cases as they combine the other approaches with the Indian approach and make suitable combinations of practices. One could also notice that there is intense corporate activity in recent years and the level of preparedness of the sector has increased many times, while there is a high level of confidence among the well-performing sections.

Evolving Indian models

There are management experts who support management styles based on the local requirements to evolve. Some of them have been articulating their views over a period. Sharma[64] notes: "Another management expert, Professor P. Singh also supports the 'evolvement' of management styles and systems, which are best suited to our requirement. In his opinion 'foisting styles which are alien to the existing way of life and thereby implicitly imposing foreign values and norms of behaviour is bound to create discord."

8.3.3 Modern Management Education in India

Modern management education in India has a background of about seventy years. Ray and Sinha[65] had noted in 2005: "Management education in India has a fairly long history dating back to the late nineteen forties. Later, the Indian government took initiatives to promote management education and set up Indian Institutes of Management ... Subsequently, as management education gained prominence, all major universities also started offering degrees in management. Privately owned business/management schools have proliferated during the last two decades offering programmes at both undergraduate and postgraduate levels. By 2000, India produced about 75,000 MBAs annually from over 700 business schools, the highest number of MBAs produced outside the US. The number of business schools including MBA granting departments of universities and the number of graduates passing out every year now are estimated to be over 1300 and 1,50,000 respectively." Now there are 13 Indian Institutes of Management and an estimated 2000 business schools and departments offering postgraduate degrees in management. It is significant to note that the numbers of business schools and management graduates are increasing every year. A study notes that the number of management institutes has grown at 16.5 per cent (CAGR) during 2005–06 to 2009–10. It also mentions that the students for management programmes have increased at 22 per cent (CAGR) during the above period[66].

A continuous increase in the demand for management professionals, especially since the 1990s, has resulted in the need for more and more qualified people with degrees in management. Tripathi and Jumani[67] note: "... the value of management professionals even in family-controlled businesses has been going up as the environment has become more competitive. Not only has the demand for the business graduate gone up several fold and is constantly growing, but also the salary and perks that he expects and is in fact offered have no resemblance with what his pre-liberlization counterpart received. This is because he is considered to be an indispensable resource to maximize the shareholder's wealth."

Though the number of institutions offering management programmes has multiplied, dissatisfaction with regard to the curriculum and approach prevails among the concerned sections. The management schools mostly teach the western concepts and practices. Ojah[68] notes: "Postgraduate management education as we know it today has been strongly influenced by similar education in the US ever since Harvard Business School and Sloan Business School, Massachusetts Institute of Technology, helped with the establishment of the Indian Institutes of Management at Ahmedabad and Kolkata respectively in the early 1960s. Continued recruitment of faculty in the IIMs, and other similar institutions, from universities in the West, particularly the US, has ensured that most of the prominent postgraduate programmes in management in India have followed the norms that emerged in the US environment, although with a lag." With more and more emphasis on western orientations, the candidates are not exposed to the realities of the functioning business systems of India. It is sad that the graduates coming out of the management schools are unaware of the native systems of working. As a result they tend to develop an inferior attitude, many times even a contemptuous one, towards the native practices. Moreover, as Ray and Sinha[69] mention: "People from many walks of life have voiced their concerns on a number of issues regarding the curriculum and its students in different forums—

journals, newspapers and magazines, and in other public pronouncements. Popular belief is that the students from leading business/management schools are impractical, impatient and arrogant." This is good neither for the management graduates nor for the economy and the country.

8.3.4 Need for India-oriented Approach

At this juncture, it is important that the management educators did some serious thinking. Of course, in the recent periods, a few voices are being raised for a 'rethinking'. With the western business and management models facing serious problems, the Indian models are beginning to attract attention. Saraswat[70] notes: "Widely publicized financial and accounting scandals at large multinational corporations such as Enron and WorldCom in recent years have brought issues of corporate governance, ethical conduct, and social responsibility to the forefront of the academic debate in the United States. Market-rigging scandals at other global corporations such as Italy's Parmalat demonstrate that the problem is not confined to any one country or culture; its dimensions are global. The growing public awareness of these transgressions has exposed the inadequacy of management education in universities and management practices in corporations. The existing parameters of academic discourse and time-honoured principles of organizational behavior seem to ignore the underlying spiritual and human values on which important management decisions are based. Consequently, individuals in positions of great responsibility in corporations are often unable to either recognize the norms and boundaries of accepted ethical behaviour or deliberately trespass them. Academic and corporate establishments in the US are, therefore, recognizing the need for a deeper discussion and understanding of the underlying causes of unethical behaviour." In this connection, it is recognized that India has better solutions to these problems than the West. As seen earlier, Indian economic and business models are different, and her management models seem to be more performing, comprehensive and humane. This is not to say that all the western models are inferior; in fact, India should try to learn the best practices from different sides. But the orientation should be invariably Indian. Moreover, in terms of management, India has a better track record than the western countries.

In the changing circumstances, it is imperative to reformulate our attitudes towards the western approaches, depending on their applicability and usefulness to India. If necessary, we might even have to challenge the models that are not relevant. In this connection, it might be useful to recollect the words of Chakraborty:[71] "... have we Indians ever thought of challenging its wholesale transmission to our students and managers? Could it be that post-independence Indian culture has been so characterless, and our intellectual spinelessness so shameful, that the well intentioned Americans have never really faced a solid and genuine challenge to review the intellectual wares they have brought over to do us good?" The challenge should not be just for the sake of it, as we should not be against any system. The challenge is more for a fresh thinking towards identifying more suitable models for a better and holistic performance.

India being a unique country with special features, it is necessary to recognize and nurture the functioning models and develop better ones suited to the prevailing conditions, wherever necessary. Chakrabotry[72] notes: "India has never been a mercenary or colonial culture like many western nations. Materialistic cultures may be glamorous, but not happy. So we are told today that 'Americans are not getting enough happiness for their money'. The 'Protestant ethic' has been associated with the promotion of several exploitative, mercenary colonial cultures. It is, therefore, likely to be unsuitable to the hidden grain of the Indian temper. The limited sociological perspective tends to miss the woods for the trees. The 'deep structure' remains untouched. Courage is required to go to the root of the matter and construct or re-construct our own models. If the endeavour is uncompromisingly honest and sincere, we need not worry about immediate results." We have to remember that India has better models that are performing well in different areas. The only thing is that they have to be recognized, nurtured and wherever necessary improvised, depending on the requirements and situations.

REFERENCES

[1] Sharma, G.D., *Management and the Indian Ethos,* Rupa and Co., New Delhi, 2001, p. 33.

[2] Chakraborty, S.K., *Ethics in Management: Vedantic Perspectives,* 3rd impression, Oxford University Press, New Delhi, 1999, pp. 2–3.

[3] Parthasarathy, Swami Dr., *Human Values Management—20 Key Principles for Modern Management,* Ane Books India, New Delhi, 2006.

[4] Chakraborty, S.K., *Management by Values—Towards Cultural Congruence,* Oxford University Press, New Delhi, 1991, p. 21.

[5] Sharma, G.D., op.cit., p. 38.

[6] Nanda, Jayanta K., *Management Thought*, Sarup & Sons, New Delhi, 2006, p. 44.

[7] Cole, Gerald, *Management Theory and Practice*, 6th ed., Thomson Asia Pte Ltd., Singapore, 2004, p. 92.

[8] Chakraborty, S.K., 1991, op.cit., p. 6.

[9] Drucker, Peter F., *Managing in the Next Society*, Butterworth-Heinemann, Oxford, Reprinted, 2003, p. 150.

[10] Salaman, Greame, India need not follow western biz model, interview, *The Hindu Business Line*, October 1, 2002.

[11] Chakraborty, S.K., 1991, op.cit., p. 41.

[12] Ibid., pp. 2–3.

[13] Brown, Andrew D., and Michael Humphreys, 'International Cultural Differences in Public Sector Management—Lessons from a Survey of British and Egyptian Technical Education Managers', *International Journal of Public Sector Management*, Vol. 8, No. 3, 1995, p. 12.

[14] Parthasarathy, Swami Dr., op.cit., p. 165.

[15] Quoted in Parthasarathy, Swami Dr., op.cit., p. 166.

[16] Chakraborty, S.K., 1991, op.cit., p. 6.

[17] Ibid., p. 5.

[18] Nanda, Jayanta K., op.cit., p. 10.

[19] Ibid.

[20] Sharma, G.D., op.cit., p. 31.

[21] Parthasarathy, Swami Dr. op.cit., pp. 166–167.

[22] Ibid., p. 167.

[23] Sharma, G.D., op.cit., p. 34.

[24] Chakraborty, S.K., 1991, op.cit., p. 6.

[25] Sharma, G.D., op.cit., p. 36.

[26] Quoted in Chakraborty, S.K., 1991, op.cit., p. 15.

[27] Pascale and Athos in Sharma, G.D., op.cit., p. 39.

[28] Sharma, G.D., op.cit., p. 39.

[29] Ibid., pp. 40–41.

[30] Ibid., p. 87.

[31] Ibid., p. 42.

[32] Chakraborty, S.K., 1991, op.cit., pp. 21–22.

[33] Chakraborty, S.K., 1999, op.cit., pp. 59–60.

[34] Ramanujam, A.K., 'Is There an Indian Way of Thinking?—An Informal Essay' quoted in Budhwar, Pawan S. and Sparrow, Paul R., 'Strategic HRM through the Cultural Looking Glass: Mapping the Cognition of British and Indian Managers', *Organisational Studies*, 2002, p. 627, EBSCO publishing 2003.

[35] Chakraborty, S.K., *Foundations of Managerial Work—Contributions from Indian Thought*, 2nd ed., Himalaya Publishing House, Mumbai, 2003, p. ix.

[36] Chakraborty, S.K., 1999, op.cit., pp. 282–283.

[37] Ibid., p. 3.

[38] Ibid., pp. 3–4.

[39] Ibid., p. 4.

[40] Ibid.

[41] Ibid.

[42] Ibid.

[43] Ibid., p. 5.

[44] Ibid., p. 60.

[45] Ibid.

[46] Ibid., p. 265.

[47] Srinivas, M.N. quoted in Chakraborty, S.K., 1999, op.cit., p. 265.

[48] Chakraborty, S.K., 1999, op.cit., p. 272.

[49] Aurobindo quoted in Chakraborty, S.K., 1999, op.cit., p. 273.

[50] Tagore quoted in Chakraborty, S.K., 1999, op.cit., p. 275.

[51] Chakraborty, S.K., 1999, op.cit., p. 275.

[52] Mahatma Gandhi quoted in Chakraborty, S.K., 1999, op.cit., p. 280.

[53] Sarkar, B.K., quoted in Chakraborty, S.K., 1999, op.cit., p. 283.

[54] Lessem quoted in Chakraborty, S.K., 1991, op.cit., p. 185.

[55] Sharma, G.D., op.cit., p. 86.

[56] Peter Cappelli, Harbir Singh, Jitendra V. Singh and Michael Useem, 'Leadership Lessons from India', *Harvard Business Review*, March 2010, pp. 90–97.

[57] Ibid., p. 91.

[58] Ibid., p. 92.

[59] Ibid.

[60] Ibid., p. 97.

[61] Ibid.

[62] Kanagasabapathi, P. and Arun Kumar, M.N., 'A Study on Sankagiri Transport Industry and Thiruchengode Rig Industry', unpublished report, P.S.G. Institute of Management Coimbatore, April 2005.

[63] Shri Shanmugavel, Velan textiles group, Dindigul, Tamil Nadu.

[64] Sharma, G.D., op.cit., p. 74.

[65] Ray, Sougata and Sinha, Anup, 'Management Education—Let a Thousand Flowers Bloom Amidst a Hundred Questions', *Decision*, Vol. 32, No. 2, July–December, 2005, p. 2.

[66] www.dreducation.com

[67] Tripathi, Dwijendra and Jumani, Jyoti, op.cit., p. 231.

[68] Ojah, Abhoy K., 'Management Education in India: Protecting it from the Ranking Onslaught', *Decision*, Vol. 32, No. 2, July–December 2005, p. 20.

[69] Ray Sougata and Sinha, Anup, op.cit., p. 4.

[70] Saraswat, Satya Prakash, 'Reflections on Spiritual Foundations of Human Values for Global Business Management', *Vision—The Journal of Business Perspective*, Vol. 9, No. 3, July–September 2005.

[71] Chakraborty, S.K., 1991, op.cit., p. 16.

[72] Ibid., p. 266.

9

EMERGING INDIA

India was a poor and underdeveloped country at the time of Independence. Sixty years later, India has emerged as a powerful economy in the world. What could be the reasons for such a high performance in just six decades? The fundamental reason is the functioning of superior economic, business and management models. These models continuously push India to move forward against many difficulties. One needs to understand these unique and performing models, as they have the potential to take India to higher levels. It is necessary to recongnize and understand them so that India could move up to reach higher limits in the years to come. Moreover, while the western models are facing serious difficulties, the Indian models offer a new hope for the other parts of the world too.

9.1 INDIA AS AN EMERGING ECONOMIC POWER

India is fast emerging as an economic power in the world. China and India are the world's fastest growing economies as well as the most populous countries. These two countries are expected to play a leading and dominant role in the affairs of the world in future. The economists predict that as Asia was dominating the world economy till the mid-nineteenth century, it would play a similar role in the future too. *The Economist* stated: "The shift in economic power towards emerging economies is, therefore, likely to continue. This is returning the world to the sort of state that endured throughout most of its history. People forget that, until the late 19th century, China and India were the world's two biggest economies...[1]." Earlier, Drucker had predicted that the future would be dominated by China and India, and India would ultimately outperform China in the long run. Performance details of the two countries show that the above conclusions are based on the study of facts. At the same time, the western countries are facing serious consequences. Their economic difficulties are compounded by problems at the social and cultural levels. It is in this situation that one has to look at India to understand the emerging dynamics.

9.1.1 Opinions on India

Let us see some of the views and information on India from diverse sources in the recent years. First, a random selection of views from outside India is presented.

In an interesting article, Muqtedar Khan[2] had earlier noted: "Fifty-eight years after independence the world is beginning to realize what most Indians always believed—that India is a great power and civilization. India's recent economic growth has attracted the attention of strategic analysts and future forecasters everywhere. A three trillion dollar economy [PPP], fourth in size after the US, China and Japan consistently growing at 6–7% per year, cannot be ignored specially when it is backed by explosive growth in the key technology of our times—InfoTech. India's phenomenal technological and economic growth in the arena of information technology is matched by developments in the nuclear sciences giving it an added strategic dimension that cannot be ignored both at the regional as well as the global level. The recent talk of India getting a permanent seat in the UN Security Council is a measure of the global recognition of India's emerging significance.

Clearly economists and politicians in the US are cognizant even concerned with India's emergence. People here are beginning to realize the growing dependence of the US economy on India's software engineers. However in all this hoopla about Digital Desis, what is being overlooked is the growing role of Indians in the management of the global economy. In the first phase of globalization that began with the transfer of low-end manufacturing to Third World countries, particularly Indonesia and China, it was believed that "they" would take the hard, labor intensive, less influential, low paying jobs, while "we" would retain the soft, high-end, managerial and control related, high paying jobs. But under the cover of the InfoTech explosion, India has also precipitated another less recognized revolution. It is slowly but steadily taking over the managerial and even research functions of the global economy.

The Business Process Outsourcing [BPO] has alone witnessed a 35% growth in the last year in India [2004–05]. The BPO industry includes not just the famous, low expertise, call centres that have become the signature of India's new foray into global business management, but they also include, high expertise endeavors such as financial management, medical diagnostic services and technology research. While last year 20,000 American tax returns were filed by CPAs* based in India, the coming year will see over 2,00,000 tax returns processed in India by Indian CPAs. More and more American medical centres are outsourcing health services to India which range from patient scheduling to accounts receivable, including the expert reading and handling of tests and diagnostic reports from the US.

Companies such as GE, Microsoft and others have established elaborate research and development facilities in India. India now produces more engineers, doctors and business managers than the US and entire Europe put together. This large pool of low-priced high expertise labor is sucking the heart of corporate America away from the continent of North America to the Indian subcontinent. General Electric's, John F. Welch Technology Center alone employs 1800 engineers [400 of them are PhDs.] This centre is located in Bangalore and provides R&D for thirteen GE divisions and has contributed 95 patents since 2000. Such developments and exploitation of India's knowledge pool requires both management and entrepreneurial skills and the revolution in these areas are keeping India's growth ticking."

Frank G Wisner, former US Ambassador to India, said: "America cannot ignore the fact that the centre of gravity is moving eastwards to Asia, away from Europe and North America, and India will be the motor force in globalization."

H Richter, the former German Ambassador to India, mentioned: "The research & development work carried out in India is of world-class standards and is now attracting German biotech companies who are keen on setting up joint ventures (JVs) and R&D facilities."

Phillippe Joubert, executive vice president, Alstom, noted: "Indian engineers are comparable to the best in the world, including the US and Europe and we will use this strength to leverage our position in the world market."

Business Week wrote: "It makes sense for pharma companies to look to India...Indian scientists are well trained...India has more pharmaceutical facilities approved by the US Food & Drug Administration (USFDA) than any foreign country."

Zakaria[3] wrote in *News Week*: "Every year at the World Economic Forum in Davos, there's a star. Not a person but a country. One country impresses the gathering of global leaders because of a particularly smart Finance Minister or a compelling tale of reform or even a glamorous gala. This year there was no contest. In the decade that I've been going to Davos, no country has

* Certified Public Accountants.

captured the imagination of the conference and dominated the conversation as India in 2006."

Now let us see the opinions of our business executives and industry captains on the performance of India.

The McKinsey Global Survey of Business Executives noted that *The McKinsey Quarterly* had asked executives from 116 countries their views about the prospects of the global economy, their national economies and their industries. It came to light that the Indian executives were far more confident than even the Chinese[4].

Anand G. Mahindra, Vice-Chairman and Managing Director of Mahindra and Mahindra, noted: "Everything you hear about India is true; in one sense, the attention is overdue[5]."

The overall assessment of diverse sections of people across the world unanimously points out that India has been fast rising as an economic power and has all the possibility to emerge as a dominant nation in the world. Why? What are the reasons? A random presentation of facts related to the recent years is enough to show the rising position of India.

A glimpse of India's recent performance

- India was one among the very few countries which was least affected by the global economic crisis.
- While the richer economies experienced negative rates of growth in 2009, India maintained its upward journey with a reasonably higher rate of growth.
- India's status has increased manifold at the global level with the emergence of G-20 as the premier economic forum.
- Among the BRIC countries, Indian firms finalized 812 deals abroad between 2000 and 2009, compared to 450 by the Chinese firms, 436 by the Russian firms and 190 by the Brazilian firms.
- By 2008, India's FDI flows to outside of Asia increased to 61 per cent[6].
- India was the largest recipient of foreign remittances in the world during 2010–11 with transfers amounting to $ 55 billion. Remittances by Indians have increased by 162 per cent during the past eight years.
- Tata Consultancy Services is the highest ranked Asia based company in the world and the second highest ranked company globally in the Information Technology and Services company category.
- The world's largest car companies are procuring their spare parts from India.

- Hero Honda is the world's largest motorcycle manufacturing company. In 2011, Hero Honda has crossed the figure of five million cumulative sales in a single year.
- Bharat Forge is the second largest forging company in the world and supplies its products to leading international players.
- Asian Paints operates in 17 countries and has 24 paint manufacturing facilities in the world servicing customers in over 65 countries.
- India has established its own Super Computer. The only other countries that have established Super Computers are the US and Japan.
- India is one among the six countries which can build and launch satellites.
- With the INSAT Organisation, India has become a very big national satellite network country in the world.
- Nine of 10 diamonds in the world are cut and polished in India, holding the No. 1 position in the world.
- Many of the global multinational companies have established their Research and Development centres in India.
- Asians were the lone exception as the number of poor in the US has risen for the fourth consecutive year across all groups last year[7].
- It is estimated that India's share of global gold usage during 2010 was 32 per cent.
- Of the skilled people who return from the US, 76 per cent of Indians and 51 per cent of Chinese note that it is the family ties that bring them back to their motherlands, reveals the Kauffman Foundation Report[8].
- A survey conducted across 17 countries revealed that Indians have the lowest concern about financial hardship in retirement and demonstrate an impressive optimism[9].

A few more facts on India's performance

- Foreign exchange reserves of the country during 2010–11 stood at $304.82 billion[10].
- IMF notes that the emerging and developing economies account for about half of global output and two-thirds of global growth in PPP terms, much of which is accounted for by China and India[11].
- India stands tenth in the world in service exports with a share of 2.9 per cent amounting to $103 billion[12].
- India continued to remain the top software services exporter with exports worth $49.4 billion in 2008[13].

- Exports and imports of goods and services as percentage of GDP have increased from 10 per cent in 1992–95 to 24 per cent in 2008[14].
- The growth rate of exports during 2010–11 (April– December) was 23.4 per cent compared to 13.6 per cent for imports[15].
- India has been ranked as the third most preferred Foreign Direct Investment (FDI) location in the world in the World Investment Prospects Survey 2010–11 of the United Nations Conference on Trade and Development[16].
- Cipla has been offering drugs to non-profit organizations at less than half of the regular prices. It has created an alternative to the high-priced AIDS drugs and has changed the way the world treats the disease. Indian pharma and biotech companies are developing unique ways of harnessing the power of medicine at an affordable cost[17].

Khanna[18] noted that Indian manufacturers were emerging as globally competitive players. "Smart Indian companies are emerging as smart leaders to the world. Just a decade ago, the idea of Indian manufacturers emerging as significant competitors in the global economy might have attracted some incredulity. Today, it has become a fact of life. From robots and computer chips to value-for-money automobile technology and high-end auto components, an increasing number of products being sold and used all over the world now flaunt the Made-in-India tag. From global laggards, a growing number of Indian manufacturers are emerging as world-beaters, so to speak."

9.1.2 Increasing Number of Cross-border Acquisitions

An increasing number of Indian companies are in an acquisition spree during the recent years. Bharti Airtel's takeover deal for the African assets of Kuwait's Zain for $10.7 billion during early 2010 was the second biggest overseas acquisition by an Indian company. This has made it the fifth largest mobile phone services company in the world. Tatas have emerged as the second most active investor in Sub-Saharan Africa. Earlier in 2007, Tatas made the headlines by acquiring the Netherlands-based steel-maker Corus for about $12.6 billion, the largest Indian takeover of a foreign company. Mittal Steel Company, promoted by the Indian-born Mittals and one of the leading producers of steel, merged with the Luxemburg-based Arcelor SA, one of the top names in the field of steel at the global level in 2006. The new company Arcelor-Mittal became the world's largest steel company accounting for nearly 10 per cent of the global share with operations in more than 60 countries. With an idea to expand its operations and reach the global markets, Sundaram Fasteners, the flagship company of the TVS group in the South, started taking over companies in the UK, Germany and China. As a result, now it has established world-class facilities in these countries. Ranbaxy Laboratories has affiliates, joint ventures and alliances in over 46 countries and manufacturing facilities in seven. Its string of acquisitions has helped the company establish its presence in Europe's pharma markets[19]. After successful acquisitions outside the country, many Indian companies have begun to earn more revenues from their international operations.

Table 9.1 provides the values of cross-border mergers and acquisitions in the world and by the Indian and Chinese companies between 1991 and 2007[20].

Table 9.1 Values of Cross-border Mergers and Acquisitions (1991–2007)

(US $ million)

	1991	1995	2000	2005	2006	2007
World	80,713	1,86,593	11,43,816	9,29,362	11,18,068	16,37,107
India	1	29	910	4958	6586	30,414
China	3	249	470	9546	14,906	4,452

Note: The data covers only those deals that involve an acquisition of an entity of more than 10 per cent.

Source: UNCTAD quoted in Reserve Bank of India Bulletin, October 2008, p. 1801.

Table 9.1 shows that the values of cross-border deals by Indian companies have been continuously increasing since 1991. In the case of India there has been a significant increase in the value of the deals particularly since 2005. As a result the share of India in the global cross-border mergers and acquisitions had touched 1.9 per cent in 2007[21]. It is relevant to note that the Indian companies have allocated investments in diverse sectors such as metals, automotive components, beverages and mobile communications, though the prominent sectors of investments are pharmaceuticals, information technology and energy.

9.1.3 Indians in Knowledge Sectors

The higher number of educated people coming out of schools and colleges is an important advantage in the emerging world order. India produces a high quantity of graduates and the maximum number of engineers in the world. The number of people knowing English in India had already crossed the number of people in England, and every year we are adding lakhs and lakhs of new numbers to this list. Internationally, the reputation of our educational institutions such as the Indian Institutes of Technology and Indian Institutes of Management are very high. Indians are respected for their high level of knowledge and hard work. Many Indians are occupying senior and important positions in diverse fields such as medicine, engineering, information technology and education at the international level. We all know that there is a high proportion of Indians as engineers, scientists and doctors in countries such as the US, and the crucial roles played by them in well-known companies such as Microsoft. India is emerging as a dominant supplier of talents in knowledge fields, including management. Khan[22] writes that "India is today exporting management expertise. Just like its engineering graduates, its management graduates too have dispersed all over the world." As more Indians are becoming chief executives in global organizations, *Time* noted that CEOs are 'India's leading exports'. As a result, Indians are emerging as leaders in different fields across the world. "Members of the enormous Indian diaspora are the thought-leaders in economics, business, philosophy, political science, religion and literature[23]."

9.1.4 Advantage of Population

India has a few additional strengths in the changing dynamics of global order. Many of the developed countries in the world are experiencing a shortage of the minimum required births. Some of them are already facing difficulties to find enough working population to keep the economy going. *World Population Policies 2005* notes: "In developed countries, 20% of the population was aged 60 or older, and by 2050 one in three persons will be aged 60 or older. The number of older persons was larger than the number of children (persons under age 15) in developed countries; by 2050, there will be two old persons for every child[24]." This is proving very difficult for these countries and they have already started increasing retirement ages and are recruiting elderly people. "While the streamlining effects of international competition are focusing attention on the need to create and keep good jobs, those fears will eventually give way to worries about the growing shortage of young workers. One unavoidable solution: putting older people back to work, whether they like it or not[25]." The cutting edge European economies like those of Finland and Denmark have already raised their retirement ages[26]. Some of the companies have started rehiring their retirees. DailmerChrysler has set up an Aging Workers Task Force, made up of human resource managers and health counselors to make sure that the employees stay productive[27]. Countries such as Japan have begun to consider the older people as the only growing asset. *Newsweek* quoted a Japanese demographer saying "Older people are Japan's only growing asset[28]."

Against this situation, India has population on its side. Economists Chandrasekhar and Jayati Ghosh[29] note that "India is and will still remain for some time one of the youngest countries in the world. A third of India's population was below 15 years of age in 2000 and close to 20 per cent were young in the 15–24 age group." The share of young population of India would be much more than all the major economies of the world. "In 2020, the average Indian will be only 29 years old compared with 37 in China and the US, 45 in West Europe and 48 in Japan[30]." A positive population gap in the working age groups is considered a 'dividend'. A population 'bulge' in the working age groups, however large the total population, is seen as an inevitable advantage and characterized as a 'demographic dividend[31].' This advantage is due to the Indian culture of family system.

9.1.5 Highest Growth Rates Expected

Due to these developments and natural advantages, Indian economy is expected to perform better in the coming years. PriceWaterhouseCoopers[32], in its study, '*The World in 2050*', has predicted that 'India has the potential to be the fastest growing large economy in the world in the period up to 2050'. Table 9.2 gives the projections.

Table 9.2 Growth in GDP of India and Selected Countries (2005–50) (% p.a.)

Country	GDP in US $	GDP in PPPs	GDP per capita (PPPs)
China	6.3	3.9	3.8
Brazil	5.4	3.9	3.2
US	2.4	2.4	1.8
UK	1.9	2.2	2.0
India	7.6	5.2	4.3

Source: PriceWaterhouseCoopers, The World in 2050, March, 2006.

The above predictions point out that India would be the most growing economy in the world in terms of GDP and GDP per capita. The Indian GDP growth rates would be more than two times the rate of US and 25 per cent higher than that of China.

9.1.6 Capability for Much More—The Unrealized Potentials and the Unrecognized Talents

Any projection by the agencies might not be the final one, as India's fundamentals lie hidden below the sight of the modern eyes. India seems to be capable of performing better than the best of the projections made through different methodologies. So the projections could at best be only the indicators, based as they are on a few exterior parameters, designed with western orientations. There is much strength that remains to be utilized for a better and more orderly development of the economy. For example, there is abundant natural resources and agricultural potential in the country. In terms of cultivable area, India is, in fact, the best-endowed country of the world. Three-fifths of our geographical area is cultivable. In most other valuable regions of the world, no more than one-fifth of the lands are cultivable. The world average is only one-tenth. India is thus blessed with extraordinary fertility within its relatively compact landmass. Measured in terms of cultivable area, India is the richest region of the world. India commands 160 million hectares of cultivable land. Cultivable area of the USA is 177 million hectares, that of the Russian Federation 126, China 124, western Europe 77, Australia 56, and Brazil 53 million hectares[33]. India not only has a larger cultivable area than all other great regions of the world; but Indian lands are also the most fertile. And the compact geography of India has always been described in superlative terms[34]. Properly planned, India could become an agricultural power in the world.

There are lots of talents that remain unorganized and, therefore, unutilized throughout the country. India's traditional knowledge systems and social capital are the biggest assets for any economy. There are communities of people who have enormous traditional knowledge and skills with them, which when properly recognized, could transform the position of the country in different fields. Textbook knowledge is universal; but the local knowledge systems are culture specific. They cannot be acquired; they are transmitted through generations. India has fortunately many such systems and skills available. They have the potential to generate wide economic prosperity. It was observed in many places that wherever possible, the local societies are using these systems and skills in the modern business contexts. But there needs a lot more to be done.

9.2 NEED TO UNDERSTAND THE PERFORMING MODELS

What is the secret behind India emerging as an economic power? The secret lies in the fact that India has superior economic, business and management models. They are not the textbook models; they are the functioning models. They are not imported from the other lands; they are home-grown and groomed in the dust and soil of India. Any attempt to study them through the popular theories would fail, as the 'modern' theories are based on the approaches of the western countries. Unless one has a proper understanding of the local environments and proceeds to study without any preconceived notions, study of the Indian models would not be fruitful. Moreover, in India, all the activities are interlinked with the social and cultural systems. Hence, one needs to have a sound knowledge of the different cultural and social systems to get a full picture of the situation. Indian models cannot be studied from a distance. They have to be studied from within. This is the reason why Anglo-Saxon minds would fail to understand India. One may not find much at the superficial level. One has to delve deeper to find out the truth. Moreover, the functioning models are not exactly the same in all parts of the country, though there is a common thread running across the lands.

All these years we have never realized that India could have her own functioning models. We were conditioned to think that India could not have her own models, as she was a poor country. This could possibly be due to two reasons. One is the lack of understanding of the economic, business and management models, as the present system of education does not help us to relate to the performing models. Second is the attitude to look at anything Indian as traditional and anti-modern. Thus, we have been attempting to look at India from a purely West-centric point of view, using only their methodologies and yardsticks. For example, we are used to assuming that wherever banking relationships are less, there cannot be any investment activity or much business activity. The studies of many centres across the country have, however, proved otherwise. It is clear that banks play only a supplementary role in the development of economic and business activities in India. There are businesses in which there is either very little or almost no banking finance at all. People have evolved their own methods of raising funds and so banking institutions are only secondary. But a modern mind would not be able to comprehend this reality as it is conditioned to look at development only from a western point of view. In none of the most successful native clusters, there are foreign investments. Take, for example, Surat. Its diamond business turnover was about ₹ 70,000 crores. Experts argue that whenever huge investments are involved, India require funds from foreign countries. But how much foreign investment is there in Surat? There are only domestic investments. The same is the case in all the successful clusters. Modern Indians find it difficult to accept that the western approaches might not be applicable in a country such as India which is different from the countries in the West. As a result, we are unable to find clues to the Indian systems.

It is time that we attempted to study the functioning models of India as they are not just the functioning ones, but the performing models. They are responsible for taking India to higher levels, in spite of all misconceptions by the policy-makers and the elite sections. The noted management expert, Prahalad[35] explains with examples as to how different types of organizations in India have grown to perform very successfully through their own business models. While writing about the Tamil Nadu-based Aravind Eye Hospital, he mentions: "It uses the most modern equipment available in any facility in the world. Its costs are dramatically brought down by its ability to use the equipment effectively, as it specializes only in eye-care and every doctor and nurse team performs an average 50 surgeries per day. Only 40 per cent of its patients pay. A cataract surgery costs $50 compared to $3000 to $3500 in the United States. In spite of these differences, Aravind's ROCE* is in the 120 to 130 per cent range. Aravind is totally free of debt. The revenues for the year 2001–02 were ₹ 388.0 million ($86 million) with a surplus (before depreciation) of ₹ 210.5 million ($46.5 million). This would be the envy of every hospital in the United States. The productivity and the volumes at Aravind are the basis for this level of profitability. Every doctor accounts for 2,000 operations per year, compared to a national average of 300 in India. The four locations in the Aravind system process more than 1.4 million patients (including 1,500 eye camps) and perform 2,00,000 surgeries. They operate with about 80 doctors and total staff, including paramedics, counsellors, and others, of 1,275."

Innovation is the key to success in the contemporary world of competitive business. Companies that make better products at cheaper costs for the large markets succeed. Prahalad and Mashelkar note that in the recent periods the Indian companies are in the forefront of innovation, making quality products at affordable costs for large sections of the society. Noting that a few companies in the developing countries are showing the way 'to do more with less for more people' as pioneers, the authors underline: "Nowhere is this more evident than in India, which was not exactly famous for innovation until recently[36]." They prefer to call innovations such as '1 cent for a one-minute telephone call and $2000 for a car' as "Gandhian innovation", because, "Affordability and sustainability were Gandhi's touch-stones six decades ago, and Indian companies have recently discovered their power[37]." Prahalad and Mashelkar mention that many companies in different sectors have been engaged in innovation. To quote: "Over the past three years, we have studied how Indian companies and organizations innovate, often backed by the government. Some are established companies,

* Return on Capital Employed.

and others are start-ups. They aren't confined to a few industries; they run the gamut of manufacturing and services—automobile manufacturing, drug development, health care, leather finishing, mobile communications, oil drilling, retailing, supercomputing, water purification, wind energy—and cover a range of capital and labor intensities. The only common link is that they're all radically innovative[38]." In many of the cases, innovations have changed the dynamics of business through creation of new business models.

The functioning models are different at various levels and in different functional areas. In many cases, these models are much better than the textbook-based techniques. Let us take the non-corporate sector and see how a modern concept is working. For this purpose, let us take the case of the now popular *dabbawallas* of Mumbai and see how the supply chain management works. The *dabba-wallas* are semi-literate people, with rural backgrounds from Pune district. They belong to the warrior caste of *Malva*, which fought for Sivaji in the earlier days. In the 1890s, one Mahado, a migrant from their area started the supply of lunch boxes. Today under the banner of Nutan Mumbai Tiffin-box Suppliers Association, more than 4500 of them are involved in supplying nearly 2,00,000 boxes every working day. Braving Mumbai weather conditions and difficulties involved in multiple transfer points, these 'ordinary' people make only one mistake for eight million deliveries[39]. It is no wonder that the *Forbes Global Magazine* gave them a Six Sigma efficiency rating on par with multinational companies such as Motorola and General Electric. In fact, the efficiency of *dabbawallas* is much better than the Six Sigma levels fixed by the experts for world class performances. As a result they are now admired as the model for the global corporations. The president of Six Sigma and Advanced Controls, Inc., USA admits: "The fascinating story of Mumbai's *dabbawallas* is an inspiration to all organizations aspiring to compete in the global market place[40]."

While mega corporations use the most modern technologies and employ highly qualified technical and management experts to reach higher levels, how could these ordinary people from village backgrounds with only their common sense and limited resources better the benchmarks fixed for the most efficient companies in the world? Is it not due to the effective teamwork and most efficient planning? Are these people not practising the most effective methods to serve their customers? In the case of modern corporate sector, they search for different methods to sell their products. In some cases, the products may not be essential to the customers. But still they try to look for different ways to attract customers and sell their products. In the case of *dabbawallas* they have devised a way to serve the customers who would like to eat home-made food, and in the process they have made it so well that they have become world-class service providers.

Let us see a different sector, namely the cooperatives. Amul is the biggest milk cooperative in the country. In the case of the western countries, there would be specific places for the rearing of cows from where the milk is procured and sent to other parts. In India, however, small families own one or two cows and the housewives themselves milk them. It is then collected from different households and sent to a centralized processing centre from where it is distributed to all the states. The widely disbursed production units are integrated with the processing and marketing systems to sell the product in diverse locations. As a result, Amul has emerged as one of the biggest cooperative enterprises in the world. So, the performing models of India are different and function at different levels. These are only three of the numerous examples of the models known to us. There are a number of cases which still remain unknown and unsung.

Let us see a case in which the economic activities are initiated and run by villagers on the community model* (see Box 9.1).

Box 9.1 Community economic models

Palamedu is a village of 8000 plus population, situated about 25 kilometres from Madurai in Tamil Nadu. The majority community of the village namely *Nadars* started a dairy farm in the 1960s to supplement their incomes. Having been successful, they started promoting community-owned grocery stores, salons, cinema hall and even toilets. Looking at this, the other communities in the village joined together and promoted another dairy, which is running successfully. A cordial relationship exists within the members of all the communities in the village. The village community does not allow liquor to be consumed within their boundaries. The community *panchayat* resolves the differences among the members and there is no room for divorces. There is complete discipline in the community.

This is a community-led economic model, planned and executed by the so-called ordinary people in a remote village. It is significant to notice that these models channelize the relationships for the economic development and social well-being. In fact, the *Nadar* community have pioneered a unique system called *Uravin Murai Mahamai* to generate funds for the development of the community and the society.

Talking about society, there was an interesting incident that took place in the village sometime earlier. In the community cinema hall, a viewer, who did not belong to the majority caste, noticed an obscene picture in the movie he was watching. He immediately wrote a letter to the community leaders objecting to the screening of the movie with that particular scene. The next day the community leaders convened a meeting and a few of their representatives were asked to see the movie. As a result, the screening of the movie was immediately stopped and a committee was formed to see that such incidents were not repeated.

* Srinivasan, R., Interview, Madurai, 2006.

Generally, it is assumed that the banking and financial institutions could be successfully promoted and run only by the highly qualified people. But there are a number of banks promoted by the local communities across the country. Even in Karur, which was made the headquarters of a district only a few years ago, the people belonging to the local *Vysya* community had promoted two scheduled banks, namely, Karur Vysya Bank and Lakshmi Vilas Bank, many decades earlier when the country was still under the British domination. In the earlier periods, banks were mainly promoted by the trading communities. But there have been exceptions. There is a highly successful bank promoted by a traditional non-trading community in the South. It is the Tamil Nadu Mercantile Bank (TMB) promoted by the *Nadar Mahajan Sangam*. As on March 31, 2010, its capital was only ₹ 28 lakhs. But its reserves were ₹ 1148.18 crores; deposits ₹ 11,639 crores and net profits ₹ 184.53 crores. It is one of the most efficient and highly respected banks in the country with an EPS of ₹ 6487. Its business per employee was estimated at ₹ 8.7 crores. During 2010–11, its net profits crossed ₹ 250 crores and net worth was ₹ 1000 crores. It proudly claims that it is the only bank in India consistently declaring higher rates of dividends from the beginning. The bank declared a dividend of 1000 per cent during 2006 and 2007 and proposed 5000 per cent dividend during 2007–08. Above all, a record interim dividend of 9000 per cent was proposed in October 2011[41]. The success of this venture and its excellent performance has proved that people from ordinary backgrounds can establish and run banking institutions that can compete effectively with the best of the financial corporations anywhere in the world.

Due to the special nature of the Indian systems, the economic, business and management models are unique. Whenever the economies of India and China are compared, it would be pointed out that China's faster growth is due to its ability to get more foreign investments. Table 9.3 gives the Foreign Direct Investment flows of India and China during 2001 to 2010[42].

Table 9.3 FDI Inflows—China and India (2001–2010)

($ billions)

Country/Year	2001	2005	2007	2010
China	46.87	72.40	83.52	105.73
India	5.47	7.62	25.35	24.64

Source: UNCTAD Statistics (www.unctadstat.unctad.org)

Table 9.3 shows that during the previous decade, FDI in India has always remained much lesser than that of China. During the

1990s, foreign direct investment as per cent of GDP was 3.6 for China while the same was only 0.5 for India[43]. Hence, experts would suggest that India should attract more such investments for higher growth rates. Governments are compelled to remove restrictions and invite foreign investments by giving all concessions and guarantees, most of the time at the cost of the domestic businesses and loss of employment. But in reality, it is becoming clearer that India's growth is not FDI dependent. Huang and Khanna[44] underline the fact that India has a better and more sustainable model than the FDI dependent model of China. To quote:

"What's the fastest route to economic development? Welcome foreign direct investment (FDI), says China, and most policy experts agree. But a comparison with long-time laggard, India suggests that FDI is not the only path to prosperity. Indeed, India's homegrown entrepreneurs may give it a long-term advantage over a China hamstrung by inefficient banks and capital markets."

China and India are the world's next major powers. They also offer competing models of development. It has long been an article of faith that China is on the faster track, and the economic data bear this out.

However, the statistics tell only part of the story—the macroeconomic story. At the micro level, things look quite different. There, India displays every bit as much dynamism as China. Indeed, by relying primarily on organic growth, India is making fuller use of its resources and has chosen a path that may well deliver more sustainable progress than China's FDI-driven approach. 'Can India surpass China?' is no longer a silly question, and, if it turns out that India has indeed made the wiser bet, the implications for China's future growth and for how policy experts think about economic development generally could be enormous.

The fact that India is increasingly building from the ground-up while China is still pursuing a top-down approach, reflects their contrasting political systems: India is a democracy, and China is not. But the different strategies are also a function of history. China's Communist Party came to power in 1949, intent on eradicating private ownership, which it quickly did. Although the country is now in its third decade of free-market reforms, it continues to struggle with the legacy of that period—witness the controversy surrounding the recent decision to officially allow capitalists to join the Communist Party.

India, on the other hand, developed a softer brand of socialism, Fabian socialism, which aimed not to destroy capitalis but merely to mitigate the social ills it caused. It was considered essential that the public sector occupy the economy's 'commanding heights,' to use a phrase coined by Russian revolutionary Vladimir Lenin, but popularized by India's first Prime Minister, Jawaharlal Nehru. However, that did not prevent entrepreneurship from flourishing where the long arm of the state could not reach.

While China has created obstacles for its entrepreneurs, India has been making life easier for local businesses. During the last decade, New Delhi has backed away from micromanaging the economy. True, privatization is proceeding at a glacial pace, but the government has ceded its monopoly over long-distance phone service; some tariffs have been cut; bureaucracy has been trimmed a bit; and a number of industries have been opened to private investment, including investment from abroad.

The real issue, of course, is not where China and India are today but where they will be tomorrow. The answer will be determined in large measure by how well both countries utilize their resources, and on this score, India is doing a superior job. Is it pursuing a better road to development than China? We won't know the answer for many years. However, some evidence indicates that India's ground-up approach may indeed be wiser and the evidence, ironically, comes from within China itself.

China and India have pursued radically different development strategies. India is not outperforming China overall, but it is doing better in certain key areas. That success may enable it to catch up with and perhaps even overtake China. Should that prove to be the case, it will not only demonstrate the importance of home-grown entrepreneurship to long-term economic development; it will also show the limits of the FDI-dependent approach China is pursuing. India is proving to the world that the native home-grown model is better and is more suitable than the universal model advocated by the west.

A nation could realize its full potential only when it nurtures and practises its own models. India, being a country of long years of experience, has her own models. So it is time for us to study and recognize the performing models of India for higher levels of performance and achievements. It is also necessary to achieve an all-round growth to the benefit of all sections of the Indian society. It is important to understand that the present rate of growth, though highly appreciable, has not benefited all sections of the country. There are certain critical areas that are neglected in this developmental process. The agricultural sector is vital to any nation and more so to India with about 60 per cent of citizens depending on it. Moreover, India is a huge country with nearly 120 crore population. India cannot depend on other countries for food. But unfortunately this sector has been suffering due to wrong policies. If it continues to stand affected, it will in turn, affect the performance of the economy in the long run. The rural economy remains largely uncared. About a quarter of the population is still living below the poverty line and there are difficulties in the social sectors. While the consumerist culture is engulfing the high earning sections of the metros and big cities, one cannot but notice the gap between the haves and have-nots widening in the recent years.

During the British rule, the economic and business policies were designed to suit their own interests. After Independence, the policy-makers have failed to utilise the opportunity to structure and frame policies based on the ground realities and social priorities of India. They tend to look outside for solutions, little realizing that India has enormous experiences and fundamental strengths that other nations do not have. During the recent decades, when the western world prescribed export-led policies, India too emphasized exports. When they said that foreign investments should play the main role for faster economic growth, India welcomed such investments. Different economists now agree that domestic funded growth is better than the foreign investment-driven growth. National Bureau of Economic Research shows that "there is no evidence of any "growth bonus" associated with increasing the financing share of foreign savings. In fact, the evidence suggests the opposite: throughout the 1990s, countries with higher self-financing ratios grew significantly faster than countries with low self-financing ratios[45]." It was observed that on an average, 90 per cent of the stock of capital in developing countries was self-financed[46].

So it is high time that India framed policies based on her own set of priorities and preferences. Writing in the context of export obsession, Jayati Ghosh[47] notes: "In this context, the only way for developing countries to get out of this trap is to stop thinking of exporting to the US as the only or even dominant means of economic expansion, and consider other ways of growth and diversification, based on the domestic market or on alternative trade patterns, perhaps within other regional arrangements. This has special significance for large economies with potentially huge internal markets. Such a shift in policy emphasis would also provide an opportunity for developing countries to cater to the citizens' needs rather than to the needs of the international market. Changing the terms of bargaining might even bring about a better deal for them in international trade negotiations." Indian experience shows that she is capable of achieving a lot more, provided a suitable framework is in place. Studies of different economic and business centres show that the potential of the unrecognized and non-corporate sectors has to be recognized. These sectors are capable of doing much better, provided a little effort is taken to understand them and a few suitable policy changes are made to allow their growth. First of all, the policy-makers should have the confidence that India could be run by Indians. All efforts should be turned towards an India-centric approach. In this respect India could learn a few lessons from China.

9.3 INDIAN MODELS FOR THE TWENTY-FIRST CENTURY

When observed carefully, one could find that India has much positive strength. A high level of entrepreneurial, technical and managerial skills exists in the country. One could see a lot of entrepreneurial activities going on at different levels. The native skills and talents of the ordinary Indians are to be seen to be believed. The clusters bubbling with activities are developed by the ordinary persons who possess excellent technical and managerial skills. Added to this are the skills acquired by the formally qualified modern Indians in the knowledge sectors. It is these skills that have already made India a major industrial and service centre in the world. Joseph M. Sigelman, Co-Chief Executive Office Tiger was quoted as saying: "We recognize the greatest strength of India is not just the number of people, not its ability to put them into seats—it's the skill level that exists here."

India's cultural background is the most significant asset. It is this traditional culture that nurtures families and communities. Fukuyama[48] notes that the role of culture extends to economic matters and international order. He writes: "Today, having abandoned the promise of social engineering, virtually all serious observers understand that liberal political and economic institutions depend on a healthy and dynamic civil society for their vitality. "Civil society"—a complex welter of intermediate institutions, including businesses, voluntary associations, educational institutions, clubs, unions, media, charities, and churches—builds, in turn, on the family, the primary instrument by which people are socialized into their culture and given the skills that allow them to live in broader society and through which the values and knowledge of that society are transmitted across the generations. A strong and stable family structure and durable social institutions cannot be legislated into existence the way a government can create a central bank or an army. A thriving civil society depends on a people's habits, customs, and ethics—attributes that can be shaped only indirectly through conscious political action and must otherwise be nourished through an increased awareness and respect for culture. Beyond the boundaries of specific nations, this heightened significance of culture extends into the realms of the global economy and international order." It is the culture of this country that compels people to work hard, lead simple lives and save money for families. It is also the culture that binds people as communities and treats all human beings as one and the same of the larger family called universe.

The high level of social capital that exists in India is a great advantage. While the West is suffering from individualistic lifestyles, which is proving to be very costly for the universe, India has an alternative system of life, which is more sustainable and balanced. India's family-based community life with a universal orientation is now being recognized as a crucial asset. As part of an international group, a Coimbatore-based textile accessories company, has business relationships in many countries across the world, including Japan.* Japanese are known for their best business practices, team spirit and perfection. When the Japanese team visited this company, they noticed the higher capabilities of the Indian employees and requested the company to send a few of their employees to train their employees in Japan. When three representatives, who are ordinary Indian village boys, went there on a one year assignment, the Japanese were surprised to see their skills and their ability to work and live as a team. Now the Japanese company wants more trainers to be sent every year, so that their employees could be trained better. It was said that it was not the higher levels of skill alone that attracted the attention of the Japanese to these Indian trainers; there were other aspects also. The Japanese were astonished to see three of their foreign trainers staying happily without any problems for months together, and mingling with them naturally.

The principle of unity in diversity is the unique feature of India since ancient times. Lehmann[49] notes: "India's one billion plus population is the most heterogeneous in the world. There are far more ethnic, linguistic and religious groups than in, say, the European Union. Yet, a far greater degree of unity has been achieved among India's disparate ethnicities than among the tribes of Western Europe... India is a microcosmic reflection of how globalization can work, especially in its remarkable ability to have managed multiculturalism to such a brilliant extent." India's ability to function as a successful democracy in spite of its multi-ethnic character is another important positive factor. Lehmann mentions

* Habasit Iakoka Limited, Coimbatore.

that "Perhaps the greatest achievement of India is to have maintained a very robust democracy in an extremely multi-ethnic environment. Contrast that with Egypt, for example, which used to have a highly multi-ethnic make-up, but which has now been mostly dissipated[50]." He says that in the contemporary world of conflicts and problems, India would prove to be an ethical model for the rest of the world. "The planet needs a sense of moral order, spirituality and an ethical compass. The Indian religious and philosophical traditions can provide a great deal of all three. But in a global environment desperate for ideas, philosophy and religion, India is the most prolific birthplace of all three—because of the great synergy of democracy and diversity, and the much greater degree of self-confidence that Indians now feel[51]."

It is due to these fundamental strengths that India is emerging as a major economic power in the world. In this context, we have to remember that the Indian diaspora of around 20 millions, is extremely successful in many countries of the world. Indians are playing a crucial role in many countries including the US and the UK, even in highly sophisticated areas such as information technology, medicine, engineering and finance. Kotkin[52] writes that "Virtually wherever they have settled, they rank among the most professionally and economically mobile of all groups. In settings as diverse as Malaysia, the United Kingdom and North America, Indians, particularly Hindus, consistently display higher-than-average levels of education, most notably in technical areas." As a result they have become crucial to the functioning of different sectors in those countries. For example, the contribution of Indians to the growth of business in the Silicon Valley is too well-known to be repeated. Indians are into businesses in many countries of the world and their presence in business is significant. They are recognized throughout the world for their high business acumen. Indians are in business in good numbers in many countries including the US, the UK, Africa and the Gulf. In some areas of business such as diamonds and motels, for example, they occupy a major share. Indians, constituting about 0.5 per cent of Hong Kong's population contribute 10 per cent to its external trade[53].

Sudipt Dutta[54] notes: "Indians abroad are still small in number compared to, say, the ethnic Chinese, who constitute 4 per cent of the population in Indonesia and control 17 of the 25 biggest business groups; in Thailand they comprise 10 per cent of the population and own 90 per cent of the commercial and manufacturing assets; and in Philippines, they constitute barely 1 per cent of the population, but own 67 per cent of the biggest companies." They are the single largest group now investing in mainland China[55]. Barnathan[56] et al. had estimated a decade ago that the Indians abroad together earned $340 billions annually, which was equal to the then official GDP of India. The success of Indians abroad is due to hard work, thrift, stability of families and the ability to adjust and function in new environments. Study on the success of the expatriate Indian community in business revealed that 'most of the values associated with the Indian family business have largely been retained' by them, though 'they may have acculturated to the host society in many outward symbols and functions.'[57]

While India has many advantages as a nation, the major economies of the rest of the world have been facing serious problems. The western capitalist model is fast collapsing under its own weight. The foundations of communist China are not strong. It is in this scenario that India is emerging as a powerful nation. India's emergence is not the emergence of another country in the world. But it is the re-emergence of a traditional power that had to lie low for historical reasons. It is the emergence of a power that could provide solutions to the contemporary issues and show the way for sustainable developmental models. Since the ancient days, Indian traditions have placed emphasis on the welfare of all living beings. Environment— friendly and inclusive approaches remained the basis of life in Indian thought. India with a very long history of thousands of years has never invaded and occupied any country. Her progress and achievements have never been at the cost of any other nation. Even when she was at the peak, it was entirely due to her own positive strengths. Throughout the history, wherever Indian thoughts went, they made the recipient lands richer. Moreover, the economic and business models of India have always had a higher orientation, even in the process of making money. The economic and business systems of India are based on stronger foundations than that of the other nations in the world. It is due to these reasons that experts from distant parts of the world expect and welcome India to take the lead role. Lehmann[58] notes: "Perhaps the most encouraging development in this early 21st century is the emergence of India as an increasingly global force, economically, politically and culturally."

REFERENCES

[1] Emerging Economies—Coming of Age,' *The Economist*, January 31, 2006, p. 13.

[2] Muqtedar Khan, 'India: The Emerging Management Giant', Muqtedar Khan Opinion Editorials, *Al-Jazeerah*, November 8, 2005.

[3] Zakaria, Fareed, 'India Rising', *News Week*, March 6, 2006, p. 20.

[4] The McKinsey Global Survey of Business Executives: Confidence Index, McKinsey Quarterly, January 2006.

[5] http://hbswk.hbs.edu/archive/5366.html.

[6] United Nations Conference on Trade and Development, FDI/ TNC database. www.unctad.org/fdistatistics.

[7] Asians Buck the Trend as Poverty Rises in US', IANS, Washington, 14, Sept., 2011.

[8] 'Grass is Indeed Greener in India and China for Returnee Entrepreneurs', Kauffman Foundation Report, US.

[9] Canara HSBC Oriental Bank of Commerce Life Insurance Survey quoted in *The New Indian Express*, 15 June, 2011.

[10] *Handbook of Statistics on Indian Economy 2010–11*, Reserve Bank of India, p. 261.

[11] *World Economic Outlook September 2011,* International Monetary Fund, p. 29.

[12] *Report on Currency and Finance 2008–09,* Reserve Bank of India, p. 266.

[13] Ibid. p. 268.

[14] Ibid., p. 13.

[15] *Economic Survey 2010–11,* Government of India, p. A-80.

[16] *World Investment Report 2009,* United Nations Conference on Trade and Development, United Nations, New York, p. 50.

[17] Ajay Khanna, 'Resurgent India Strikes Back with Confidence', *The Hindu Business Line,* April 26, 2006.

[18] Ibid.

[19] Ibid.

[20] United Nations Conference on Trade and Development quoted in Reserve Bank of India Bulletin, October 2008, p. 1801.

[21] Ibid.

[22] 'India: The Emerging Management Giant', Muqtedar Khan Opinion Editorials, op.cit.

[23] Ibid.

[24] United Nations, *World Population Policies 2005*, Academic Foundation, New Delhi, 2006, p. 11.

[25] Stefan Theil, 'The New Old Age', *Newsweek*, January 30, 2006, p. 21.

[26] Ibid.

[27] Ibid.

[28] Ibid.

[29] Chandrasekhar C.P. and Ghosh, Jayati, 'India's Potential Demographic Dividend', *The Hindu Business Line*, January 17, 2006, p. 11.

[30] Ibid.

[31] Ibid.

[32] Price Waterhouse Coopers, '*The World in 2050*', March 2006.

[33] Bajaj, J.K. and Srinivas, M.D., *Timeless India Resurgent India*, Centre for Policy Studies, Chennai, 2001, p. 7.

[34] Ibid.

[35] Prahalad, C.K., *The Fortune at the Bottom of the Pyramid*, First Indian Reprint, Wharton School Publishing, Pearson Education (Singapore) Pte Ltd., Delhi, 2005, p. 56.

[36] Prahalad, C.K. and Mashelkar, R.A., 'Innovation's Holy Grail, *Harvard Business Review*, July–August 2010, p. 134.

[37] Ibid.

[38] Ibid.

[39] Thakker, Pradip, 'Mumbais Amazing Dabbawalas', *Smart Manager*, November 11, 2005.

[40] Deshpande, Pradeep B., President of Six Sigma and Advanced Controls, Inc. and Professor of Chemical Engineering, University of Louisville.

[41] www.tnmbonline.com and www.mydigitalfc.com.

[42] *www.unctadstat.unctad.org*.

[43] Quoted in Kumar, Nagesh, 'Liberalization, Foreign Direct Investment Flows and Development: Indian Experience in the 1990s', *Economic and Political Weekly*, Vol. 40, No. 14, p. 1462, 2005.

[44] Huang, Yasheng and Khanna, Tarun, 'Can India Overtake China?', *Foreign Policy*, July/August 2003.

[45] Aizenman, Joshua, Brian Pinto and Artur Radziwill, 'Sources for Financing Domestic Capital: Is Foreign Saving a Viable Option for Developing Countries?', Working Paper, National Bureau of Economic Research, June 2004. www.nber.org.

[46] Ibid.

[47] Ghosh, Jayati, ' The Export Obsession', *Front Line,* December 2, 2005, p. 110.

[48] Fukuyama, Francis, *Trust,* Free Press Paperbacks, New York, 1996, p. 4.

[49] Lehmann, Jean-Pierre, 'The Dangers of Monotheism in the Age of Globalization', *The Globalist,* March 30, 2006.

[50] Ibid.

[51] Ibid.

[52] Kotkin, quoted in Sudipt Dutta, op.cit., p. 236.

[53] Sudipt Datta, op.cit., p. 231.

[54] Ibid.

[55] Ibid.

[56] Barnathan, Joyce, et al., quoted in Sudipt Dutta, op.cit., p. 231.

[57] Jacob, Rahul, quoted in Sudipt Dutta, op.cit., p. 232.

[58] Lehmann, Jean-Pierre, op.cit.

10

CONCLUSION

India's first Prime Minister Jawaharlal Nehru[1] had noted: "... that vision of five thousand years gave me a new perspective, and the burden of the present seemed to grow lighter." A historical study of the Indian economy and business gives new perspectives and throws ideas for new hopes. But the past alone cannot help, especially in the highly complex and dynamic affairs of the modern business and economics. One has to see the functioning systems of the contemporary times. The international economic and business systems are dominated by the western thinking since the eighteenth century. In the recent decades, the economic and business affairs of different countries are becoming closely intertwined with the global markets and the developments in other nations.

An objective study of the different economic and business systems over the years helps to understand the following points:

1. The available sources indicate that India was a very prosperous country since the ancient days. During the last two millennia for which the economists have calculated the GDP of different countries of the world, India remained at the top for most part of the period, till the British interfered with the native systems. India's economic prosperity was accompanied by achievements in diverse fields such as mathematics, medicine, education, literature, agriculture, industry and trade. In all their activities, including business and trade, a higher sense of character and responsibility was visible. The prosperity of India was always on the superiority of her products and services, and never in her history, did India disturb or attack any other nation for trade or business. The foreign travellers and observers had noted the prosperity, high character of the people and the higher quality of life in India.

2. For more than sixteen centuries since 0 CE, China was following India in terms of economic performance. Europe entered the map of the global GDP only in the sixteenth century. Beginning from mercantilism, the different economic models of the West lasted only for a few centuries or decades. There is no continuity of the models as each of them seemed to have suffered without solid foundations. Moreover, these models have survived only at the cost of the other sections of societies. The success of these models almost always depended on the use of resources of other nations through distorted policies and unequal competition. In the earlier centuries, it was achieved through colonialism and exploitation of resources of other nations.
3. The developments over the last few decades have clearly proved that there could be no uniform model for the economic development of different countries. Moreover, experts agree that there are different factors that influence the economic development of nations. These include the cultural and social backgrounds, historical developments and availability of resources.
4. India became one of the poorest countries during the British rule. Even after Independence, the Indian policy-makers leaned heavily on the western models. As a result, the full potential of India is yet to be realized. But in spite of the official attitudes, the people of India started their own initiatives, and it is largely through their efforts that India is fast emerging as an economic power. The emergence of India as a powerful economy is due to the fundamental strengths and character of the local societies.
5. The business models of different countries are shaped by the economic ideologies, cultural and social backgrounds, historical developments and availability of resources. Resultantly, the business models of different countries have differences.
6. The Indian business models are unique. Family and community systems play a major role in the economic and business decisions. The non-corporate sector plays a dominant role in the economy and business of India. The growth of the economy and business is largely influenced by the family-based non-corporate and corporate sectors.
7. The management models of India seem to be different from the management models of the other countries, especially the West.

8. There are no universal models as such for all the countries in the world. The western models do not seem to be suitable for all the countries. India, being a unique country with different priorities and a universal outlook, has her own functioning models evolved through historical and cultural experiences.
9. While the western models are facing serious difficulties, many of the Indian models are performing better. As a result, experts have come to recognize the superiority of the Indian models. In fact, the Indian models are expected to show the way for a better economic, business and management systems.
10. It is imperative that the performing models of India are recognized and allowed to function, wherever they are doing well, for the overall economic development of the country. Moreover, the Indian models could be considered as alternatives to the western models which are facing a crisis.

The basic difficulty with the western systems is that they view everything from a purely monetary point of view. They assume that people always pursue their self-interests, whereas in practice, it is not really so. Fukuyama[2] notes: "There is no doubt that human beings are, as the economists say, fundamentally selfish and that they pursue their selfish interests in a rational way. But they also have a moral side in which they feel obligations to others, a side that is frequently at cross-purposes with their selfish instincts. As the word "culture" itself suggests, the more highly developed ethical rules by which people live are nurtured through repetition, tradition, and example. These rules may reflect a deeper adaptive rationality: they may serve economically rational ends; and in the case of a few individuals, they may be the product of rational consent. But they are transmitted from one generation to another as rational social habits. These habits, in turn, guarantee that human beings never behave as purely selfish utility maximizers postulated by economists." The judgement based on western economics is not complete; it is only partial. Schumacher[3] had earlier said: "The judgement of economics, in other words, is an extremely fragmentary judgement; out of large number of aspects which in real life have to be seen, judged together before a decision can be taken, economics supplied only one—whether a thing yields a money profit to those who undertake it or not." In real life, decisions are not always taken on the basis of economic aspects alone.

Moreover, critics argue that there is no such thing as free trade with integrated global markets. Instead, the international business is dominated by a few countries led by the US. Rugman[4] writes: "No credible evidence can be found to support the viewpoint that a system of global capitalism exists. There is no evidence for globalization, that is, of a system of free trade with fully integrated world markets. Instead, the evidence on the performance and activities of multinational enterprises demonstrates that international business is triad-based and triad-related. Virtually, all of the world's largest 500 multinational enterprises are operating in a strong triad home base, with some access to another triad. Almost none of them have true global strategies. Multinational enterprises actually organize production, marketing, and other business activities by triad." The world is in difficult times. On the one hand, it is dominated by the modern theories that are not sound and on the other hand, the free trade mechanism is not working for the benefit of all the nations. Soros[5] says that the markets are not moral and the American domination of the globalization system is deficient. "What I am asserting is that the moral base of globalization and American domination is deficient. Markets are amoral, the untrammelled pursuit of self-interest does not necessarily serve the common interest, and military might is not necessarily right." It is important to note here that both the popular western economic models have been proved wrong.

The failure of the two dominant western models requires a different set of policies for the future. Drucker[6] had noted: "These new realities require different economic theories and different international economic policies." But countries have to be careful, as once again they should not adopt wrong policies. In this regard, the western thinker Guenon[7] had cautioned: "So long as western people imagine that there exists a single type of humanity, that there is only one type of 'civilization' at different stages of development, no mutual understanding will be possible." The new theories and policies should be based on the backgrounds and realties of different countries.

It is clear that the different countries of the world have different economic, business and management models. As we have seen, these models are shaped by historical, cultural, social and other factors. India, with a long history of civilization, was an acknowledged economic power till the eighteenth century, the longest number of years for any nation in the recorded history. An achievement of such a high magnitude of sustained economic status would not have been possible without a superior economic, business and management model. No doubt, a lot of changes have taken place during the last three centuries due to large scale industrialization and developments in technology and information. But India is performing better in most of these modern sectors as well, catching up with the western countries in a very short time. The difficulty for India during the last three centuries was mainly with the policies and approaches. The realities of India being different, the country requires a different kind of approach. Mahatma Gandhi[8] had noted: "My Swaraj (self-rule or independence) is to keep intact, the genius of our civilization. I want to write many new things but they must all be written on the Indian slate. I would gladly borrow from the West when I can return the amount with decent interest."

It does not mean that India should follow an isolationist approach; it only means that India needs a self-reliant and India-centric approach. No country could remain as an island; more so a country such as India. India has always considered the whole world as a family. But every nation should aim for a self-reliant economy. International transactions should be on a mutually beneficial basis. Self-dependence has always remained an Indian ideal ever since ancient times. Writing two thousand years ago, Thiruvalluvar[9] wrote in one of his couplets: "A country which relies on internal strength, without undue exertion or dependence on outsiders, rises in respect." It is highly unfortunate that the Indian policy-makers have failed to realize the full potential of India. Aurobindo[10] had squarely blamed the educated sections for this situation. To quote: "But our educated class have become so unfamiliar with the deeper knowledge of their forefathers that it has to be translated into modern European terms before they can understand it. For it is the European ideas alone that are real to them and the great truths of Indian thought seem to them mere metaphors, allegories and mystic parables." Media personality Mark Tully[11] echoes the same views: "India is no longer a land dominated by brown *sahibs* imitating the ways of the white *sahibs* who used to rule them. But India is still a land dominated by foreign thinking, and I would suggest that that thinking is just as alien as the brown *sahibs*. Colonialism teaches the native elite it creates to admire—all too often to ape—the ways of their foreign rulers. That habit of mind has survived in independent India."

There is a large-scale failure to understand the realities of India and frame suitable policies to realize the full potential. Better late than never, the exercise should start at least now, especially when the other systems are failing and India is fast emerging as an economic power. India has many needs to fulfil within the country, as sections of people are waiting for results and the present growth is not inclusive. So the immediate step could be to start thinking afresh to learn the realities and plan further course of actions. India should assimilate all thoughts and practices, but apply only those that are most suitable. Home-grown models could be preferable in all possible areas, as they are the outcomes of the local initiatives and experiences. They would be able to function naturally in the native environments and deliver optimum results. Fortunately for India, there are performing models. It is these models that are mainly responsible for taking the country to higher levels. Simultaneously we could adopt and improve superior methods and practices from other places, wherever necessary. When the rest of the world is searching for clues to their difficulties, India has solutions with her. It has been a long time since Indians fully understood her potential. The time has come now; it is up to us to comprehend the issues and go forward, for India has all the potential to emerge, in fact, re-emerge, as a dominant power again. In the contemporary world of confusions and calamities, India is destined to play a larger responsibility, not just for her people, but for the rest of the world as well.

REFERENCES

[1] Nehru, Jawaharlal, *The Discovery of India*, Penguin, New Delhi, 2004, p. 44.

[2] Fukuyama, Francis, *Trust*, Free Press Paperbacks, New York, 1996, p. 41.

[3] Schumacher, E.F., '*Small is Beautiful—A Study of Economics as if People Mattered*, Vintage, London, 1993, p. 28.

[4] Rugman, Alan, *The End of Globalization*, AMACOM edition, New York, 2001, p. 218.

[5] Soros, George, *Open Society—Reforming Global Capitalism*, Viva Books Private Limited, New Delhi, 2004, p. 165.

[6] Drucker, Peter, 'Peter Drucker Sets Us Straight,' interview by Brent Schlender, *Fortune*, 2004, January 12, 149(1), pp. 114–118.

[7] Guenon quoted in Chakraborty, S.K., '*Foundations of Managerial Work—Contributions from Indian Thought*,' Himalaya Publishing House, 2nd ed., Mumbai, 2003, p. 11.

[8] Mahatma Gandhi quoted in Mark Tully, *No Full Stops in India*, Penguin Books, New Delhi, 1991, p. 11.

[9] Thiruvalluvar, *Thirukkural,* couplet 739.

[10] Aurobindo quoted in Chakraborty, S.K., *Foundations of Managerial Work—Contributions from Indian Thought,* Himalaya Publishing House, 2nd ed. reprint, Bombay, 2003, p. 101.

[11] Mark Tully, *No Full Stops in India*, Penguin Books, New Delhi, 1991, pp. 3–4.

Bibliography

Books, Journals and Papers

Agarwala, P.N., *A Comprehensive History of Business in India—from 3000* BC *to* 2000 AD, Tata McGraw-Hill Publishing Company Limited, New Delhi, 2001.

Aizenman, Joshua, Brian Pinto and Arthur Radziwill, 'Sources for Financing Domestic Capital: Is Foreign Saving a Viable Option for Developing Countries?', Working Paper, National Bureau of Economic Research, June 2004.

Bajaj, Jitendra (Ed.), *Food for All,* Centre for Policy Studies, Chennai, 2001.

Bajaj, Jitendra and Srinivas, M.D., *Annam Bahu Kurvitha,* Centre for Policy Studies, Madras, 1996.

Bajaj, Jitendra and Srininvas, M.D., *Timeless India Resurgent India,* Centre for Policy Studies, Chennai, 2001.

Basham, A.L., *The Wonder that was India,* Rupa & Co., New Delhi, 2001.

Brown, Andrew D. and Humphreys, Michael, 'International Cultural Differences in Public Sector Management—Lessons from a Survey of British and Egyptian Technical Education Managers', *International Journal of Public Sector Management,* Vol. 8, No. 3, 1995, p. 12.

Budhwar, Pawan S. and Sparrow, Paul R., 'Strategic HRM through the Cultural Looking Glass: Mapping the Cognition of British and Indian Managers', *Organizational Studies, 2002,* EBSCO Publishing, 2003.

Chadha, G.K., *Rural Industry in India, Policy Perspectives, Past Performance and Future Options,* South Asia Advisory Team, International Labour Organization, New Delhi, 2003.

Chakraborty, S.K., *Ethics in Management: Vedantic Perspectives*, 3rd impression, Oxford University Press, New Delhi, 1999.

Chakraborty, S.K., *Foundations of Managerial Work—Contributions from Indian Thought*, Himalaya Publishing House, 2nd ed. reprint, Bombay, 2003.

Chakraborty, S.K., *Management by Values—Towards Cultural Congruence*, Oxford University Press, New Delhi, 1991.

Chakravarty, Ranabir, *Trade in Early India*, Oxford University Press, New Delhi, 2001.

Chandra, Bipan, *The Rise and Growth of Economic Nationalism in India,* Revised & Abridged edition, Anamika Publishers & Distributors (P) Ltd., New Delhi, 2004.

Chari, Sharad, *Fraternal Capital*, Permanent Black, Delhi, 2004.

Cole, Gerald, *Management Theory and Practice*, 6th ed., Thomson Asia Pte Ltd., Singapore, 2004.

Corsi, Marco, 'Modernity, Modernisation, Development: The Karur Industrial District', Paper presented at the workshop on Asia-Pacific Studies in Australia and Europe: A Research Agenda for the Future, Australian National University, Canberra, July 5–6, 2002.

Daya Krishna, *India's Planned Poverty*, Bharatiya Agro Economic Research Centre, Delhi, 1989.

Daya Krishna, *Golden Age to Globalisation—7000 Years of Indian Economy*, Swadeshi Jagran Prakashan, New Delhi, 2002.

Dew-Becker, Ian and Gordon, Robert, 'Where Did the Productivity Growth Go?—Inflation Dynamics and the Distribution of Income', *National Bureau of Economic Research*, Working Paper No. 11842, December 2005, www.nber.org.

Dharampal, *The Beautiful Tree*, 2nd ed., Keerthi Publishing House Pvt. Ltd., and AVP Printers and Publishers Pvt. Ltd., Coimbatore, 1995.

Dharampal, *Science and Technology in the Eighteenth Century*, Other India Press, Goa, 2000.

Drucker, Peter F., *Managing in the Next Society*, Butterworth-Heinemann, Oxford, Reprinted, 2003.

Duncan, Richard, *The Dollar Crisis—Causes, Consequences, Cures,* John Wiley and Sons (Asia) Pte Ltd., Singapore, 2005.

Durkheim, Emile, *The Division of Labor in Society,* The Free Press, New York, 1997.

Dutt, Romesh, *The Economic History of India—Under Early British Rule,* Vol. I, 2nd ed., Kegal Paul, Trench, Trubner, Great Britain, 1906.

Dutt, Romesh, *The Economic History of India—In the Victorian Age,* Vol. II, 2nd ed., Kegal Paul, Trench, Trubner, Great Britain, 1906.

Dwivedi, Mridula, 'Nature of Trust in Small Firm Clusters: A Case Study of Kanpur Saddlery Cluster', Paper presented at the conference on '*Clusters, Industrial Districts and Firms: The Challenge of Globalisation*', Modena, Italy, 2003.

Frank, Andre Gunder, 'Asian-based World Economy 1400–1800: A Horizontally Integrative Macro-history', University of Amsterdam, November 12, 1995.

Frank, Andre Gunder, *ReOrient: Global Economy in the Asian Age,* Vistaar Publications, New Delhi, 1998.

Fukuyama, Francis, *Trust,* Free Press Paperbacks, New York, 1996.

Georges Ifrah, *Histoire Universelle des Chiffres,* Vol. 2, Robert Laffont, Paris, 1994.

Gurucharan Das, *India Unbound—From Independence to the Global Information Age,* Penguin Books, New Delhi, 2002.

Hamilton, Clive, *Growth Fetish,* South Asian Edition, Allen & Unwin, Australia, 2004.

Harriss-White, Barbara, 'India's Informal Economy: Facing the Twenty-first Century', in Kaushik Basu (Ed.), *India's Emerging Economy—Performance and Prospects in the 1990s and Beyond,* Oxford University Press, New Delhi, 2005.

Hayami, Yujiro, *Development Economics—From the Poverty to the Wealth of Nations,* Clarendon Press, Oxford University Press Inc., New York, 1998.

Huang, Yasheng and Khanna, Tarun, 'Can India Overtake China?', *Foreign Policy,* July/August 2003.

India Brand Equity Foundation, 'Hinterland India: The Real Source of India's Entrepreneurship', Department of Science and Technology, Government of India, New Delhi. www.ibef.org.

International Monetary Fund, 'Is India Becoming an Engine for Global Growth?', *World Economic Outlook: September 2005,* IMF, Washington.

International Monetary Fund, *World Economic Outlook April 2010*, IMF, Washington.

International Monetary Fund, *World Economic Outlook September 2011: Slowing Growth, Rising Rates*, IMF, Washington, 2011.

Jodhka, Surinder S., 'Dalits in Business: Self-Employed Scheduled Castes in North-West India', *Economic and Political Weekly*, Vol. XLV, No. 11, March 13, 2010.

Kanagasabapathi, P., 'Ethics and Values in Indian Economy and Business', *International Journal of Social Economics*, Special Issue on India, Part I, Vol. 34, No. 9, pp. 577–585, 2007.

Kanagasabapathi, P., *Unorganised Finance Sector: The Engine for Economic Growth—A Study with Reference to Karur, Tamil Nadu*, Swadeshi Academic Council, Coimbatore, 2002.

Kennedy, Paul S., *The Rise and Fall of the Great Powers—Economic Change and Military Conflict from 1500–2000*, Fontana Press, London, 1988.

Khanna, Vikramaditya S., 'The Economic History of Corporate Form in Ancient India', 1997, http://ssrn.com/.

Khor, Martin, *Rethinking Globalization*, Books for Change, Bangalore, 2001.

Korten, David C., *When Corporations Rule the World*, The Other India Press, Goa, 1998.

Korten, David C., *Agenda for a New Economy*, Tata McGraw-Hill, New Delhi, 2009.

Kumar, Nagesh, 'Liberalization, Foreign Direct Investment Flows and Development: Indian Experience in the 1990s', *Economic and Political Weekly*, Vol. 40, No. 14, pp. 1459–1469, 2005.

Kumarappa, J.C., *Economy of Permanence*, 6th ed., Sarva Seva Sangh Prakashan, Varanasi, 1997.

Macaulay's Minute on Indian Education dated February 2, 1835.

Maddison, Angus, *The World Economy—A Millennial Perspective*, 1st Indian Edition, Overseas Press (India) Private Limited, New Delhi by arrangement with Organization for Economic Cooperation and Development, 2003.

Maddison, Angus, *The World History* (Two-in-One Edition), Indian Edition, Academic Foundation, New Delhi in arrangement with the Organization for Economic Cooperation and Development, 2007.

Makkhan Lal with Rajendra Dixit, *Educating to Confuse and Disrupt*, India First Foundation, New Delhi, 2005.

Mark Tully, *No Full Stops in India*, Penguin Books, New Delhi, 1991.

Marglin, Stephen A., *The Dismal Science: How Thinking Like an Economist Undermines Community,* Oxford University Press, New Delhi, 2009.

Meier, Gerald M. and Stiglitz, Joseph E. (Eds.), *Frontiers of Development Economics—The Future in Perspective*, World Bank and Oxford University Press Inc., New York, 2002.

Michel Danino, 'Indian History & Civilization: Recent Discoveries and Their Significance', Paper presented at the national symposium on '*Philosophy and Practice of Education for India*', organized by Sri Aurobindo Samiti at Kolkata, November, 2004.

Mookerji, Radha Kumud, *Ancient Indian Education,* 4th ed., Motilal Banarsidas, Delhi, 1969.

Mukund, Kanakalatha, *The Trading World of the Tamil Merchant—Evolution of Merchant Capitalism in the Coromandel*, Orient Longman Limited, Hyderabad, 1999.

Munusamy Varadarasan, *Thirukkural Thelivurai,* The South India Saiva Siddhanda Works Publishing Society Tinneveli Ltd., Chennai, 2002.

Nanda, Jayanta K., *Management Thought*, Sarup & Sons, New Delhi, 2006.

Naoroji, Dadabhai, *Poverty and Un-British Rule in India*, 2nd ed., Ministry of Information and Broadcasting, Government of India, New Delhi, 1966.

Nayyar, Deepak, 'Economic Growth in Independent India—Lumbering Elephant or Running Tiger?', *Economic and Political Weekly,* Vol. XLI, No. 15, pp. 1451–1458, 2006.

Nehru, Jawaharlal, *Discovery of India*, Penguin Books, New Delhi, 2004.

OECD Fact Book 2011: *Economic, Environmental and Social Statistics,* Organization for Economic Development and Cooperation, Paris, www.oecd.org.

Ojah, Abhoy K., 'Management Education in India: Protecting it from the Ranking Onslaught', *Decision*, Vol. 32, No. 2, July– December, 2005.

Palley, Thomas I., 'A New Development Paradigm: Domestic Demand-Led Growth—Why it is Needed & How to Make it Happen',

Foreign Policy in Focus Discussion Paper, September, http://www.fpif.org/.

Parthasarathy, Swami Dr., *Human Values Management—20 Key Principles for Modern Management,* Ane Books India, New Delhi, 2006.

Patel, Parvin J. and Rutten, Mario, 'Patels of Central Gujarat in Greater London', *Economic and Political Weekly,* Vol. 34, Nos. 16 and 17, pp. 952–954, 1999.

Pereira, Winin, *Tending the Earth,* Earthcare Books, Bombay, 1993.

Peter Cappelli, Harbir Singh, Jitendra V. Singh and Michael Useem, ' Leadership Lessons from India', *Harvard Business Review,* Vol. 88, No. 3, March 2010, pp. 90–97.

Prahalad, C.K., *The Fortune at the Bottom of the Pyramid,* Wharton School Publishing, Pearson Education (Singapore) Pte Ltd., Delhi, First Indian Reprint, 2005.

Prahalad, C.K. and Mashelkar, R.A., 'Innovation's Holy Grail', *Harvard Business Review,* July–August 2010, pp. 133–141.

Rakshit, Mihir, 'On Liberalizing Foreign Institutional Investments', *Economic and Political Weekly,* Vol. 41, No. 11, pp. 991–1000, 2006.

Rangarajan, L.N., *Kautilya—The Arthashastra,* Penguin Books, New Delhi, 1992.

Ray, Sougata and Sinha, Anup, 'Management Education—Let a Thousand Flowers Bloom Amidst a Hundred Questions', *Decision,* Vol. 32, No. 2, July–December, 2005.

Robins, Nick, *The Corporation that Changed the World—How the East India Company Shaped the Modern Multinational,* Orient Longman, Hyderabad, 2006.

Rudner David West, *Caste and Capitalism in Colonial India—The Nattukkottai Chettiars,* University of California Press, Berkeley, 1994.

Rugman, Alan, *The End of Globalization,* AMACOM edition, New York, 2001.

Russo, Fabio, Strengthening Indian SME Clusters: UNIDO Experience, Case Study, Project: US/GLO/95/144, UNIDO, July 1999. http://www.unido.org/userfiles/RussoF/Vie. 3pdf.

Saith, Ashwani, *Rural Industrialization in India—Some Policy Perspectives,* South Asia Multidisciplinary Advisory Team, International Labour Organization, New Delhi, 2000.

Saraswat, Satya Prakash, 'Reflections on Spiritual Foundations of Human Values for Global Business Management', *Vision—The Journal of Business Perspective,* Vol. 9, No. 3, July–September 2005.

Schumacher, E.F., *Small is Beautiful—A Study of Economics as if People Mattered,* Vintage, London, 1993.

Sharma, G.D., *Management and the Indian Ethos,* Rupa and Co., New Delhi, 2001.

Shirur Srinivas, *Strategic Alternatives for Family Business Houses,* Deep and Deep Publications Pvt. Ltd., New Delhi, 2005.

Shutt, Harry, *A New Democracy, Alternatives to a Bankrupt World Order,* Zed Books, London, 2001.

Soaring High—Kites and Community Endeavour, Swadeshi Academic Council, Coimbatore, 2004.

Soros, George, *The Crisis of Global Capitalism*, Public Affairs, New York, 1998.

Soros, George, *Open Society—(Reforming Global Capitalism),* 1st Indian ed., Viva Books Private Limited, New Delhi, 2004.

Stiglitz, Joseph E., *Globalization and its Discontents,* Penguin Books, New Delhi, 2002.

Sudipt Dutta, *Family Business in India*, Response Books, New Delhi, 1997.

Tomilson, B.R., *The Economy of Modern India, 1860–1970,* First South Asian Paperback ed., Cambridge University Press, U.K., 1998.

Tripathi, Dwijendra and Jumani, Jyoti, *The Concise Oxford History of Indian Business*, Oxford University Press, New Delhi, 2007.

Uma Kapila (Ed.), *Indian Economy since Independence*, 14th ed., 2002–03, Academic Foundation, New Delhi, 2002.

Uma Kapila, *Understanding the Problems of Indian Economy*, 4th ed., 2003–04, Academic Foundation, New Delhi, 2003.

United Nations, *World Population Policies 2005,* Academic Foundation, New Delhi, 2006.

Virmani, Arvind, *Propelling India from Socialist Stagnation to Global Power—Vol. 1: Growth Process*, Academic Foundation, New Delhi, 2006.

Will Durant, *The Case for India,* Simon and Schuster, New York, 1930.

Williamson, Jeffrey, 'De-industrialization and Underdevelopment: A Comparative Assessment around the Periphery 1750–1939', Paper prepared for the Harvard Economic History workshop, Harvard University, December 2004.

Winters, Alan L. and Yusuf, Shahid (Eds.), *Dancing with Giants—China, India and the Global Economy*, The World Bank and the Institute of Policy Studies, Singapore, 2007.

———*Pride of India*, Samskrita Bharati, New Delhi, 2006.

Reports

Ali, Akbar M. and Kanagasabapathi, P., 'A Study on Leather Tanneries in Dindugul', unpublished report, P.S.G. College of Technology, Coimbatore, April 2004.

'Breakdown Britain—Interim Report on the State of the Nation', Social Justice Policy Group, London, December 2006. www.povertydebate.com.

Global Entrepreneurship Monitor 2002 Summary Report, Babson College, Ewing Marion Kauffman Foundation and London Business School, November 2002. www.gemconsortium.org.

Goli, Venkat Raju and Kanagasabapathi, P., 'A Socio-economic Study of the Entrepreneurs of Visakhapatnam', unpublished report, P.S.G. College of Technology, Coimbatore, July 2003.

Human Development Report 2005, Oxford University Press, New Delhi.

International Monetary Fund, 'Islamic Bonds in Malaysia', *Global Financial Stability Report—Market Development and Issues*, Washington, 2005.

International Monetary Fund, *Global Financial Stability Report*, Washington, 2011.

Kanagasabapathi, P., 'A Study of Pattinavar Community', unpublished report, Swadeshi Academic Council, Coimbatore, 2005.

Kanagasabapathi, P. and Anuradha, R., 'A Study on Reasons Behind the Success of Knitwear Industry in Tirupur with Regard to the Ancillary Units', unpublished report, P.S.G. College of Technology, Coimbatore, April 2004.

Kanagasabapathi P. and Arun Kumar, M.N., 'A Study on Namakkal Transport Industry', unpublished report, P.S.G. Institute of Management, Coimbatore, April 2006.

Kanagasabapathi, P. and Arun Kumar, M.N., 'A Study on Sankagiri Transport Industry and Thiruchengode Rig Industry', unpublished report, P.S.G. Institute of Management, Coimbatore, April, 2005.

Kanagasabapathi, P. and Gopalsamy, R., 'A Study on Supply Chain Practices and Performances in the Printing Industry of Sivakasi', unpublished report, P.S.G. College of Technology, Coimbatore, April 2006.

Kanagasabapathi, P. and Menakha, I., 'A Study on Powerloom Textile Export Industry of Palladam', unpublished report, P.S.G. College of Technology, Coimbatore, April 2005.

Kanagasabapathi, P. and Ramanathan, A.R., 'A Study on Butter and Ghee Industry in Kangayam with Special Reference to Sozhiya Chetty Community', unpublished report, P.S.G. Institute of Management, Coimbatore, March 2006.

Kanagasabapathi, P. and Rathishree, P., 'A Study on Karur Textile Export Industry', unpublished report, P.S.G. Institute of Management, Coimbatore, April 2005.

Kanagasabapathi, P. and Reddy, Senthil V., 'A Study on Entrepreneurship among Reddiars', unpublished report, P.S.G. College of Technology, Coimbatore, April 2004.

Patel, Sharad and Kanagasabapathi, P., 'A Study on Gujarat Diamond Export Industry', unpublished report, P.S.G. Institute of Management, Coimbatore, April 2005.

Project OASIS Report, Ministry of Social Justice and Empowerment, Government of India, 1999.

Reserve Bank of India, *Annual Report 2008–09*, RBI, Mumbai.

Reserve Bank of India, *Annual Report 2010–11*, RBI, Mumbai.

Reserve Bank of India, *Handbook of Statistics on the Indian Economy* 2010–11, RBI, Mumbai.

Reserve Bank of India, *Report on Currency and Finance 2003–04*, RBI, Mumbai.

Reserve Bank of India, *Report on Currency and Finance 2006–08*, RBI, Mumbai.

Reserve Bank of India, *Report on Currency and Finance 2008–09*, RBI, Mumbai.

Securities and Exchnage Board of India, *Annual Report 2010–11*, SEBI, Mumbai, 2011.

The Boston Consulting Group, 'The New Global Challengers—How 100 Top Companies from Rapidly Developing Economies are Changing the World', BCG Report, The Boston Consulting Group Inc., May 2006.

The State of Human Development, United Nations Development Report 1998, United Nations, New York.

The State of the National Report—Indebtedness, Social Justice Policy Group, London, December 2006. www.povertydebate.com.

United Nations Conference on Trade and Development, *World Investment Report 2009*, United Nations, New York.

World Development Report 2001, World Bank, Washington.

World Development Report 2012: Gender Equality and Development, World Bank, Washington.

Government of India Publications

Annual Report 2009–10, Ministry of Company Affairs, Government of India, New Delhi.

Annual Report 2010–11, Ministry of Micro, Small and Medium Enterprises, Government of India, New Delhi.

Economic Census 1998, Ministry of Finance, Government of India, New Delhi.

Economic Census 2005, Ministry of Finance, Government of India, New Delhi.

Economic Survey 2009–10, Ministry of Finance, Government of India, New Delhi.

Economic Survey 2010–11, Ministry of Finance, Government of India, New Delhi.

Employment and Unemployment Situation in India 2009–10, NSS 66th Round, Ministry of Statistics and Programme Implementation, Government of India, 2011.

Final Results: Third All India Census of Small Scale Industries 2001–02, Ministry of Small Scale Industries, Government of India, New Delhi, 2004.

Fourth All India Census of MSME Sector, Ministry of Micro, Small and Medium Enterprises, Government of India, New Delhi.

Newspapers

Chandrasekhar, C.P. and Ghosh, Jayati, 'India's Potential Demographic Dividend', *The Hindu Business Line*, January 17, 2006.

Economic Times Intelligence Group Analysis, 'Capital Strength—Desis Beat MNCs in Use of Money', *The Economic Times*, Chennai, August 2, 2006.

Khanna, Ajay, 'Resurgent India Strikes Back with Confidence', *The Hindu Business Line,* April 26, 2006.

Krugman, Paul, 'Debt and Denial', *The Hindu*, February 14, 2006.

Meena Menon, 'Dharavi Residents Wary of New Project', *The Hindu*, August 8, 2004.

Murali, D., E. Dimension, 'Globalization is Now Officially Dead', *The Hindu Business Line,* February 4, 2006.

Rigby, Elizabeth, *The Financial Times*, November, 17, 2003.

Shashi Tharoor, 'Why Indian Science Scores', *The Hindu*, June 8, 2003.

Swaminathan S. Aiyar, 'Harness the Caste System', *The Times of India*, June 4, 2000.

Swaminathan S. Aiyar, 'Social Capital—An Idea Whose Time Has Come', *The Times of India,* May 28, 2000.

The Economic Times, Chennai, August 25, 2006.

The Financial Express, January 29, 2008.

The Hindu Business Line, October 1, 2002.

The Hindu, February 20, 2006.

The Hindu, February 24, 2006.

The Hindu, June 11, 2007.

The Hindu Business Line, December 8, 2008.

The Hindu, April 17, 2011.

The New Indian Express, June 15, 2011.

The Wall Street Journal, Asian Edition, November 25, 2009.

Vaidyanathan, R., 'Bias Against the Self-Employed', *The Hindu Business Line*, February 24, 2005.

Vaidyanathan, R., 'Capital Formation and P&P Sector—The Inconsistencies and Adjustments', *The Hindu Business Line*, August 26, 2004.

Vaidyanathan, R., 'End Consumption, Nurture Savings', *The Hindu Business Line*, May 5, 2005.

Vaidyanathan, R., 'Gold, Savings and P&P Sector: Foolish Governments, Smart Women', *The Hindu Business Line*, September 9, 2004.

Vaidyanathan, R., 'Stock Market: Barometer of Economy?', *The Hindu Business Line*, March 24, 2005.

Vaidyanathan, R., 'Success of Unorganized Services', *The Hindu Business Line*, July 1, 2004.

Vaidyanathan, R., 'The Least Acknowledged Big Savers', *The Hindu Business Line*, July 15, 2004.

Vaidyanathan, R., 'Understanding the Unorganized Sector', *The Hindu Business Line*, June 3, 2004.

Magazines

Bhattacharya, S.K., 'Organisational Culture: An Indian Perspective', *Business World*, February 1–14, 1998.

Business Today, January 16, 2005.

Ghosh, Jayati, 'The Export Obsession', *Front Line*, December 2, 2005.

India Today, November 28, 2005.

Lehmann, Jean-Pierre, 'The Dangers of Monotheism in the Age of Globalization', *The Globalist*, March 30, 2006.

Stefan Theil, 'The New Old Age', *Newsweek*, January 30, 2006.

Thakker, Pradip, 'Mumbai's Amazing Dabbawalas', *Smart Manager*, November 11, 2005.

The Economist, August 31, 2001.

The Economist, January 31, 2006.

The Economist, July 16, 2009.

The Economist, August 15, 2009.

Zakaria, Fareed, 'India Rising', *News Week*, March 6, 2006.

Other Publications

Centre For Monitoring Indian Economy, Corporate Sector, CMIE, Mumbai, February, 2009.

Economic Intelligence Service—Monthly review of the Indian Economy, *Centre for Monitoring Indian Economy*, Mumbai, May 2010.

Editorials, *Al–Jazeerah,* November 9, 2005.

Farrel, Diana and Lund, Susan, 'Reforming India's Financial System', 2005, Special Edition, *Mckinsey Quarterly.*

Handbook of Statistics on the Indian Securities Market 2010, Securities and Exchange Board of India, Mumbai.

Muqtedar Khan, 'India: The Emerging Management Giant', Muqtedar Khan Opinion Editorials, *Al–Jazeerah,* November 8, 2005.

PriceWaterhouseCoopers, '*The World in 2050*', March 2006.

Reserve Bank of India Bulletins, March 2006, October 2008 and November 2008, Reserve Bank of India, Mumbai.

Reserve Bank of India, *Macro–economic and Monetary Developments in 2010–11,* RBI, Mumbai.

Seminar 482—October 1999.

The McKinsey Global Survey of Business Executives: Confidence Index , *McKinsey Quarterly,* January 2006.

World Bank, *Global Development Finance I: Review Analysis, and Outlook 2008,* World Bank, 2008.

Surveys

Business Today Annual Survey 1994, *Business Today,* July 22–August 6, 1994.

Interviews and Speeches

Galbraith, John K., Interview, *Outlook,* August 20, 2001.

'Peter Drucker Sets Us Straight', Interview by Brent Schlender, *Fortune 2004,* January 12, 149(1), pp. 114–118.

Ramadorai, S., Speech at the Ahmedabad Management Association, April 22, 2003.

Websites

www. britannica.com
www.censusindia.net
www.cso.org
www.dreducation.com
www.gemconsortium.org
www.hbswk.hbs.org
www.imf.org
www.mca.gov.in
www.mydigitalfc.com
www.narayanhospitals,com
www.nbr.org
www.oecd.org
www.pewforum.org
www.povertydebate.com
www.rbi.org
www.tnmbonline.com
www.unctad.org

NAME INDEX

Subject Index